GENERAL BUSINESS
CONCEPTS □ VALUES □ SKILLS

Herbert L. Lyon

Professor, Business Administration, Department of Business Administration, University of Kentucky, Lexington, Kentucky; Associate Dean, Graduate School, University of Kentucky, Lexington, Kentucky

John M. Ivancevich

Professor of Organizational Behavior and Management, Department of Organizational Behavior and Management, College of Business Administration, University of Houston, Houston, Texas

Consultant: **Daniel H. Kruger**

Professor of Industrial Relations, School of Labor and Industrial Relations, Michigan State University, East Lansing, Michigan; Associate Director, Manpower Program Service, School of Labor and Industrial Relations, Michigan State University, East Lansing, Michigan

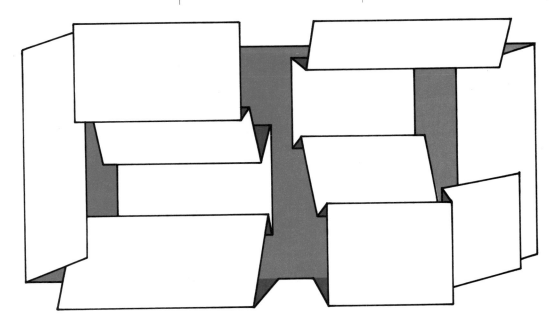

 HARCOURT BRACE JOVANOVICH
NEW YORK CHICAGO SAN FRANCISCO ATLANTA DALLAS *and* LONDON

ISBN 0-15-377420-7   Printed in the United States of America

Acknowledgments:

Grateful acknowledgment is made to *Changing Times,* The Kiplinger Magazine, for permission to reprint "The High Cost of Aging" (April 1972), copyright © 1972 by The Kiplinger Washington Editors, Inc., and "Name Brands vs. House Brands" (August 1973), copyright © 1973 by The Kiplinger Washington Editors, Inc., Editors Park, Maryland, 20782; and to the *Institute of Life Insurance* for permission to reprint pp. 106-107 from the *Life Insurance Fact Book,* 1969.

Picture Credits:

Front cover, clockwise from top: Harbrace; Shostal; Erich Lessing from Magnum; Burt Uzzle from Magnum; Harbrace.

Back cover, clockwise from top: Harbrace; Scott D'Arazien; Harbrace; Ron Benveniste from Magnum; Harbrace.

Text: p. 4, The British Museum; p. 5 left, Porterfield-Chickering, Photo Researchers; p. 5 right, Esaias Baitel, Rapho-Photo Researchers; p. 6 left, John Zoiner; p. 6-7 center, John Zoiner; p. 7, R. N. Milacron, Louis Mercier; p. 8 all, John Zoiner; p. 9 left, Harbrace; p. 9 right, Larry Mulvehill, Photo Researchers; p. 10, Harbrace; p. 18, John Zoiner; p. 19, Shostal; p. 20, Joern Gerdts, Photo Researchers; p. 21 left, Bill Powers, Nancy Palmer; p. 21 right, Herb Levart, Photo Researchers; p. 25 both, Harbrace; p. 26 top, Culver; p. 26 bottom, Wide World; p. 34, The Carnegie Institute; p. 35, The Pittsburgh Chamber of Commerce; p. 46, Courtesy of Pepsi-Cola, Inc.; p. 52 left, Courtesy of African Fabric Prints; p. 52 top, Harbrace; p. 52 bottom, Courtesy of Caltex; p. 53, Courtesy of Federal Reserve Bank of N.Y.; p. 61-68, Harbrace; p. 74 left, Courtesy of RCA; p. 74 right, Courtesy of Ford Motor Co.; p. 77 left, Bettmann; p. 77 middle, Esaias Baitel, Rapho-Photo Researchers; p. 77 right, UPI; p. 78 all, Courtesy of Gulf & Western; p. 85, Harbrace; p. 86, Larry Mulvehill, Photo Researchers; p. 87, Courtesy of Kentucky Fried Chicken Corp.; p. 88, Marc St. Gil, Black Star; p. 92, British Crown Copyright, Science Museum, London; p. 96, Harbrace; p. 102, John Zoiner; p. 108, Bettmann; p. 110 left, NYPL; p. 110 right, Chase Manhattan Bank Museum; p. 111, Harbrace; p. 112, Courtesy of Federal Reserve Bank of N.Y.; p. 113, Harbrace; p. 120, Culver; p. 124, Sygma; p. 125 top, Culver; p. 125 bottom, Harbrace; p. 126, Courtesy of Sears Roebuck & Co.; p. 133, Culver; p. 136, Harbrace; p. 158 all, Harbrace; p. 161, Courtesy of Bulova Watch Co.; p. 162, Courtesy of American Tourister; p. 173, Courtesy of the Kellogg Company; p. 183 left, Dennis Brack, Black Star; p. 183 right, Werner Wolff, Black Star; p. 184, Wide World; p. 185 top, Harbrace; p. 185 bottom, Courtesy of the Ford Motor Co.; p. 186, Harbrace; p. 188 left, Peter Borsari, Camera 5; p. 188 right, James Pickerell; p. 190-191, Courtesy of Campbell Soup Co.; p. 194 left, Harbrace; p. 194 right, Guy Gillette; p. 195, USDA; p. 204, Harbrace; p. 206, Courtesy of Mazda Motors; p. 207, Harbrace; p. 208, Harbrace; p. 209, USDA; p. 216, Bettmann; p. 218 left, John Zoiner, p. 218 right, Rapho-Photo Researchers; p. 219, Harbrace; p. 223, UPI; p. 233, Bettmann; p. 246-247, Harbrace; p. 269, Rothco; p. 270, Bettmann; p. 287, Bettmann; p. 288, C. Ray, Photo Researchers; p. 291 right, Courtesy of the American Express Co.; p. 291 left, Larry Mulvehill, Photo Researchers; p. 297, Courtesy of *Changing Times,* The Kiplinger Magazine; p. 315, Bettmann; p. 316, Sydney Harris; p. 328, Edward C. Topple; p. 334, Harbrace; p. 336, Guy Gillette; p. 345, Sydney Harris; p. 351, Harbrace; p. 365, Laurie Dietz; p. 367, Sydney Harris; p. 376, Harbrace; p. 391, Shostal; p. 396, N.Y. Life Insurance Co.; p. 397, Shostal; p. 400, © The New Yorker Magazine, Inc.; p. 404, Doizer Mobley, CNA; p. 406 left, Peter Arnold; p. 406 middle, UPI; p. 406 right, Monkmeyer; p. 407, Peter Arnold; p. 413, James H. Karales, DPI; p. 422, NYPL, © The New Yorker Magazine, Inc.; p. 424, Guy Gillette; p. 426 left, Harbrace; p. 426 right both, Guy Gillette; p. 435 left, DPI; p. 435 right, Pete Ariessohn, DPI; p. 441, © The New Yorker Magazine, Inc.; p. 444 top left, Mimi Forsyth, Monkmeyer; p. 444 middle, Sybil Shackman, Monkmeyer; p. 444 bottom right, Sybil Shackman, Monkmeyer; p. 450, Hugh Rogers, Monkmeyer; p. 457, George S. Zimbel, Monkmeyer; p. 459 right, Shostal; p. 459 left, DPI; p. 469 left, John Zoiner; p. 469 right, Peter Arnold; p. 470, Harvey Lloyd, Peter Arnold; p. 472, John Zoiner; p. 490, Sydney Harris; p. 497 left, Raytheon Corp.; p. 497 right, UPI; p. 508, Wide World; p. 518 both, Guy Gillette; p. 525 left, John Zoiner; p. 525 right, Guy Gillette; p. 528 both, Guy Gillette.

PREFACE

General Business
Concepts Values Skills has been purposely written for the student who must live in a world influenced by business. Business is a major force in our society. It is the primary source of goods and services, income, and jobs. Business, therefore, is an area of study that is of tremendous practical value for all students.

OBJECTIVES

There is general agreement among educators on the several objectives a business course and textbook must achieve. First, there is a *consumer-education* objective. Achievement of this objective involves improving the knowledge of all students about business in the United States and how it relates to our economic system. Second, there is the *consumer-awareness* objective. This objective is met by improving students' understanding of the marketplace and how to use the goods and services business provides. Third, there is the *personal-utilization* objective, met by improving students' understanding and use of money, credit, investment opportunities, and insurance protection. Finally, there is the *career-awareness* objective, the achievement of which includes helping students in selecting a career for the future. This textbook was prepared with these four objectives in mind.

CONTENT

The book is organized into ten self-contained units, with the four above-listed objectives serving as their foundation. Each of the units can be read in total or in part without loss of comprehension or continuity. Because of the self-contained type of format, the units can be rearranged to meet the educational style and preference of the individual instructor. The material selected for inclusion in the ten units contains a significant degree of practical business orientation. We have used numerous examples to teach students the vocabulary of business, the problems of business, and the theme of business in today's society. The examples are realistic in that they use current facts and figures to teach a particular subject or concept. Of course, due to the dynamic nature of society and the rapid inflation in the marketplace, some of these facts and figures will become outdated. As this happens, however, the presentation of the underlying business concepts, values, and skills will remain sound, and only the outdated facts and figures will need appropriate modification.

The ten major units of the textbook include the following:

Unit I—THE BUSINESS ENVIRONMENT informs students about the nature of the business world and the economic system within which business in the United States operates. International competition and trade, major forces influencing the decisions made by United States business firms, are discussed.

Unit II—THE ORGANIZATION OF BUSINESS examines the different kinds of business firms that exist. The various levels of management found in corporations are explained to students. The computer, which has become a major force in many business organizations, is also discussed.

Unit III—GOOD MONEY MANAGEMENT focuses on money and budgeting. Many citizens in our economic society lack an adequate understanding of the value of money and the processes of budgeting. This lack of knowledge can create financial burdens that might be difficult to correct completely.

Unit IV—MARKETING AND THE CONSUMER discusses in a realistic manner the consumer and his or her problems and gratification. Each student is already an important consumer. Thus, the lessons presented in these chapters are especially valuable.

UNIT V—BANKS AND THEIR SERVICES identifies the functions banks perform in our society and illustrates how banks serve the individual.

Unit VI—FUNDAMENTALS OF CREDIT presents some of the important issues involving credit. Student awareness of the dangers of becoming a "crediholic" is considered. This knowledge is extremely critical during the present era of abuse and overuse of credit-card purchasing.

Unit VII—INVESTING MONEY discusses some of the potential outlets for investing extra dollars. The success or failure of investing is directly related to careful planning and understanding on the part of the investor.

Unit VIII—INSURANCE PROTECTION explains some of the types of insurance protection that can be purchased. Because many people have limited and often incorrect viewpoints of insurance, this unit provides useful and necessary information for the potential insurance buyer.

Unit IX—GOVERNMENT, LABOR UNIONS, AND BUSINESS discusses the function of these three major forces in our society. Also, it points out how these forces must work together if the economy is to be healthy.

Unit X—THE CHALLENGE OF THE FUTURE ties the course together for the key people—the students. Career planning and some suggestions on finding a job are the main topics in this unit.

These ten units contain a number of topics not covered in most other business textbooks. These include international competition, the management team in business firms, the computer, home and other real estate investments, and the need for a greater social orientation among business leaders. These areas, along with the other topics, are continually discussed in a practical-example style.

STUDENT ACTIVITIES

Each chapter has four sections of specific activities for students. These are designed to reinforce what has been presented in the chapters. The first section is used to highlight key vocabulary by using a fill-in-the-blanks format. The second section contains short questions which help review main points covered in the chapter. In the third section, students apply their understanding of the material by answering questions not specifically covered in the chapter. Finally, section four uses exercises, such as reporting, debating, and interviewing, to reinforce what has been learned. These four distinct sections allow the instructor to probe the understanding of the students and give students an opportunity to display some creativity in dealing with business-related issues.

ACKNOWLEDGMENTS

Many people aided us in preparing *General Business/Concepts Values Skills*. Dr. Daniel Kruger of Michigan State University, Dr. Celestine Mongo of the Detroit Public Schools, Dr. Paul F. Brandwein of Harcourt Brace Jovanovich, Inc., and Dr. Robert Callis of the University of Missouri each offered suggestions on format, content, and style. Their help was invaluable in improving the textbook.

We would like to acknowledge the assistance provided by Mr. Douglas P. Johnson, First Security National Bank and Trust Company, Lexington, Kentucky, on Units III and V. Also, our thanks go to the International Consumer Credit Association (St. Louis, Missouri) and Household Finance Corporation (Chicago, Illinois) for permission to use selected materials from their organizations in Units III and VI.

HERBERT L. LYON
JOHN M. IVANCEVICH

TABLE OF CONTENTS

Unit 1
The Business Environment

Business is important to everyone in the United States. Many people, however, do not understand how important it is or how it affects their daily lives. Chapter I discusses the meaning and objectives of business, what it produces, and its size and growth. It also discusses business as a field of study.

All consumers have certain needs and desires that business tries to satisfy. Chapter 2 shows that business can meet these needs and wants through production and marketing activities.

The decisions about what to produce, how to produce, and how to share the goods and services produced are called *economic decisions*. How these decisions are made depends on a country's economic system. Chapter 3 treats the various kinds of economic systems and the ways in which decisions are made within each system.

Chapter 4 takes a detailed look at the economy of the United States. Some of the topics included are the goals of the nation's economic system, the relationship between profits and economic growth, and how economic growth can be measured. Finally, the future of the United States economy is discussed.

The United States economy does not operate by itself. It is closely related to the economies of many other nations. Chapter 5 considers international trade. It answers such questions as Why do nations trade? How do nations pay for international trade? What are the barriers to international trade?

UNIT PREVIEW

2

AS YOU STUDY THIS UNIT YOU WILL BE ENGAGED IN

* **DISCOVERING** how business is a basic part of your life and living

* **DETERMINING** how a nation's needs are met by business

* **OBSERVING** how decisions that affect the economy are made

* **PROBING** why economic growth is necessary if the nation's standard of living is to rise

* **ANALYZING** the likenesses and differences in national and international trade

* **UNDERSTANDING** the environment in which national and international business is conducted.

A FOCUS FOR YOUR STUDY

THE NATURE OF BUSINESS

In the early days, people hunted and farmed for food, made clothes, and built different kinds of shelters. Some people, of course, could do certain things better than others. For example, some were better at farming, while others were better at making clothes. As a result, most people began to do the types of work they did best. They then traded whatever extra food, clothing, and other things they produced with their neighbors.

This type of trading is called *bartering*. Bartering means that things are exchanged without using money. For example, a farmer gives a shoemaker twenty pounds of potatoes for one pair of shoes. At first, trading was limited to nearby neighbors. When people started to travel, they began trading with people in distant places.

A trade route from a publication dated 1374.

This making and trading of goods is called *business.* Business exists all over the world but not exactly the same way in every country. For example, in countries where people are mainly farmers, business is a fairly simple process. On the other hand, business activities in industrial countries, such as Canada, Japan, West Germany, the Soviet Union, and the United States, are complicated. Because business is complicated, your study of business should begin with an idea of what business is all about.

THE MEANING OF BUSINESS

There is no simple definition of *business.* In fact, the word *business* may now have no particular meaning to you. This is not surprising since business in the United States is both big and complicated.

You know that business exists and affects your life each day. However, you probably are not completely sure what business does. Three meanings of the word *business* will be discussed so that you will have an idea of what business is all about.

The dog-walker is providing a service.

This woman is making sound equipment in a factory.

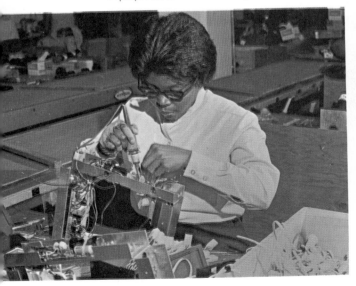

Very often the word *business* is used to describe all of the economic activity that takes place in the United States. The term *economic activity* means all of the banking, transportation, construction, mining, and other activities conducted by small and large organizations. From this viewpoint business is an environment that surrounds all of us.

A second definition of the word *business* is *any organization that provides different things for the public*. For example, American Motors makes small cars, such as the Gremlin. By providing cars for the public to buy, the company is considered to be a *production* business. The Kroger Company makes food products available to the public. It is considered to be a *distribution* business. The H and R Block Company prepares income tax forms for people. It is considered to be a *service* business.

Business can also be defined as *all of the activities that take place between people when money changes hands*. For example, service station managers are paid when they put gas in your car. Similarly, doctors are paid for their services when they examine you.

These three definitions should help you to understand how the word *business* is used. In this book, usually the third—the more personal—meaning of the word will be used. However, the other meanings of *business* will be used when necessary.

Making hamburger buns, knitting latex material, and manufacturing heavy industrial equipment are production activities that provide goods.

OBJECTIVES OF BUSINESS

There are four basic objectives of most business organizations in the United States. First, a business organization must *survive.* This means that the organization continues to exist. No other objective can be reached if the organization does not survive.

Not all business organizations survive. Large ones as well as small ones go out of business every year. One established business organization that recently failed was the Penn Central Railroad. This was the largest railroad in the United States.

A second important objective in business is *growth.* Business does not stand still. It either gets larger or smaller. By growing larger, businesses can provide new jobs for many workers. The McDonald's Corporation is an example of a business organization that has grown rapidly since it was founded.

Making a *profit* is a third objective of business. To make a profit means that goods and services are sold for more money than it costs to produce them. Profit provides the money business organizations need for growth. Some people, however, feel that business organizations make too much profit. There is no easy way to explain this. The problem is that no one knows what *too much* means.

Finally, business organizations must also have an objective of meeting their *social responsibilities*. Only in recent years has this become an important objective for many business organizations. This means that businesses must consider their effect on the quality of life. To help improve the quality of life means not to pollute the air and water, not to discriminate against women and minority groups, to make products that are safe, and to be fair to customers.

SOME ASPECTS OF BUSINESS

People are different from one another in many ways. They differ in their politics, color, size, and religion, to name just a few. All people, however, have two things in common: *needs* and *wants. Needs* are basic things people must have to exist. *Wants* are things people would like to have but are not required in order for people to exist. Needs include food, clothes, and shelter. Wants are things such as color televisions, stereo tapes, and sports cars.

These pictures show producer goods, consumer goods, and services.

BUSINESS PRODUCES GOODS AND SERVICES

Business is the main source of supply to satisfy needs and wants. Think of the things you need and want. If you add them to those needs and wants of the other people in the United States, you can begin to see how important business really is.

To satisfy people's needs and wants, business produces *goods* and *services.* Goods are things you can touch and see, such as watches, cars, shoes, airplanes, and car generators. There are two major types of goods: *consumer goods* and *producer goods.* Consumer goods are used to satisfy personal wants. They include pocket watches, shoes, and cars. Producer goods are used in producing other goods or services. For example, steel is used to produce new automobiles. Even though you do not usually buy producer goods, these goods are necessary to help satisfy consumer needs and wants by being part of a consumer product.

Can you think of a way cars could be considered producer goods? One way is if the cars are used by salespeople who sell a service, such as insurance. The way products are used determines if they are producer goods or consumer goods.

Services are produced by people doing things for you. They include mowing lawns, cutting hair, painting houses, and being treated by a doctor. Even baby-sitting is a service.

CONTRIBUTIONS OF BUSINESS

Business makes three major contributions to society by producing goods and services: It provides jobs for people; it pays taxes to local, state, and Federal governments; and it contributes to the general well-being of the citizens of the country. These contributions are important for several reasons. First, by providing jobs, business enables workers to earn money. With this money the workers can buy the goods and services they need and want. In the United States, business provides jobs for about six out of every seven workers. The other workers work for Federal, state, and local governments. Of course, the exact number of jobs depends largely on how many goods and services are bought by consumers.

Second, by paying tax money to governments, business helps pay for many services that governments provide. Business taxes help support fire departments, public schools, parks, and roads. Another very important type of business tax is the social security tax. This money is used to help support retired people, widows with children, and other people in need. When you retire, you will benefit from these taxes by receiving social security checks every month. Third, the goods and services provided by business raise the standard of living.

This is an individual business.

THE SIZE OF BUSINESS

In the United States there are more than 12 million individual business firms. They account for about 90 percent of all the goods and services produced in this country. About 30 percent, or 3.5 million, of these businesses are farms.

There are different ways to measure the size of business firms. An easy way to measure the size is to count the number of people working for each firm. Some business firms, such as the local grocery store, consist of only one person. Other business firms, such as the American Telephone and Telegraph Company (AT&T) and General Motors, are very large. AT&T employs over 900,000 people.

Think for a moment about the different size business firms in your town. You have probably thought of more small firms than large ones. Most businesses in the United States are small. This is also true for other countries. Figure 1–2 shows that about 90 percent of all business firms in the United States have less than 20 workers. These are the types of firms that you go to most often. They include such places as Ann's Knitting Shop, David's Music Store, Linda's Dance Studio, or Scott's Bike Shop.

FIGURE 1-2
PERCENT OF BUSINESS FIRMS
EMPLOYING LESS THAN 20 PEOPLE

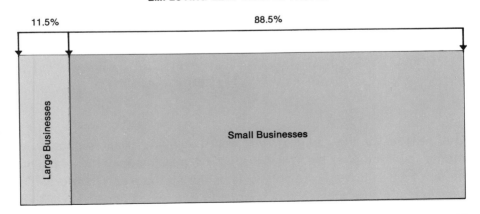

11.5%   88.5%

Large Businesses

Small Businesses

Large firms often do business throughout the United States. Some, such as General Motors, even do business in many other countries. Although these large companies make up only 10 percent of the total number of businesses, they do about half of all the business in the United States. Examples of other large firms that sell their goods or services throughout the United States are Exxon (gas and oil), Holiday Inn (motels), Prudential (life insurance), and Westinghouse (electrical equipment).

THE GROWTH OF BUSINESS

Business has grown very fast since World War II. Compare the periods before and after World War II in the United States (Table 1–1). After the War (after 1945) there was an increase in the number of business firms. In fact, between 1945 and 1969 the number of firms almost doubled.

This increase in the number of business firms was not caused entirely by the increase in the number of people. By dividing the number of firms into the number of people you can find out the number of business firms for every thousand people (Table 1–1). The number increased more than three times during World War II (1939 to 1945). After the War, from 1945 to 1969, the population increased more than 50 percent, but the number of business firms grew almost 80 percent. Thus, the number of business firms grew much faster than the population.

TABLE 1–1
BUSINESS GROWTH IN THE UNITED STATES

Year	Number of Firms	Population (in Thousands)	Business Firms per Thousand People
1939	1,793	130,880	13.7
1945	6,737	132,481	50.7
1969	12,021	201,385	57.1

One reason for the rapid growth was that many families had more money to spend after the War. This was because many of the items the people wanted to buy were not available during the War. Therefore, the people could save their money to spend when goods became available again. When people have more money, new businesses are formed to give the people the new products and services they want to buy.

WHY STUDY BUSINESS?

Now that you have read about some different aspects of the business world, you may be wondering if learning about business is useful. After all, you can drive a car without understanding how the transmission works. It is also true that you can buy and sell goods and services without fully understanding the business system.

There are several reasons why you should have a good understanding of how business works. Most of the reasons result in either a personal or social benefit.

One reason for studying business is because it is all around you. It is impossible to lead a normal and active life in the United States without coming in constant contact with business. Since you will be in close contact with many different aspects of business you should understand it. This understanding will permit you to better deal with it.

In addition, business is exciting. It is dynamic; that is, it is constantly changing in many ways. New laws are being passed, new products are being introduced, and people's habits and customs are changing. You can help effect changes in business if you understand it.

Studying business can also help you become a better shopper, or consumer. You will learn where to get basic buying information about different kinds of goods and services. You will also learn how governments work to protect the rights of consumers.

Every person and family should learn how to save money for the future. Business offers several different ways to save money. By studying business you can get the information that will help you decide the best way for you to save. In short, understanding business is the first step in becoming a good money manager.

Finally, understanding business may also help you select a career in business. If you think you have an interest in a business career, study the subject carefully. Learning about the organization and functions of business can better prepare you to choose the type of company you might want to work at and the type of job you might want to do.

So far, all of the reasons for studying business have been personal ones—personal, in that you benefit directly from the study. However, there is another important reason—a social benefit. There are many business problems that are basically political. To answer them intelligently you need to understand basic business concepts and operations.

An example of a political problem is whether a tax should be placed on extra profits made by oil companies during an energy crisis. The oil industry does not think so. Some government officials think a tax should be placed on extra profits. Who is right? To understand this problem you must understand certain facts about the oil industry and how the tax would affect it.

Another reason for learning about business is because many social problems are very difficult to solve. Business, however, has both the intelligent people and the financial resources to help the government try to solve some of these problems. With a better understanding of business, you too can eventually help make the United States a more satisfying country in which to live.

SUMMARY

Business is almost as old as the existence of people. Today, *business* has three basic meanings. First, it can mean all the economic activity conducted by large and small organizations. Second, it can mean any organization that provides goods and services for the public. Third, business can mean all the activities that take place between people when money changes hands.

Business has four objectives: survival, growth, profit, and social responsibility.

The study of business will lead to 1) an understanding of its functions, 2) an appreciation of its problems, 3) better shopping habits, and 4) a better career choice.

I. REVIEW OF TERMS

Which words complete the statements below?

small	services	large	social
goods	personal	jobs	producer

1. Business produces _____ and services to satisfy wants.
2. _____ are produced by people doing things for you.
3. There are more _____ firms than _____ firms in the United States.
4. Goods used in making other goods are called _____ goods.
5. The main types of benefits from studying business are _____ and _____ .
6. One way business contributes to the United States economy is by providing many _____ .

II. REVIEW OF MAIN POINTS

1. List and explain three different meanings of *business*.
2. List the different objectives of business. Select one and explain why you think it is the most important.
3. How can business help support the community?
4. Why has business grown so fast since World War II?
5. How can consumers influence what goods and services a company sells?
6. Why do you think there are more small businesses than large businesses in the United States?
7. Explain why it is to your advantage to have a good understanding of business.

III. THE NATURE OF BUSINESS: CONCEPTS

1. Do you think businesses should have social responsibilities? If the product a business is producing can be dangerous or

destructive, should the company be permitted to continue producing it?

2. Do you think businesses should be permitted to grow as large as they want to, or should there be limitations on size?

IV. THE NATURE OF BUSINESS: EXERCISES

1. Prepare a list of 15 items and tell whether the items are goods or services. Also, see if you can list a business that produces each one.

2. Look in the Yellow Pages of the local telephone book and make a list of ten business firms that are unfamiliar to you. Find out what they produce and if the item is a product or a service. If it is a product tell if it is a producer or consumer product.

3. A former classmate writes to you and asks why you are studying business. Prepare a letter that will answer this question.

SATISFYING THE CONSUMER 2

Business satisfies people's needs and wants in two ways. First, it produces many goods and services in large quantities. People often talk about *mass-produced* goods. When items are made in large amounts they are said to be mass-produced. One mass-produced item that many people want is the automobile. If cars were made by hand, they would cost so much that only very rich people could afford them.

The second way business meets consumer needs and wants is by moving goods and services to places where people can buy or use them. For example, after tape cassettes are made, they must be sent to stores before people can buy them. Such a business activity as the moving of cassettes to stores is called *distribution*.

SATISFYING NEEDS AND WANTS

Production is the way a business firm changes *raw materials* into goods and services. Raw materials are such things as wood, coal, and iron ore. Nature provides the basic raw materials, but they are usually not in the proper form to meet a particular need. For example, if you want to get wood to build a house, you would go to a lumberyard, not to a forest. The reason for this is simple. The wood at the lumberyard has already been changed into a form that can be used to build the house.

PRODUCING GOODS AND SERVICES

An example of producing a service is the process used to make electricity. Even though you cannot see or hold electricity, a production process is used to make it. In one method, coal is first burned to heat water. The heated water becomes steam, which then turns large generators that actually produce the electricity. This electricity is sold to people who use it in their everyday life.

As mentioned earlier in this book, some people are able to do certain types of work better than other people. For example, some people are better farmers, while others are better tailors. These differences encourage people to do special types of work, particularly what they do best. This division of labor is also true of business. Business firms often specialize in certain types of work.

This work specialization, however, can be either simple or complex. For example, one person may run a clothing store, while another person might run a law office. On the other hand, many people are needed to build a color television set. Some workers specialize in finishing the wood cabinet, others produce the tubes and transistors, others assemble the various parts of the television set, and still others test the finished set and package it for shipment.

PRODUCTION USES RESOURCES

All of the production processes described use *resources*. If you think about the example of producing electricity, this should become clear.

Natural resources usually must be processed.

Producing electricity requires the use of coal, water, workers, generators, and buildings. These items are all called *factors of production.* Each item is a resource. Coal and water are natural resources, generators and buildings are capital resources, and workers are labor resources.

Natural resources are things nature supplies. Such resources include iron ore, coal, trees, zinc, copper, oil, and water. Natural resources usually must be *refined* or *processed* before they can be used to make goods or services. For example, before copper can be used to make electrical wiring, the copper has to be extracted (removed) from the copper ore. This is done by heating the copper ore so that the metal separates from the rock.

Capital resources are man-made things used in production. They are producer goods and include such things as railroad cars, heavy machinery, typewriters, and buildings. These things are actually a type of capital resource called *fixed capital.* They can be used many times to produce other goods. For example, a railroad car can be used over and over to carry steel from the mills in Pittsburgh to the automobile plants in Detroit. Capital resources that cannot be used again but are used up in the production process are called *working capital.* Glue, paper, cardboard boxes, tape, nails, fuel, and money are examples of working capital.

These railroad cars are capital resources, also called fixed capital.

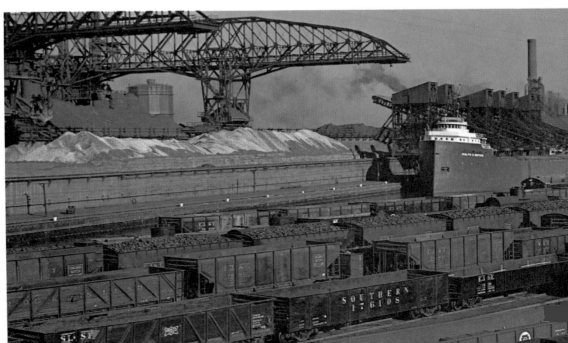

Without human resources, the other two resources would be of little value.

The third economic resource is the *labor,* or *human, resource.* The term *labor* means all work done for pay. It includes both physical and mental skills. A worker on the auto assembly line in Detroit performs *physical labor.* A lawyer representing a person in court performs *mental labor.* The human resource is probably the most important of the three resources because without human resources to use the other resources, both natural and capital resources would be of little value.

DISTRIBUTING GOODS AND SERVICES

The distribution part of business is very important because it makes goods and services available to the people who want them. The *distribution process* includes all the business activities involved in moving goods and services from producers to consumers. People and businesses involved in distribution are called *distributors*.

When color television sets are made in a Chicago plant, they are shipped from the manufacturer to many distributors. These distributors may be located in Chicago or in distant cities. The distributors, in turn, send the sets to the stores in their city (or cities). In this example, all three aspects of business (producers, distributors, and stores) are involved in marketing color television sets.

Coffee awaits distribution.

Trucks start to distribute goods in the early dawn.

Services also have to be distributed. Businesses that distribute services include banks, motels, insurance firms, and transportation companies. For example, banks distribute two basic services: making loans and accepting money for savings and checking accounts. Transportation companies distribute the service of moving goods and people from place to place.

There are several million businesses that distribute goods and services. They represent a very large part of the nation's economy. Because the distribution process is so important, it is discussed in more detail in Unit IV.

SUMMARY

To meet consumers' needs and wants, business performs two basic functions: production and distribution. These two functions work together as a system to make goods and services available to consumers. To make the system work, many economic decisions must be made by both producers and consumers. What these decisions are and how they are made are discussed in Chapter 3.

I. REVIEW OF TERMS

Which words complete the numbered statements?

labor	division of labor
production process	factors of production
capital	fixed capital
distributing	natural
producing	working capital

1. Business firms convert raw materials into goods and services by a _____.
2. Business meets consumer needs and wants by _____ and _____ goods and services.
3. Resources used only once in a production process are called _____.
4. The three kinds of resources used in production are 1) _____, 2) _____, and 3) _____.
5. Resources used many times in a production process are called _____.
6. Economic resources used in producing goods and services are called _____.
7. The idea of people doing specialized jobs is called _____.

II. REVIEW OF MAIN POINTS

1. Why do you think it is important to mass produce goods and services in order to meet the needs and wants of consumers?
2. Three economic resources were discussed. Which one do you think is the most important? Explain your answer.
3. What is meant by the term *production*?
4. What is meant by the term *distribution*?
5. Explain how production and distribution can be combined by business to meet consumer needs and wants.

III. SATISFYING THE CONSUMER: CONCEPTS

1. Business produces and distributes goods and services to meet consumer needs and wants. In doing this, business uses resources—natural, human, and capital. Suppose one of these resources was not available. What do you think would happen to the country's economy?

2. Choose one product or service that you often use in daily living. Show how each of the three basic resources was used to produce it.

3. For the product or service selected in Question 2, list at least two examples of both the fixed capital and working capital resources used to produce it.

IV. SATISFYING THE CONSUMER: EXERCISES

1. Prepare a list of ten business firms in your community and indicate if the business produces goods, distributes goods, or does both.

2. Choose one product produced in your community and list the raw materials needed to produce it. Also, tell if the raw material is found in your state.

3. Families use more services today than ever before. Make a list of ten services your family might have used in the last year.

4. Prepare a list of three business firms that sell only goods, three that sell only services, and three that sell both goods and services. Are the firms different in any way? For example, are they different in the size of the building they use? Are they different in the number of people they employ? Can you explain why they might be different?

5. Ask five different people to make a list of five wants. Answer the following questions:
   a. Do the wants differ with the ages of the people?
   b. Are the wants different for each sex?
   c. Are there any wants that appear on all five lists?
   What does this tell you about consumer wants?

3 MAKING ECONOMIC DECISIONS

The people in the United States attempt to use enough natural resources, capital resources, and human resources to satisfy everyone's needs. There are people, however, whose basic needs are not satisfied. This is not because the nation does not have the necessary resources. Instead, it is because some people do not have enough money to buy the necessary food, clothing, and shelter.

Even though it is possible to satisfy our basic needs, wants are another matter. There is no limit to people's wants. As soon as one want is satisfied a new want usually arises. For example, when you buy a tape cassette player, you soon want a large collection of tapes. In fact, there is really no limit to the number of tapes you might want to buy. Once you buy a large number of tapes, you will probably want several storage racks. Thus the cycle continues.

Even though there is no limit to people's wants, there is a limit to the resources that can be used to satisfy them. For example, there is a definite limit to the amount of coal in the ground. It is possible, therefore, to run out of this natural resource. However, before this happens another thing will probably occur. Before all the coal is removed, coal mining will become very expensive. This will happen because the remaining coal may be too deep in the ground or in too small quantities for the coal miners to get. The important thing is that all natural resources, including coal, oil, natural gas, iron ore, clean air, and clean water, are limited. Also, because some natural resources are in short supply, there is a limit to the products that can be made from them.

Because wants are often greater than natural resources, nations must be economical, or economize, when using their resources. To economize means to get as much value as possible from something. An important question for every nation is how to use its resources in a way that will satisfy as many people's wants as possible. The way this question is answered depends on the nation's *economic system.* An economic system, therefore, is a way in which a nation uses its economic resources. Different types of economic systems are discussed later in this chapter.

ECONOMIC DECISIONS

In order to balance wants with resources, a country must make some important economic decisions. No matter what type of economic system a nation has, these decisions are made by answering these three questions:

1. What goods and services should be produced?
2. How should goods and services be produced?
3. How should goods and services be shared, or divided, among the people?

Read these questions and think about what they mean.

WHAT GOODS AND SERVICES SHOULD BE PRODUCED?

This question is very difficult to answer because people have many different ideas about what is important. The people of a nation must

Constructing buildings and performing medical research are results of economic decisions.

decide what goods and services are necessary to them at a certain moment in time. For example, do they need covered wagons or automobiles? They must also decide how the resources should be divided between producer and consumer goods, and what types of producer and consumer goods should be produced. The people might decide to use most of their nation's resources to make military supplies, such as guns, airplanes, warships, and tanks. However, there will probably not be enough resources left over to make enough other goods and services, such as better housing, improved medical care, better schools, cars, television sets, and similar goods. Answering the question with these two extreme cases is often referred to as deciding if a nation shall produce *guns or butter.* In World War II the United States produced *guns* to such a degree that many of the other goods and services had to be *rationed* (given out in small portions) by the Government. Even a nation as wealthy as the United States cannot produce large amounts

Rationing was necessary during World War II.

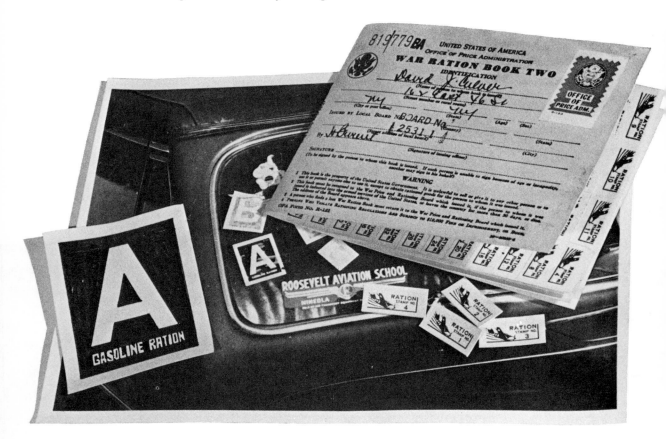

of both guns and butter over a long period of time. Within limits, however, many nations, including Canada, Japan, the Soviet Union, and the United States, can produce military supplies as well as goods and services for the consumer.

HOW SHOULD GOODS AND SERVICES BE PRODUCED?

Production involves combining natural resources, capital resources, and labor resources in some way to produce goods and services. It is often possible to combine these factors in different ways to produce the same goods or services. Consider the case when the United States decided to build a cross-country highway system. There were two ways this could have been done. The highways could have been built using a large amount of capital resources and little labor. This means that only a few people (labor) would have been used, along with large numbers of bulldozers, dump trucks, and earth movers (capital). The other way would have been to use a large number of people and a few capital resources. The first way was chosen because at that time the country did not have a lot of extra workers. It was more practical to replace people with machines so that the workers could do other useful jobs, such as building houses, parks, schools, and offices.

HOW SHOULD GOODS AND SERVICES BE SHARED, OR DIVIDED, AMONG THE PEOPLE?

There are at least two basic ways to answer this question. One way is to have the goods and services shared equally by every person in the society. A second way is to let the people share the goods and services according to the amount of work they do and the amount of money they earn. This money is then used to buy goods and services. The amount of money people earn depends on factors such as their abilities and skills and the demand for these abilities and skills.

The way a nation answers these economic questions is directly related to the type of economic system it has. For example, in the United States, the consumer largely determines what will be produced. In the Soviet Union, the government decides.

ECONOMIC SYSTEMS

There are three basic types of modern economic systems: communism, socialism, and capitalism. There are some very important differences among these three systems. It is difficult, however, to define and explain the three systems in an exact way. This is because none of these systems exists in a pure form. For example, regulating industries is a feature of a socialistic economy. The United States has a capitalistic system, but the government does regulate certain industries. Among those industries that are regulated in some way by the government are the telephone, gas, electric, water, and transportation (trains, airlines, and buses) industries.

THE COMMUNISTIC SYSTEM

Communism is a type of economic system in which the government tightly controls all of the country's economic resources. The government owns all of the resources and operates all of the businesses. All economic decisions are made by a central economic planning group. Although individual people can decide what they will or will not buy, they have no say in determining what will be produced. In other words, the consumer's opinion is not important. The two largest countries using this type of economic system are the People's Republic of China and the Soviet Union.

THE SOCIALISTIC SYSTEM

Under *socialism* the government may own and operate many of the country's basic industries. These industries include the railroads, steel mills, airlines, television stations, and power plants. An important difference between socialism and communism is that under socialism the people may determine the degree of government ownership and control. In fact, some of the country's basic industries are often owned by individuals, and the people have many of the economic freedoms found in capitalism. Examples of countries that have socialistic systems are Great Britain and Sweden.

THE CAPITALISTIC SYSTEM

Capitalism is the economic system used in the United States. Some important features of capitalism are the right to own property and the freedom of economic choice. These rights apply to both producers and consumers. Businesses can produce what they want to and sell it when and where they want to as long as they meet the requirements of the law. Consumers can buy what they want to as long as they have enough money.

In a capitalistic system the consumers can be very important when it comes to taking part in the nation's economic decisions. If a new product is put on the market and consumers do not buy it, the producers will soon stop making it. Thus, each time you buy a product or service you cast an *economic vote.* This economic vote also affects the production of capital goods (goods used to make consumer goods and services). So the consumers have a vote, even though it is indirect, on whether or not capital goods should be produced.

The right to *private ownership of property* is basic to capitalism. This means that producers and consumers have the right to buy, own, use, and sell items of value. These include such things as homes, cars, clothes, tools, office buildings, or the goods a business produces. Whenever you buy goods you must pay for them. Whenever you sell goods, however, you keep the money from the sale.

If you buy and sell goods, you are in business. You are free to choose the type of business you enter and the goods or services you sell. This freedom is called the *right of private enterprise*. Private enterprise is very important to the success of capitalism.

An important feature of private enterprise is that a business is entitled to make a profit if it produces useful goods or services. *Profit* is the difference between what it costs to produce a product or service and what the product or service sells for. The reason a business should be allowed to make a profit is because each firm must usually compete with other firms that sell the same or similar products. This involves some risk and a firm can lose money and go out of business. In general, the consumer benefits from such competition. Competition often leads to lower prices, more services, or better products.

SUMMARY

Every nation has more needs and wants than it has resources to satisfy these needs and wants. This means that nations must decide what goods and services should be produced, how they will be produced, and how they will be shared by the people. A nation's economic system generally provides the answers to these basic questions. The three types of modern economic systems are communism, socialism, and capitalism. Although the United States uses the capitalistic economic system, the government does regulate certain industries.

REVIEW   MAKING ECONOMIC DECISIONS

I. REVIEW OF TERMS

Which words complete the sentences below?

private enterprise   wants
socialism   capitalism
economic system   economize
profit   resources
communism

1. Nations use an _____ to balance economic wants with economic resources.

2. Under capitalism, business firms take risks. In order to get them to take risks, firms must be able to make a _____.

3. The United States uses an economic system called _____.

4. _____ refers to an individual's freedom to decide what business to enter.

5. To _____ means a nation uses its resources wisely.

6. _____ refers to an economic system that has both private and government ownership of business firms.

7. Most nations have unlimited _____ and limited _____.

8. The type of economic system that uses a central economic planning group is called _____.

II. REVIEW OF MAIN POINTS

1. Explain how consumers in a capitalistic economic system can have a voice in the nation's economic decisions.

2. Why is it important that business firms be allowed to make a profit?

3. Which of the three economic systems do you think is best? Why?

4. What are the three basic economic questions every nation must answer?

5. How do you think people should share the goods and services produced in a nation, equally or according to the work they do? Why?

III. MAKING ECONOMIC DECISIONS: CONCEPTS

1. Prepare a list of natural resources that are now in danger of being used up. If the country runs out of one of these resources, how might it affect the way we live?

2. The government controls or sets the prices for many items consumers buy. Explain why it is important, and to the benefit of consumers, that the government regulate the retail price of the following goods and services:
postage stamps   electric power

telephone calls   interstate bus fares

airplane tickets   water

3. Explain why it is more accurate to call the United States economic system modified capitalism rather than pure capitalism.

IV. MAKING ECONOMIC DECISIONS: EXERCISES

1. List five items your family wants today that probably would or could *not* have been on the list when your parents were your age.

2. Do you think profits made by United States companies are too large? Explain your answer.

3. Often you hear that people only go into business "to get rich quick." Do you agree with this statement? Can you think of other reasons why people would go into business?

4. Prepare a list of advantages and disadvantages of living in communistic and capitalistic economic systems. Which system would you prefer? Why?

UNITED STATES ECONOMY

The United States uses an economic system called *modified capitalism.* This system is based on two concepts: profit and competition. In several important industries, however, unlimited profit and competition are not permitted. Government regulates the prices these industries are permitted to charge for their services. Because of this, the profits these industries make are also regulated. Examples of government-regulated industries are public utilities, such as the water company and gas company. Because the services these companies provide are so important to the people who live in the United States, the government wants to make sure that the people can afford to buy them.

Now that you know why the United States has an economic system and what type of economic system the United States has, you might want to think about these two questions:

1. What do the people of the United States expect from their economic system?
2. How does the United States satisfy these expectations, or goals?

GOALS OF THE ECONOMIC SYSTEM

Many people agree that the most important goals of the United States economic system are

1. To distribute resources effectively
2. To provide jobs for all people who want to work
3. To avoid big price increases
4. To divide the wealth of the country fairly among all the people

33

5. To care for those people who cannot help themselves
6. To conserve natural resources by using them wisely
7. To improve the country's environment.

These are not easy goals to reach, and it is not easy for people to agree on how the United States should try to reach them.

The United States tries to reach these goals through its political and economic systems. It is important to understand that the two systems—the political and the economic—must be used together. For example, the Government can use income taxes to divide the nation's wealth

Corporations faced their social responsibility and helped turn "old Pittsburgh" into a "new Pittsburgh."

more evenly among the people. This can be done by making people who earn large incomes pay high taxes and making people who earn small incomes pay low taxes. Exactly how the people are taxed in the United States is decided by the Congress, whose members are elected by the people.

Another way the political system can help the nation reach its economic goals is by setting up programs to care for people who need economic help. In the United States, these programs include Social Security and Medicare.

Assume that a very small nation has a certain standard of living. *Standard of living* means the amount of money, goods, and services a family normally has to use for everyday living. In this example, the country has 100 people and each one earns $1,000 a year. This means the total yearly income for the nation is $100,000. Now suppose the number of people in the nation increases by 10 percent; that is, the *population* grows to 110. What then happens to the nation's standard of living if there is no economic growth? Or what if there is a 10 percent economic growth? Or a 20 percent economic growth? All of these possibilities are listed in Table 4–1. Notice what happens to each person's income when the population increases 10 percent and the total income remains

TABLE 4-1
POPULATION AND A NATION'S ECONOMIC GROWTH

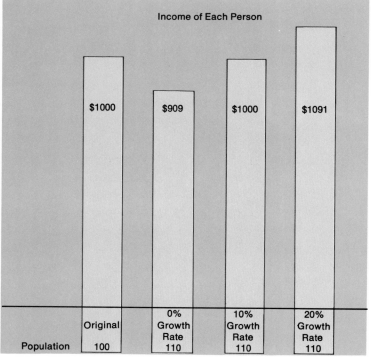

the same. It drops from $1,000 to $909. In other words, the nation's standard of living drops. However, if the nation's income and population grow at the same rate, the standard of living stays the same. If the country's income grows faster than its population, the standard of living increases. This is what happens when the income increases by 20 percent and the population grows only 10 percent. Thus, some economic growth is necessary if a nation is to raise its standard of living while its population is growing.

The United States has set a national goal of improving the standard of living and the quality of life of its citizens. Thus, the United States has decided that some economic growth is necessary.

UNLIMITED VERSUS LIMITED ECONOMIC GROWTH

For many years there was unlimited economic growth in the United States. It was widely believed that the United States would be better off if its population and economy grew very fast and became very large. You may even remember when cities and states boasted about how fast their populations were growing and how many new industries they attracted. The idea of unlimited economic growth was popular until about 1965.

After 1965 many people started to seriously question the idea of un-limited growth. Over a period of several years they began to realize that it would be better to control both population and economic growth. Why? The answer lies in the quality of life the people want. If the population continues to grow very fast, the people's standard of living might fall because the economy might not grow fast enough. Even if the economy could keep up with population growth, a large area of the nation might become unfit for living. Many places might become unfit because of air, water, and noise pollution.

It is important to realize that limited growth is not the same as no growth at all. There must be some economic growth to provide the money for reaching the economic goals mentioned earlier. The objective of the United States now is to have some economic growth but to control it so that the standard of living and the quality of life can improve at the same time.

PROFIT AND ECONOMIC GROWTH

How has economic growth been affected by the idea of working for a profit? Working for a profit is often called the *profit motive*. The profit motive has been very important to the success of capitalism and economic growth in the United States. It has helped keep the economy strong by encouraging people to invest their money in business. Without being rewarded for their work, people probably would not have worked to develop large businesses, such as the computer and automobile industries.

But what do people think of the profit motive? Many people approve of the idea but some do not. In a study made by the Illinois State Chamber of Commerce, high school students thought business profits were too high. More than two-thirds of the students mistakenly thought that profits were at least 16 percent of company sales; that is, for every dollar a company received, 16 cents was thought to be kept as profit. Actually, this figure is usually closer to 6 cents. Very few firms even come close to the 16 percent guess made by these students.

Another way to understand the effect of the profit motive on economic growth is to look at the nation's standard of living. By any economic yardstick, the people of the United States have the highest standard of living of any people in the world. In the United States the profit motive has been the basis for the economic growth, which has resulted in improving the standard of living.

MEASURING ECONOMIC GROWTH

Economic growth means an increase in the nation's production of goods and services. If a nation wants to raise its standard of living, economic growth must be faster than the growth of the population. Measuring a country's economic growth can be done several ways. One way is to measure the value of goods and services in terms of dollars. Another way to measure economic growth is by how much (goods and services) the average person produces. A third way is to measure how much is produced for each man-hour of work.

MEASURING IN DOLLARS

The total dollar value of all the goods and services produced in the United States in a year is called the *gross national product* (GNP). This figure includes producer goods, such as machines and factories, and consumer goods and services, such as airplane rides, cars, bread, and greeting cards. If the GNP increases each year, it is a sign that the economy is growing.

Table 4–2 shows the GNP for certain years from 1929 to 1973. It gives a good idea of how the nation's economy has grown in modern times. The average annual growth of the economy over this period was slightly over 3 percent.

TABLE 4–2
GROSS NATIONAL
PRODUCT FOR SELECTED
YEARS BETWEEN
1929–1973

Year	Total in Billions
1929	203.6
1940	227.2
1945	355.2
1955	438.0
1960	487.7
1965	617.8
1970	722.1
1971	741.7
1972	789.7
1973	837.3

*All values are in 1958
dollars.*

In Figure 4–1 you can see that the largest part of the GNP is money spent for consumer goods and services. Together they make up about 65 percent of the total GNP.

FIGURE 4-1
PARTS OF THE GROSS NATIONAL PRODUCT

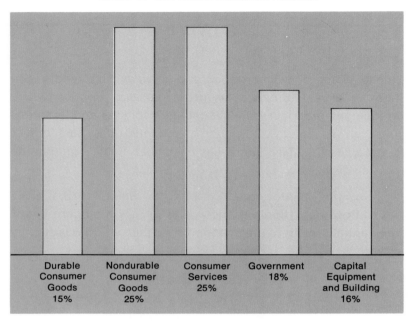

| Durable Consumer Goods 15% | Nondurable Consumer Goods 25% | Consumer Services 25% | Government 18% | Capital Equipment and Building 16% |

Notice that the GNP total is in dollars. This is done so that it is possible to add goods and services together. It would be impossible to add one washing machine, one car, and one visit to a doctor. However, if the

TABLE 4–3
PER CAPITA GROSS NATIONAL PRODUCT FOR
SELECTED YEARS BETWEEN 1929–1973

Year	GNP (in Billions)	Population (in Millions)	Per Capita GNP
1929	$203.6	121,767	$1,672
1940	227.2	132,122	1,719
1945	355.2	139,928	2,538
1955	438.0	165,931	2,640
1960	487.7	180,671	2,700
1965	617.7	194,303	3,179
1970	722.1	204,879	3,525
1971	741.7	207,049	3,582
1972	789.7	208,837	3,781
1973	837.3	210,404	3,979

car is worth $4,000, and the washing machine is worth $300, and the visit to the doctor is $15, then the total value is $4,315.

PRODUCTION PER PERSON

Probably the best way to measure the economic growth of a nation is to divide the total value of its goods and services by the number of its people. This figure is called the *per capita* (per person) *GNP*. It is a good measure of economic growth because it tells if the economy is growing faster than the population. In fact, the per capita GNP of the United States in 1973 was over two times greater than that in 1929.

TABLE 4–4
PER CAPITA GNP FOR SELECTED COUNTRIES
IN 1965

Country	Per Capita GNP
United States	$3,557
Canada	2,464
France	1,924
West Germany	1,905
United Kingdom	1,804
Soviet Union	1,288
Italy	1,101
Japan	857
India	99
China, People's Republic of	98

WORKER PRODUCTIVITY

Another way to measure how the economy is growing is to determine how much is produced per worker in an hour. This is called *worker productivity.* During the period from 1960 to 1970, worker productivity in the United States increased 35 percent. This increase in productivity was the result of using new machines and better production methods.

What are the benefits or advantages of increasing worker productivity? Often it lowers production costs and thus lowers the price of goods and services. If cars were made by hand they would cost so much that only the very rich could buy them. Using modern machines and assembly lines, cars can be made cheap enough for many people to afford them. Also, as workers produce more, labor costs go down. This saving can be passed on to the workers in the form of higher wages (salaries).

ECONOMIC GROWTH OF THE UNITED STATES

Using any of these yardsticks, it is easy to see that the United States' economic growth since 1929 has been very great. You can also see that the United States has the highest standard of living of any country in the world. To better understand this, look at the per capita GNP figures for the United States and various other countries in Table 4-4. These figures show the different types of foreign money *converted* (changed) to United States dollars using the value of one dollar in 1965 as the base. The country closest to the United States is Canada, but even here, the United States figure is almost 50 percent higher.

The economic wealth of the United States is the result of several factors.

1. Natural resources were available.
2. People worked hard.
3. Modern machines were available to produce goods efficiently.
4. The profit motive.

SUMMARY

A nation's standard of living depends on the relationship between two things: its economic growth and its population growth. If the standard of living of the United States is to be raised, one of two things has to happen. If the population grows very fast, the nation must produce goods and services even faster. This can cause many pollution problems that affect the quality of life. The other possibility is to slow the population growth so there are fewer new people. In fact, some people believe that there should be *zero population growth*; that is, the number of people born each year should exactly equal the number of people who die.

Although the nation's birth rate is declining and may eventually reach a growth rate of zero, it does not necessarily mean that there is zero economic growth. It does mean, however, that the standard of living can be improved. If the rate of population growth is less than the rate of economic growth, there are more goods available. More people can move out of poverty while the economy grows at a slower rate. If the United States moves toward zero population growth and also continues to have economic growth, the future of the nation is bright.

REVIEW UNITED STATES ECONOMY

I. REVIEW OF TERMS
Which words complete the following statements?

services	change
worker productivity	goods
economic growth	per capita
gross national product	profit motive
	standard of living

1. The total dollar value of all goods and services produced in the United States during one year is called the _____.
2. A nation's _____ represents the amount of money, goods, and services an individual family has to use for everyday living.
3. The _____ has been very important to the success of capitalism and economic growth in the United States.

4. The one word that best describes the United States economy is _____ .

5. The best way to tell if the economy is growing faster than the population is to use _____ figures.

6. An increase in the production of goods and services is called _____ .

7. One way to measure economic growth is to determine the output per man-hour of labor. This measure is called _____ .

8. The largest part of the United States GNP is represented by the dollars spent for _____ and _____ .

II. REVIEW OF MAIN POINTS

1. Explain how population and economic growth can affect the country's standard of living.

2. What are the major goals of the economic system of the United States?

3. Explain why it is important for businesses in the United States to make a profit.

4. What are the three ways used to measure economic growth? Explain each one and tell which one you think is best.

5. How can the political system be used to help reach the goals people have set for their country's economy?

III. UNITED STATES ECONOMY: CONCEPTS

1. Economic growth is needed if the United States is to improve the standard of living of its poorer citizens. If this is so, explain why many people say that the United States cannot afford to have unlimited economic growth in the future.

2. You have probably heard people say that the younger generation today has more opportunity to do and invent new things than any other generation in United States history. Do you agree? Explain your answer.

IV. UNITED STATES ECONOMY: EXERCISES

1. Discuss with people who were adults during the period of 1930 to 1932 how they lived. Compare their standard of living with yours today. What advantages did they have that you do not have today? What advantages do you have that they did not have? In which time period do you think it would be best to live?

2. Explain why it is important for the United States to move toward the economic goals listed in this chapter.

3. Explain how slowing the population growth and economic growth of the United States can still result in an improvement in the nation's standard of living.

5 INTERNATIONAL TRADE

Each day people buy many things to meet their needs and wants. Whatever they buy must be sold by another person or a business firm. The buying and selling of goods and services is called *trade*.

Today many of the things traded in one city are not made in that city. Because of this, communities and their people depend on other communities and people. Any community in the United States depends on other locations in the world for many kinds of goods. For example, suppose you are in Jackson, Tennessee, and are buying gasoline for your car. The oil may have come originally from the Middle East or South America. It could then have been refined into gasoline at Baton Rouge, Louisiana, and shipped up the Mississippi River on a large tanker to Memphis, Tennessee. From the harbor in Memphis the gasoline would have been carried by truck to the local gas station in Jackson.

People would find it hard to buy gasoline in Jackson, Tennessee, if the United States did not trade with other countries and if there were no trade with other cities in the United States. Trade within one country, say between Baton Rouge and Jackson, is called *domestic trade*. Trade between countries, as between the United States and Iran, is called *international trade.*

WHY DO NATIONS TRADE?

Probably the main reason for international trade is that trading with other nations can raise a country's standard of living. International trade can raise a nation's standard of living because nations, like people, cannot usually do everything for themselves. The United States depends on various countries for a large part of its oil and other natural resources.

Pepsi-Cola is now manufactured under license in the Soviet Union.

Nations tend to specialize in the things they do best. This way, they can produce more than enough of their specialty goods and then sell or trade the *surplus* (extra) with countries that produce other items. The reason countries specialize in doing certain things is that natural, human, and capital resources are not evenly divided among the countries of the world. For example, Norway does not have a warm enough climate (natural resource) for growing lemons, oranges, and other citrus fruits. Norway does, however, have a big fishing industry. This means that Norway must trade some of its fish with a fruit-producing nation, such as Spain.

A country's human resources depend on many things, including the size of the population, the health of the people, and the school system. If a nation does not have good schools and a growing population, it will probably not have a large number of skilled workers.

A country's capital resources are usually the result of a long history of economic development. Countries such as Japan, the United States, and West Germany are rich in capital. India and Uganda are examples of nations that are poor in capital. Poor nations can improve their capital resources by buying or building more machines and factories. As they do this they can start to produce new and different products for international trading.

Because of the differences in a country's resources, some countries can make products cheaper than others. This is called an *absolute cost advantage*. The example of Norway and Spain illustrates this point. It is impossible to grow citrus fruits in Norway as cheaply as in Spain.

The basis of international trade is that countries use their own particular advantages. By using these advantages wisely a nation can produce certain things more cheaply than other nations.

THE UNITED STATES AND INTERNATIONAL TRADE

Even though the United States is a rich country, it depends on other countries for many things. All of the goods that are bought from other countries are called *imports*. Examples of such goods that are bought in large quantities are tea, coffee, crude rubber, silk, bananas, spices, and sugar. The United States also imports many important metals and minerals, such as tin, aluminum, chrome, industrial diamonds, and manganese. Without international trade many of the things the United States needs and wants would cost more than they do now or would not be available at all.

Just as the United States buys things from other countries, it also sells things to many countries. Those goods that are sold to other countries are called *exports.* Exports are good for both the United States and for the other countries. For example, many computers used by business firms in France are made in the United States. The United States also exports large amounts of chemicals, food, farm machinery, medicines, plastics, earth-moving equipment, jet planes, and air conditioners. In 1972 the United States made one of the largest single export sales ever made. Millions of bushels of wheat were sold to the Soviet Union.

The country's exporting efforts affect its economy in two ways. First, the jobs of millions of workers, both in industry and on farms, depend on how much the United States exports. Also, the profits of many companies depend on how much their goods and services are wanted by other nations. The computer industry of the United States, for example, will benefit greatly if the Soviet Union and other countries decide to use United States computers instead of making their own.

TABLE 5–1
UNITED STATES IMPORTS AND EXPORTS
TO WORLD REGIONS AND SELECTED
COUNTRIES, 1973

Region	Millions of Dollars	
	Exports	Imports
Africa	$ 2,307	$ 2,350
Asia	18,426	17,775
Australia and Oceania	1,744	1,554
Canada	15,073	17,443
Europe		
—Western	21,361	19,162
—Eastern	1,797	519
South and Central America	9,931	9,338
Unidentified Countries	677	981
TOTAL	$71,316	$69,122

Exports from the United States are only about 4 to 5 percent of the value of the country's total goods and services. In Belgium exports are 38 percent of the total, in Sweden they are 20 percent, and in England they are 14 percent. Although the United States sells a fairly small amount of its total goods and services to other countries, the dollar amounts are not small. For example, in 1972 the exported goods and services amounted to almost $50 billion.

Looking at Table 5–1, note that western Europe, which includes many industrial (capital-rich) nations, is the United States' biggest export market. Canada and the Asian countries, mainly Japan, are the next largest markets.

PAYING FOR INTERNATIONAL TRADE

Countries, like people, must pay for the goods they buy. They must also collect money for the goods they sell. Unfortunately, paying for international trade is not as easy as paying local business firms. Local business firms are paid with money that can be used anywhere in the United States. However, suppose that different states used different types of money, each with a different value. Think of the trouble you would have if you lived in Rhode Island and went shopping in Vermont. You would have to change your Rhode Island money into Vermont money. If you then went on vacation to Massachusetts, you would have to change both the Vermont money and Rhode Island money into Massachusetts money. This is what happens when a person travels to another country or when one country trades with another.

Since each country has a different type of money (currency), rates of exchange must be established. A *rate of exchange* is the price at which one country's money is converted (changed) into another country's money. For example, one British pound sterling, a unit of money in the United Kingdom, is equal to about $2.30 in United States money. The changing of one money into another takes place in *foreign exchange markets*. These markets are not in any one place but are wherever banks buy and sell the monies of different countries. Two of the most important foreign exchange markets are in London, England, and New York City. These markets are very important in making it possible for international traders to make and receive payments.

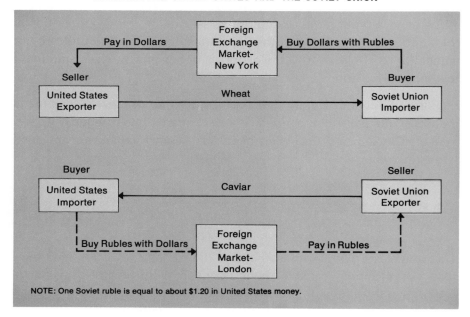

FIGURE 5-1
INTERNATIONAL TRADE
BETWEEN THE UNITED STATES AND THE SOVIET UNION

To show how the system works, consider international trading between the United States and the Soviet Union. The United States buys caviar from the Soviet Union and sells farm products, such as wheat, to the Soviet Union. This trading is shown in Figure 5–1.

Notice that the London foreign exchange market makes it possible for the United States importer (buyer) of caviar to pay the Soviet exporter (seller) in rubles. In the same way, the Soviet importer of wheat pays in United States dollars by working through the New York foreign exchange market.

THE BALANCE OF INTERNATIONAL TRADE

The difference in dollar value between a country's total exports and its total imports is called that nation's *balance of trade.* If a country exports (sells) more than it imports (buys) it has a favorable balance of

TABLE 5-2
BALANCE OF TRADE OF THE UNITED
STATES 1959-1973 (IN BILLIONS OF
DOLLARS)

Year	Net Exports	Year	Net Exports
1959	$ .1	1966	5.3
1960	4.0	1967	5.2
1961	5.6	1968	2.5
1962	5.1	1969	1.9
1963	5.9	1970	3.6
1964	8.5	1971	.7
1965	6.9	1972	−4.6
		1973	4.0

NOTE: *Net exports is the value of exports of goods and services minus the amount of imports of goods and services.*

trade. On the other hand, if a country imports (buys) more than it exports (sells) it has an unfavorable balance of trade.

Looking at Table 5-2 you can see that the United States had a favorable balance of trade during the last decade. However, in 1972 the United States imported more than it exported. Thus, in that year it had an unfavorable balance of trade. (Except for the period during World War II, this was the first time since 1893 that the United States had an unfavorable balance of trade.) The reason this happened was that many United States goods were too expensive for foreigners to buy. This price increase did not happen in just one year. The balance of trade started to decrease in 1968 and finally became unfavorable four years later.

THE BALANCE OF PAYMENTS

The balance of payments works very much like the personal buying you do each year. Just as you try to balance the money you earn with the money you spend, so must nations. A country's *balance of payments* is the dollar value of all the economic activities that take place between that country and the rest of the world during one year.

The balance of payments is not the same as the balance of trade. The balance of trade is only part of the balance of payments. Other money that goes into the balance of payments includes the money United States tourists spend in foreign countries, the money involved in the purchase and sale of foreign stocks and bonds, and the money spent by United States soldiers overseas. To understand the things that make up the balance of payments, it is helpful to divide them into two groups: outpayments (minus items) and inpayments (plus items). *Outpayments* include imports, overseas military spending, and United States investments abroad. *Inpayments* are such things as exports, foreign money invested in United States companies, and money spent by foreigners visiting the United States.

These goods represent some of the imports and exports of the United States.

Table 5-3 shows the balance of payments of the United States for the years 1960 through 1973. In certain years the figure is shown with a minus sign, meaning that in those years the United States spent more than it received from other countries. When this happens the United States is said to have a *deficit* in its balance of payments. In those years when the United States received more than it spent, the balance of payments shows a *surplus*. This difference is covered by the flow of gold and financial claims between countries.

TABLE 5-3 UNITED STATES BALANCE OF PAYMENTS POSITION 1960-1973 (In Billions of Dollars)	
Year	Balance of Payments
1960	$- 3,400
1961	- 1,300
1962	- 2,700
1963	- 1,900
1964	- 1,500
1965	- 1,300
1966	200
1967	- 3,400
1968	1,600
1969	2,700
1970	- 9,800
1971	-29,800
1972	-10,400
1973	- 5,300

Gold bricks in a New York bank. Gold serves as a basis for the United States money supply.

An important point to remember is that the balance of payments account is always made to balance. If the United States has a deficit, the difference is usually settled by an exchange of gold and financial claims with other countries. The United States Government keeps most of its gold at Fort Knox, Kentucky. This gold is worth many billions of dollars and serves as a basis for the money supply of the United States.

BARRIERS TO TRADE

Free trade is the buying and selling of goods and services between nations without anything to hinder or restrict it. This is the type of trading that takes place between two or more states. For example, if you live in Hammond, Indiana, you can shop in Chicago, Illinois, without paying a special tax to the State of Illinois.

Barriers to international free trade are meant to help businesspeople sell their products in their own country. The two main types of barriers are tariffs and import quotas. A *tariff* is a tax that is put on imported goods or services. Suppose you want to buy a camera. The Japanese manufacturer sets a price of $100 on the Japanese camera. The United States manufacturer sets a price on a similar camera at $110. To protect United States businesspeople, the United States Government could put a 15 percent import tariff on the Japanese camera, which would make the price $115. Thus, the United States consumer would probably buy the camera from the United States manufacturer, rather than from the Japanese (or any other foreign) manufacturer.

An *import quota* puts a limit on the amount of a particular product that can be imported during a certain period of time. Quotas have been used in the United States to control the import of many things, including oil, cattle, and sugar. In 1973 President Nixon changed the oil import quota so that more oil could be brought into the United States. This was because the United States was facing a serious shortage of gasoline and heating oil.

SUMMARY

Trade between nations is called international trade. Nations trade with one another because it is to their economic advantage. Nations tend to specialize in producing certain goods because natural, human, and capital resources are not evenly divided throughout the world. Even though there are some advantages to free international trade many countries have established trade barriers, such as tariffs and import quotas.

I. REVIEW OF TERMS

Which words complete the sentences below?

absolute cost advantage
international trade
foreign exchange markets
balance of trade

domestic trade
exports
balance of payments
import quota
rate of exchange

1. Goods and services that are sold to other nations are called _____ .

2. The difference between a country's exports and imports is called its _____ .

3. Trade between nations is known as _____ , while trade within a country is known as _____ .

4. An _____ places a limit on the amount of a particular product that can be brought into a country.

5. The price at which one nation's money is changed into another country's money is the _____ .

6. When one nation can produce certain goods more cheaply than another nation can, this is called an _____ .

7. _____ play an important role in making it possible for international traders to make and receive payments.

8. The money value of all economic transactions between one country and the rest of the world is called the _____ .

II. REVIEW OF MAIN POINTS

1. Explain why nations trade with one another.
2. The United States is a very rich country. Explain why it is necessary for the United States to become involved with international trade.
3. Define the terms *balance of trade* and *balance of payments*. Are they the same? Explain.

4. What are two barriers to free international trade? Explain how each works.
5. When does a country have a favorable balance of trade?

III. INTERNATIONAL TRADE: CONCEPTS

1. Since the end of World War II the United States has stationed thousands of military troops in Europe. Explain how this has had a negative (minus) effect on the United States' balance of payments.
2. Locate the foreign exchange section of the *Wall Street Journal* or the financial section of a large city newspaper. Prepare a list of the current exchange rates for the countries listed below and show how their rates have changed.

   Australia (dollar)   Italy (lira)
   Great Britain (pound)   Japan (yen)
   Canada (dollar)   Switzerland (franc)
   Denmark (krone)   West Germany (mark)

3. Explain why a decline (devaluation) in the dollar exchange rate would make it easier for United States companies to sell their goods in Great Britain.

IV. INTERNATIONAL TRADE: EXERCISES

1. Find five items in your home that were imported or that have some imported part. List where you think these items could have come from. If you did not have these five items, how would your life be affected?
2. Trace the basic steps involved in the export of United States products (such as plywood) to Japan and the import of Japanese products (such as cars) to the United States. Show in a diagram how the exporters and importers convert United States dollars and Japanese yen in order to make payments.
3. Go to one of the following businesses and talk to the owner or manager about the types of goods he or she imports for sale in your community. Prepare a list of at least ten things and show from where the items were imported and if any tariffs were paid.

   jewelry store   drugstore
   grocery store   clothing store
   gift shop   appliance store

Unit II
The Organization
of Business

If you were setting up a business, you would first want some important questions answered. Among these questions are How should the business be set up? Who will run it? How much money will be needed to start and continue it? How much money will be lost if the business fails? How successful will the business be in five years? Is special equipment needed to help run the business?

There are no simple answers to these questions. There are, however, some basic characteristics of business organizations. Understanding these characteristics can help you answer these questions.

In Chapter 6 you will learn about the oldest form of business organization, the business owned by one person, or the sole proprietorship. Over 75 percent of all businesses in the United States are sole proprietorships. Sole proprietorships are often depended upon for shoes and clothing. Chapter 6 will also point out the advantages and disadvantages of sole proprietorships.

The second section of Chapter 6 covers partnerships. The advantages and disadvantages of partnerships are explained.

Chapter 7 discusses the corporation and its history. The reasons why corporations are attractive to many people will be given as well as some of the unfavorable features of corporations.

All three types of businesses—the sole proprietorship, the partnership, and the corporation—need a manager or management team. Chapter 8 looks at the need for managerial know-how in business organizations.

The final chapter of this unit discusses the computer. Small businesses and giant corporations alike have found the computer to be a valuable aid. You will learn how a computer works and how it is used in business.

UNIT PREVIEW

AS YOU STUDY THIS UNIT YOU WILL BE ENGAGED IN

* **DISCOVERING** the advantages of a sole proprietorship as compared with a partnership

* **ANALYZING** the nature of a company and contrasting a profit and non-profit corporation

* **IDENTIFYING** the persons in authority and with responsibility by analyzing the organization chart of a business

* **DESCRIBING** the differences in duties for top-, middle-, and lower-level managers

* **UNDERSTANDING** the functions of the computer in serving management and employees.

A FOCUS FOR YOUR STUDY

6 SOLE PROPRIETORSHIPS AND PARTNERSHIPS

Whenever a business is started, whether it will sell motor bikes, tape cassettes, fishing equipment, or women's wigs, one important question must be answered: What type of business should be formed? This chapter examines two types of business firms—those owned by *one* person, a *sole, or individual, proprietorship* and those owned by *two or more* people, a *partnership.* The next chapter covers the third type of business. This business is usually owned by many people and is called a *corporation*. Figure 6-1 shows these three major types of business organizations.

FIGURE 6-1
FORMS OF BUSINESS ORGANIZATION IN OUR SOCIETY

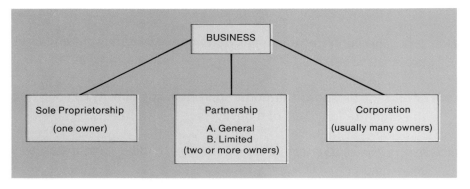

SOLE PROPRIETORSHIP

The *sole proprietorship,* a business owned by one person, is the oldest type of business. This is also called a *sole ownership*. In this type of business, the owner usually plans what the business is going to try to accomplish and is responsible for the success or failure of the business.

The sole proprietorship is the major type of business found in most *industrialized* nations. Industrialized nations have many industries that make a wide variety of products, such as cars, food, and clothing. Therefore, the sole proprietorship is the major business organization in Canada, Japan, West Germany, and the United States.

FIGURE 6-2
TYPES OF BUSINESS OWNERSHIPS

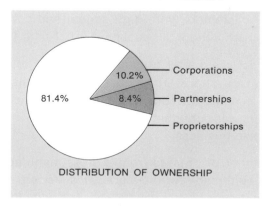

DISTRIBUTION OF OWNERSHIP

You probably do business with many sole proprietors. You purchase your school supplies, your lunch, or have your clothes cleaned by businesses that are sole proprietorships.

STARTING A SOLE PROPRIETORSHIP

To learn more about the sole proprietorship business, read about the experiences of a young woman who started her own business. Jill

Brightly, when she was seventeen years old, had worked part-time for one year in a local drugstore. Every week she saved part of the money she earned. Her goal was to own her own business someday; that is, she wanted to be a sole proprietor.

Jill took as many business courses as her high school offered, and when she was eighteen she became a salesworker in a women's clothing store. She enjoyed selling the elegant evening clothes and sportswear, and most of her customers were high school and college girls. After graduation from high school Jill accepted a full-time job in the store.

During the first six years after graduation, Jill was able to save some money from each paycheck. Through her job she also learned a lot about the women's fashion business. When she had finally saved enough money and was confident of her ability to sell women's fashions, she started her own business.

Jill bought a number of dresses from a dress manufacturer, rented a store, and had a sign made for the store, *Jill's Modern Women's Wear.* From the very start of the business, the responsibility for either making or losing money was Jill's since she was the sole proprietor.

In the beginning of her venture, Jill did not have enough money in her savings to buy all of the dresses she wanted to have in her store. She also did not have enough money to buy the cash register and all of the clothing display racks she wanted. She had saved $6,000 and had to borrow $2,000 from the bank. This borrowed money, however, had to be paid back to the bank within one year after she borrowed it. During that first year Jill had to earn enough money to pay back the borrowed money and still have enough left over to earn a living.

ADVANTAGES OF SOLE OWNERSHIP

There are several reasons why this type of business arrangement is so popular. The most important reasons are

1. *The sole owner receives all of the profits.* In Jill's case, all of the profits belonged to her. She did not have to share the profits with any other owner. Part of the profits could be kept by Jill as her

salary. The remaining profits could be used to purchase things for the store.

2. *The sole owner does not answer to anybody else.* Jill did not have to discuss with any other person what style of dresses she would buy and display in her store. She was her own boss and could do as she pleased. This feeling encouraged her to work harder to make the business a success.

3. *The sole owner is free from filing legal papers.* A person can usually start or end a sole proprietorship without having to file legal papers with a state or city government. This saves the owner the expense of hiring a lawyer. Restaurant owners, however, must have a license in order to operate, and government inspectors regularly check the restaurant for cleanliness.

4. *The sole owner knows the employees and customers.* Since most sole proprietorships are small, the owner can get to know each worker, or employee, personally. Also, the owner gets to know the customers better. For example, if Ms. Wilcox does not like the color blue, Jill would show her only dresses of other colors. Most customers enjoy this personal touch.

5. *The sole owner usually pays less income tax.* In most sole proprietorships, the income tax paid to Federal and state governments is usually less than a corporation would pay.

DISADVANTAGES OF SOLE OWNERSHIP

Although the advantages of sole ownership are certainly attractive, there are also a number of disadvantages.

1. *The sole owner absorbs all losses.* Just as the sole owners get all the profits, they also absorb all of the business losses. If Jill's business had gone so badly that she could not have paid back the bank, the bank could have had her sell her personal property to raise the money she owed them. For example, Jill may have had a beautiful jade bracelet she could have sold. Thus, Jill may have lost not only the money she invested in the business but also her personal property, such as the bracelet. Jill had the full responsibility of paying the debts of the business.

2. *The sole owner may not be able to do many jobs.* The sole owner, in many cases, must be able to do many jobs. Jill, for example, must buy and sell the dresses, plan the newspaper advertisements, help solve the salesworkers' arguments about who will work on Saturdays, and handle customers' complaints. If she cannot do all of these jobs fairly well, the business could fail. For any sole owner to do so many things well is a large order. Thus, it is easy to understand why so many sole proprietorships end in failure.

3. *The sole owner has a limited amount of money.* Jill invested all of her savings in her store. If she suddenly needed more money, Jill might have trouble raising it. For example, if she wanted to buy a particular new style of dress, she might need $2,000. If she could not borrow this money she would have to cancel her plans for buying the dresses.

4. *The sole owner's death or long illness may close the business.* Since the sole owner is the boss, his or her death or long illness usually forces the business to close.

SOLELY OWNED BUSINESSES IN THE COMMUNITY

Even a quick look at the businesses in your community will immediately point out the large number of solely owned businesses that you deal with every day. They usually include barbershops, beauty parlors, real estate agencies, restaurants, and repair shops for radios, televisions, cars, and appliances.

A type of business that is well suited for a sole proprietorship is one that sells goods but does not need a large number of employees or a lot of money. Such businesses include roadside fruit and vegetable stands, grocery stores, dress shops, and dry-cleaning stores.

PARTNERSHIPS

Jill, the sole proprietor of a dress store, was eventually faced with the problem of expanding her store so that she could sell many more styles.

In order to expand, Jill had to get more money. She also needed more experience in how to buy dresses. Since Jill did not want to borrow more money, she decided that a partnership was the best type of business arrangement for her.

A friend of Jill's, Amy Smartly, had worked for the past eight years as a buyer of women's fashions in a large department store in New York City. She studied retailing (selling) in high school and was known to be hard working and honest. After discussing a partnership, Jill and Amy hired a lawyer to draw up an agreement called the *articles of partnership.*

Actually there are two basic types of partnerships. Amy and Jill formed a *general partnership.* The second type is a special type of partnership called a *limited partnership.*

In forming their general partnership, Jill and Amy agreed to the following:

1. The name of the store would be "The Jill and Amy Fashion Store."
2. Jill and Amy would each invest $5,000 in cash.
3. Each partner would draw a salary of $700 a month.
4. Profits or losses, after all salaries were paid, would be shared equally by Jill and Amy.
5. Jill would handle the sales within the store, the customer complaints, the financial records, and the hiring of employees. Amy would be responsible for buying dresses from manufacturers, advertising, and helping Jill with selling the dresses.
6. Any business checks written must be signed by both Jill and Amy.
7. If either Jill or Amy were to leave the business, the other partner would have the right to buy the departing partner's share of the ownership.

ADVANTAGES OF PARTNERSHIP

As with the sole proprietorship, the general partnership also has advantages and disadvantages. Some of the advantages are

1. *The pooling of funds* Jill had used all of her savings and had no more money to invest. By establishing a partnership Jill could combine, or pool, her money with Amy's. This ability to pool money is a major reason why partnerships are so attractive to many people.
2. *The talents of different people are brought together.* It is often necessary to use the talents of different people to make sure the business earns money. A partnership lets the owners use their best talents. Jill used her skill of working with people, while Amy used her buying skills. They hoped that the combining of talents would result in a more efficient and more profitable business.
3. *The credit rating is better.* Because there are two or more owners in a partnership, more people are responsible for its success or failure. A bank that loans money to the business would look at the number of responsible owners and then judge the partnership to be a better credit risk than a sole proprietorship. Thus, the bank would feel that it is taking less of a risk in loaning the partnership money because there are two people—Amy and Jill—responsible for paying the bank back, not just one.

4. *There is a joint effort in running the business.* Partners often suggest plans of action to each other. This type of discussion seems to create a greater concern for the business. Both individuals have an interest, namely an investment of money and time, and this causes them to work harder toward improving the business.

5. *The partnership usually pays less income tax.* Although the partnership must file a federal income tax report, it does not pay as much tax as a corporation.

DISADVANTAGES OF PARTNERSHIPS

Some of the more important disadvantages of the general partnership are

1. *Each partner is responsible for the firm's debts.* Unless some type of legal agreement is reached when the partnership papers are drawn up, each person in a general partnership is responsible for the money that the partnership owes, no matter how much he or she has personally invested. If the business does not pay the money it owes, the debt must be paid by the individual partners. If one partner does not have enough money to pay his or her share of the debt, the other partners have to pay it. If Jill and Amy's partnership failed after three years and the business had a $12,000 debt, the two partners would have to combine their money. For example, Jill may have $9,000 worth of personal property—including her car, jewelry, and clothing—to sell and Amy may have only $3,000 worth. Thus, although Jill and Amy are equal partners in the business, Jill would have to pay 75 percent of the money owed, while Amy would have to pay only 25 percent.

2. *The power and authority are divided.* Since each partner has something to say about making decisions, there will be times when the partners will not agree with each other. As a result, poor decisions may be made. Disagreements between partners can also lead to making slower decisions since the disagreement must be settled before the partners can act.

3. *The lifetime of the partnership is uncertain.* If one partner dies the partnership must go out of business. The partners who live may reorganize and form a new partnership, but they must buy the

dead partner's share of the business. In most states, the death of a partner or the bankruptcy (inability to pay debts) of a partner is a cause for ending the partnership.

THE LIMITED PARTNERSHIP

In a limited partnership, the *general partners* have unlimited responsibility (or liability) for any business debts and the *limited partners* have limited responsibility. The limited partners are only responsible, or liable, for the amount of money they contributed to the partnership.

It is impossible to form a limited partnership without at least one general partner. The limited partner is bound by law not to become involved in managing the business. The major advantage of a limited partnership is that it attracts people who want to contribute money to a business but do not want the responsibility of making business decisions.

PARTNERSHIPS IN THE COMMUNITY

Businesses that are suited for partnership arrangements include barbershops, beauty parlors, radio and television repair shops, restaurants, grocery stores, dress shops, dry-cleaning establishments, and landscaping firms.

68

SUMMARY

The major type of business organization in most industrialized nations today is the sole proprietorship. Over 75 percent of the businesses in the United States are owned by sole proprietors. The next most popular type of business organization is the partnership, of which there are two kinds: general and limited. Both advantages and disadvantages of sole proprietorships and partnerships are discussed. In Chapter 7 the third type of business organization, the corporation, is examined.

REVIEW   SOLE PROPRIETORSHIPS AND PARTNERSHIPS

I. REVIEW OF TERMS

Which words complete the statements below?

sole proprietorship   general partnership

limited partner

1. In a _____ each person is responsible by law for the money that the business owes.
2. A partner who has no say in running the business but only contributes money to it is a _____.
3. A business that is owned by only one person is a _____.

II. REVIEW OF MAIN POINTS

1. Name at least two disadvantages of a sole proprietorship.
2. What generally happens to a partnership when a partner dies?
3. What is a general partner?
4. What is a limited partner?
5. What are articles of partnership?

6. How are profits divided in a partnership?
7. Name at least two advantages of a sole proprietorship.
8. If a business fails and one of the partners goes bankrupt, what must the other partner or partners do?
9. Why might a sole proprietor want to form a partnership?

III. SOLE PROPRIETORSHIPS AND PARTNERSHIPS: CONCEPTS

1. Why is it good to have a legal partnership agreement?
2. What should a person know about unlimited liability?
3. Suppose Jill and Amy have failed in their partnership and the business owes $20,000. Jill has personal property worth $18,000, but Amy has nothing. How much of the store's debt will Jill probably have to pay?
4. Why would a person want to become a limited partner in a profitable (money-making) restaurant?
5. Why is a sole proprietor considered to be the boss of a business?
6. It is said that a dry-cleaning establishment can be either a sole proprietorship or a partnership. Is this correct? Why?
7. If you were to go into business with a partner, what personal and financial characteristics would you consider?

IV. SOLE PROPRIETORSHIPS AND PARTNERSHIPS: EXERCISES

1. If you were going to draw up articles of partnership, what factors would you be sure to cover? List them and explain each one.
2. Name some partnerships that exist in your community.

CORPORATIONS

Most large businesses are *corporations.* A corporation is made up of a number of owners that have the right to do business as a single legal unit. Compared to the sole proprietorship and the partnership, a corporation is more difficult to start and to operate. In this chapter you will learn how a business is started and operated as a corporation. In addition, some of the advantages and disadvantages of corporations will be discussed. Businesses that are similar to corporations will also be discussed.

CORPORATIONS

Throughout your lifetime you will probably buy many products and services produced by corporations. You may buy a car made by the Chevrolet division of the General Motors corporation. You may buy film as well as a camera and a movie projector made by the Eastman Kodak corporation. You may travel on a coast-to-coast flight in a plane manufactured by the Boeing corporation. The corporate business form is certainly a part of your daily life.

How did General Motors, Eastman Kodak, Boeing, and other corporations become established? A corporation is regulated by a state government which passes *corporation laws.* Each state has slightly different laws concerning the formation of a corporation. These laws differ in the amounts the corporation will be taxed by the state and the steps that have to be taken to establish a corporation. Some states make it very easy to form a corporation, or to become *incorporated.* Other states make it more difficult because of legal problems. For example, some states require that the backgrounds of the company's officers be carefully checked before a *charter* can be issued.

A corporation does not exist except in law. The right to do business is not given by the state to a sole owner or to a partner but to the corporation. Instead of granting Jill, the owner of a dress store, the right to operate, the state would grant these rights to a corporation owned by her. When the owner dies, the corporation continues for it is treated as a single legal unit. Compare this with the sole proprietorship, which usually ceases to exist when the owner dies.

HISTORY OF CORPORATIONS

It is believed that corporations date back to the fifth century when the corporate form was used to establish Roman military and religious organizations. In the United States, the early settlers did business with trading companies in England. These trading companies resembled corporations and had the right to do business in a particular part of the country. In 1811, the State of New York passed laws that limited a person's responsibility in a corporation, making sure the person could not lose any more than the person had invested. For example, if Claude Betteroff invested $100 in a corporation that produced stereo tapes and the corporation failed, Mr. Betteroff would lose only the $100 invested. In Jill and Amy's partnership, both women were responsible for business losses and had to pay off debts by selling their personal property. The New York laws helped make the corporation a popular type of business organization. Corporation laws continued to improve, and, as the country grew, the increased demands for more products, such as cars, airplanes, dishwashers, and furniture, encouraged the growth of corporations.

THE CORPORATION'S OWNERS

Few individuals or partnerships could raise the money needed to start a large airline like American Airlines, a steel company like United States Steel, or an appliance company like General Electric. For a business that needs a lot of money for machinery, raw materials, and salaries, the corporation is a good type of organization. The people who put money into a corporation are the owners. General Motors, the

FIGURE 7-1   THE CREATION AND GROWTH OF A CORPORATION

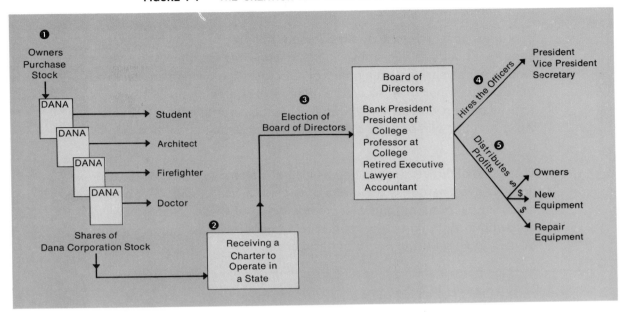

largest manufacturing company in the United States, has over one million owners; that is, more than one million people have invested money in General Motors.

To start a corporation, people hire a lawyer to help them request a charter from the state. Each state issues *charters* or *certificates,* which generally tell what type of business the corporation can do and how many shares of *stock* it can sell. The shares of stock are sold for money, and each person buying a share becomes an owner. A *stock certificate* is an actual piece of paper that is evidence of ownership.

THE MANAGERS OF THE CORPORATION

Every type of business must have decisions made for it every day of the week. The people who operate the business must decide what to buy, how to advertise, and whom to hire. The people who make these crucial decisions are called the *management.* In the example of the sole proprietorship the management was Jill. In the partnership example the management was Jill and Amy.

In a large corporation it would be impossible for every owner to make important business decisions. To make decisions for them, the owners meet once a year to elect a *board of directors*. The owners are allowed the same number of votes as the number of shares of stock they own. Thus, a person who owns 4,200 shares of stock is entitled to 4,200 votes, while another person who owns one share of stock is entitled to only one vote.

The board of directors picks people, called *officers,* to manage the corporation. The board may appoint a president, a vice president of operations, an accountant, and a secretary. None of these officers have to be owners. Although it is to their advantage, it is not necessary for owners to vote for the board of directors.

PROFIT AND NONPROFIT CORPORATIONS

Corporations such as General Motors, International Business Machines (IBM), Proctor and Gamble, and Sears are in business to earn a profit. However, there are corporations that do not earn profits. Many religious organizations, charities, and educational institutions are nonprofit corporations. These will be discussed in more detail in later chapters.

A stockholders' meeting and an original stock certificate, which belonged to the founder of the Ford Motor Company.

The board of directors of a profit-making corporation decides how the profits will be used. For example, the Dana Health Foods Corporation earned a profit of $500,000 one year after paying all expenses (salaries, etc.). More than half of the profit money was needed to pay federal and state taxes. Of the remaining profits, the board of directors decided to distribute $100,000 to the *stockholders,* or owners. These payments to the owners are called *dividends.* Owners can receive dividends on each share of the company's stock they own. The rest of the profit was used to replace old equipment, repair broken equipment, hire more sales-people, and do similar things to improve the corporation.

The steps in forming a corporation include raising money, receiving a state charter or certificate, electing a board of directors, picking managers, and distributing and using profits. Some of the important things to remember are

1. The stockholders own the business.
2. Any person of legal age (eighteen or over) can become an owner if stock is available.
3. The corporation is granted the right to operate by a charter or a certificate from the state.
4. The owners elect a board of directors.
5. The directors hire the officers—the people who actually run the corporation.
6. The officers have the responsibility of running the business and of hiring more workers if necessary.
7. The directors distribute the profits.
8. If the company earns enough money, the owners can receive a part of the profits in the form of dividends.

ADVANTAGES OF CORPORATIONS

There are advantages and disadvantages of owning a part of a corporation. Some of the advantages are

1. *Limited liability of the owners* If the corporation fails, the owners' responsibilities are limited; that is, they can lose only the money they paid for their shares of stock. The owners do not have to sell their personal property to pay money owed by the corporation.

2. *The ability to raise money* A corporation usually can get money more easily than any other type of business. There are usually many people who might want to become owners. People are willing to buy stocks because of the opportunity of making money (dividends), because they, as owners, have limited liability, and because they do not have to run the business.

3. *Specialized management* Corporations are usually much larger than sole proprietorships or partnerships and can be run by people who specialize in certain areas. In a corporation, *specialists* are in charge of production, advertising, selling, accounting, research, and other areas. In a sole proprietorship or a partnership, only one person or a few people must do all of these jobs.

4. *Owners can sell their shares of stock.* The stock that people buy to become owners in a corporation can be sold. For example, if the owners wanted to get back the money they had spent for their stock, they could sell their shares without having to get anyone's approval. A *stockbrokerage* company could handle the sale of the stock.

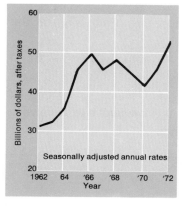

FIGURE 7-2
CORPORATE PROFITS

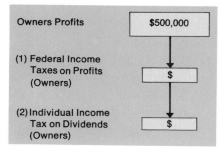

FIGURE 7-2
DOUBLE TAXATION OF CORPORATIONS

DISADVANTAGES OF CORPORATIONS

Corporations have a number of disadvantages. These disadvantages apply to the corporation as a business organization, however, and not to the owners.

1. *More difficult to organize* It is often more difficult to organize a corporation than it is to organize a sole proprietorship or a partnership. People wishing to form a corporation must follow the legal requirements of the state in which the company becomes incorporated. A lawyer handles all of the legal work involved when a company incorporates, and legal fees can be expensive. Also, in some states, special fees to incorporate and various taxes must be paid when the incorporation begins.

2. *Taxes are often higher.* A corporation may have to pay taxes in each state in which it does business. For example, if the Dana corporation sells health foods in 20 states, it may have to pay a tax in each state. The profits of a corporation are also taxed by the Federal Government. The dividends that the owners get are also taxed as part of each owner's income tax.

3. *Lack of interest* The proprietor or partners of a business are eager to do their best because failing means that they will go out of business. The owners of corporations, however, usually have little interest in the workings of the business. They are mainly interested in the dividends they will receive. This lack of interest can cause poor corporate management.

OTHER TYPES OF BUSINESSES

There are several other types of business organizations. From time to time, state and Federal governments have formed *government corpora-*

Each of these stores has formed a cooperative to take advantage of buying larger quantities at lower costs.

tions. These organizations provide services to the public. The Federal Government has formed such organizations as the Tennessee Valley Authority and the Federal Deposit Insurance Corporation. Organizations dealing with water systems and banking have been incorporated by state and even city governments. These government corporations do not make profits. They earn only enough money to pay for their expenses.

A small number of businesses in the United States are run as *cooperatives.* A cooperative is a business owned by its customers. One example of a cooperative is the Sunkist Growers, Inc. Its purpose is to supply goods and services to its customers. If there are profits, the money is given to the customers (or owners). There are also *consumer cooperatives* in which people get together to buy goods. Each member then buys part of the goods. By buying in large amounts, customers are usually able to buy the goods cheaper than if they purchased them in smaller amounts.

Gulf & Western is a conglomerate that manufactures a variety of products.

There are also stores that form a cooperative to take advantage of buying larger amounts at lower prices. The store cooperative then sells its goods to its members at lower prices than other stores selling the same goods. For example, if you bought an orange in a regular grocery store it might cost ten cents. However, if you belonged to a cooperative store that bought in large amounts, the orange might cost only eight cents.

Another form of business is the *conglomerate.* A conglomerate develops when one business firm gets control of a number of other firms, often by buying large amounts of the other firms' stock. In some cases, an organization gets control of 20 firms. These firms may be in 20 different regions and they may produce many different kinds of products. For example, a food company may buy control of a clothing company, a tool manufacturer, a computer manufacturer, and a small airline. Two large conglomerates in the United States are Litton Industries and Gulf and Western.

Conglomerates have a number of advantages and possible disadvantages. One advantage is that conglomerates make it possible to bring together people with different talents and experience. Also, the money of many different companies can be combined so that research in many different areas can be conducted. The Federal Government makes sure that firms in a conglomerate do not do business only with each other. It is against the law to exclude competing firms from the business market.

SUMMARY

The form of ownership of a business organization is important to consumers, employees, and society. The most difficult form of business to start and run is the corporation. Corporations are responsible for more than 75 percent of all the business done in the United States. The corporation is also found in government organizations, such as the Tennessee Valley Authority and the Federal Deposit Insurance Corporation.

I. REVIEW OF TERMS

Which words complete the statements below?

Roman	owner
board of directors	charter
officers	votes

1. An _____ of a corporation has limited liability, or responsibility.
2. A corporation is granted the right to operate by a _____ or a certificate from the state.
3. The history of corporations dates back to the _____ Empire.
4. The _____ is elected by the owners of a corporation.
5. The _____ of a corporation are appointed by the board of directors.
6. The owners of a corporation are allowed as many _____ as they own shares of stock.

II. REVIEW OF MAIN POINTS

1. What is a conglomerate?
2. What things do you purchase from a corporation?
3. Can the officers of a corporation receive dividends? If so, when?
4. Who can become an owner of a corporation?
5. The president of General Motors is the only owner of this corporation. Is this a true statement? Why?
6. Can a person lose money by investing in a corporation?
7. What is limited liability?
8. Can a corporation raise money from many different people? If so, how is this done?
9. What is a corporation charter?

10. Name two corporations in each of the following fields:
   a. oil production   **c.** food manufacturing
   b. air travel   **d.** automobile production

III. CORPORATIONS: CONCEPTS

1. Discuss some of the reasons why a person would want to invest in a corporation.
2. Why would it be helpful to form a cooperative to buy food?
3. If a person owned 100 shares of stock and the company gave a dividend of $2.25 a share, would an owner receive more than $200 in dividends?
4. Is it possible for one person to be the only stock owner in a corporation? If so, describe how this could happen.
5. How can the board of directors be changed in a corporation?
6. Do state governments know who is doing business as a corporation within the state?

IV. CORPORATIONS: EXERCISES

1. Each year one issue of *Fortune* magazine lists the 500 largest industrial corporations in the United States. Review a library copy of this year's issue and determine the top ten firms based on
   a. sales
   b. profit
   c. growth rate
2. If a corporation with a profit of $250,000 is taxed at a 60 percent rate, how much of the profit is left for dividends and other things?
3. What foreign corporations are competing with United States corporations for the dollars of consumers in your community?
4. What corporation impresses you the most? Explain why it is your favorite corporation.
5. Visit the library and prepare to discuss the products produced by the Litton Industries conglomerate.

8 MANAGEMENT

Within any type of business organization, people work with each other and do a number of tasks. The success of the business depends on how well the people do their jobs. It is also important that the workers organize their job duties. The company's management—the people who run the company—decide how the jobs are to be organized and who is to do each job.

The term *management* is generally defined as *getting things done through people*. Managers' jobs include planning, organizing, and controlling the activities within a business.

ORGANIZING

A school teacher, a housewife, a company president, a student, and anyone else who has specific job duties must do some organizing. Organizing helps people do things more efficiently. If your homework is 50 pages of reading and five math problems, you have to organize your time so that you can finish the assignment. Almost everyone does some organizing and planning every day. Poor planning or none at all often results in a job that is poorly done or not done at all.

In organizations, such as Jill's dress store or General Motors, the duties of all workers must be outlined. Jill was organizing her business when she said, "Donna, you're in charge of the store on Saturdays. Handle any customer questions or problems the best way you can. On Saturdays I will not be able to discuss any business matters."

82

This example shows how Jill assigned responsibility and authority to a worker. *Responsibility* is the duty, or obligation, to do the assigned job. In this case, Donna must run the store on Saturdays. *Authority* is the right to make decisions concerning the job. Donna has the authority to solve any problems that come up on Saturdays.

It is important to notice that the owner, Jill, gave authority to a worker, Donna. In order for Donna to do her job well she must know three things: 1) what her duties are, 2) what authority she has to make decisions, and 3) to whom she is responsible; that is, who is her boss. If these three points are not clear there is a good chance she will do a bad job, and Jill will be unhappy with her work.

THE ORGANIZATION CHART

To avoid misunderstandings about who has what responsibility and authority, companies usually have *organization charts.* An organization chart shows which people are in which jobs and who has authority. It also shows who each person's boss is. Figures 8–1, 8–2, and 8–3 are organization charts for the three businesses described earlier in this book. Each chart shows the structure of the organization and some of the relationships between the people.

In the first chart, Jill is the sole proprietor and must do a variety of jobs. She must buy dresses, put price tags on them, advertise the

FIGURE 8-1
JILL'S MODERN WOMEN'S WEAR – A SOLE PROPRIETORSHIP

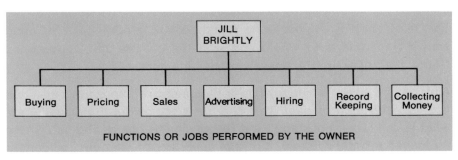

FIGURE 8-2
JILL AND AMY FASHION STORE — A PARTNERSHIP

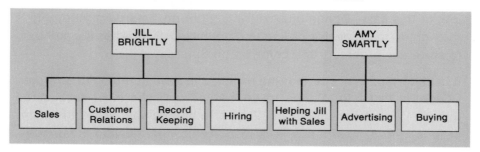

dresses, hire help, keep records, sell the dresses, and collect money from the customers. When part of a partnership (Figure 8-2), Jill shares the work, the responsibility, and the authority with Amy.

FIGURE 8-3
DANA HEALTH FOOD CORPORATION

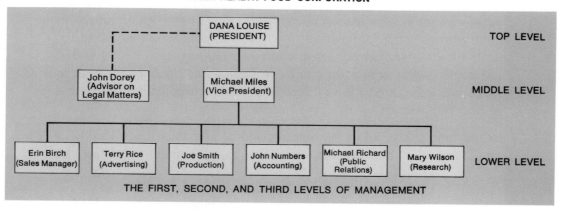

The third chart is for the Dana Health Food Corporation. This chart shows who reports to whom and who the owners and workers are. Notice that there are three levels of management.

Another aid used to show what is happening within an organization is an *organization manual.* This is a book or booklet that usually tells what each worker does and what responsibilities he or she has. These are called *job descriptions.* For example, the job of vice president in charge of sales might be described in the manual as:

VICE PRESIDENT OF SALES
of San Francisco Region

The vice president is to supervise, direct, and control the eighteen sales managers in the San Francisco region. The vice president is to review the work, recommend for promotion, and recommend for salary increases the eighteen sales managers. The vice president will report directly to the president of operations and will have his or her performance reviewed by the president. The performance of the vice president will be based on the sales records of the people of whom he or she is in charge.

THE MANAGEMENT TEAM

In a corporation, management is often divided into three groups: *top, middle,* and *lower management.* (See Figure 8–3 for kinds of job levels.)

TOP MANAGEMENT

At the top management level, there are the top executives of the organization. These executives are usually the highest paid people in the organization and often have the title of president or vice president. These executives make all of the general overall policy decisions and

At the top management level, executives make policy decisions and determine the company's goals.

decide on the company's goals. Decisions to buy out a competitor, to produce a new product, or to hire handicapped employees are examples of policies and goals decided by top management.

Another area that has become of major concern to top management is the pollution of the environment. For example, top managers of United States Steel Corporation are working on a program to cut down the pollution caused by their steel mills in such areas as Clairton, Pennsylvania; Gary, Indiana; and Chicago, Illinois.

MIDDLE MANAGEMENT

At the middle management level, there are the superintendents and managers of various departments, such as production and accounting. The middle manager is a tie between the top and lower managers. Middle managers supervise the jobs and activities of lower-level managers.

In corporations, management is divided into different levels to help business function smoothly.

LOWER MANAGEMENT

At the lower management level, there are the supervisors who work directly with the workers. The lower managers are very important since they are responsible for making sure the work of the corporation is done. The top and middle managers are concerned mostly with developing company policies. The lower-level managers put these policies and plans into action by supervision, or managing the workers.

THE PROPRIETORSHIP BECOMES A CORPORATION

Sometimes a sole proprietorship becomes a corporation. A good example of this type of growth is the development of the Kentucky Fried Chicken Corporation. For 25 years, Colonel Harland Sanders operated a restaurant that specialized in chicken dinners. In 1952 a new highway was built nearby, and traffic was routed away from the restaurant. Instead of closing the restaurant, Colonel Sanders began traveling and asking people if they would like to buy his *secret blend of herbs and spices* that made his chicken so good.

After ten years of traveling and selling his recipe, the Colonel had convinced over 700 people that selling chicken with this blend was a good business. In 1964, the Colonel realized that his business was too large

The Kentucky Fried Chicken Corp. shows how one man's idea became a multi-million dollar business.

Have a
**Good Meal
Good Deal
Good Time**
barrel of fun

Colonel Sanders' sole proprietorship became a corporation.

to operate by himself. He sold his organization to three investors for $2 million and a lifetime contract to act as public relations ambassador for the company.

The Kentucky Fried Chicken example shows how a small business grew so much that it became too hard for the owner to manage it. The three investors who purchased the business from the Colonel recently sold it to a large corporation.

SUMMARY

An organization must be managed. Generally, the work is divided among the workers. How this work is divided is shown in organization charts. Special organization manuals usually have descriptions telling what each person does and how much authority the person has.

In corporations, the management is divided into top, middle, and lower levels. The top-level managers generally make major policy decisions and plan the goals of the corporation. The lower-level managers give orders to the workers who actually produce the products. The middle-level managers are a link between the top and lower levels.

Sometimes a sole proprietorship becomes a corporation. This happens when the business grows. An example of this is the Kentucky Fried Chicken Corporation.

I. REVIEW OF TERMS

Which words complete the numbered statements?

lower   management team

policies   authority

responsibility

1. The top managers in a corporation generally develop company _____ .

2. _____ is the right to make decisions with respect to an assigned job.

3. _____ is the obligation to do an assigned job.

4. The _____-level manager has the most contact with the workers.

5. The _____ consists of top-, middle-, and lower-level managers.

II. REVIEW OF MAIN POINTS

1. Why is it necessary to manage an organization?

2. Can you tell from an organization chart who has authority in an organization?

3. What would be a job description for the president of the Dana Corporation shown in Figure 8–3?

4. Describe what the term *management responsibility* means.

5. In an organization, who makes decisions about such issues as air pollution?

6. Why must a person have a clear understanding of his or her authority in an organization?

7. Do sole proprietors manage their businesses?

8. What policy decisions might the top managers of a company such as General Motors make?

III. MANAGEMENT: CONCEPTS

1. It is said that every individual in an organization, from the lowest paid worker to the president, is responsible to some other individual. Do you agree with this statement? Why?
2. Are businesses responsible to the communities in which they operate? Why?
3. How do organization manuals help the employees of an organization?
4. Should organization charts tell you what a person's feelings are about another person on the chart? Why?

IV. MANAGEMENT: EXERCISES

1. Colonel Sanders is called a public relations ambassador. Do other companies in society have these types of ambassadors? Discuss some of these firms and their public relations people.
2. Visit your library and find an organization chart for a large corporation. List the jobs of the people who are directly responsible to the president.
3. At what level of management is your teacher working? Explain your answer.
4. At what level of management is the principal of your school working?

COMPUTERS IN BUSINESS

All business firms keep records. This is true for the small, solely owned businesses, such as Buck's Furniture Repair Store, as well as for giant corporations, such as the Ford Motor Company and IBM. Businesses keep records for three major purposes:

1. To operate the business on a day-to-day basis. For example, companies must make sure that customers' orders are filled and that bills are sent promptly.
2. To manage and control the business efficiently. Managers must know how much business the company is doing and how much it costs to do the business.
3. To prepare reports for stockholders and government agencies. For example, most companies file income tax returns four times a year.

Although the amount of record keeping varies with the size and type of business, all businesses must keep records of certain information, or data. The collecting, classifying, summarizing, reporting, and storing of this information is called *data processing.*

The people and machines used to process data are called *data processing systems.* There are three basic ways to process data:

1. *Manual data processing* With this method all of the work is done by hand, usually by a bookkeeper.
2. *Machine data processing* With this method adding machines and calculators are used to process business records.
3. *Electronic data processing (EDP)* This method uses electronic computers to process data quickly.

Most data processing systems today combine at least two of these methods. None of these systems are totally automatic since some of the work must always be done by hand (manually).

The system that is best for a company depends on the amount and type of paperwork that must normally be done. Large, complex companies generally use the EDP system. However, when small companies use EDP systems, they usually share the cost of the system with other small companies.

COMPUTERS

The system you are going to study in this chapter is the EDP system. In particular, you will learn about the five basic units (machines) that make up the EDP system and how these units work. You will also find out how computers are instructed to do their tasks.

WHAT IS A COMPUTER?

A computer is at the center of the EDP system and serves as the system's *brain.* A *computer* is actually a series of machines that process (handle) data according to instructions stored in a special part of the computer. These machines are connected to each other by wire cables much like those used to connect telephones.

Computers are not a recent invention. A computer similar to the modern electro-mechanical computer was designed by the English mathema-

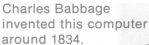

Charles Babbage invented this computer around 1834.

Today, both large and small businesses use computers.

tician Charles Babbage around 1834 but was never put successfully into operation. It was called Babbage's Analytical Engine. Babbage was about 100 years ahead of his time because the first electro-mechanical computer was not built until 1944 at Harvard University. Shortly afterward, an electronic computer was built at the University of Pennsylvania. It was named ENIAC. The first computer made for business data processing was UNIVAC I, built in 1954.

The basic idea of a modern computer is not complicated or difficult to understand. Figure 9-1 shows that a computer consists of five units. By following the arrows and dotted lines you can see how the data flow through the system.

FIGURE 9-1
A COMPUTER SYSTEM

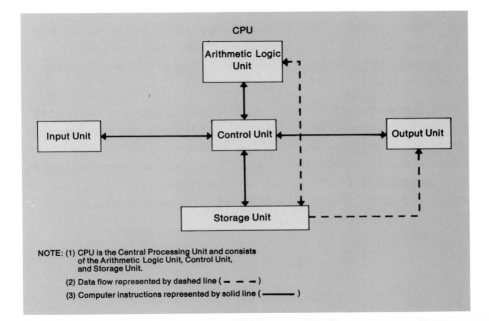

NOTE: (1) CPU is the Central Processing Unit and consists of the Arithmetic Logic Unit, Control Unit, and Storage Unit.

(2) Data flow represented by dashed line (— — —)

(3) Computer instructions represented by solid line (———)

A very important point to realize is that <u>people</u> must always put the data into the computer and interpret and use the data produced by the computer. People are also needed to tell the computer what to do. In other words, *people are necessary to make the EDP system work.*

CHARACTERISTICS OF COMPUTERS

Computers come in many different types and sizes. Some are faster than others and some can handle more complicated problems. Even though computers do vary, some characteristics are the same.

First, computers do not think. While they can process mountains of data in short periods of time, computers must be told exactly what to do by people. Often you hear someone say that a computer made a mistake. Actually, the mistake was made by the people who operated the computer. In the future, computers may be able to think in some way, but for now they depend entirely on people for their direction.

Second, computers can process data and solve problems faster and more accurately than people can. For example, if you had to divide the number 1,764,391,820 by the number 6,176,711, it might take you five minutes or longer. A computer could divide the same numbers in a fraction of a second. This example, however, is basically a simple problem that you could do correctly in a reasonable amount of time. But what about very hard and large problems that are really impractical to solve by hand?

An example of a very difficult problem easily handled by computers is the launching of rockets to hit specific points on the moon. Each time astronauts have been sent to the moon, large computers have quickly determined when to launch the rockets so that they would land in the right places.

Finally, computers do not understand human speech and cannot talk. Engineers are working on ways to make computers communicate with people by voice. When this happens more people will be able to use computers in new and different ways. You might someday be able to tell a computer to divide the numbers mentioned earlier and have the answer appear on a television screen a fraction of a second later.

HOW COMPUTERS WORK

The five basic units that make up a computer are (1) the input unit, (2) the arithmetic logic unit, (3) the control unit, (4) the storage unit, and (5) the output unit. The arithmetic logic, control, and storage units make up the *central processing unit* (CPU).

INPUT UNIT

Information can be put into a computer in two basic ways: punched cards and magnetic tape. Most computer systems use a combination of these two methods.

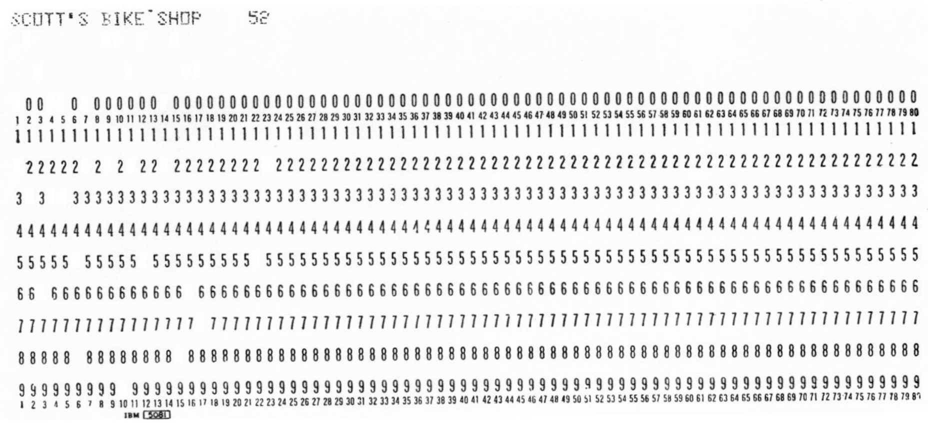

Figure 9-3.

For example, assume that the data put into a computer are the seasonal sales of a certain type of bicycle at Scott's Bike Shop. Specifically, 52 Pinto bikes were sold in the spring. The sales data were punched into the 80-column computer card shown in Figure 9-3. The holes were punched in the card by a special *card key punch machine.* This machine can punch one or more holes in each of the 80 columns. Every hole on the card stands for a number, a letter of the alphabet, or some other special symbol. In the card in Figure 9-3, the company name is punched in columns 1 through 17. The date is punched in columns 10 through

28, the product name is in columns 30 through 34, and the sales figures are in columns 36 and 37.

Another way the same data can be put into the computer is through *magnetic tape* and a *magnetic tape drive* (shown in Figure 9–5). There are two reasons for using magnetic tapes. First, the data from several thousand punched cards can be placed on only one roll of magnetic tape. In other words, a great deal of information can be stored on a small amount of tape. Second, the computer can read the data from tape faster than it can read the data from punched cards.

People prepare magnetic tapes to be used by computers.

The tape used for computers is much like the tape used in tape recorders and tape cassettes. By *magnetizing* a tiny part of the tape, the data can be put on the tape. People cannot see these magnetic spots, but the computer can *sense* them. (When you record music on a tape, you cannot see the music, and yet the machine can *sense* the music and change it to sound.)

It is difficult to say which input method is the best. Both have advantages and disadvantages. When speed is important and large amounts of data have to be stored, magnetic tapes are probably best. However, it is possible to see what is punched on cards so that data can be corrected, if necessary, more easily than on tapes. An important point to remember is that, no matter which method is used, people have to put the data on the cards or tape.

Once the data are on cards or tapes, the cards or tapes are *fed* into the computer by either a tape drive or card reader. Large computer systems usually have both machines so that either method can be used.

CENTRAL PROCESSING UNIT

The central processing unit (CPU) is the *nerve center* of a computer system. It controls the entire system. The CPU contains three of the five basic units that make up a computer system. These are the arithmetic logic unit, the storage unit, and the control unit.

When a company processes data, a lot of arithmetic is often necessary. Also, the data must often be rearranged and compared. The *arithmetic logic unit* can do all of these things in any order.

Suppose at Scott's Bike Shop, Scott wants to know how many different spare bicycle parts are on hand at the end of each week. He also wants to know the cost of each part. This could be done for every type of spare part by (1) subtracting the number of parts used during the week from the previous week's total, (2) multiplying the new total by the cost of the part, and (3) adding up the dollar values for every part. This way, Scott could get the total value of the company's supply of spare parts.

The arithmetic logic unit can also do *logical operations,* such as comparing two numbers and determining if one is larger. For example, suppose at Scott's Bike Shop it is important never to run out of 20-inch rubber tires. Also, suppose that it takes one week to get the tires after they are ordered and that about eight of these tires are sold each week. Therefore, when only eight tires are left in stock, it would be time to order more tires. The computer's logic unit can compare the number of 20-inch tires in stock with the reorder number (eight) to decide if any new tires should be ordered. As soon as the number of tires drops to eight or less, the computer would indicate that it is time to order more tires.

The *storage unit* stores the data and the instructions that tell the computer what to do. Often, the storage unit is called the computer's *memory.* Once data are stored, the computer can remember where they are until they are erased. The computer can recall the data from the storage unit as often as commanded.

Every system needs something to make sure all of the parts are working correctly, just as business organizations need management. In a computer system, the *control unit* tells all the other parts of the computer what, when, and how to do their job. You might think of the control unit as a traffic director. The control instructions are fed into the computer as input data.

OUTPUT UNIT

When the computer completes the processing of the data, the results are released by the computer in a form that people can easily read. The three major forms of computer output are (1) punched cards, (2) magnetic tape, and (3) paper printout. The paper printers are very fast and can print 2,000 lines of words and numbers a minute. A line on a computer printout is about twice as wide as this page.

COMMUNICATING WITH COMPUTERS—PROGRAMING

A *computer program* is nothing more than a set of instructions that a computer follows to do a specific job. For example, a program told the computer to check the spare parts for Scott's Bike Shop.

Computer programing requires very exact planning and logical thinking. It takes time to develop a program because every step in the program must be considered. Telling a computer how to figure out a worker's paycheck takes much longer than telling an individual bookkeeper. However, once a program is written and put into the computer, the computer can do the job faster and with fewer mistakes than a person can.

COMPUTER LANGUAGES

Because a computer must be told what to do, there has to be some way to give the computer its instructions. In other words, if people must *talk* to computers they need a *language*—a code—that the computer can *understand*. There are many computer languages. Two are

FORmula TRANslation, also called FORTRAN, and COmmon Business-Oriented Language, or COBOL.

Once the complete computer program is written, it is normally key punched on computer cards. The program is then fed into the CPU one card at a time and stored in the storage (memory) unit. Next, the data (also in the form of key punched cards) are fed into the machine. The data are then processed, and the results are printed out.

SOME SAMPLE COMPUTER PROGRAMS

Suppose you want to have a computer add three numbers—524, 72, and 1040—and then print the answer. The program needs only one statement:

```
1   PRINT   524 + 72 + 1040
```

When a computer gets this program it will print the answer: 1,636. (The number 1 written to the left of PRINT is the program's statement number.)

Notice how a plus sign (+) is used to add the three numbers. A minus sign (−) to subtract, a slash (/) to divide, and an asterisk (*) to multiply are also used. The following program contains all of these symbols:

```
1   PRINT   10 + 5
2   PRINT   16 − 6
3   PRINT   4/2
4   PRINT   5 * 4
```

The computer printout would have the following answers:

```
15   (10 plus 5)
10   (16 minus 6)
 2   ( 4 divided by 2)
20   ( 5 times 4)
```

To write programs for more complicated problems, you only have to add more instruction statements or make one statement longer. Suppose you want to know the area of a circle. The formula for finding the area of a circle is πR^2. (π is the Greek letter *pi* and it is approximately 3.14.) If the circle's radius (R) is 10 inches, the computer program could be written:

```
1  PI = 3.14
2   R = 1Ø.Ø
3  PRINT PI  * R * R.
```

The printed answer would be 314 square inches.

COMPUTERS HELPING BUSINESS

Given the correct set of instructions (program) and data, an electronic data processing (EDP) system can quickly provide business firms with accurate information. This information can be used by a business in two essential ways. First, accurate and timely information can help managers operate the business better. For example, when production costs for a certain product get too high, this information can be quickly reported to the production manager. The production manager then analyzes the information and figures out why the costs have increased. It could be due to a problem in the production line or to increases in the costs of raw materials. Whatever the problem, managers need to know the facts quickly so that action can be taken right away.

A second way EDP systems can be helpful to business is in making decisions. Suppose Buck wants to know how his furniture repair service might be affected if he raises his hourly labor charge to $4.75. By programing the computer to answer this type of question, Buck would be in a better position to decide whether or not to raise his rates. This particular use of the computer and EDP system can be very complicated, particularly for a large business. The important point to realize is that computers can be useful in all types of business decisions, from deciding where to locate a new plant to figuring out how much a product's price should be raised.

In addition to the uses already mentioned, computers are valuable for other business purposes. Computers are used in manufacturing companies, publishing houses, ticket sales agencies, retail companies, insurance firms, banks, designing companies, and automobile and motel reservation agencies. To illustrate just one of these uses—ticket sales—suppose you live in Miami, Florida, and want to buy a ticket from Eastern Airlines to travel on a particular flight from Miami to

Atlanta. When you ask for the ticket, the salesperson feeds the information into a special input unit connected to a computer in Charlotte, North Carolina. If the computer sends back a message that there are seats available on the flight, you could buy the ticket.

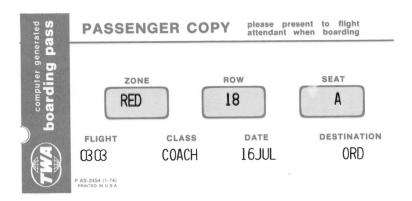

Banks use computers to keep track of the checks written on an individual account. This way, the bank knows exactly how much money is in the account at all times. Newspapers are sometimes typeset by computer, and machine tools are sometimes operated by computer.

THE FUTURE OF COMPUTERS

It is quite possible that the future of computers will be more exciting than their past. The reason for this is that in the past, the main interest was in making computers bigger and faster. Now the interest is shifting toward finding new ways to use the computer. This is where people in the day-to-day operation of a business or government agency can use their influence to improve computers. These are the people that must gather and process the data.

Even though computers and EDP systems are very helpful and have a bright future, they could be used against people. With the computer's ability to store large volumes of data, it is possible to build complete information files on people and businesses. Some people in the Federal Government have suggested that files on people should be put into a national data bank. Many congressional representatives and senators have disagreed. They believe that much of this information is too personal and could possibly be used in the wrong way. Do you think it is possible to know so much about a person that his or her privacy is violated? This is a very important question that will have to be answered now that computers can build and store complete files on every person in the United States.

SUMMARY

All businesses keep records so that the management can see if the company is operating profitably. Records are also kept so that reports to stockholders and government agencies can be made easily. Because there is so much information to be handled (processed), data processing systems have been developed. The largest and often the most efficient system is the EDP system, which uses electronic computers. Computers are also used to help managers make business decisions, such as where to locate a new plant or what would happen to sales if the price of a product were raised.

Some of the more important businesses that have used computers are motels, airlines, banks, department stores, and manufacturing companies. The future of computers is probably brighter today than it was 25 years ago. The reason for this is that companies are now more interested in finding new ways to use computers, rather than building computers that are bigger and faster.

This railroad yard is run by computers to help simplify its management.

I. REVIEW OF TERMS

Which words complete the sentences below?

computer program	manual
storage unit	magnetic tape
electronic	control unit
data processing systems	memory
punched cards	arithmetic logic unit
computer	machine

1. The people and machines used to process company records are called _____.

2. A _____ is a series of machines that process data according to a set of instructions.

3. The three major parts of the computer's central processing unit are the _____, _____, and _____.

4. The two major ways to enter data into a computer are _____ and _____.

5. Three types of data processing systems are _____, _____, and _____.

6. The storage unit in the computer is often called the computer's _____.

7. A set of step-by-step instructions that tell a computer what to do is called a _____.

II. REVIEW OF MAIN POINTS

1. Explain the characteristics that all computers have in common.

2. What are the three specific reasons all businesses keep records and process data?

3. What are the major units of a computer? Explain the purpose of each unit.

4. Why is the future of computers brighter today than at any time before?

III. COMPUTERS IN BUSINESS: CONCEPTS

1. It is generally believed that computers and EDP systems help business operate better today than in past years. Do you agree? Why or why not?

2. Many people complain that when companies or governments use computers in their day-to-day business activities, people are no longer individuals but become *just a number.* Do you agree with this complaint? Why or why not?

3. Suppose the Federal Government did not use computers to process income tax returns. What advantages would there be for the taxpayers? What disadvantages would there be?

IV. COMPUTERS IN BUSINESS: EXERCISES

1. Select five adults and find out their opinions about a national data bank. Ask them if they think it is a good idea and why they think it is or is not. Compare their answers with your own ideas.

2. Select one of the businesses or government agencies listed below and find out how computers help them in their day-to-day operations. Prepare a short report to explain what you find out.

   a. motel   d. Internal Revenue Service
   b. police department   e. bank
   c. hospital   f. airline

3. Go to the library and find the names of four corporations that make computers.

4. Write a computer program to do the following problem: find the area of a triangle if the formula for the area is $\frac{1}{2}$ bh and b = 16 and h = 29.

Unit III
Good Money Management

Money is important because of what it can buy. For this reason, every-one should understand the meaning of money, the changing value of money, and the management of money.

Chapter 10 discusses the nature of money. Since money was invented, a variety of objects have been used as money. You will first look at what people use for money today. Next, you will learn about money's functions in a modern economy.

The value of money—how much it will buy—does not stay the same, but changes over time. Chapter 11 explains why the value of money changes. It is important that the value of money be kept fairly stable. You will learn the various ways the Government can help keep the value of money stable.

Good money management is important to individuals and families. In Chapter 12 you will learn about steps in becoming a good money man-ager. A family budget, one of these steps, is described in detail.

UNIT PREVIEW

AS YOU STUDY THIS UNIT YOU WILL BE ENGAGED IN

* DETERMINING the role of money in a modern economy

* ANALYZING the various functions of money in the economy

* INTERPRETING the concepts of inflation and deflation and how they affect money's buying power

* CONSIDERING why good money management is important to both individuals and families

* PLANNING AND DEVELOPING a complete family budget.

A FOCUS FOR YOUR STUDY

10 THE MEANING OF MONEY

In ancient times, people traded different types of goods with their neighbors. This kind of trading is called *bartering*. Bartering is the exchange of goods without using money. For example, a soapmaker and a candlemaker could easily trade their products. People agreed on how much each item was worth in terms of the other. One chunk of soap, for example, might have been worth ten candles.

As more and more people became involved in bartering, it became harder to put values on different products. Also, this type of trading took a lot of time. It became harder to find a person who wanted to trade a particular item for the item you were trading.

Because people had trouble deciding how to set values for different goods, they came up with a new idea. Why not sell every item for something that was acceptable to *all* sellers? This "something" was *money*.

At the Hudson Bay Co., items were bartered.

It is important to understand certain basic concepts about money. You use money every time you buy something. So do other people. Without money, the country's economy could not work. In this chapter, you will learn how money developed, the functions of money, the different kinds of modern money, and money's buying power.

THE NATURE OF MONEY

Money is anything that is generally acceptable as payment for goods or services. Throughout history, money has taken many shapes and has been used in many different ways.

In early times, such things as tobacco, wheat, fishhooks, beads, cattle, and stones were used as money. American Indians used wampum or shells for money. In Haiti, gourds were once used for money, and today the monetary unit of Haiti is called a *gourde.* Examples of various items that have been used for money are shown in Figure 10–1. The important point to remember is that as long as an item is *acceptable* to people, it can be used as money.

The first use of gold coins for money was in Lydia around 600 B.C. Lydia was an important commercial center in Asia Minor on the Mediterranean Sea. As countries grew larger and their economies became more complicated, a new medium of exchange developed. This new medium was paper money. The oldest known paper money was used in China around 1370 A.D. Today paper bills, as well as a few kinds of coins, are used for money.

TYPES OF MONEY

The major forms of money currently used in the United States are (1) currency (paper money and coins) and (2) checkbook money. These same forms are also used in many other countries, including Great Britain, West Germany, Japan, Brazil, Australia, Egypt, and Mexico.

July 14_3.
Prices of Goods
Supplyed to the
Eastern Indians,
By the several Truckmasters; and of the Peltry received by the Truckmasters of the said Indians.

One yard Broad Cloth, *three* Beaver skins, *in season*.
One yard & half Gingerline, *one* Beaver skin, *in season*.
One yard Red or Blew Kersey, *two* Beaver skins, *in season*.
One yard good Duffels, *one* Beaver skin, *in season*.
One yard & half broad fine Cotton, *one* Beaver skin, *in season*.
Two yards of Cotton, *one* Beaver skin, *in season*.
One yard & half of half thicke, *one* Beaver skin, *in season*.

Four Pecks Pease, *one* Beaver skin, *in season*.
Two Pints of Powder, *one* Beaver skin, *in season*.
One Pint of Shot, *one* Beaver skin, *in season*.
Six Fathom of Tobacco, *one* Beaver skin, *in season*.
Forty Biskets, *one* Beaver skin, *in season*.
Ten Pound of Pork, *one* Beaver skin, *in season*.
Six Knives, *one* Beaver skin, *in season*.
Six Combes, *one* Beaver skin, *in season*.
Twenty Scaines Thread, *one* Beaver skin, *in season*.
One Hat, *two* Beaver skins, *in season*.
One Hat with Hatband, *three* Beaver skins, *in season*.
Two Pound of large Kettles, *one* Beaver skin, *in season*.
One Pound & half of small Kettles, *one* Beaver skin, *in season*.
One Shirt, *one* Beaver skin, *in season*.
One Shirt with Ruffels, *two* Beaver skins, *in season*.
Two Small Axes, *one* Beaver skin, *in season*.
Two Small Hoes, *one* Beaver skin, *in season*.
Three Dozen middling Hooks, *one* Beaver skin, *in season*.
One Sword Blade, *one & half* Beaver skin, *in season*.

Figure 10–1

Beaver skins and other items were worth definite amounts before coins and paper bills were in common use.

PAPER MONEY

All of the paper money in the United States is printed by the Treasury Department of the United States Government. When it becomes worn or damaged, it is collected and returned to the United States Treasury Department. It is then burned and new currency is printed to take its place.

This machine sorts and counts dimes.

COINS

Coins are made from various metals. They are used for paying small amounts of money. All coins used in the United States are *minted* (manufactured) by the Treasury. The *face value* (stated value) of coins is always greater than the value of the metal used to mint them.

CHECKBOOK MONEY

Money placed in checking accounts at banks is called *checkbook money.* A *check* is actually an order telling a bank to pay a certain amount of money to another person. Because a check is an order, the money in checking accounts is called a *demand* deposit. Demand deposits account for about 80 percent of all the money used in the United States.

Figure 10-3 shows a check that Freddy Alfonso used to pay Buck's Furniture Repair. The reason checkbook money accounts for so much of the money in circulation is that governments, business firms, and individuals use checks to pay for almost everything they buy. It is much easier and safer to pay by check than to carry around a lot of currency.

THE FUNCTIONS OF MONEY

Money serves four important functions. These four functions can be remembered from an old rhyme:

> Money is a matter of functioning four,
> A medium, a measure, a standard, a store.

No one function is more important than the others.

MEDIUM OF EXCHANGE

Money serves as a medium of exchange because it allows you to pay other people for the goods or services you want or need. For example, suppose Lynn Spruill mows a neighbor's lawn for $5. Lynn could then take this money to David's Music Store and buy a tape cassette for $4.50. Without money, it would be very hard for Lynn to quickly exchange her lawn-mowing services for a tape cassette. People seldom want money for money's sake. Instead, they want money for what it will buy.

MEASURE OF VALUE

Rulers are used to measure length. Scales are used to measure weight. In the United States, money is used to measure the value of goods and services. The value of any product or service is measured in dollars and cents and is called its *price.* The value of Lynn Spruill's lawn mowing was $5. The tape cassette was valued at $4.50 by David's Music Store. By using money as a measure of value, you can easily tell how much the lawn-mowing service is worth in terms of the tape cassette.

Another advantage of this function of money is that business records based on money values can easily be compared. If David's Music Store sold $55,000 worth of goods and Scott's Bike Shop did $42,000 worth of business this past year, then David's business earned $13,000 more than Scott's. Of course, each store owner can look back at earlier records to see if his or her own business is growing.

STORE OF VALUE

Money serves as a store of value because it lets you save money for future spending. Suppose Lynn did not want to spend the $5 right away but wanted to save the money for two weeks and then buy a new shirt. By saving the $5, Lynn would store its value—or buying power—to use at a future time.

This is a very important feature of money. The reason is that services cannot be stored, and many goods spoil if they are stored for a long time. Money, on the other hand, can be stored. Thus, money does not have to be spent right away for fear that it will lose all of its value. The value of money, however, can often change somewhat. This is discussed further in Chapter 11.

STANDARD OF FUTURE PAYMENT

Money also serves as a standard for future payment. This means that you can lend or borrow money that will be paid back with interest (extra money) at some future date.

For example, when Bill Sartoris bought a new car for $4,700, he had only $1000 to use as a down payment, leaving a balance of $3,700. The car dealer agreed to let him repay the $3,700 plus interest over three years (36 months). The amount Bill has to pay each month is decided when the car is bought, not later on. The monthly payment is figured by dividing the $3,700 plus interest by 36. This makes paying for the car more convenient for Bill. He will repay only the amount agreed upon at the time of the sale.

MONEY'S BUYING POWER

The only real value money has is its buying power. *Real value* refers to the money's buying power in exchange for other goods; in other words, how many goods and services can be bought with each dollar.

This becomes clear when you think about why you work. If you have a job delivering papers, baby-sitting, or packing groceries, you earn money. You work for money because of what it will buy. When you think of the value of money you earn in terms of what it will buy, the money is called *real wages.*

SUMMARY

For centuries people traded goods to get the things to meet their needs and wants. This trading is called bartering. Bartering worked until many people became involved in the trading. When bartering became complicated, money was invented. Money is anything people will accept as payment for goods and services. Over the years many things have been used for money including salt, cows, beads, and shells.

Today, the major forms of money in most countries are (1) currency (paper money and coins) and (2) checkbook money. Checkbook money has become very important in the United States. About 80 percent of all the money used in the United States is checkbook money.

Money serves many useful functions in modern business. It is a medium of exchange, a store of value, a standard of future payment, and a measure of value. The money you use today has very little or no value of its own. It is only a convenience. Money's only real value is in its buying power.

REVIEW THE MEANING OF MONEY

I. REVIEW OF TERMS
Which words complete the statements below?

checkbook money   medium of exchange
acceptable   bartering
real value   demand deposit
money

1. Anything that is _____ for paying for goods and serv-ices is called _____ .
2. The _____ of money is measured by what it will buy.
3. Trading goods for other goods is called _____ .
4. _____ represents about 80 percent of the money used today.
5. One function of money is to serve as a _____ .
6. The money in checking accounts is called a _____ .

II. REVIEW OF MAIN POINTS
1. What are the major functions of money?
2. Why was money invented?
3. Explain what is meant by money's buying power.
4. What are the two types of money used in many nations?
5. Explain the differences between the three different kinds of money.
6. What determines whether or not something is money?
7. Who mints (manufactures) the coins used in the United States?

8. What is the most widely used kind of money in the United States?

III. THE MEANING OF MONEY: CONCEPTS

1. People often think that bartering is something that only took place in the past. Many things, however, are still traded.
   a. Look in the local newspaper classified ads and prepare a list of ten items that people want to trade.
   b. Are there any special reasons you can think of that make people want to trade these items? You may want to ask your parents for help with this answer.

2. Have you ever wondered how much currency is in circulation in the United States? To answer this question, look at the following table. The figures are as of July, 1974.

Currency	Amount in dollars
Coin	$ 8,039,627,206
$1 bills	$ 2,531,942,239
$2 bills	135,354,660
$5 bills	3,439,429,945
$10 bills	9,878,258,260
$20 bills	24,348,444,304
$50 bills	6,762,773,500
$100 bills	18,295,573,900
$500 bills	182,475,000
$1,000 bills	213,026,000
$5,000 bills	2,200,000
$10,000 bills	4,010,000
TOTAL	$73,833,115,014

   a. Which paper money ($1, $5, $10, etc.) has the largest number of bills in circulation?
   b. Why do you think there are more of this particular bill in circulation than any of the others?
   c. How many $50 bills are in circulation?

3. It is said that checkbook money (demand deposits) accounts for about 80 percent of all the money in circulation in the United States. Study the following table and answer the questions:

	MONEY IN CIRCULATION (in billions of dollars)		
Year	Currency	Demand Deposits	Total
1941	$ 9.6	$ 39.0	$ 48.6
1945	26.5	75.9	102.4
1950	25.4	92.3	117.7
1955	28.3	109.9	138.2
1960	29.5	115.2	144.7
1965	37.1	134.9	172.0
1970	50.0	177.7	227.7
1974	61.9	225.5	287.4

a. Determine what percentage demand deposits are of the total money in circulation in the United States for each year in the table.

b. Did this percentage grow between 1941 and 1974?

c. What was the average percentage from 1941 to 1974?

d. What are some of the advantages of checkbook money over the other kinds of money?

IV. THE MEANING OF MONEY: EXERCISES

1. Prepare a short answer to the following question:
   How would business be affected if everyone had to pay in currency? There would be no checkbook money.
   Discuss this question with your parents and a banker.

2. Write a short report explaining now paper money is made. Trace all the steps from start to finish and explain the importance of each step.

3. Select ten countries around the world and find out the names of their monetary units. In the United States, the monetary unit is the dollar. Look up the exchange rates for these currencies in terms of dollars. Check the *Wall Street Journal* or the financial page of a large city newspaper for the exchange rates.

THE CHANGING VALUE OF MONEY

1

The value of money depends on what you can buy with it. However, the value of money does not remain the same forever. In fact, it changes constantly. This chapter will examine why the value of money changes and how this change is measured. It will also cover inflation, deflation, and their effects. Finally, it will consider what can be done to help keep money's value stable.

These ideas are important. They affect how you live now and how you will live in the future. Studying them will help you understand many of the nation's current economic problems.

CHANGES IN MONEY'S BUYING POWER

One of the functions of money is to serve as a measure of value. This measure of value lets shoppers say that one item costs more, or is worth more, than another. Unfortunately, the value of a dollar does not remain the same. No doubt you have heard your parents say that today's dollar is worth only 50 cents—maybe even less. This means that it takes a dollar today to buy what you could have bought for about 50 cents years ago.

The change in the dollar's value is measured against its value at some time in the past. You can measure the value of today's money in terms of the money's value in 1950, 1964, 1975, or any other year for which there are records.

This old photograph shows how the general price level of goods has changed.

Why does the buying power of money change? The buying power of money is related to the general price level of all goods. The term *general price level* is used to describe the *average* level of prices in a country at any given time. This price level is never constant. When it rises, each dollar buys less. When it falls, each dollar buys more. Thus, the buying power of money varies from time to time.

Measuring changes in the general price level is not easy. In fact, no one consumer can do it. The *Bureau of Labor Statistics* (BLS) of the United States Department of Labor does the job.

PRICE LEVEL CHANGES: THE CONSUMER PRICE INDEX

The BLS publishes the *Consumer Price Index* every month. A *price index* compares the amount by which the price level changes during a particular time period. One year is chosen as the base year—the year used for comparison. Prices in other years are measured as percentages of the base year prices. Thus, the *Consumer Price Index* (CPI) measures changes in the general price level for all goods and services.

Figuring out the CPI is complicated. First, the BLS gets the prices of about 400 goods and services in 39 large cities and 17 smaller cities.

Included are the prices of foods, rents, gas and electricity, clothes, transportation, medical care, and recreation. Some of the large cities are Boston, New York, Detroit, St. Louis, Denver, Los Angeles, Seattle, and Dallas. The small cities include Florence, Alabama; Logansport, Indiana; Kingston, New York; McAllen, Texas; Orem, Utah; and Green Bay, Wisconsin. The prices are collected from about 18,000 establishments, such as hospitals, gas stations, and grocery stores. They are obtained by both personal visits and mailed questionnaires. Once the prices are collected, they are added together and averaged to form the CPI.

The CPI measures price changes from a particular base year. This base year is assigned a value of 100 percent. The CPI for other years is expressed as a percent of the base year. Suppose the price level rises 5 percent in one year. The CPI for that year would be 105 percent.

TABLE 11-1
UNITED STATES CONSUMER PRICE INDEX
1950-1973
(IN PERCENTAGES)
(1967 = 100 PERCENT)

Year	CPI	Year	CPI
1950	72.1%	1962	90.6%
1951	77.8	1963	91.7
1952	79.5	1964	92.9
1953	80.1	1965	94.5
1954	80.5	1966	97.2
1955	80.2	1967	100.0
1956	81.4	1968	104.2
1957	84.3	1969	109.8
1958	86.6	1970	116.3
1959	87.3	1971	121.3
1960	88.7	1972	125.3
1961	89.6	1973	130.7

Table 11-1 shows the CPI for the years 1950 to 1973. The year 1967 is used as the base year by the U. S. Department of Labor. From 1967 to 1973 you can see that prices rose about 31 percent. If Gene Dixon made $1,000 a month in 1967, he would need an income of $1,310 a month to be just as well off in 1973. That is, he would have to spend $1,310 in

1973 to buy the same goods and services that cost $1,000 in 1967. If Gene made more than $1,310 a month in 1973, he would have a real increase in his standard of living. Suppose, for example, that Gene made $1,400 a month in 1973. The buying power of his wages grew faster than the general price increases over this period. He had $90 more a month to spend. This $90 represents the real increase in his standard of living.

Sometimes it is hard to notice price increases from one year to the next. From 1960 to 1966, prices rose about 9 percent. This increase over seven years was not a heavy burden for most families because wages generally rose at least as fast. Decreases in the dollar's buying power were more than made up for by increases in wages.

Note the period from 1966 to 1973 in Figure 11-1. The price increase was almost 34 percent. Much of this was due to the war in Vietnam.

FIGURE 11-1   U.S. CONSUMER PRICE INDEX 1950-1973 (1967 = 100.0)

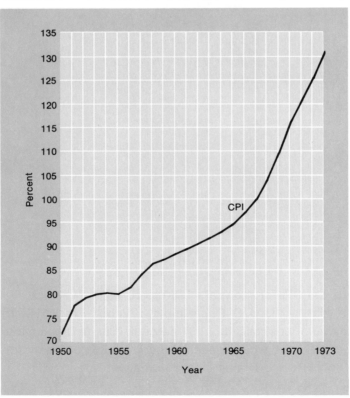

The reason for this increase will become clear after reading the next section. But no matter what the reason, the increase was a burden on the consumer. Many consumers found it hard to make ends meet.

Increases in the CPI are a sign of *inflation.* During inflation, the buying power of the dollar falls. A decrease in the CPI is a sign of *deflation.* During deflation, the dollar's buying power increases. In Table 11-1, you will note that the price level decreased in one year only, 1955. In all other years it rose. This means that in recent years inflation has been more of a problem to consumers than deflation has been.

INFLATION

Inflation is a rise in the average level of prices of all goods and services. Inflation always means rising prices. Therefore, inflation cuts the value, or buying power, of the money you earn. If the average price level triples, your dollar will buy only one third as much.

This does not mean that all prices rise, only that the average price level rises. Some prices may actually fall, but these decreases are more than offset by increases in other prices.

WHAT CAUSES INFLATION?

People do not always agree about what causes inflation. There are several ideas on the subject. One reason that is often given as a cause of inflation is discussed here.

When the total demand (consumers + industry + government) for goods and services is more than can be supplied, inflation occurs. This is called *demand-pull inflation.* This happens when the nation's ability to produce goods and services cannot grow fast enough to keep up with increases in demand. There are simply not enough goods and services to go around.

The reason that the demand increases is that most people have jobs and are earning money. They, therefore, have the money to spend. Since there are not enough goods and services on the market, people will pay what is asked. They do not watch price increases closely be-

Paper bills are printed by the United States Government in large quantities and distributed under careful control. The picture shows $1,000,000,000.

cause they have the money to spend. The result is inflation, or price level increases.

Unless it is controlled, inflation becomes a vicious circle. As the prices rise, wages also tend to rise. This makes more money available for consumers to spend. If the nation's production of goods and services is not increased to offset the wage rise, the imbalance between demand and supply continues. The result is more inflation. Without controls, an economy can have a high rate of inflation, or *runaway inflation.* This happened in Germany, China, and Greece after World War II.

The United States normally has had what is called *creeping inflation.* This was especially true during the period from 1960 to 1966. In the period from 1966 to 1973, the nation had *trotting inflation.*

This old photograph shows money being carried in carts in Germany following World War I. The value of money changed constantly.

EFFECTS OF INFLATION

Is inflation good or bad? That depends. Some people are helped by inflation and some people are hurt by it. Generally, more people are

Inflation affects chewing gum prices.

hurt than helped. People with fixed incomes, such as retired people receiving pensions, suffer the most. People that lend money are hurt because loans are repaid with dollars that are worth less than when they were first borrowed. Also, people who save money are hurt. The interest paid on savings accounts is often less than the percentage rate of inflation.

CONTROLLING INFLATION

The major reason for controlling inflation is to keep the dollar's buying power stable. Keeping the value of the dollar stable is important to almost everyone.

Unfortunately, no single person can do very much to control inflation. If prices get too high, you might decide not to buy a new television or car. If enough people stopped buying these kinds of items, there would be an impact on inflation. However, people cannot put off buying food, clothes, and shelter. Dollars spent for these needs represent the major part of most people's wages. So, a single consumer has little choice in putting off large amounts of spending.

The most effective way to control inflation is through group action.

This means that the Federal Government must step in. What can it do on behalf of all the people?

First, the Government can *cut spending* thereby helping to decrease the nation's total demand. The Government is the largest single spender in the nation. Every year it spends billions of dollars for military supplies, public buildings, highways, office supplies, transportation, and other goods and services.

Another way to control inflation is to *increase income taxes.* Any tax increase takes money away from consumers, so that consumers have less money to spend on major purchases. Although a tax increase will help control inflation, it is hardly ever used. The reason is that tax increases are unpopular with the people, and the politicians who must vote for the increases know it. The politicians would not want to risk losing the votes of the people just because of tax increases.

Third, the Government can *increase interest rates.* With higher interest rates, consumers have to pay more to borrow money for houses, cars, or large appliances. As a result, consumers often delay buying many expensive items. Higher interest rates also force businesses to slow down their expansions and major purchases.

Another way to control inflation is for the Government to control wages, salaries, and the prices of goods and services sold for a certain length of time. The Government decides when to put controls into effect and when to take them off.

It is impossible to say that any one method of controlling inflation is the best. During 1973, when there was rapid inflation, President Nixon reduced government spending and forced interest rates up. Probably the best approach is to use a combination of methods.

DEFLATION

Deflation is the opposite of inflation. During *deflation,* the general price level falls and the buying power of money rises. Your first reaction might be to think this is good. But is it?

TABLE 11–2 UNITED STATES CONSUMER PRICE INDEX SELECTED YEARS, 1929–1943 (1967 = 100 Percent)	
Year	CPI
1929	51.3%
1933	38.8
1939	41.6
1940	42.0
1941	44.1
1942	48.8
1943	51.8

In Table 11–2, you can see that the CPI was 51.3 percent in 1929 and 38.8 percent by 1933. This was a price level decrease of about 12 percent. So in 1933 the value of a dollar increased by 12 percent compared to 1929.

The deflation in this period was not good. In 1933, the United States was in its worst economic depression. Millions of people were out of work and had little hope of finding jobs. Business firms were failing every day. The gain in money value made little difference. It makes no difference how valuable money is if you have no hope of earning any.

When the economy enters a period of deflation, the Government must take action. It must increase government spending, cut income taxes, and lower interest rates. The Government is likely to take quick action during a period of deflation. This is because the effects of deflation are more quickly noticed than the effects of inflation.

SUMMARY

The value of money depends on what it will buy. What money will buy depends on the general price level of the economy.

Measuring the general price level is not easy. The Bureau of Labor Statistics does the job by means of the Consumer Price Index (CPI).

This index is published monthly. It is based on prices of about 400 goods and services in 56 cities.

Increases in the CPI show periods of inflation. When the CPI falls, there is a period of deflation. Throughout the history of the United States, inflation has been much more common than deflation. There is some disagreement about the causes of inflation. However, as a result of inflation, the value (buying power) of the dollar is reduced.

Unless it is controlled, inflation can hurt the economy. To fight inflation and keep the dollar's buying power stable, the Government must take action. This action can include (1) cutting government spending, (2) increasing taxes, (3) raising interest rates, and (4) controlling wages, salaries, and prices.

When the economy is in a period of deflation, the Government can reverse the actions taken to fight inflation. Periods of deflation are bad, even though the value of money increases. These periods are bad because businesses fail and people cannot get jobs.

REVIEW   THE CHANGING VALUE OF MONEY

I. REVIEW OF TERMS
Which words complete the statements below?

deflation   demand-pull
CPI   price index
buying power   rising prices
depression   inflation
increasing taxes

1. The value of money is determined by its _____.
2. A _____ compares the amount by which the price level changes over a particular period of time.
3. The _____ measures changes in the price level for all goods and services.

4. During a period of deflation, the economy usually is in a _____ .

5. Increases in the CPI show _____ .

6. Inflation always means _____ .

7. One type of inflation often discussed is _____ inflation.

8. The Government can fight inflation by _____ .

9. _____ happens when the CPI falls.

II. REVIEW OF MAIN POINTS

1. What are three ways the Government can fight inflation?
2. How is the value of money determined?
3. Explain the purpose of the CPI.
4. How is the CPI figured out?
5. What is meant by *deflation*?
6. How is inflation shown in the CPI?
7. Explain the term *demand-pull inflation.*
8. What is the main purpose for trying to control inflation?
9. What causes the value of money to change?
10. What does the term *creeping inflation* mean?

III. THE CHANGING VALUE OF MONEY: CONCEPTS

1. You learned earlier about worker productivity; that is, a worker's output for each hour of labor. Why is it important that worker productivity rise faster than wages if there is to be a stable economy?

2. Explain how increased government spending without a tax increase can cause inflation. Has this happened in recent years?

3. During the depression of the 1930's, many people hid money in cans. Suppose D. I. Clarke, who lived during the depression, still refuses to put his money in a bank savings account. One year he placed $500 in a bank safety deposit box for safe-keeping. Explain why his money's value is likely to be less than $500 three years later.

4. Would Verna Philpot, who made $400 a month in 1955, be equally well-off with a monthly paycheck of $550 in 1971? If your answer is no, how much would Verna need to earn? (Use Table 11−1.)

IV. THE CHANGING VALUE OF MONEY: EXERCISES

1. Use Table 11−1 to answer the following questions:
   a. What was the percentage increase in the CPI between 1950 and 1953?
   b. What was the percentage increase between 1965 and 1972?
   c. What was the percentage increase from 1958 to 1963?
   d. What important events took place during the periods 1950−1953 and 1965−1972 that made them different from 1958−1963? How did these events affect increases in the CPI?
2. Talk to people who remember the period from 1929 to 1940.
   a. Ask them to compare life in that period with life between 1967 and 1975. Remember, the last period was one of high inflation.
   b. Ask them which period they preferred living in. Ask them to explain why.
   c. Prepare your answers in a short report.
3. Many people are interested in the economic events that affect the nation. Look through newspapers and magazines (U.S. News & World Report, Time, or Newsweek) for some articles dealing with current economic events. Bring these to class and be prepared to explain the meaning of two articles. Indicate why you think these two articles are important.

2 FAMILY MONEY MANAGEMENT

Managing money is not easy, especially when prices are always rising. There is hardly a family or individual who is not concerned about money. Good money management does not depend on how much or how little money you have. It depends on how you use what you have.

Good money management is a personal matter. Each family or person must decide how to use his or her own money. Each one must set his or her own financial goals and find ways to reach them. A good money management plan can help you avoid financial mistakes.

This chapter discusses why money management is needed and how you can become a good money manager. It also considers the purpose of a family budget and the steps to follow in making a budget. Finally, you will see how a budget for the Sutton family was made.

GOOD MONEY MANAGEMENT

Money management is planning how to use your dollars. This does not always mean saving lots of money. You often read of people who save money and live very poor lives. One such person was Henrietta Green, who left an estate of $95 million when she died in 1916. She ate cold oatmeal because she would not spend the money to cook it. Even though she left millions of dollars, she was not a good money

Henrietta Green lived as a pauper and left an estate of millions.

manager. Similarly, people who spend all of their money without thinking are not good money managers either. Money management involves getting the most for your dollars and understanding why you spend or save dollars as you do.

WHY MONEY MANAGEMENT IS NEEDED

You need to manage money just as you need to manage your time and other valuable resources. Good money management helps you to

1. Check how you use money.
2. Live within your income.
3. Avoid foolish or impulsive spending.
4. Get the most for the dollars spent.
5. Reach financial goals.
6. Have financial security.

You should start learning to manage money at an early age. During your lifetime, you will be handling various sums of money. When you become an adult, the exact amount of money you will handle depends on many things, including the amount of education you have. For example, if you stop your education at high school, you are likely to earn

TABLE 12-1
EXPECTED LIFETIME INCOME
BASED ON YEARS OF EDUCATION
(1972 Dollars)

Years of Education	Expected Annual Income	Total Expected Lifetime Income
Less than 8	$ 7,825	$316,000
8 years	9,121	356,000
9–11 years	9,594	398,000
12 years	10,938	465,000
13–15 years	12,780	554,000
16 or more	17,515	723,000

NOTE: *This respresents income received by a person from eighteen years of age to sixty-five years of age.*

about $465,000 over your lifetime. However, if you continue your education after high school, your total earnings could be as much as $723,000. These estimates do not allow for inflation. The actual dollars earned would be higher.

The data in Table 12–1 are for men. Women have usually earned less money than men. This is changing because of new laws that require equal pay for equal work. In recent years, women have experienced marked gains in income. For example, during the 1960's the number of women earning over $10,000 per year increased more than seven times. Thus, a woman's ability to earn money in the future should be closely related to her educational achievement.

So, the sooner you learn to manage your money, the better off you will be.

HOW TO BECOME A GOOD MONEY MANAGER

There are two key steps to becoming a good money manager. First, it is important to plan wisely to make sure your dollars buy what you need and want. If you do not plan your spending, you may spend foolishly. Second, you must shop carefully for the goods and services you buy. How to become a careful shopper is discussed in Unit IV.

Making a plan for spending and saving does not necessarily mean you will have more money to spend or that you will save more. Nor does it mean that you will not run short of money sometimes. A *financial plan* is a guide to spending and saving. For most families and individuals the plan should be simple. If it is not easy to understand, you will soon stop using it. This defeats the purpose of having a plan.

The best way to develop a money management plan is to use a *budget*. Nearly every business, government, school system, or other organization has budgets. To be successful, you too must conduct your financial affairs in a businesslike manner and have a budget.

THE FAMILY BUDGET

When people hear the word budget, they often think of pinching pennies. A budget does not mean this at all. A *budget* is a plan for personal spending and saving. It is a guide to use to plan ahead for good money management.

The most important thing that influences making a budget is people. Each family is different from every other family. Its income, tastes, needs, goods, size, friends and neighbors, debts, and health are only a few of the things that make budgeting a personal matter. What is important to one family may mean nothing to another. For example, the O'Dell family is quite happy with one old car. To them, buying a second car would be a waste of money. The Apperson family, however, finds it necessary to own two new cars.

No matter how well-planned a family budget is, the budget must be followed to be helpful. To be used, a budget must
1. Be easy to understand
2. Include the family's financial goals
3. Be personal (planned for one family)
4. Provide a way to save regularly.

PURPOSES OF A BUDGET

Budgets have several purposes. First, budgets help families understand their financial position. A good budget shows how much income a family has to spend each month. It also shows how much money a family owes. Second, budgets help families to live within their means (income). This is very important because it is easy to get deeply in debt. It is easy to borrow money but difficult to repay.

Saving a certain amount of money is not easy. However, budgets can help families put money away every month. A budget can also help a family decide in advance what major items to buy. For example, a family might decide to buy a new television. By following a budget, no money would be spent for a new car until the television was bought. Finally, a budget often serves as a family's *money conscience*. When starting to spend money carelessly, a person is likely to stop and think if this kind of spending is within the family budget.

STEPS IN MAKING A BUDGET

To make a budget, a family must answer the following questions:

1. What are the family's savings goals?
2. How much money does the family have to spend?
3. What are the family's fixed expenses? Fixed expenses include rent, house payments, taxes, and heating.
4. What are the family's flexible expenses? These include clothes,

The Sutton family discuss their budget.

gifts, and furniture.

5. How much money can be saved?

Answering these questions takes time, but it is time well spent. Once a family answer them, they have taken a big step toward practicing good money management. With some additional work, they can make a budget that guides them in managing their money.

MAKING A BUDGET: THE SUTTON FAMILY

The Sutton family has four members: Dick, Betty, Mary, and Jim. They live in Topeka, Kansas, where they own their home. Dick works as a driver for the local milk company.

Each year the family plans a budget that is followed closely. The Suttons have found that this is the only way they can buy what they need and want.

THE FAMILY'S SPENDING GOALS

The first step in planning a budget is to decide what the family want their money to buy. This means outlining their present and future needs and wants.

To fill in the outline, the family must set goals for the future. These goals must be reasonable. If the family's income is $10,000 a year, it is foolish for the family to set a goal of buying a $25,000 cabin cruiser. Also, it is important for the entire family to help set the goals. Making a budget is a family affair because each member benefits from the rewards.

There are two types of goals the Sutton family can set. One is the *near-future goal.* This is for things they want soon, usually within the next month or year. Examples of things that can be near-future goals are a new car, a color television, a dress, a coat, or a bike. Getting out of debt can also be a near-future goal. A *long-range goal* is for major items that may not be needed for years. Examples include a college education, a new home, or a retirement income.

The Sutton family have already planned their long-range goals. They put money aside each month for their home and the children's college education. Dick's retirement income will be paid by the milk company. He will also receive monthly social security checks.

At a family meeting, the Suttons discussed buying a new car or a color television as a near-future goal. The family decided the next goal should be a new car. They felt this was more important, since the family was planning a vacation trip to the Lake of the Ozarks in Missouri. Dick did not think the old car would make the trip safely.

After setting its goals, the family had to figure out how much money could be spent for the car. To answer this question, they had to add up their monthly income and their expenses.

THE FAMILY INCOME

Estimating the family's income is important when planning a budget. It tells the family how much money they have to spend. Dick is the only member of the family with a permanent full-time job. His salary of $11,400 is the family's only regular income.

Betty does bookkeeping at home for a small hardware business in town. For the last two years she has received an average of $215 every three months. Betty expects this job to last until she decides to quit. The

TABLE 12-2
THE SUTTON FAMILY'S ANNUAL INCOME ESTIMATES
(GROSS AND NET)
MONTHLY INCOME

Income Sources	Jan	Feb	Mar	Apr	May	Jun
Dick Sutton	$ 950	$950	$950	$ 950	$950	$950
Betty Sutton	215	—	—	215	—	—
Savings Account Interest	66	—	—	—	—	—
Dividends on AT&T Stock	—	35	—	—	35	—
GROSS INCOME	$1,231	$985	$950	$1,165	$985	$950
(−) INCOME TAXES	246	197	190	233	197	190
NET INCOME	985	788	760	932	788	760

family also has $2,400 in a bank savings account and owns 50 shares of American Telephone and Telegraph (AT&T) common stock.

Based on this information, Betty prepared a summary of the family's estimated total income for the next year. This estimate, which was prepared for each month, is shown in Table 12–2. Although Dick expects a raise in July of $75 a month, Betty did not include this money. Until actually received, expected raises or other extra money should not be counted.

The Sutton family expects to have a total income of about $12,530 next year. The highest income per month ($1,231) occurs in January and July. In these two months, the family receive Dick's check ($950), pay for Betty's work ($215), and interest on their savings account ($66). The dividends on the AT&T stock are paid four times a year and add up to a total of $140 a year.

The total income figures do not represent what the Sutton family has to spend. This total, or *gross,* income is what they receive. What the family can spend is their *net* income. This is their income after taxes are subtracted. Their net income for the year is estimated to be $10,026. Each year, the Suttons have to decide how the money is to be spent.

THE FAMILY EXPENSES

Figuring out how money is spent is usually harder than estimating the family income. One good way is to keep track of all the family spending for several weeks, usually six or eight weeks. Never depend on one week's spending to be a good estimate. To get an idea of how the family spend their money, figures over the six or eight weeks should be aver-

Jul	Aug	Sep	Oct	Nov	Dec	Year Income
$ 950	$950	$950	$ 950	$950	$950	$11,400
215	—	—	215	—	—	860
66	—	—	—	—	—	132
—	35	—	—	35	—	140
$1,231	$985	$950	$1,165	$985	$950	$12,532
246	197	190	233	197	190	2,506
985	788	760	932	788	760	$10,026

aged. This should give a good estimate of how much is spent in a single week.

Most families have different types of records they can use to help figure out where their money is spent. Such records are tax forms, cancelled checks, sales receipts, and credit card bills. Some families keep books showing how they spend their money.

Families have three types of expenses: (1) fixed, (2) flexible, and (3) emergency. *Fixed expenses* must be paid at certain times and in specific amounts. Fixed expenses such as rent, house payments, and gas, telephone, and electric bills have to be paid each month. Others may be paid only once or twice a year. Some of these are insurance premiums, income taxes, property taxes, and real estate taxes. Many of these expenses require large sums of money to be paid. In order to have the money to pay these expenses when they are due, families need to set aside money each month. This money should be put in a bank savings account specially set up for these expenses.

Flexible expenses change from month to month. They vary as to when they have to be paid and in the amounts that have to be paid. Some typical flexible expenses are clothing, food, gifts, transportation, entertainment, and household supplies. Some flexible expenses have

TABLE 12–3
THE SUTTON FAMILY'S ANNUAL FIXED EXPENSE ESTIMATES

Fixed Expenses	Jan	Feb	Mar	Apr	May	Jun
Mortgage	$110	$110	$110	$110	$110	$110
Insurance						
Car	—	36	—	—	—	—
Life	15	15	15	15	15	15
Home	22	—	—	22	—	—
Taxes, Property	17	17	17	17	17	17
Telephone	10	10	10	10	10	10
Gas	22	22	17	17	10	8
Electricity	12	12	12	14	15	18
Water	8	8	8	8	8	8
Car License	—	—	13	—	—	—
Emergency Fund	10	10	10	10	10	10
Educational Fund	50	50	50	50	50	50
TOTALS	$276	$290	$262	$273	$245	$246

to be paid each month, while others may be due only once a year. For example, a family must buy food each month but may pay a doctor's bill only three times a year.

Emergency expenses cannot be predicted. They are unexpected and often involve large amounts of money. They include repair bills for the family car, the television, the clothes dryer, or the hot water heater. A small amount of money should be set aside to cover such expenses when they happen. The Sutton family put money into their savings account for this purpose.

After reviewing their cancelled checks for the past year, Dick and Betty estimated the family's fixed, flexible, and emergency expenses. The fixed expenses totaled $3,158 for the year. They ranged from $245 (May) to $290 (February). When averaged, the monthly fixed expense was about $263.

Fixed expenses such as mortgage payments, property taxes, and the educational fund do not change each month. Thus, these expenses are easy to estimate for the year. Other expenses, such as telephone and water services, are budgeted for the same amount each month. However, they do vary slightly each month. But the totals of $120 (telephone) and $96 (water) represent normal yearly costs for these services. Other expenses, such as gas and electric bills, are also pre-

Jul	Aug	Sep	Oct	Nov	Dec	Year Total
$110	$110	$110	$110	$110	$110	$1,320
—	36	—	—	—	—	72
15	15	15	15	15	15	180
22	—	—	22	—	—	88
17	17	17	17	17	17	204
10	10	10	10	10	10	120
5	5	6	8	17	22	159
21	23	21	14	12	12	186
8	8	8	8	8	8	96
—	—	—	—	—	—	13
10	10	10	10	10	10	120
50	50	50	50	50	50	600
$268	$284	$247	$264	$249	$254	$3,158

dictable. Therefore, the different amounts budgeted for each month are likely to be close to the actual expense. Remember, you should be realistic and accurate in making a budget if it is to be a useful guide.

The amount of money needed for the emergency fund each month cannot be predicted. You never know when a financial emergency will happen. In reviewing his cancelled checks for three years, Dick found that the family spent about $120 each year for unexpected problems. He decided to set aside $10 a month to cover emergencies. If no emergencies happen, the money is left in the savings account until it is needed.

The Sutton family's flexible expense estimate is $5,975 for the year. The monthly estimates range from a low of $470 to a high of $660 per month. (See Table 12–4.) The monthly average is about $500. The three highest months have extra expenses—vacations, holiday gifts, and getting the children ready for school. July's budget estimate, for example, contains $200 for the family's vacation trip to Missouri.

Notice that most of the flexible expense estimates do not change from month to month. Exact monthly estimates are hard to make for flexible expenses. Therefore, Dick divided the yearly total for each flexible

TABLE 12–4
THE SUTTON FAMILY'S ANNUAL FLEXIBLE EXPENSE ESTIMATES

Flexible Expenses	Jan	Feb	Mar	Apr	May	Jun
Food and Drink	$180	$180	$180	$180	$180	$170
Clothing	40	40	40	40	40	30
Personal Care	25	25	25	25	25	25
Household						
Operation	30	30	30	30	30	30
Upkeep	25	25	25	25	25	25
Equipment	15	15	15	15	15	15
Furnishings	15	15	15	15	15	15
Medical Care	40	40	40	40	40	40
Transportation	70	70	70	70	70	70
Recreation	20	20	20	20	20	20
Gifts	—	—	10	—	—	—
Vacation	—	—	—	—	—	—
Miscellaneous	10	10	10	10	10	10
TOTALS	$470	$470	$480	$470	$470	$450

expense item by 12 to get a monthly figure. This means that the amount of money spent for a certain item in any month may not agree with the budget estimate. However, over the year, enough money will be budgeted to cover the total expenses.

The Suttons now have estimates of their expenses and income. An important point is finding out if their income will be more than expenses or if expenses will be more than income. To consider this issue, the estimates must be compared. Only after comparing the figures can the Suttons decide if they have enough money to buy a new car.

TESTING THE BUDGET

To test a budget, you should check both the year's total and monthly totals. By looking at each month, you can spot those that are likely to be troublesome—that is, those months where expenses are likely to be greater than income. When such a month appears likely, you must plan to have extra money. This extra money can be saved from months when the family income is greater than its expenses. Or you can try to adjust your flexible spending in the troublesome months. Each flexible expense must be checked to see if it can be cut. By cutting several items a little, expenses can often be reduced to make the budget balance.

Jul	Aug	Sep	Oct	Nov	Dec	Year Totals
$170	$175	$175	$180	$180	$180	$2,125
30	30	40	40	40	40	490
25	25	25	25	25	25	300
30	30	30	30	30	30	360
25	25	25	25	25	25	300
15	15	15	15	15	15	180
15	15	15	15	15	15	180
40	60	40	40	40	40	500
70	70	70	70	70	70	840
20	20	20	20	20	20	240
10	—	20	—	—	100	140
200	—	—	—	—	—	200
10	10	10	10	10	10	120
$660	$510	$485	$470	$470	$570	$5,975

The Sutton family's estimates for income and expenses are shown in Table 12–5. The Sutton family should have enough money to meet its expenses during the year. Looking at the yearly difference between income and expenses (line 5, Table 12–5) shows $893 extra income. This is income they can save or use for some purpose other than the expenses listed in Table 12–5.

In August and December, however, the family will not have enough money. December's income is $760, but the total estimate of fixed and flexible expenses is $824. In December, the family will need an extra $64. This shows an important advantage of family budgeting—plans can be made to have extra money on hand when the family is likely to need it. The reason December is over the budget is because of the holidays. The Suttons plan an extra expense of $100 for gifts in this month. The extra money for December can be taken from a month like October, which is free of gift-giving holidays.

In a month where there is money left over in the budget, the money should be put in a bank savings account. When extra money is needed, it can be taken out of savings. The advantage of putting it in a bank savings account is that the money will be there when needed. If extra money is not put away, it may be spent on something the family does not really need.

DECIDING ABOUT A NEW CAR

Now that a budget has been made, the family can decide if they have enough money to buy a car. The family wants a compact car. They think the price of the car is within their budget. Also, Dick says the car

TABLE 12–5
THE SUTTON FAMILY'S TEST BUDGET

Items	Jan	Feb	Mar	Apr	May	Jun
1. Total Income	$985	$788	$760	$932	$788	$760
2. Fixed Expenses	276	240	262	273	245	246
3. Flexible Expenses	470	470	480	470	470	450
4. Total Expenses (Line 2 + Line 3)	746	760	742	743	715	696
5. Difference (Line 1 − Line 4)	$239	$ 28	$ 18	$189	$ 73	$ 64

is not expensive to operate. With a limited budget and the rising cost of gasoline, a compact seems to be the family's best bet.

To help the family make its decision, Dick put the financial facts together. (See Table 12–6.)

TABLE 12–6 THE SUTTON FAMILY'S NEW CAR FINANCIAL FACTS							
Income				**Expenses**			
Savings Account Withdrawal	$1,500			New Car		$3,700	
Extra Income	893			Sales Tax		185	
Trade-in Value of Old Car	790			License		13	
TOTAL	$3,183			Extra Car Insurance		40	
				TOTAL		$3,938	

Jul	Aug	Sep	Oct	Nov	Dec	Year Total
$985	$788	$760	$932	$788	$ 760	$10,026
268	284	247	264	249	254	3,158
660	510	485	470	470	570	5,975
928	794	732	734	719	824	9,133
$ 57	$ −6	$ 28	$198	$ 69	$−64	$ 893

The Suttons plan to take $1,500 from their bank savings account to help pay for the new car. This cuts the family savings account to $900. Betty did not think the family should let its savings account go below $900. This amount should be kept on hand in case of family emergencies.

The trade-in value of the old family car is $790. The annual budget summary (Table 12–5) shows that there should be $893 left over after all family expenses are paid. This money can be used for the car. Thus, during the budget year there will be a total of $3,183 that can be spent on a new car. The expenses for a new car will be about $3,938. (See Table 12–6.) This leaves $755 to be paid. The family will have to pay this amount out of the next year's budget. This means that the family is building a fixed expense into the budgets for the next two years. Since cars are so expensive, it is common for families to take more than one year to pay for them. The Suttons finally decided to buy the compact.

CHANGING THE FAMILY BUDGET

The test budget (Table 12–5) shows that $893 will be left over at the end of the year. Such extra money can be put in a savings account or used to buy a major item. The Suttons are planning to use their extra money to buy the new car.

If the budget shows expenses to be greater than income, it is called a *deficit budget.* One way to help a deficit budget is to get extra income. However, this is not easy for most families unless another member of the family gets a job.

A better approach to correct the deficit is to cut family expenses. First, try to decrease or completely cut out some of the flexible expenses. Things that can often be reduced are vacations, furniture, clothing, and gifts. By cutting a few dollars from these items, it may be possible to balance the budget. Another approach is to reduce fixed expenses. This is harder because these expenses cover many of the family's basic needs.

The important point is that all family budgets should be tested to see if they balance. When the test shows expenses greater than income, the budget must be changed. Since it is hard to get extra income, the best approach is to cut expenses. This is another way of saying a family must live within its income.

SUMMARY

Money was invented to help people trade for goods and services. Many things have been used for money, including shells, rocks, salt, paper, and cows. The major types of money used today are (1) currency (paper money and coins) and (2) checkbook money. In the United States, about 80 percent of all money in use is checkbook money.

Money functions as (1) a medium of exchange, (2) a measure of value, (3) a store of value, and (4) a standard of future payment. Without money, business, as it is known today, could not be carried on.

The only value money has is what it will buy. What money will buy depends on the general price level. The general price level represents the cost of all goods and services. In the United States the general price level is measured by the Consumer Price Index (CPI).

Increases in the CPI represent inflation. The effect of inflation is to decrease the value (buying power) of money. If not controlled, inflation can ruin an economy. The most effective way to fight inflation is for the Government to take action. This action includes (1) cutting government spending, (2) increasing taxes, and (3) raising interest rates.

Because inflation is common in the United States, good money management is important. Good money management does not depend on how much money you have, but on how you use what you have. Good money management means planning how to use your money wisely.

There are two basic steps to becoming a good money manager. First, you must plan wisely to make sure your money is spent for what you need and want. Second, you must shop carefully for what you buy. You must get the most for your dollar.

You can plan the use of money by making a budget. A budget is a plan, or guide, a family or an individual can follow. A budget is a personal matter. Each person or family should develop their own. The major purpose of a budget is to help a person or a family understand and control how their money is spent. In short, budgets help people live within their income.

REVIEW FAMILY MONEY MANAGEMENT

I. REVIEW OF TERMS

Which words complete the statements below?

emergency   budget
near-future goal   flexible
fixed   guide
personal   money management

1. A financial plan is a _____ to spending and saving.
2. _____ is planning how to use your dollars.
3. A _____ is something you want soon.
4. _____ expenses cannot be predicted.
5. A family budget is _____ and should be planned for a specific family.
6. _____ expenses change from month to month.
7. A _____ is a plan for personal spending and saving.
8. _____ expenses must be paid at certain times and in specific amounts.

II. REVIEW OF MAIN POINTS

1. Why is money management important to every family?
2. What are the key steps to becoming a good money manager?
3. Why should a family's financial plan be simple and easy to understand?
4. What is a budget?
5. Name four specific purposes of a family budget.
6. What are the steps in preparing a budget?
7. What are three types of expenses each family must face?
8. Explain the differences among the three types of family expenses.
9. Why should a family budget be tested?

10. What is the most practical way to make a family budget balance?

11. What are the characteristics of a good budget?

III. FAMILY MONEY MANAGEMENT: CONCEPTS

1. Lowell Hobbs says, "I know how much I make, how much I spend, and how much I want to save. There is no reason to keep any financial records."

   a. Do you think Lowell is a good money manager? Explain.

   b. How would you try to show Lowell that he could be a better money manager.

2. From the following list of items, select those that are fixed, flexible, or emergency expenses.

   a. clothing
   b. taxes
   c. television repairs
   d. rent
   e. gas bill
   f. gifts
   g. books
   h. magazine subscriptions
   i. tobacco
   j. telephone bills
   k. dancing lessons
   l. life insurance
   m. state income tax
   n. cable TV

3. The first step in making a budget is to set goals. Make a list of five items you want in the next few weeks. Talk with your family and list five items the family wants in the next few weeks.

   a. What types of goals are these? Explain.

   b. Do your personal goals match the family's? Explain your answers.

   c. Go through your list and rank the most important one first, etc. Have your family do the same thing. Do the lists more closely agree now?

   d. Which list do you consider to be the more important? Why?

4. Talk with your parents about flexible and fixed expenses. Know what these terms mean.

   a. Prepare a list of ten items that are fixed expenses in your family.

   b. Now list ten items that are flexible expenses in your family.

IV. FAMILY MONEY MANAGEMENT: EXERCISES

1. Steve Daniel's family wants to buy a new electric stove instead of having the old one repaired. They can buy one for $35 a month for 18 months. With $90 of Steve's take-home pay being used to pay for carpeting and a recently bought TV, they are doubtful about adding another debt. To help the family decide, Steve kept records of how they spent their money for two months. The following data show how the family spent their income. Steve's take-home pay is $900 a month.

Item	Monthly Expenses
Food and Household Supplies	$280
Rent	200
Utilities	60
Clothing	75
Car	65
Time Payments	90
Medical Care	20
Gifts	10
Recreation	25
Emergency Fund	10
Miscellaneous	15
TOTAL	$850

    a. Looking at these expenses, do you think a $35 monthly expense for 18 months is too much for the Daniel family? Explain.

    b. If your answer to (a.) is yes, what items can be cut to add the electric stove payment?

    c. What is the purpose of making a study of the ways a family spends its money?

2. How do you think you spend your money? Do you really know? To answer these questions, copy and complete the following table. First fill in Column 1 with what you think you spend. For one week, keep a record of how you actually spend your money. Then fill in Column 2.

| Item | Expenses | |
	Column 1	Column 2
Lunches		
School Supplies		
Recreation		
Personal Expenses		
Gifts		
Hobbies		
Bus Fares		
Other		
Savings		
TOTALS	___	___

    a. How do the two columns compare? Are you surprised at the results? Explain your answer.

    b. Do you think the way you actually spend your money should be changed? Why or why not?

3. The following table shows how three city families with different budgets spend their money. Each budget represents a different level of living for a family of four: a husband, a nonworking wife, a boy, and a girl.

Item	Lower Budget	Middle Budget	Higher Budget
Food	$1,964	$ 2,532	$ 3,198
Housing	1,516	2,638	3,980
Transportation	536	964	1,250
Clothing & Personal Care	848	1,196	1,740
Medical Care	609	612	638
Other Family Consumption	368	684	1,129
TOTAL FAMILY CONSUMPTION	$5,841	$ 8,626	$11,939
Other items	357	560	937
Taxes	1,016	1,785	3,033
TOTAL ANNUAL BUDGET	$7,214	$10,971	$15,905

Answer the following questions:

    a. What is the amount of money spent on total family consumption and other items for the three different budgets?

b. What percentage of each total in question (a.) is spent for food? For housing? For medical care?

c. Explain why the higher-budget family spends a lower percentage of its budget on medical care than the other two families.

d. Explain why the higher-budget family spends a greater percentage of its budget on housing (furnishings and operation included) than the lower-budget family.

Unit IV
Marketing and the Consumer

All people have needs and wants. While needs—food, clothing, shelter —are the same for all people, wants are not the same. To meet both needs and wants, business produces a wide variety of goods and services.

In Chapter 13, you will see how goods and services are made available to consumers. In particular, you will learn about marketing and certain basic marketing activities, such as packaging, advertising, and selling. You will also learn how goods can be moved from producer to consumer and how much it costs to move them.

The marketing of goods and services changes all the time because consumers constantly change. Chapter 14 covers the ways in which consumers change.

Consumers also change their opinions about business. Chapter 15 discusses consumerism, a popular movement based on the idea that shoppers should be treated fairly. The chapter also takes a look at how an individual can be important in the consumer movement. Finally, the roles of business and governments in consumerism are described, as well as the future of consumerism in the United States.

One way shoppers can get their money's worth is by being well informed. Chapter 16 considers several types of buying aids. These aids can help consumers get information on different products before actually buying them.

Understanding how the marketing system works and what aids and agencies are available to help and protect consumers is important. Combining this knowledge with some common-sense buying guides can help you become a smart buyer. In Chapter 17, you will learn why and what consumers buy. You will also learn some general buying rules that can help you avoid making costly mistakes.

The major goal of this unit is to help you learn how to become a smart shopper. Once you learn the material in this unit, you will have taken a giant step toward reaching that goal.

UNIT PREVIEW

AS YOU STUDY THIS UNIT YOU WILL BE ENGAGED IN

* DISCOVERING how the marketing system works

* IDENTIFYING the basic marketing activities

* DETERMINING why consumer markets change and how these changes affect consumers

* FINDING different sources of information for consumers

* UNDERSTANDING the role of government and business in the consumerism movement

* EVALUATING different consumer buying aids

* TESTING the USDA grading system when buying groceries

* FINDING the best values in different products with respect to price and quality.

A FOCUS FOR YOUR STUDY

3 THE MARKETING SYSTEM

To meet people's needs and wants, business produces a large variety of goods and services. Simply producing goods and services, however, is not enough. The goods and services must be moved to places where they can be bought by consumers. This moving of goods and services is called marketing, and it is always related to buying and selling.

Marketing, however, is much more than just buying and selling. This chapter discusses the meaning of marketing, the basic elements of marketing, how goods and services reach the consumer, and how much marketing costs.

THE MEANING OF MARKETING

It is not easy to define *marketing.* This is because marketing means different things to different people. Consider the shopper who buys a carton of Coca-Cola in the supermarket. To her, marketing means going to the supermarket to buy food, in this case, the Coca-Cola. The supermarket does its marketing by bringing the Coca-Cola to the store, advertising it, and storing it so the shopper can buy it when she goes shopping. To the bottling company, marketing means deciding what drinks consumers want and then bottling them and moving them to the supermarket. On the other hand, the South American farmer who grows cola nuts or cola plants thinks of marketing as shipping the nuts or the coca leaves from the area where they are grown to the factory that makes the cola syrup for the bottling company.

These people and businesses are all involved in marketing. Yet each is only a small part of the total marketing system. Marketing involves a lot more than buying and selling. It includes packaging, transporting, storing, and advertising. *Marketing,* then, is a series of activities that move goods and services from the producer to the consumer.

MARKETING ACTIVITIES

The most important marketing activities are (1) buying, (2) packaging, (3) pricing, (4) transporting, (5) storing, (6) advertising, and (7) selling.

BUYING

Buying is a basic marketing activity. In every marketing transaction someone buys a product or a service. However, people do not always buy for the same reason. For example, the shopper who bought the Coca-Cola for her family to drink was a *consumer-buyer.* The supermarket and bottling company bought the Coca-Cola for resale—not for final use. Such businesses are called *resale-buyers* because they buy something for the purpose of selling it to someone else.

Governments are buyers who buy for *use* and not for resale. For example, city and state governments buy large fleets of cars for their police to use. Governments also buy such things as computers, gasoline, office supplies, and insurance for city workers.

No matter why buyers make their purchases—to use them, to make other goods, or to resell them—they all have one thing in common. They all want to get the most value for their money. This is often difficult, especially for individuals. Businesses and governments usually have certain standards that must be met before goods can be bought. People called *purchasing agents* work full-time to enforce these standards. They often consider the offers of several companies before deciding which is the best.

Suppose the State of Ohio planned to buy 500 new patrol cars. The state government would set minimum standards and requirements for the new cars. Several car dealers would be asked to tell the state how much they would charge for the 500 cars and what type of equipment and servicing they would include. It would then be the job of the purchasing agent to decide which dealer's offer was the best buy for the money.

PACKAGING

Packaging is an important marketing activity. Some of the reasons for packaging are

1. To help sell goods
2. To protect goods
3. To make goods easier to use
4. To give consumers a container they can use again.

These purposes make it necessary to package goods in different ways. Products are packaged in cans, cartons, glass jars, plastic wrappers, paper, wooden boxes, and various other materials.

Packaging can help sell goods by catching the shopper's eye, identifying a product, or protecting a product from misuse. For example, parents with young children are concerned about their children's safety.

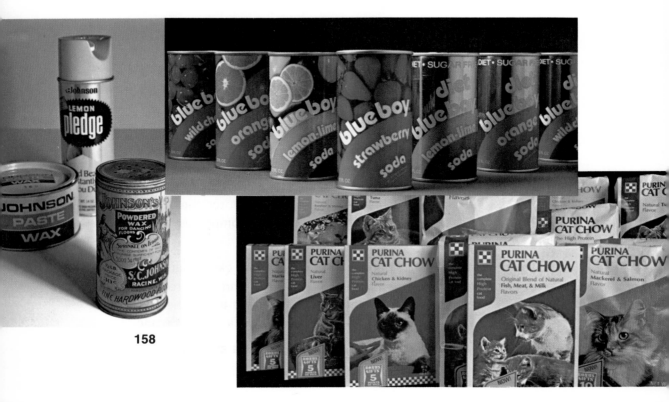

158

Children's aspirin is now sold in containers with special tops that are hard for small children to remove. This is an important safety feature, and many parents will buy children's aspirin packaged in these containers instead of in bottles with regular screw-on tops.

For many years, the major aim of packaging was to protect the product. Today this is still important because consumers will not buy products that are dirty or damaged. For example, packaging light bulbs in corrugated containers helps prevent the bulbs from breaking. Also, wrapping bread in plastic wrappers keeps it fresh and clean.

Making products easier to use and giving consumers reusable packages are also important. One type of package that makes something easier to use is the aerosol spray can. This type of package is used for hair spray, suntan lotion, insecticides, and many other products. This type of package, however, is not reusable and must be disposed of with care. Examples of reusable packages are coffee cans that can be used as canisters and jelly jars that can be used as drinking glasses.

PRICING

Since buyers often shop for the best value, businesses must price their products realistically or people will not buy them. Setting the price of a product or a service is not always easy. Two things that affect the price of a product are how much it costs to make and how much other companies charge for the same thing. If two products are the same quality, you will probably buy the cheaper one.

TRANSPORTING

If goods are to be sold they must be moved to where people can buy them. This moving of goods must often be done quickly and at little cost. Most fruits and vegetables must be moved quickly or they may spoil. Fresh strawberries, for example, are brought daily from farms into the cities. If the cost of transporting the strawberries is high, their price will be increased and consumers may not buy them.

When talking about transportation, you usually think of a product being moved. However, services can also be transported. For example, the television repairer comes to your home or a rug cleaner shampoos wall-to-wall carpets in your home. Thus, transportation is also very important in selling services.

STORING

Storing is closely related to transporting because goods must often be stored whenever they are transported in large quantities to a particular location. The importance of storage is to make goods readily available to consumers. Many things are needed the year around, not just when they are produced. Wheat, for example, is stored in grain elevators and is shipped to flour mills and other food processors any time during the year. Other types of goods, such as soap, are made in one place, say Cincinnati, and shipped to large warehouses around the United States. Storing the soap in many locations saves costly delays in getting the product to the consumer.

There are many different types of storage for different types of products. These include (1) yard and ground storage for coal, lumber, or bricks; (2) cold storage for foods; (3) commodity warehouses for grain, cotton, and tobacco; and (4) merchandise warehouses for various packaged goods.

ADVERTISING

Advertising's major purposes are to create a demand for new goods or services and to increase the demand for existing goods or services. One advantage of advertising is that it can reach large numbers of customers. Another advantage is that advertising often can *presell* customers on a particular product. This means that customers decide to buy a certain product before they even go into the store.

There are many ways to advertise products. Often the same products are advertised on radio and television, in magazines and newspapers, and on billboards. Some television advertisements may be seen by more than 40 million people at one time during such events as the Super Bowl or World Series. Not every advertising method is suitable for every

Advertising creates or increases demand for a product or service. This is a magazine ad for watches.

product. For example, if you were selling children's toys you would not run ads in sports magazines but would probably run television ads during Saturday morning cartoon shows.

A still from a television commercial for luggage.

Businesses spend over $20 billion a year for advertising. The largest amounts go into newspapers (over $6 billion) and television (over $4 billion). Between 1950 and 1970 the money spent on advertising each year increased from about $6 billion to almost $20 billion.

SELLING

Selling is the last step in the marketing process. Even though marketing is more than just selling, this activity is probably the most important. Most selling is done by people who can show the advantages of a product, help customers reach a decision, and close the sale. This is called personal selling, and it is the most important and effective way to sell goods and services. For example, when you buy a stereo set or a car, it is important for you, the customer, to have a salesperson demonstrate the product and answer your questions.

CHANNELS OF DISTRIBUTION

The link between the producer and the buyer is called a *channel of distribution*. Another way to view a channel of distribution is to think of it as a route that goods take in moving from the producer to the consumer.

The producer is at one end of the channel and the consumer is at the other end. People or businesses that move the goods between the producer and consumer are called *distributors*. They help the goods and services move more easily to the consumer.

Producers move their products in one of two ways: directly or through distributors. The first method is called a *direct channel of distribution*. The second is called an *indirect channel of distribution*.

DIRECT CHANNELS OF DISTRIBUTION

A direct channel of distribution is in effect when goods move directly from the producer to the consumer. This form of distribution is shown in channel 1, Figure 13-1. Notice there is no distributor in this distribution channel.

FIGURE 13-1
TYPES OF DISTRIBUTION CHANNELS
FOR CONSUMER GOODS

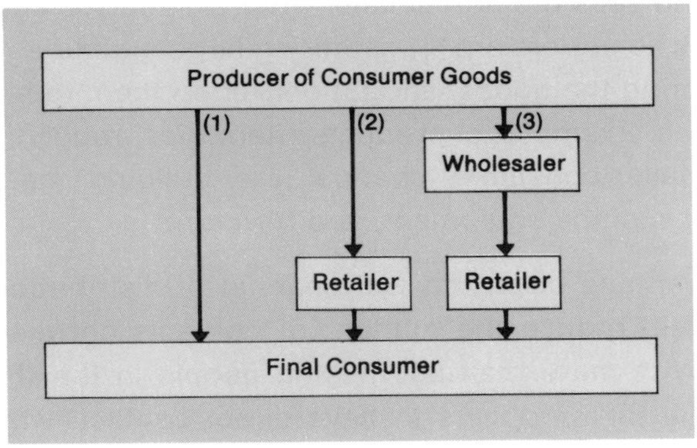

Most producer goods are sold this way by highly trained industrial salespeople. These salespeople contact other manufacturers, hospitals, universities, hotels, and boards of education. Examples of goods sold this way are computers, chemicals, cleaning supplies, dry docks, and heavy machinery.

Consumer goods are sometimes sold directly to the consumer by door-to-door salespeople. Products sold in this way include encyclopedias, spices, vacuum cleaners, cosmetics, cookies, and cooking utensils.

INDIRECT CHANNELS OF DISTRIBUTION

An indirect channel of distribution is in effect when distributors stand between the producer and consumer. The two most common types of indirect channels involve retailers and wholesalers. Channels 2 and 3 in Figure 13–1 represent indirect channels.

A *retailer* is the more familiar type of distributor. A retailer is the one from whom consumers buy almost all their goods and services. Retailers, of which there are about 1.8 million in the United States, range in size from small neighborhood grocery stores to large department stores. Retailers, who sell almost every product made, have played an important part in helping the United States reach its present high standard of living. Examples of goods often sold through the producer-retailer-consumer channel are men's and women's clothing and perishable foods, such as meat.

A *wholesaler* is a distributor who buys large quantities of goods from a producer and sells them in smaller quantities to retailers. The main jobs done by wholesalers are (1) gathering large quantities of goods together, (2) storing the goods, and (3) delivering them to retailers when they are needed. Examples of products often sold through the producer-wholesaler-retailer-consumer channel are building materials, food, barber supplies, office equipment, and furniture.

The main advantage of an indirect channel of distribution is that the distributors help reduce the number of contacts between producers and buyers. With more than 200 million people in the United States, it is impossible for producers to have direct contact with all of their possible customers.

This is shown in Figure 13–2. By using direct channels, each producer maintains contact with three consumers. As the number of consumers grows, this soon becomes impractical. Also, as the number of producers increases, it becomes impossible for consumers to keep up with them.

FIGURE 13-2   DISTRIBUTORS REDUCE THE WORK OF PRODUCERS

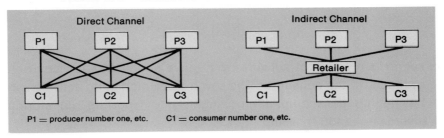

A solution to the problem is to use indirect channels—to put distributors between the producers and the consumers. Notice in the example that the retailer makes it possible for each producer and consumer to maintain only one contact point.

Though there are advantages to using distributors, there is also a cost. Wholesalers and retailers are in business to make a profit. To make a profit, they must increase the cost of the goods you buy.

THE COST OF MARKETING

The marketing services of distributors, since they cannot be seen, are often not appreciated by consumers. Many people feel that marketing does nothing but raise the price of goods. The question of how much marketing costs is not easy to answer. In fact, it varies depending upon the type of goods you buy. It has been estimated that the cost of marketing is about one-half (50 percent) of the selling price. In other words, if a suit costs $90 the marketing costs are about $45.

Another way to think about marketing is to look at the value marketing adds to goods. Suppose the material and labor to make the suit cost $25, and the producer sells the suit for $45. As long as the suit remains at the factory, it is worthless to the consumer because the consumer cannot buy it. Now assume the suit is shipped through the producer-retailer-consumer channel and the consumer is asked to pay $90 for it. The $45 the retailer added to the price of the suit represents the value added by marketing and is sometimes called the *mark-up*.

SUMMARY

Marketing is a series of activities that move goods and services from the producer to the consumer. The seven basic marketing activities are (1) buying, (2) packaging, (3) pricing, (4) transporting, (5) storing, (6) advertising, and (7) selling.

Goods and services reach the consumer through channels of distribution. There are two basic kinds of channels: direct and indirect. The indirect form, which uses distributors, is most often used for consumer goods. The distributors perform an important marketing service and add value to the goods. The value they add, however, raises the price of the goods.

REVIEW THE MARKETING SYSTEM

I. REVIEW OF TERMS

Which words complete the sentences below?

wholesalers
advertising
indirect channel
marketing
retailers
purchasing agents
selling
resale-buyers
channel of distribution
consumer-buyers
direct channel

1. The major purpose of _____ is to create or increase the demand for goods or services.
2. The link between the producer and consumer is called the _____ .
3. Distributors that final consumers buy most of their products from are called _____ .
4. The activities that take place in moving goods and services from the producer to the consumer are called _____ .

5. In marketing there are two types of buyers. The type of buyer a person or business is depends on how the goods or services are used. These types of buyers are called _____ and _____.
6. People whose job it is to find the best buy for governments and businesses are known as _____.
7. Distributors who buy large quantities of goods from producers and businesses are known as _____.
8. An _____ of distribution has distributors between the producer and consumer.
9. Probably the most important marketing activity is _____.
10. Most industrial goods are sold through a _____ of distribution.

II. REVIEW OF MAIN POINTS
1. List the seven marketing activities and explain the purpose of each.
2. Explain why marketing is just as important as production in meeting consumer needs and wants.
3. What is the purpose of channels of distribution in the United States economy?
4. Explain the difference between direct and indirect channels of distribution. What types of goods are best suited for each channel?
5. What does *cost of marketing* mean?

III. THE MARKETING SYSTEM: CONCEPTS
1. All of the different marketing activities add costs to the retail price of goods. Explain the reasoning behind a company's decision to use self-service stores as a way to lower marketing costs.
2. Mr. Larry Reid thinks, that in most cases, distributors are not needed in our marketing system and that they only add extra costs to goods. His son, Blaine, argues that this is not true. Blaine says distributors perform an important service and their costs are worthwhile. Decide which one you think

is correct. Prepare a report explaining the reasons for your choice.

3. One purpose of advertising is to sell goods and services. Explain how advertising can make your shopping easier and less time consuming. Do you think the cost of advertising is justified? Explain your answer.

IV. THE MARKETING SYSTEM: EXERCISES

1. Talk with friends who have shopped in a small neighborhood retail store. Ask them to describe how the goods were packaged, advertised, and displayed, and to make a list of as many goods as possible that were sold in the store. Compare the list with the goods sold in a modern department store. Does the department store provide any better service than the small retail store? Put your answers in report form to share with your class.

2. Trace the channel of distribution for one of the following goods. Go to a local business that sells the product and ask for help to complete this exercise.

   a. gasoline
   b. frozen orange juice
   c. fresh oranges
   d. automobile
   e. bar of soap

   f. sofa
   g. television set
   h. encyclopedia set
   i. can of pipe tobacco
   j. milk

THE CHANGING CONSUMER MARKET

Businesses often have to change to continue making a profit. They have to create and produce new products or change the way old products are marketed. The reason businesses must change is that people—the consumers—change. For example, as people grow older they may stop buying a certain product or using a particular service. No matter what the reason, when people change, the market for goods and services changes.

The term *market* can mean many different things. In business, it means a group of people who buy a particular product or service. Often you will hear businesspeople speak of the new car market, the market for new homes, or the color television market. In the last example, this means the people who may buy a color television set within a certain time period, such as one year.

The things that change in consumer markets include such things as the total population, education levels, income, and age. These changes are important to businesses for planning how to sell their goods and services. By studying these characteristics, businesses can locate the markets in which they are most likely to sell their products.

POPULATION

Since consumer markets consist of people, you will first look at certain important population characteristics. These include the total population, the percentage of people in different age groups, the racial and national origins of the population, and the percentage of people living in the country or in cities.

Suppose you make a product, such as men's razors, that is not wanted or needed by everybody. You are interested in only that part of the total consumer market that can use the razors. You will therefore want to know how many men in the United States are over fifteen years of age, because they are your most likely customers.

TOTAL POPULATION

Every minute of the day people are born and people die. Over the past several years in the United States about eight people have been born each minute and three people have died. This means, that on the average, the nation's population has gained about five new people every minute.

Table 14-1 shows how the nation's total population has changed during the period from 1900 to 1970. During this period the total population grew from 76 million to about 203 million. This is an increase of over 160 percent. These figures on total population are important to companies that make products nearly everyone can use, such as soap and toothpaste. By paying attention to the increase in population, a manufacturer can figure out how much of a product may be sold in the future.

Most companies, however, do not make products intended to be sold to every person. It is important for these companies to study different parts, or segments, of the population.

TABLE 14-1
TOTAL UNITED STATES POPULATION
1900-1970
(in millions)

Year	Population
1900	76.0
1910	92.0
1920	105.7
1930	122.8
1940	131.7
1950	150.7
1960	179.3
1970	203.2

Knowledge of the way the population changes by age groups is very important to businesses. Table 14–2 shows how the total population was divided by age groups during the time from 1900 to 1970. The figures in the table are percentages. For example, in 1970, 28.3 percent of the total population was less than fourteen years old.

Looking at Table 14–2, you can see that the percentages of people in different age groups are always changing. For example, in 1900 about 4 percent of the population was over sixty-five. By 1970 this percentage had more than doubled, to almost 10 percent. This happened because better medical care enabled people to live longer. Certain areas of the country, such as Florida and Arizona, because of their mild weather have large numbers of people in the sixty-five-and-over group. About one-fourth (25 percent) of the people in St. Petersburg, Florida, are in this age group.

Businesses often use age-group percentages to help them plan their advertising programs. One company that has been very successful in selling its product in the youth market is Pepsi-Cola. This company has appealed to the youth market through its ads about "The Pepsi Generation—You've Got a Lot to Live."

The growing numbers of older people have been very profitable for many companies. For example, older people buy many leisure goods, medicines, and convenience foods. One reason why older people have become an important market is because they have more money to spend during retirement than older people had in past years.

TABLE 14–2
DIFFERENT AGE GROUPS OF TOTAL POPULATION
(1900–1970)
(in percentages)

Age Group	Year							
	1900	1910	1920	1930	1940	1950	1960	1970
Under 14	34.4	32.1	31.8	29.4	25.0	27.2	31.4	28.3
14–44	47.6	48.9	47.3	47.7	48.3	44.6	39.6	41.4
45–64	13.7	14.5	16.1	17.4	19.8	20.6	20.3	20.5
65–over	4.3	4.5	4.8	5.5	6.9	7.6	8.7	9.9

RACIAL AND NATIONAL ORIGINS

The population of the United States is made up of people with different ethnic origins. In fact, the United States is often called a *melting pot* because so many German, Scottish, Italian, Serbian, Chinese, African, Spanish, and other foreign people came to live here. By dividing the population according to ethnic backgrounds, separate markets can be studied.

Of all the ethnic markets, the market for Blacks is the most important at the national level. Table 14-3 shows the numbers of Black and White

TABLE 14-3
BLACK AND WHITE
CONSUMERS IN THE UNITED STATES
(in millions)

Group	Year		
	1950	1960	1970
Black	15.0	18.8	22.7
White	135.2	158.8	177.6

consumers for the period from 1950 to 1970. In 1970, Blacks made up about 13 percent of the population. They make up a major market for many products. For example, Blacks buy about 20 percent of the men's shoes sold in cities. In addition, Blacks use more cooked cereals and soft drinks per person than other groups.

Another important group in the United States is the Mexican-American group. There are now about 5.7 million Mexican-Americans in the country. In 1930, there were only 1.3 million. Most Mexican-Americans live in the Southwest. However, thousands of Mexican-Americans live in large cities, such as Chicago. As income rises for all groups, these groups represent potential new markets for business firms.

COUNTRY POPULATION VS. CITY POPULATION

Another way the United States population has changed is in the number of people who have left the country (rural areas) and moved to the cities

Great-tasting nutrition.

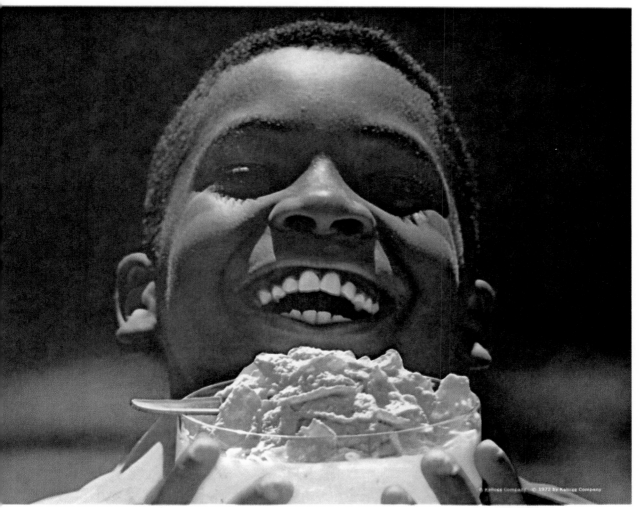

Would you believe there's somebody who gets a bigger kick out of Freddy's breakfast than Freddy?

Sure, he gets the good nutrition of a breakfast built around Kellogg's Sugar Frosted Flakes and milk. And he gets it as he likes it ... in a hurry, and delicious.

But while Freddy gets the nourishment, Mother gets his million-dollar smile. That alone makes a mother's morning a success. Besides, she'll probably sit down later to the same good breakfast herself.

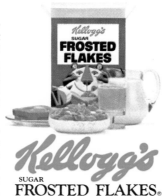

Kellogg's
SUGAR
FROSTED FLAKES®

Advertising is often directed to a special ethnic market.

**TABLE 14–4
UNITED STATES POPULATION
IN RURAL AND URBAN AREAS
(in percentages)**

	Year		
Area	*1950*	*1960*	*1970*
Rural	36.0	30.1	26.5
Urban	64.0	69.9	73.5

(urban areas). For many years, most of the people in the United States lived on farms. Around 1920, however, more people lived in the cities (51.2 percent) than on the farms. By 1970, over 70 percent of the people lived in cities.

Various states have different percentages of city dwellers. New Jersey and California are the most urban, with about 80 percent of their people living in cities. On the other hand, Arkansas, North Dakota, and West Virginia have less than 33 percent of their people in cities.

The way the population is divided between country (rural) and city (urban) areas is important to business. People in the country buy less food than city people because the country people can grow much of their food. Generally, rural markets have become less important because about 75 percent of all retail sales are made in urban areas. Most advertising dollars, therefore, are spent on urban areas.

EDUCATIONAL LEVELS

One of the most quickly changing characteristics of the consumer market is its level of education. More people are completing high school and college than ever before. This means that the consumer is becoming better educated. Table 14–5 shows that in 1940 the average number of years of school completed by people twenty-five and over was 8.6. By 1970, this figure had increased to 12.2. This means that the average person twenty-five or over had completed high school.

TABLE 14-5
EDUCATIONAL ACHIEVEMENT
OF POPULATION 25 YEARS OF AGE AND OVER
IN UNITED STATES, 1940–1970

Year	Years of School Completed
1940	8.6
1950	9.3
1960	10.6
1970	12.2

Usually, the more education people have, the more money they make. Since it takes money to buy goods and services, you can see why studying levels of education is so important to business. Also, the better educated people are, the better shoppers they become.

INCOME

Another very important characteristic of consumer markets is the amount of income people have. Income is money. Various sources of income include wages, salaries, interest, rents, and dividends. People usually cannot keep all of the money they earn. Taxes have to be paid— federal and state income taxes as well as a social security tax. A worker who makes $175 a week might have to pay $25 for federal income tax, $10 for state income tax, and $10 for social security. These taxes are taken out of the worker's earnings, leaving the worker only $130 to take home. This money that is left after taxes is called *buying income*. It is used for food, clothes, housing, insurance, and other needs and wants.

GROWTH OF BUYING INCOME

The best way to measure the growth of buying income is on a *per family* basis. This is done by dividing the total buying income of a group by the total number of families in the group.

TABLE 14–6
BUYING INCOME PER FAMILY
IN THE UNITED STATES, 1961–1971

Year	Buying Income
1961	$10,165
1962	10,485
1963	10,789
1964	11,447
1965	12,086
1966	12,560
1967	12,858
1968	13,339
1969	13,459
1970	13,777
1971	13,967

NOTE: *Buying income is in 1971 dollars.*

The buying income for the average family for the years 1961 to 1971 is shown in Table 14–6. During this period, buying income per family increased by about 37 percent. On the average, each family had 37 percent more money to spend after taxes in 1971 than in 1961.

SPENDING THE BUYING INCOME

People spend their buying income to satisfy their needs and wants. Needs, such as food, clothing, and shelter, are essentials to keep alive. To some people, transportation and medical care are also thought of as needs.

After needs are satisfied, the money left over is used for wants. Wants are "extras" such as insurance, gifts, movies, and restaurant meals. People spend their money on wants in different ways. The way it is spent can tell you about a person's values—that is, the things that are important to him or her. Some people spend money for paintings and books, while others buy speed boats. Some prefer to go out to eat in a French restaurant, while others might choose to buy a color television set. The main point is that people can spend their buying income for anything that seems worthwhile to them.

The U. S. Government has studied how the average city family spends its buying income for needs and wants. (In this study, every town with more than 2,500 people was included, not just the large cities. Thus, the study included over 70 percent of the total population.) The way the money was spent in 1960 is shown in Table 14–7. Notice that the average city family spent 55 percent of its buying income for food, clothing, and shelter. The largest single item was housing. By including transportation and medical care as needs, each family spent about 74 cents of each dollar on needs. The 26 cents left over were spent about evenly on such wants as recreation, personal care, and gifts.

Families living in the country may spend their buying income differently from city families. For example, rural families probably spend less for food because they can raise some of their own food, and less for housing because land for houses costs less in the country. In general, however, the figures in the table give you a good idea of how families in the United States spend their buying income.

TABLE 14–7
FAMILY SPENDING OF BUYING
INCOME
(in percentages)

Item	Percent of Buying Income	
NEEDS		
Housing	25	
Food	21	
Transportation	13	
Clothing	9	
Medical Care	6	
TOTAL		74
WANTS		
Personal Insurance and Investments	8	
Recreation and Education	5	
Gifts and Contributions	5	
Personal Care	3	
Miscellaneous	5	
TOTAL		26
TOTAL NEEDS AND WANTS		100

THE DISTRIBUTION OF BUYING INCOME

The way that buying income is divided among families is called the *income distribution*. It can tell you if only a few families have most of the income or if it is divided evenly. The more evenly divided the income is, the fewer poor families there are.

How buying income was distributed during 1961 and 1971 is shown in Table 14–8. Between these years there was a great change in income distribution. In 1961, for example, about 67 percent of the families had buying incomes of less than $9,999. By 1971, this figure had fallen to about 48 percent. This means that almost 20 percent of the families moved into the top three buying income groups. Also, notice that the percentage of families with buying incomes over $15,000 more than doubled from 1961 to 1971.

TABLE 14–8
FAMILY BUYING INCOME DISTRIBUTIONS
FOR THE UNITED STATES
(in percentages)

Yearly Income	Percent of Families	
	1961	1971
$ Less than $3,000	14.7	8.3
3,000—4,999	13.4	10.2
5,000—6,999	15.3	11.2
7,000—9,999	23.5	18.5
10,000—11,999	11.4	12.5
12,000—14,999	10.0	14.4
15,000 and over	11.7	24.9

NOTE: These figures are based on 1971 dollars.

The increase in buying income is very important to business. As more families increase their buying incomes, they can spend more money on wants. In other words, more families can afford to buy color television sets, meals in restaurants, or sports cars.

SUMMARY

In this chapter you have learned how consumer markets change. They change in total population, in educational levels, in the amount of buying income, and in the age-group distribution. You have examined how the total consumer market can be divided into various ethnic markets or rural or urban markets.

You also saw how buying income per family has increased in the United States and how the income distribution for families has changed. Finally, you learned how the average city family spends its buying income.

REVIEW   THE CHANGING CONSUMER MARKET

I. REVIEW OF TERMS
Which words complete the sentences below?

buying income   market   income distribution

1. Money left after taxes have been taken out is called _____.
2. A _____ is a group of people that buy a particular product or service.
3. The way income is divided between families is called the _____.

II. REVIEW OF MAIN POINTS
1. Explain how the total population can be divided into separate markets for different products.
2. Explain why a knowledge of the educational levels of markets is important to business.
3. Explain how changes in the buying income distribution can be used to tell whether or not more families are enjoying a higher standard of living.

III. THE CHANGING CONSUMER MARKET: CONCEPTS

1. Mr. and Mrs. Ray Earls and their one child live in Quincy, Illinois. Suppose the family pays a state income tax and a city sales tax. The Joel Broussard family lives in Austin, Texas. They have no children and pay no city or state income taxes. Assume both families make $15,000 per year. Will both families have the same buying income? Do you think the two families might spend their buying incomes differently? How?

2. Suppose a company produces a sports car that costs $15,000 and plans to advertise the car in local newspapers. The company, however, does not have enough money to buy ads in all newspapers. What marketing characteristics should the company consider in deciding where to run the ads?

3. Explain why it is often necessary for businesses to change either their products or their marketing methods. Give examples of industries that have made major changes in their products or marketing methods during the past 20 years.

IV. THE CHANGING CONSUMER MARKET: EXERCISES

1. Recent government figures show the following about income and schooling:

Years of Schooling Completed	Average Income Per Person
8	$ 6,261
11	7,988
12	9,566
15	11,045
16	14,158
17 or more	16,276

Looking at these data, do you think that school is a worthwhile investment of your time?

2. The chart shown gives the estimated percentage of buying income that two typical families spend on each item in Table 14–7.

Item	The Platt Family (two children at home)		The Grey Family (no children at home)	
NEEDS				
Housing	28		27	
Food	23		22	
Transportation	14		13	
Clothing	10		8	
Medical Care	7		7	
TOTAL		82		77
WANTS				
Personal Insurance and Investments	7		9	
Recreation and Education	6		5	
Gifts and Contributions	2		4	
Personal Care	2		3	
Miscellaneous	1		2	
TOTAL		18		23
TOTAL NEEDS AND WANTS		100		100

How do these percentages compare with the national averages in the table? In what ways are the estimates made by the two families different? What are some of the things that might account for the differences?

3. For many years, families spent about 96 percent of their total buying incomes and saved the other 4 percent. In more recent years families have been saving about 8 percent and spending the rest. If the trend continues, how do you think this will affect spending patterns in the United States? Look at the items in Table 14–7 and indicate how each might be affected—that is, will each item have a higher, a lower, or the same percentage spent on it as people save more of their buying income?

15 CONSUMERISM

Knowing how consumers' opinions change is important to business. It is also important for businesspeople to know how consumers feel about business. Their opinions, however, are hard to measure for two reasons. First, changes in opinion usually take place slowly and are not easy to measure on a year-to-year basis. Second, it is very hard to measure consumers' opinions exactly. Nevertheless, these changes do take place and have important effects on business.

CONSUMERISM

For the past several years there has been a rising interest in consumerism in the United States. The term *consumerism* means different things to different people. The basic idea of consumerism is that it is an effort on the part of individuals, governments, and businesses to protect consumers from bad business practices.

Two things that unite people in the consumer movement are their anger and frustration. People are angry about the poor quality of many products, bad service, products that are not safe, and high prices. People are frustrated because they cannot deal with giant corporations. When something goes wrong with a product they have bought, consumers have a hard time finding anyone who will take responsibility for the problem.

It is difficult to say just when and where the consumer movement started in the United States. It probably began in 1965 when Ralph Nader criticized the Corvair auto produced by General Motors. He accused General Motors of refusing to let the public know about the

182

Corvair's rear-end suspension system. Nader believed that this suspension system made the car unsafe, and that executives of General Motors knew this. Despite this attack, General Motors made no effort to recall the cars and fix the suspension system.

CONSUMER COMPLAINTS

It is impossible to list all the things of which business has been accused at one time or another. There are, however, five common complaints that people often make.

One consumer complaint is that *marketing costs too much.* In other words, business charges too much to get goods to the consumer. This is probably not true in most cases. Even though marketing costs are about 50 percent of a product's price, marketing does add value to the product. The value is having the product available at the time the consumer wants to buy it. The complaint that marketing costs too much is hard to prove but it is also hard to disprove.

Another common complaint is that *business fixes prices.* Price fixing means that two or more businesses which offer the same kinds of goods

Consumers picket for fairer prices.

or services will agree to charge the same price for the goods or services they sell. This practice can eliminate competition. There is no argument against this' charge. Businesspeople have been found guilty of price fixing and been sent to jail. This means that some businesspeople do break the law, but it does not mean that all businesspeople get together and fix prices.

A third complaint is that *business makes some products that are not safe.* This is completely true. Examples include unsafe children's toys, poorly designed automobiles, and medicines with harmful side effects. Businesses do not purposely make products that are unsafe, but some turn out that way. For many years, car makers made dashboards with many sharp edges. By 1968 all cars were required by law to have padded dashboards without sharp edges. This helped cut down on the number of people hurt in accidents. Today, more and more businesses are becoming concerned about the health and safety of consumers.

This is Consumers Union Laboratory where products are tested for quality and safety and reported on in a magazine.

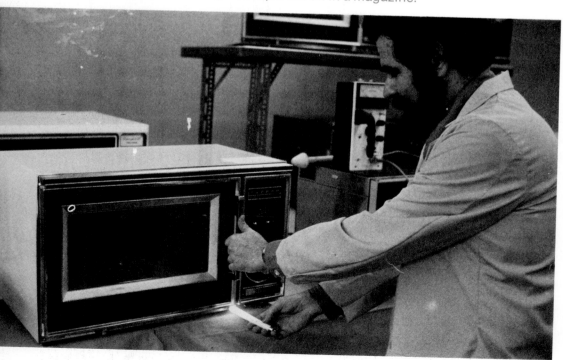

The fourth complaint is that *product quality and service are poor.* This charge has merit. It is not hard to find poor quality products made by companies that also have poor service departments to support their warranties. This is most often the case with such products as washing machines, cars, and color television sets. Some businesses have taken effective steps to correct this problem of servicing. For example, the Ford Motor Company has made a special Service Convenience Card. The purpose of the card is to help owners of Ford products get help in servicing their cars. The company will even help motorists get motel reservations if the people are forced to stay away from home overnight while their cars are being repaired.

Businesses are attempting to correct the problem of poor servicing.

Finally, many shoppers feel they *do not get enough product information.* Labels are often confusing, and different package sizes make it hard to compare prices. Again, business has to plead guilty in many cases. For example, a one-pint can (16 ounces) of charcoal starter-fluid may sell for 33 cents, while another can labeled as 2 pints (32 ounces) may sell for 69 cents. The larger can actually costs 3 cents more than two small cans together would cost, even though most consumers think larger cans are a better buy.

Wise consumers read *all* labels carefully.

RIGHTS OF CONSUMERS

Perhaps the best comment on consumer rights was made by President John F. Kennedy in 1962. He said that consumers have

1. The right to *safety*
2. The right to *be informed*
3. The right to *choose*
4. The right to *be heard.*

These rights became the basis for many of the consumer laws passed since 1962. Some of these laws give consumers

1. The right to clean air and water
2. The right to good lawyers if needed
3. The right to good health care
4. The right to government protection and information when needed.

Almost every consumer, business, and government agrees that consumers should have these rights. What they do not agree on is how to make sure consumers actually receive these rights.

REACTIONS OF THE PUBLIC

Since President Kennedy outlined the consumer's rights, the public has reacted in many ways. Some of these reactions have included
1. Providing consumers with easy ways to start legal action against businesses
2. Forming consumer protection agencies
3. Improving consumer education
4. Passing more federal and state laws to protect consumers.

The most powerful of these reactions has been item 1—the consumer's right to sue a business for damages. The most promising reaction over the long run is item 3—improved consumer education. A better-educated consumer is a better buyer.

THE INDIVIDUAL AND CONSUMERISM

A well-known spokesman for the consumer in the United States is Ralph Nader. Mr. Nader is a lawyer who has crusaded for consumer rights over the past several years.

Recently he set up the Center for the Study of Responsive Law. The purpose of the Center is to make government agencies more directly answerable to the public. This is done by first studying a government agency, such as the Food and Drug Administration. The results of the

Ralph Nader and his associates work hard for consumer rights.

study are then reported to the public. So far, the studies that have been released have suggested that government agencies may have more concern for businesses than for consumers.

Ralph Nader has been very successful in getting politicians to pass laws that favor the consumer. Nader's success is partly due to the hard work of the many young lawyers and college students who are on his staff. The changes "Nader's Raiders" have helped bring about show that individuals, if they are willing to work hard, can often affect important decisions.

ROLES OF GOVERNMENTS IN CONSUMERISM

Governments help consumers in two ways: (1) by passing laws and (2) by setting up agencies to protect consumers. Both the laws and the agencies help consumers get their money's worth when they buy goods and services.

LAWS THAT PROTECT THE CONSUMER

Two important laws passed by Congress to help consumers are the *Truth in Packaging Act* (1966) and the *Truth in Lending Act* (1969). Both laws are important to you as a consumer.

The Truth in Packaging Act makes it easier for consumers to get the best possible buys when they shop. Under this law all labels must tell

1. What is in the package
2. How much is in the package, in weight or volume
3. How many servings are in the package (if the label says anything about servings).

Looking at the reproduction of the label for Campbell's Chunky Soup on page 191, you can see the effects of the Truth in Packaging Act. Notice that the label says the can contains 19 ounces of Chunky Clam Chowder Soup, ready to serve. The label also shows that the can has two servings of 9 ounces each. This label does what the law requires because it does not deceive or mislead the buyer about what is in the package (can).

The Truth in Lending Act makes sure that consumers are told about all the charges they have to pay for charge accounts and loans. This law applies to both individuals and credit companies. It covers both monthly charge accounts and long-term loans, such as car loans.

If you have a charge account, the business must tell you

1. The unpaid balance (how much you still have to pay) at the start of the credit period

2. The dates on which you bought things and how much they cost
3. The payments you have to make
4. Any finance charges in dollars and cents, and the monthly and annual interest rates to the nearest one-fourth of 1 percent
5. The unpaid balance on which any finance charges were made
6. The date of the end of the billing period, and the unpaid balance on that date.

In Figure 15–3, you can see how this information is given to the consumer. The unpaid balance—the money left to pay from the month before—was $138.19. There were 26 charges made, totaling $229.71, and a payment of $147.91 was made during the month of June. A list of the purchases is also given, each with its exact cost. There were no monthly finance charges, but the annual percentage rates are noted at the bottom of the form. Finally, the new balance—$219.99—is given.

Note the list of ingredients on the soup label in p. 191. The Truth in Packaging Act requires that manufacturers list contents in decreasing order of their volume.

FIGURE 15-2

Campbell's ®
CHUNKY SOUP
Chunky Clam Chowder
DIRECTIONS:
DO NOT ADD WATER.

Just pour contents of this can into a saucepan. Heat to boiling; simmer a few minutes to blend flavors. Stir often. Makes two 9 oz. avdp. servings.

Nutritive composition of all Campbell's Soups is available on request.

RECIPE
Vegetable Clam Chowder

1 can Campbell's Chunky Clam Chowder Soup
1 cup cooked peas
1 teaspoon lemon juice

In saucepan, combine all ingredients. Heat; stir occasionally. Makes about 3 cups.

Chunky soup is so chunky you'll be tempted to eat it with a fork! (But use a spoon. You'll want to get every drop.)

If this amount is paid before July 11, 1975, no finance charges will be added to the bill.

There are many public agencies run by the United States Government to help protect consumers. These agencies include the *Federal Trade Commission* (FTC), the *Food and Drug Administration* (FDA), the *Department of Agriculture* (USDA), and the *United States Postal Service.*

The main purpose of the FTC is to make sure the free-enterprise system is not hurt by dishonest business practices. The FTC was established in 1915 and is the nation's oldest consumer protection agency. The FTC also enforces the Truth in Packaging Act and the Truth in Lending Act.

One dishonest practice the FTC has investigated many times is *phony pricing.* Suppose an appliance dealer sells products in three states and

FIGURE 15-3

CHASE MANHATTAN BANKAMERICARD ®

2000 Marcus Avenue
New Hyde Park, New York 11040

JOHN M. MALONE
18350 S. MITCHELL AVENUE
CLEVELAND, OHIO

Please indicate
any change of
name and address

Make your check or money order payable to **BANKAMERICARD**.

CLOSING DATE	ACCOUNT NUMBER	NEW BALANCE	MINIMUM PAYMENT DUE	AMOUNT ENCLOSED
06-10-75	2220-569-087-987	219 99	11 00	$

Return this portion of statement with payment. Our address on back must show in window of enclosed envelope.

Statement Closing Date   Direct inquiries concerning this statement to   or by writing
BankAmericard, P.O. Box 1111, New Hyde Park, N.Y. 11040. Include your account number and telephone number in all correspondence

TRANS-ACTION OR *POSTING DATE	CREDIT LINE TOTAL	CREDIT LINE UNUSED	ACCOUNT NUMBER	PURCHASES ADVANCES AND DEBITS	PAYMENTS AND CREDITS	REFERENCE NUMBER
	800.00	580.01	2220-569-087-987			
04/08/75	PAYMENTS APPLIED TO PURCHASES				147 91	4973950
05/22/75	CREDIT - K MART				4 07	4973958
05/22/75	NATIONAL FABRIC			8 74		4952307
05/26/75	TOBACCO LANE OF TURFLAND			1 58		4951224
05/29/75	IRELAND S INTERNATIONAL #			7 30		4944241
05/31/75	CREDIT - MR WIGGS NICHOLASVILLE R				1 46	4920700
05/31/75	BEARDS ART NEEDLEWORK INC			14 70		4922402
05/31/75	DICKENS LINOLEUM & CARPET CO			2 36		4930812
06/01/75	MR WIGGS NICHOLASVILLE ROAD			9 74		4920835
06/01/75	K-MART NICHOLASVILLE RD			21 12		4942707
06/02/75	MR WIGGS NICHOLASVILLE ROAD			2 45		4935982
06/02/75	MR WIGGS NICHOLASVILLE ROAD			5 67		4935913
06/04/75	BEGLEY DRUG CO #24			3 81		4930967
06/04/75	PET GALLERY			2 08		4944344
06/07/75	K-MART NICHOLASVILLE RD			5 40		4974107
06/08/75	TINDER KRAUSS TINDER BURT ROAD			5 25		4956366
	SEE PAGE 2					

If the Retail Purchases New Balance is paid within **25** days of the Closing Date, there will not be a **finance charge** on that balance
The **finance charge** on Cash Advances continues to accrue until the date of payment.

	PREVIOUS BALANCE	PAYMENTS AND CREDITS	PURCHASES ADVANCES AND DEBITS	AVERAGE DAILY BALANCE	FINANCE CHARGE	ANNUAL PERCENTAGE RATE	NEW BALANCE	AMOUNT PAST DUE	MINIMUM PAYMENT DUE
RETAIL PURCHASES	138 19	147 91	229 71		00	18 %	219 99		
CASH ADVANCES	00	00	00	00	00	12 $	00		
TOTAL	138 19	147 91					219 99	00	11 00

NOTICE: See reverse side and accompanying statement(s) for important information.

advertises a washing machine as "regularly priced at $300, now only $175 for a Special Sale." If the machine has never sold for $300, the FTC can stop this advertising because $300 is a phony price. This could be misleading to the consumer because it could make him or her think the saving is greater than it really is. Another product often the object of phony pricing is carpeting. Unless you buy from an established dealer, it is difficult to know the usual price of the carpet.

The FTC has also stopped companies from showing *false advertising* on national television. Often advertisements use substitute products to present pictures that are not completely true. For example, shaving cream has been used for whipped cream because the shaving cream looks thicker and richer than the whipped cream really is.

Some claims made in advertisements are often hard to back up. When the advertising claims are false or misleading, the FTC can stop the advertising. In 1971, for example, the auto companies were told to prove many of the claims they made on television. Many companies could not prove all their claims and had to cancel some of their advertisements.

The FDA was established in 1927, when the Federal Food, Drug, and Cosmetic Act was passed. The FDA makes sure that foods, drugs, and cosmetics are not harmful. The FDA also enforces labeling laws. This is a very important consumer agency, since it checks on products for which the public normally spends 20 to 30 percent of its income.

One of the largest jobs of the FDA is to make sure that our food is clean and free of harmful germs and chemicals. This is done by regularly checking the factories where food is packaged. Occasionally, the FDA finds that some canned foods contain bacteria that cause *botulism,* a serious, sometimes fatal disease. In nearly all cases, the contaminated cans have been collected and destroyed before they reached the public. This quick action has saved thousands of people from serious illness and possible death.

Another important job for the FDA is the control of the sale of drugs in the United States. Before a drug can be used, it must undergo a long period of testing. Once a drug is considered safe, it can then be used to treat patients. The long period of testing can be very helpful to the safety of consumers.

While many drugs do a good job of curing illness, they sometimes have harmful side effects. These side effects must be discovered before a drug is used. A well-known instance of the FDA acting to protect the consumer involved a drug called thalidomide. Even though the drug (used as a sedative) was made and widely used in Europe, the FDA would not allow it to be sold in the United States until certain rigorous tests were completed. The results of these tests showed that thalidomide had serious side effects.

In the meantime, in Europe, pregnant women who had taken the drug were giving birth to deformed babies. Because the FDA would not approve the use of this drug, United States consumers avoided this tragedy.

The FDA also makes certain that products that are harmful or that burn easily are labeled as such. If foods contain artificial flavors or colors, these must be noted on the label. Also, if two or more foods are used in a product, they have to be listed on the label in the order of quantity. Looking at the soup label in Figure 15-2, you can see that there is more clam broth in the soup than actual clams.

Manufacturers spend large amounts of money to test products for safety. The woman is testing a garment for flammability.

FIGURE 15-4

The USDA services that are of particular value to consumers are the inspecting and grading of foods of all kinds—meat, fish, poultry, eggs, fresh and processed fruits, and butter.

Meat inspection is one of the USDA's important jobs. Meat is inspected to make sure it is wholesome, clean, and of a certain quality. Figure 15–5 shows three common USDA meat inspection stamps. You should always look for these seals on the meat products you buy.

Although many food products carry a grade label, it is not required by law. The purpose of grading is to show quality. The grading system uses

There are many USDA inspection labels. To understand them, consumers should know about the USDA's grading system.

FIGURE 15-5

the letters A, B, and C, with grade A usually being the best. For a complete understanding of these grades, read the book *What Grades Mean,* published by the USDA. You can send for it from the Superintendent of Documents, Washington, D.C. 20402.

FIGURE 15–6
USDA GRADES FOR SELECTED PRODUCTS

Product	1st Grade	2d Grade	3d Grade	4th Grade
Beef	USDA Prime	USDA Choice	USDA Good	USDA Standard
Lamb	USDA Prime	USDA Choice	USDA Good	USDA Utility
Mutton	——	USDA Choice	USDA Good	USDA Utility
Poultry	U.S. Grade A	U.S. Grade B	U.S. Grade C	——
Eggs	U.S. Grade AA	U.S. Grade A	U.S. Grade B	U.S. Grade C
Swiss Cheese	U.S. Grade A	U.S. Grade B	U.S. Grade C	U.S. Grade D
Processed Fruits and Vegetables	U.S. Grade A (Fancy)	U.S. Grade B (Choice or Extra Standard)	U.S. Grade C (Standard)	——

NOTE: There are lower grades (USDA Commercial for beef, USDA Cull for lamb and mutton), but meat of these grades seldom appears in the retail market except in processed meat items, such as hot dogs.

The *United States Postal Service* enforces postal laws that are designed to protect consumers. For example, it is illegal to use the mails to defraud people. This means you cannot trick or cheat people through the mail. Postal inspectors check on thousands of consumer complaints each year. Some of the more common complaints concern high school-equivalency correspondence courses, obscene materials, worthless health insurance, and chain letters. A violation of postal laws often carries a heavy fine and a prison sentence.

STATE AND LOCAL PROTECTIVE AGENCIES

State and local government agencies pick up where the Federal Government leaves off. One reason is that federal agencies can act only when goods or services are sold between states. The sale of goods and services between states is called *interstate commerce.* Also, the job of protecting consumers is too large for only the Federal Government to undertake.

Several states have established agencies to speak up for the consumer in state government and also to prevent consumer fraud. Some states having such agencies are California, Illinois, Kentucky, Massachusetts, New York, Ohio, and Washington. These agencies have been successful in stopping some consumer frauds. For example, used-car dealers can no longer change the mileage on cars, and companies cannot attract buyers by saying they are giving away free gifts.

Many local city and county governments have some consumer protection programs. For many years, local governments have checked the scales in meat markets and grocery stores, the meters in gasoline pumps, taxi meters, and other kinds of measuring devices. This checking helps protect the consumer from being cheated.

A leader in consumer protection is New York City, which has a Department of Consumer Affairs. This department studies consumer complaints and makes sure consumers are treated fairly. So far the New York City effort has been very successful.

LOOK FOR THE ORANGE

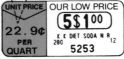
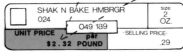

The Unit Price is printed on the Orange Panel of the Price Labels you find on the shelves of your food market.

With the Unit Price you can compare values. The Unit Price helps you get the most for your money.

Smart Shoppers Check Unit Prices!

City of New York, Department of Consumer Affairs, 80 Lafayette Street, New York, N.Y. 10013 — *Any questions? Call 566-2020*

BUSQUE LA ETIQUETA DE COLOR NARANJA

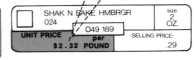

El Precio por Unidad está impreso en la sección naranja de la etiqueta que usted puede ver en los estantes del supermercado.

Precio por Unidad le permite comparar el valor de los alimentos. El Precio por Unidad le ayuda a obtener lo máximo por su dinero.

El Comprador Sabio se Aprovecha del Precio por Unidad.

Departamento de Asuntos del Consumidor de la Ciudad de Nueva York, 80 Lafayette Street, New York, N.Y. 10013 - *Preguntas? Llame 566-2020*

As the importance of consumerism grows, the job of the *Better Business Bureau* (BBB) will increase. The BBB is a private, nonprofit agency with branches in about 150 United States cities. These branches are often relied upon as local consumer protective agencies.

The BBB *protects consumers* by uncovering misleading advertising by local stores. The BBB *informs consumers* about these local businesses. The BBB also *handles complaints* from consumers. Many BBB branches have a special panel of local citizens who listen to both sides of a complaint and make a fair and quick decision. This process does not favor either side—the consumer or the business. As a result, both businesses and consumers benefit.

If the BBB can continue to provide these services, it can help prevent misleading business practices. In fact, strong action at the local level by the BBB and local agencies may be the best hope for consumerism.

ROLE OF BUSINESS IN CONSUMERISM

Most businesses are interested in serving their customers and making sure their customers are pleased with what they buy. Many consumers, however, feel that business does not care. In 1971, about 60 percent of the consumers studied said they felt forgotten by business. Only 40 percent of the consumers felt this way in 1964.

Several businesses have tried to change this attitude by setting up ways to provide consumers with information and to handle complaints. The Whirlpool Corporation was the first company to set up toll-free telephone service for consumer problems. Established in 1967, this "Cool-Line" handles about 70 percent of all customer complaints. Ford Motor Company uses a similar program called "We listen better."

In almost every business, there are some people who do care about the consumer. Trouble develops when consumers cannot easily find these people. This problem can be corrected by establishing "hot lines" for consumers, setting up consumer listening posts, or having a top-level executive handle consumer problems.

THE FUTURE OF CONSUMERISM

The present emphasis on consumerism by the United States public will most likely continue. In fact, it may grow stronger, even though past history suggests that it could very well grow weaker. This is what happened during the 1920's and 1930's, after a brief interest in consumerism. The reason we may not see a repeat of that earlier experience is that consumers today are better educated, are better buyers, and have more money to spend. They are now demanding their money's worth.

Business cannot ignore consumer demands for safe, dependable products. All businesses have a moral obligation to meet these two consumer demands. To ignore them will only result in more consumer protection laws being passed. If businesses will not take care of the consumer, governments will. Thus, the future of the consumer movement is bright, and it could result in better and safer products.

SUMMARY

Consumerism is the combined effort of individuals, governments, and businesses to protect people from bad business practices. The most common consumer charges against business are that

1. Marketing costs too much.
2. Business fixes prices.
3. Business makes unsafe products.
4. Product quality and service are poor.
5. Consumers do not get all the necessary product information.

The role of government in the consumer movement was also discussed. In particular, emphasis was placed on the need for laws and agencies that protect the consumer.

I. REVIEW OF TERMS

Which words complete the sentences below?

arbitrate complaints   inform consumers

FTC   FDA

interstate commerce   safety

USDA   informed

consumerism   marketing costs too much

    sue for damages

1. Two important functions of the BBB are to _____ and _____.
2. The _____ inspects and grades meat products.
3. A frequent consumer charge is that _____.
4. Two consumer rights are _____ and to be _____.
5. The most powerful consumer reaction against bad business practices is to _____ against such practices.
6. An effort on the part of individuals, government, and businesses to protect consumers from bad business practices is called _____.
7. The oldest consumer protective agency in the United States is the _____.
8. Business that is conducted in two or more states is called _____.
9. The _____ is charged with making sure that food, drugs, and cosmetics are not harmful to people.

II. REVIEW OF MAIN POINTS

1. List and explain the major complaints consumers have made against businesses.
2. What does the term *consumerism* mean to you? Explain your answer in detail.
3. What is the role of business in the consumer movement?
4. How does the Federal Government protect the rights of individual consumers? Explain your answer in detail.

5. What are the basic rights of all consumers?

6. Why were state and local government consumer agencies established? Do you think they can be more effective than federal protective agencies? Why or why not?

7. Who is Ralph Nader and what does he do?

III. CONSUMERISM: CONCEPTS

1. Suppose you buy a record player from a local music shop. The music shop makes certain claims about the sound quality and tone of the record player in its advertisement. When you buy the record player, the salesperson even says it will last longer than other brands sold elsewhere. Later you find that none of these claims are true.

   a. Do you think you have any rightful claim against the owner of the music shop?

   b. What are the different ways you might try to get your money back?

   c. If the record player was shipped in the mail from San Francisco, California, to your home in another state, would you have different ways to try to get your money back?

2. We have talked about the rights consumers have when dealing with businesses. Do you think that consumers also have responsibilities to business? Explain the reasoning behind your answer.

3. Suppose you buy a color television set for $525 from a local appliance dealer. You plan to pay for the television set by monthly payments. You want to know

   a. The amount of money you are being loaned to make the purchase

   b. All finance charges

   c. All other charges.

   The owner tells you that because he is running a small business, he does not have to give you all of this information. Besides, he tells you that all of these charges are not important, that what you pay each month is what counts.

a. Is the shop owner required by law to answer all your questions?

b. If he refused to answer the questions, would you still want to buy the television set from him? Why or why not?

IV. CONSUMERISM: EXERCISES

1. Make a list of several advertisements that seem to be false or misleading. Find out what part of the advertisement is misleading. You may find these examples by talking with your parents, the Better Business Bureau, or the local Chamber of Commerce. Report your findings to the class.

2. When consumers shoplift (steal from a store), the business has to charge higher prices to cover the loss. Also, shoplifters can be fined and sent to jail.

   a. Do you think businesses should pass on the expense of shoplifting to other customers? Explain your answer.

   b. Explain why some people shoplift. What can you do to prevent or deal with the problem of shoplifting in your community?

3. Go to a supermarket and make a list of as many foods as you can that have USDA grades on the package or label. See if there are any foods that do not have USDA grades. Are there any foods that have more than one grade on different brands?

4. Read the article "Does Consumer Arbitration Really Work?" in *Changing Times* (July 1973), pp. 19–21. Prepare a report on this article for your class by answering the following questions:

   a. What is consumer arbitration?

   b. What is the purpose of consumer arbitration?

   c. How does consumer arbitration work?

   d. Has it been helpful in solving consumer problems?

BUYING AIDS

Before consumers can get the most for their money, they need information. Becoming an informed consumer is the first step in becoming a smart buyer. An informed consumer usually gets better buys.

What kind of information does a consumer need? To be well informed, a consumer needs answers to the following questions:

1. What products and services can be bought?
2. What are the different features of the available goods and services? These features include price, quality, guarantee, and repair service.
3. How can the products or services be used? What care or treatment is necessary to keep the products in good condition?

In this chapter each of these important questions will be considered. They will be called the *basic buying questions*. The answers to them are known as *product information.*

Product information can be obtained from many sources. The major problem a shopper faces is how to tell the difference between factual information and promotional (advertising) information. Promotional information may be helpful, but it must be remembered that the main purpose of such information is to sell goods or services.

This chapter discusses various information sources. These sources include business firms, government agencies, advertising, magazines, and private testing agencies. The information these sources provide is called *consumer information*.

Consumer information can be of two types. The first is *product information*—the answers to the basic buying questions. The second is *personal information* about such things as money management and budgeting.

Many businesses and organizations that represent businesses publish consumer buying aids. These aids are often helpful in answering the basic buying questions.

One company that provides information on money problems is the Household Finance Corporation (HFC). This company started an educational program in family economics in 1930. It was designed to teach good money management. As part of this program, HFC puts out a series of booklets describing different ways individuals can better manage their personal finances. These include *Your Automobile Dollar, Your Housing Dollar, Your Clothing Dollar, Reaching Your Financial Goals,* and *Your Food Dollar.* All of these booklets stress wise planning and careful shopping as the keys to getting what you really need and want. You can get any of the booklets by writing to the Money Manage-

All government agencies publish informative booklets and bulletins for the public.

ment Institute, Household Finance Corporation, Prudential Plaza, Chicago, Illinois 60601.

The Better Business Bureau publishes material to help you shop for clothes, new and used cars, jewelry, and home appliances. For a complete list of their booklets and how much they cost, write to the National Better Business Bureau, Chrysler Building, New York, New York 10017. The purpose of these booklets is to help consumers become better informed about shopping for goods and services.

Another organization representing business is the *trade association.* There are thousands of trade associations in the United States. Each one represents companies that produce similar products or services. For example, the National Cotton Council is the trade association for producers of articles made from cotton.

Trade associations have a lot of information on the products they represent. The National Cotton Council can tell you about clothes made from cotton and how they compare with clothes made of other materials. Trade associations do not try to sell a particular brand of a product, but they do try to sell the product itself (cotton, milk, orange juice, etc.). Their information can help you make buying decisions, but remember that their information is designed to sell a product.

GOVERNMENT AGENCIES

The United States Department of Agriculture (USDA), in addition to protecting consumers, also gives them information. The USDA publishes over one hundred booklets that are excellent buying aids for consumers.

Probably no public or private group has done more to provide consumers with information than the USDA. You can write to the USDA's Office of Information, Washington, D.C., 20250, for a complete list of their publications. Most of the booklets deal with family money management and buying tips.

The cooperative extensions of state land-grant universities also provide consumers with information.

The main purpose of advertising is to sell goods and services. It can, however, be a source of information that helps consumers buy wisely. By looking at different advertisements you can sometimes get answers to the basic buying questions. The best source of advertisements is your local newspaper. By reading the newspaper, you can get an idea of what store has the best buys for the particular products and services you want.

Suppose you are interested in buying a new economy car. By looking at car dealers' advertisements you can find the ones that sell the model you want. For a major purchase such as a car you will go to the dealers' showrooms. The advertisements tell you where to start shopping. They also give you an idea of the car's price.

Advertising is especially helpful in telling consumers about new products. It is probably the best way to make information on new products available to consumers. When the Japanese-made Mazda automobile

Advertisements can inform consumers of new products on the market, such as the Wankel engine.

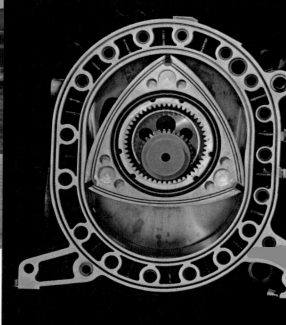

was introduced to United States consumers, millions of dollars were spent on newspaper and television advertising. The reason for this was to tell consumers about the advantages of the new rotary Wankel engine that powers the car.

Since the major purpose of advertising is to sell, you should always be careful when reading ads. This is especially true since the claims made in ads cannot always be supported. Keep this in mind and use other buying aids to help you when you shop.

MAGAZINES

Most newspapers publish various types of consumer information. Sometimes there are articles on such topics as (1) family money management, (2) new products, or (3) how to care for and repair such home products as clothing and household equipment. "Hints from Heloise" is one of the most popular columns about the care of home products.

One magazine designed to help families get their money's worth is *Changing Times.* This magazine has no advertising and does not permit its name to be used for selling any product or service. Some of the products and services covered in the magazine are house buying, life insurance, cars, electronic calculators, and record players.

Some of the books and guides available to the consumer are shown below.

It is unusual to find a newspaper or magazine that contains no consumer product information. Some of the information can be helpful, but often it is nothing more than advertising. Because of this you should check several private sources of information. These sources include consumer-sponsored services, professional associations, and independent testing agencies.

PRIVATE SOURCES

A private source of consumer information is never associated with any company that produces and sells a product or service. Private sources are thus more likely to give you truthful facts about products.

PROFESSIONAL ASSOCIATIONS

Among the most effective of the professional associations that provide consumer information to the public is the *American Home Economics Association* (AHEA). For almost sixty years, the AHEA has supported many laws to help consumers. The AHEA makes general buying guides available to consumers through its Consumer Interest Committee. For a list of these buying guides, write to the American Home Economics Association, 2010 Massachusetts Avenue, N. W., Washington, D.C. 20036.

Two health associations, the *American Medical Association* (AMA) and the *American Dental Association* (ADA), also make useful information available to the public. The AMA publishes the magazine *Today's Health,* which contains information on medical products. A special AMA committee tests these products.

Certain products are accepted by professional associations.

The ADA established the Council on Dental Therapeutics to tell consumers about dental products. This council studies products that claim to help consumers. If a toothpaste or other product is accepted by the council, it carries a special seal indicating it has met certain standards.

SEALS OF APPROVAL

Other types of approval seals can also be effective consumer buying aids. These seals are awarded by either independent or association testing laboratories. An example of a seal that is helpful to consumers is shown in Figure 16-5. When a product carries a seal, it has been tested or inspected to make sure it meets certain standards for quality and safety.

FIGURE 16-5

The two main advantages of seals are

1. They are placed on products only after tests have been made by independent agencies.
2. They tell you something about the product at the time you are buying it.

For example, when buying a small electrical item, such as a radio or hot comb, you should always make certain it carries the Underwriters Laboratories, Inc. seal. This means that the radio or comb meets certain electrical safety and performance standards.

CONSUMER-SPONSORED TESTING SERVICES

It is often hard to find factual information about different brands of the same product. Each consumer cannot afford to buy and test the different brands.

There are two consumer-sponsored testing organizations—Consumers Union and Consumers' Research—which test various products and report their findings by brand names each month in *Consumer Reports* (published by Consumers Union) and *Consumer Bulletin* (published by Consumers' Research). These magazines are usually kept on file in school and public libraries.

To cover costs of the testing, individual consumers pay annual dues to the organizations. Each person who pays these dues receives a year's subscription to the magazine published by the organization.

For example, *Consumer Reports* rates portable typewriters according to brand name. This rating includes such features as keyboard feel and operation of shift key. A mark after a particular brand indicates that it is considered to be a good buy.

Besides reporting on products, both magazines also have reports on movies. You may also find articles dealing with topics of special interest to consumers. For example, *Consumer Reports* has notes on government action taken to enforce consumer-protection laws.

Both Consumers Union and Consumers' Research are very important to you as a consumer. This is because their tests are (1) independent and (2) reported by brand name. Every brand of a particular product cannot be tested because it would cost too much. As a result, only leading brands are tested.

CONSUMERS AND THE LAW

Once in a while consumers have serious problems with producers. When this happens the consumer may have to see a lawyer. The laws protecting consumers are very technical. Therefore, good legal advice can only be given by people who understand the laws.

Laws are made for everybody. If you cannot afford to pay a lawyer you may still have the benefit of one. In many large cities, for example, legal aid societies help consumers with legal problems.

Some of the matters that may cause buyers problems are

1. Items received in the mail that were not ordered. In some states, if you did not order the goods, either orally or in writing, you do not have to pay for the goods received. You may use them or dispose of them as you see fit, without any obligation on your part to the sender. However, the best action is to refuse delivery. The U.S. Postal Service will return the goods to the sender, at the sender's expense.

2. Buying goods on approval; that is, taking goods home before making a final decision. If you keep the goods longer than the approval time, you must pay for them. However, the seller must be responsible for the goods during the approval time.

3. Warranties on products that are not backed by the seller. You should study a warranty or guarantee very closely before buying a product. Also, be sure to keep the warranty and a dated receipt for the purchase. If you have a problem, those two items will help you in making a claim.

Also, if you have to sign a contract for buying or selling property, have a lawyer read it before you sign. It is easier to avoid problems than to correct them after they happen.

SUMMARY

There are several sources of information that can be useful consumer buying aids. These sources include (1) business organizations, such as trade associations and the Better Business Bureau; (2) government agencies; (3) advertising; (4) newspapers and magazines; (5) professional associations; (6) seals of approval from independent and association laboratories; and (7) consumer-sponsored testing services.

There is no one best source of consumer information. Consumers should consider many sources when shopping. Trade associations have information that can help you choose among products made from different types of materials; for example, clothing made from cotton fabrics and clothing made from synthetic fabrics. Independent testing laboratories can also provide information on different types of products. Finally, consumer-sponsored testing services can be helpful in getting information on specific brands. Thus, a good shopping rule is to always consider several different sources of information. This will help keep you from making costly mistakes.

Sometimes consumers have serious difficulties with producers. When this happens it is usually best to get the advice of a good lawyer.

I. REVIEW OF TERMS

Which words complete the following sentences?

brand name   seal of approval

trade associations   newspaper

basic buying questions   advertising

product information

1. A well-informed consumer needs answers to the three _____.
2. The way to identify the product of a certain producer is to look for a _____.
3. _____ is a source of consumer information, but its main purpose is to sell goods and services.
4. Answers to the basic buying questions are known as _____.
5. The best source of advertising in your hometown is the local _____.
6. When a product carries a certain _____, it means it meets certain standards for quality and safety.
7. _____ represent groups of producers that make the same kind of product.

II. REVIEW OF MAIN POINTS

1. By answering the three basic buying questions, what information will a consumer have to aid in making a purchase?
2. What is the difference between factual and promotional (advertising) product information?
3. What is the main purpose of advertising?
4. What types of consumer product information are published in newspapers?
5. Name three private sources of consumer product information.
6. Why is it hard for consumers to get factual product information about different brands of the same product?

7. Name three reasons why consumers may have to get legal assistance.
8. What are the most trusted consumer-sponsored testing organizations in the United States?
9. How do the consumer-sponsored testing organizations distribute their information on brand name products? Explain your answer in detail.

III. BUYING AIDS: CONCEPTS

1. Some businesses try to destroy a buyer's trust in the findings of both Consumers' Research and Consumers Union, while others completely approve of them. How do you explain this difference in attitude?
2. Go to several stores in your area and make a list of ten goods which have a seal of approval. Tell which types of seals are on which goods. If you find a seal you do not recognize, find out the conditions under which it is awarded.
3. Examine ten ads in your local newspapers. Divide them into (a) factual ads and (b) promotional ads. What types of products are associated with the different groups of ads? Do you think some of the advertisements are meaningless? Explain.
4. Why do you think *Changing Times, Consumer Reports,* and *Consumer Bulletin* do not permit their names to be used in promoting a particular brand of product or service?
5. Suppose a door-to-door salesperson tries to sell you a product. Where could you find out about the person's reliability and get information on the product?

IV. BUYING AIDS: EXERCISES

1. Select one advertisement that is carried on radio or television or printed in a newspaper. Answer the following questions:
   a. Do you like or dislike the ad? Why?
   b. Does the ad contain any factual information about the product? Explain.
   c. Is there any other information in the ad that is helpful to shoppers? Explain.

2. Suppose you are planning to buy a small appliance such as a transistor radio or hair dryer. Make a list of the features you want the item to have. Go to three stores that sell the item and do the following:

    a. Ask for product information on the different brands of this item.

    b. Analyze the information to see if it helps you to make a buying decision. Explain how it does or does not help.

    c. Compare the information the stores gave you with information contained in *Consumer Reports* or *Consumer Bulletin*. Which is the best source? Why?

3. Read the article "Electronic Calculators" in *Changing Times* (July 1973, pp. 39–41). Prepare a report for the class that explains what types of information contained in the article would help a consumer interested in buying a small calculator.

4. Read these automobile advertisements closely.

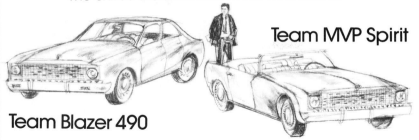

IF QUALITY'S THE NAME OF YOUR GAME, TRY US.

The extras are standard in the 1975 Teams.

Team MVP Spirit

Team Blazer 490

MVP Standard Interior has everything for total comfort, including room enough for a 6-footer to stretch out. Team's new instrument panel and king-sized glove compartment mean maximum passenger/driver convenience. And the wiper-mounted windshield washers are a safety plus.

Added passenger protection with Team's redesigned impact-absorbing bumper system and steel-reinforced side doors.

Every '75 Team comes fully equipped with power steering, disc brakes, automatic transmission, air conditioning, and a 378 V-8 engine for smooth driving. See them today at your local Team Dealer's.

POPULAR CAR voted the '75 Teams "The Year's Best."

PACER TESTING named Team MVP "Convertible of the Year."

TEAM knows the score when it comes to quality.

Answer the following questions:

a. Which ad contains the most factual information?

b. Which ad appeals most to convenience and looks? Explain your answer.

c. Compare the two Roadster ads. Do you see any differences in them? Explain.

d. Select one ad and tell why you think it is the best consumer buying aid.

17 BUYING HINTS

Was it worth the price? When shoppers ask themselves this question after buying something, they are really asking if they got their money's worth. Getting your money's worth is the key to being a smart buyer.

Becoming a smart buyer does not just happen. It takes time, work, some careful thinking, and planning. Most people are willing to work hard to learn about their jobs and hobbies. Few, however, are willing to spend the time to learn how to buy wisely.

Getting your money's worth is not easy. There are so many items to choose from that it is often hard to know which one is the best buy. Also, prices keep going up but quality does not seem to improve. Getting your money's worth is not just a matter of luck.

Making poor buying decisions can result in having to sell hastily.

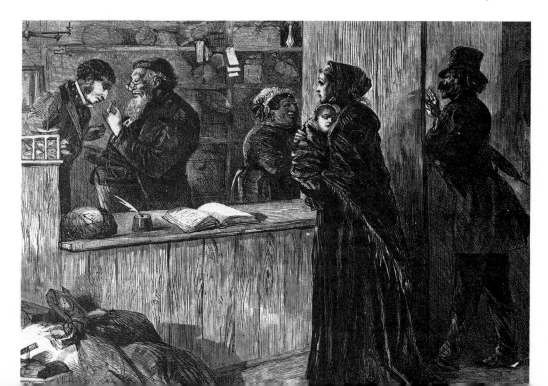

WHY CONSUMERS BUY

People buy goods and services for many reasons. All of these reasons are either needs or wants. A need is something you must have to survive, such as food. A want is something that makes life more pleasant; for example, a color television set.

The reasons why people buy and some examples of what they buy include

1. Hunger (food)
2. Personal grooming (hair spray, cosmetics)
3. Information (schooling, books)
4. Status (expensive jewelry)
5. Exercise (golf clubs, health club membership)
6. Comfort (air conditioning)
7. Recreation (speed boats, motorcycles)
8. Transportation (cars)

WHAT CONSUMERS BUY

The three basic types of goods and services that consumers buy are (1) convenience, (2) shopping, and (3) specialty. Most of the things people buy belong to these groups. But do not be surprised if you can think of a product that fits into more than one group.

Convenience goods and services often are bought with little or no shopping effort. Because people do not like to spend time buying these items, brand names become important. No doubt you have heard consumers say, "Give me a pack of Kleenex," or "I'll take a bottle of St. Joseph's Aspirin." These items do not cost very much, which is a characteristic of convenience goods. Other examples of convenience goods and services are candy, milk, bread, dry cleaning, gasoline, and shoe repairing.

Shopping goods and services are usually bought only after buyers compare the price, color, quality, and style of several items. These items cost enough to make it worthwhile to shop and compare. Shopping goods and services include house painting, carpet cleaning, women's clothing, radios, automobiles, record players, and bicycles.

Specialty goods and services have certain unusual, very special features that interest the buyer. A buyer will often go to great lengths to visit a particular store to see a specialty item or to discuss a specific service. Specialty goods and services often cost more than other items. Examples of specialty items or services are cameras, art objects, sports cars, home termite and pest control services, and gourmet food.

In general, the group that a particular product or service fits into depends on its cost. If it is costly, people usually spend time comparing different brands. You may think of exceptions, but usually cost is important in determining into which group an item fits.

Careful shopping is important.

GENERAL BUYING RULES

The reason for becoming a smart buyer is to get your money's worth. Seven general buying rules that can help you get your money's worth and also be satisfied with a purchase are

1. Know what you want.
2. Take your time.
3. Get product information.
4. Compare prices and services.
5. Choose your seller.
6. Decide the best way to pay for your purchase.
7. Time your buying wisely.

Buying sale items can sometimes save you money.

KNOW WHAT YOU WANT

Before you go shopping, decide what you want. Many shoppers fail to do this. People often see an item in a store window and buy it. This is called *impulse buying*. Impulse buying involves buying without thinking or planning. It can be very costly.

Suppose that Nathan Novack recently bought an AM/FM radio for his car. It was on sale. When he got home he found that the radio did not fit properly. After much extra work, Nathan finally put the radio in his car. Later in the week, he found a radio made exactly for his car. The price was $10 less than he paid for the first radio. If he had known exactly what he wanted, Nathan could have bought the correct radio. He would have shopped until he found the correct radio. He would also have saved $10.

Knowing what you want is important when buying anything. Before buying new clothes you should decide what is needed. Otherwise, you may buy a hat, a pair of shoes, a belt, or a coat that does not go with your other clothing. When grocery shopping, always make a shopping list first. Without a list, people often buy things they do not need. This increases their grocery bills.

TAKE YOUR TIME

Knowing what you want and avoiding impulse buying means taking your time. Smart shoppers always are willing to take their time. It saves them money. For example, by waiting to buy, you often can pay cash or make a larger down payment. You also can look for the best values. This makes your money go further. Never be hurried into making a purchase! Resist any pressure from salespeople and advertising.

GET PRODUCT INFORMATION

The more you know about the things you buy, the better shopper you are. In Chapter 16, you read that a well-informed shopper gets the answers to the basic buying questions before making a purchase. These answers provide the buyer with product information. By having this information, you can (1) tell what item meets your particular needs, (2) compare the price and quality of different goods, and (3) avoid being influenced too much by advertising. Knowing the facts, you can become a smart buyer because you are guided by facts and not by impulse.

COMPARE PRICES AND SERVICES

Most goods and services are sold by more than one producer. This lets you compare the price and quality offered by different producers.

Comparing the price and quality of different goods is not easy. Cheap goods often turn out to be expensive because they do not last as long as more costly items. Lee Ann Reid decided to buy two suitcases, one for $36 and the other for $15. The first one lasted six years, while the second was worn out after two years. The cheaper suitcase turned out to be the more expensive when its cost was compared to its life. Can you explain why this is true?

Smart buyers also check the customer services offered by stores. Honest sellers try to provide good service; however, the quality varies. Some customer services you should check for are

1. Does the merchant sell for cash or for credit (time payments)?
2. Does the merchant deliver to your home?
3. Does the merchant service what he or she sells?

You should always get answers to these questions when buying shopping or specialty goods.

Sometimes, good customer service is enough of a reason to pay more for a particular product. Suppose you have two prices for the same model car, say $3,500 and $3,650. If the $3,650 price is from a local dealer who gives good service, this could be your best buy. Certainly this is true if the $3,500 price is offered by a dealer located in a city 75 miles away. The time saved in getting service would be well worth it.

Good customer service is always important. But do not pay too much for it or buy service you do not need. For example, do not buy a merchant's service contract for a new kitchen stove if the stove is covered by a manufacturer's guarantee.

CHOOSE YOUR SELLER

You should always buy from sellers you trust. This is very important if you are not sure which goods or services are your best buys. Reliable merchants want to help you make good choices. First, they are interested in their customers' satisfaction. Second, if you are pleased with your purchases you will probably return to their stores and recommend them to your friends.

Many new products need service after they are sold. Often the service is only minor, but it is important to the buyer. If you buy from dependable merchants, they will make sure you get good service. Many businesses have built their reputations on the idea of selling quality goods and providing excellent service. One such company is Sears Roebuck, Inc. If a family buys a Kenmore (Sears) washer in Seattle and then moves to Omaha, the Sears store in Omaha will see that it is repaired free under the warranty.

DECIDE THE BEST WAY TO PAY FOR YOUR PURCHASE

How you pay for a product or service can affect the final price. Before you shop for an expensive item, know how you are going to pay for it. This can save you many dollars. For example, James Webb is planning to buy a color television set. The set he wants costs $600. Paying cash is the cheapest way for James to buy the set. In fact, the seller will let him have it for $585 if he pays cash. By paying cash James also avoids paying any interest charges on a loan.

Suppose James has to borrow the money from a bank to pay for the set. Say he has to pay 8 percent interest on a one-year loan. This amounts to $48 interest. James then pays $648 for the television set instead of $585. By paying cash, he saves $63.

If you have to get a loan to pay for something, shop for loan money. Loans do not always cost the same. Companies charge different interest rates. Usually banks have the lowest interest rates. They are a good place to start shopping when you have to borrow money.

TIME YOUR BUYING WISELY

There is usually a best time to buy any product or service. Cars are cheaper just before new models arrive. Air conditioners usually cost less in the winter. In fact, many large companies run special sales on air conditioners in January and February.

Time also affects price. For example, long distance telephone rates vary at different times of the day. A three-minute station-to-station call from Lexington, Kentucky, to New York City may cost $1 between 8:00 A.M. and 5:00 P.M. The same call may cost 60 cents if made between 5:00 P.M. and 11:00 P.M., and only 20 cents between 11:00 P.M. and 8:00 A.M.

You should also look for sales. These can save you a lot of money. There are two types of sales: (1) special sales and (2) end-of-season sales. *Special sales* occur when merchants want to promote special items in their stores. The purpose of the sale is to get people to try a particular product or service or simply to get customers into the store. In other words, make sure sales are genuine.

End-of-season sales are used to clear out merchandise. This is a familiar type of sale for clothing stores, car dealers, and sporting goods shops. Often you can find very good buys at these sales.

A problem with end-of-season sales is that your choices are limited. When a car dealer closes out one year's models, you have to select

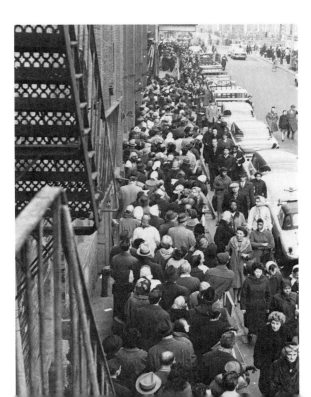

People wait in line to enter the stores on special sale days, such as Washington's Birthday.

from whatever cars are in stock. You usually cannot order a car with special features.

A word of caution on sales. Always make sure the sale price is lower than the regular price. Some stores advertise a sale but do not lower the price. Do not buy a sale item unless you know it is what you want. Many items bought on sale cannot be returned. This means the sale is final. Also, get to the sale early. By doing this you will have a better choice of goods.

SUMMARY

Marketing takes place every day in the United States. Goods and services are moved to markets so people can buy them. Consumer markets change, and sellers must change with them. The ways in which markets change include consumers' ages, the amount of money people have to spend, the educational level of consumers, and the total number of people in the market.

In order to protect consumers from bad business practices, the Government has formed several protective agencies. These agencies include the Food and Drug Administration, the Federal Trade Commission, and the U. S. Department of Agriculture. State and local governments also have consumer protective agencies.

If consumers are to make good buying decisions, they need information. There is much product information available from a variety of sources. Places providing this information include business organizations, government agencies, newspapers and magazines, and private sources, such as Consumers Union and Consumers' Research.

Understanding the marketing system, knowing how consumers are protected, and knowing what product information is available make you better prepared to go shopping. Being a smart shopper is not easy. It takes time, work, and careful planning. However, it is worthwhile to learn how to be a smart buyer. It saves you money and prevents you from making costly mistakes.

I. REVIEW OF TERMS

Which words complete the sentences below?

impulse	wants
needs	special
specialty	convenience
end-of-season	shopping

1. People buy to satisfy _____ and _____ .
2. _____ sales promote either a certain product or the store's name.
3. _____ goods usually do not cost much, and brand names are important.
4. Buying without first getting product information is called _____ buying.
5. When buying _____ goods, it is best to compare styles, prices, quality, and colors.
6. _____ sales are used to clear out merchandise.
7. _____ goods are usually expensive and are of very special interest to buyers.

II. REVIEW OF MAIN POINTS

1. Give five reasons why consumers buy, and list some of the goods they buy.
2. Why is it worthwhile to become a smart buyer?
3. What are the seven general buying rules?
4. What type of customer service should you ask about when buying a product?
5. Why is it important to decide how to pay for purchases before making them?
6. Explain the difference between end-of-season sales and special sales.
7. Why is it important to buy from a seller (merchant) you can trust?

III. BUYING HINTS: CONCEPTS

1. Look at the information presented below for certain name-brand and store-brand items. The prices quoted are for 1973.

	STORE A		STORE B	
Items	Price of name brand	Price of store brand	Price of name brand	Price of store brand
1. coffee— 32 oz.	$2.09	$1.85	$2.05	$1.83
2. toothpaste— 7 oz.	.84	.59	.84	.55
3. salt— 26 oz.	2/.25	.10 ea.	2/.25	2/.21
4. sugar— 5 lbs.	.73	.69	.73	.69
5. shortening— 48 oz.	1.03	.97	.97	.89
6. flour— 10 lbs.	1.37	1.29	1.37	.95
7. tomato juice— 46 oz.	.41	.41	.37	.36
8. peas— 8.5 oz.	.19	.17	.19	.19
9. ketchup— 20 oz.	.37	.31	.41	.34
TOTALS				

Answer the following questions:

a. Figure out how much the goods cost at each store if only name brands are bought.

b. How much do the goods cost at each store if only store brands are bought?

c. Which store is the least expensive place to shop? (Assume you buy all of the goods in one store.)

d. Prepare a table of the nine items using the following headings:

ITEMS	LOWEST PRICE	STORE

Add up the lowest prices to see how much it will cost to buy the nine items at the cheapest prices.

    e. Compare the total price in (d) with the total price in (c). Is it worthwhile to buy part of the items in one store and the rest in another if the stores are two miles apart? Explain.

2. Explain why store brands usually cost less than name brands. (Hint: Go to the manager of a large chain grocery or other retail store for information.)

3. People usually do not spend much time shopping for convenience goods. Explain why it is important for producers to create loyalty for their brand of products.

4. Name five types of convenience goods that you buy on the basis of brand name.

5. Jim's Steak House serves a complete T-bone steak dinner for $2.25. Located across Union Avenue is the Four Flames Restaurant. A T-bone steak meal there costs $6.50. Both places do a good business.

    a. Why doesn't Jim's Steak House get all the business?

    b. Are the people who decide to eat at the Four Flames necessarily poor shoppers? Explain by giving several reasons why some people might prefer the Four Flames over Jim's Steak House.

IV. BUYING HINTS: EXERCISES

1. Labels on all types of goods can help you to get your money's worth. Read the following article. Explain how this new labeling practice ordered by the USDA helps shoppers get the most for their money.

    "HOT DOGS." Under the Department of Agriculture rules effective September 7, frankfurters hereafter must carry labels giving better descriptions of contents, by three types. Type A must contain only regular meat plus the normal ingredients needed for processing. Type B may contain by-products such as heart or tripe, but must be labeled "with by-products." Type C may contain certain nonmeat binders

but the label must specify each such ingredient. And for the first time, frankfurters may be labeled "hot dogs."

2. Often people think that smart buyers always save money by buying in large quantities.

   a. Try to find three products in a grocery store that cost more when bought in large quantities. What types of goods did you find? Try to explain why there is sometimes no economy in buying large quantities.

   b. Explain why it might be more costly to buy large quantities than to buy smaller quantities of the same product but more often.

Unit V
Banks and Their Services

Money is so important that our economy cannot work without it. Money is used to buy and sell goods and services every day. Over 80 percent of the payments for all goods and services sold in the United States are made with checkbook money. Banks play an important role in helping transfer checkbook money from the buyer to the seller. The use of banks and their services will no doubt increase in the future. It is, therefore, to your advantage to learn about the services banks offer.

Chapter 18 explains what a bank is and describes the different types of banks in the United States. It also discusses the different types of services offered by commercial banks. Finally, it explains the purpose of the Federal Reserve System and shows how it works.

One important service of a bank is the personal checking account. In Chapter 19 you will learn how to open your own checking account. You will also find out about the service fee that banks often charge for such checking accounts. Finally, you will learn why it is important to save your cancelled checks.

How to use a personal checking account is covered in Chapter 20. This chapter also discusses some problems you may have when using personal checking accounts. You will learn how to endorse personal checks that are made out to you. Finally, you will learn how a personal check is cleared; that is, what happens to a check from the time it is written until the time it is paid.

In Chapter 21 you will learn how to open a personal savings account. You will also learn why people save money and the different ways in which they can save it. Also, you will see how compound interest helps a savings account grow.

UNIT PREVIEW

AS YOU STUDY THIS UNIT YOU WILL BE ENGAGED IN

* **IDENTIFYING** the functions of the three different types of banks in the United States

* **EXPLAINING** the major consumer services offered by commercial banks and how these services assist you in managing your money

* **UNDERSTANDING** the Federal Reserve System and how it works to protect bank deposits

* **EVALUATING** the uses of various checking accounts in commercial and savings banks

* **UNDERSTANDING** the importance of savings in your future, and in the economy generally.

A FOCUS FOR YOUR STUDY

8 THE BANK IN SOCIETY

Nearly everyone uses a bank and some of its services. You may already have a bank account. If not, you will almost certainly have one in a few years. To use a bank and its services properly you should have some understanding of banks and what they do.

Banks are important to all local communities. They can help communities grow economically by providing financial services. In fact, the local economy of most towns and cities could not work without banks. Banks also provide other important services. For example, they often sponsor community improvement projects. They also lend money to governments at low interest rates.

WHAT IS A BANK?

A bank is a corporation that performs many different financial services. A bank is a private company in business to make a profit. Banks usually have the word *National* or *State* in their names, such as the First Security National Bank or the Millington State Bank. If a bank has the word *National* in its name, it means that the Federal Government gave the bank a license to do business. If a bank is licensed by the state, the word *State* will probably be part of its name.

Banking is not new. Many ancient societies used banks of one kind or another hundreds of years ago. In the seventh century B.C., Assyria had a banking system, even though coins and checks were not used. Both the Greek and Roman empires had banking systems. Two of the oldest and most famous banks in the world are the Bank of Amsterdam, founded in 1609, and the Bank of England, started in 1694. In the United States, it was not until the early 1800's that a national banking system was begun.

232

This 15th century bank performed some of the same functions as a commercial bank does today.

TYPES OF BANKS

All banks do not provide the same services. Different banks do different things. The three basic types of banks are (1) investment banks, (2) savings banks, and (3) commercial banks.

Investment banks work mainly with large businesses to get them their machinery, land, office buildings, and other capital goods. These banks are usually located in large cities.

Savings banks are set up to accept personal savings accounts. These banks also make loans to people who are buying or building homes. Sometimes these banks use the word *Savings* in their names, such as the Leader Federal Savings and Loan Association.

Most banks in the United States are *commercial banks*. These banks serve both individual people and businesses. Commercial banks have different departments that provide different services. These departments usually include a savings department, a personal loan department, a commercial loan department, an investment department, and a trust department. Many services of these banks may be of use to you now and in the future.

THE BANK IN SOCIETY   **233**

SERVICES OF A COMMERCIAL BANK

Commercial banks often have been called *supermarkets of finance.* This is because they offer such a wide variety of services. Large banks usually provide more services than small banks; sometimes as many as 30 or 40 different services. Most commercial banks, however, provide many of the following services:

1. Accept cash deposits for checking and savings accounts
2. Make loans
3. Transfer funds
4. Provide trust services
5. Rent safe deposit boxes.

Banks that provide all of these services are usually called *full-service banks.*

ACCEPTING MONEY DEPOSITS

Every month, Dick Sutton puts his paycheck for $950 in a checking account at the First National Bank of Topeka. When Dick puts the money in the bank, he makes a *deposit.* Money put in a checking account is called a *demand deposit.* Money can be taken out of a demand deposit account at any time; it is done by writing a check.

Each month Dick also deposits $50 in a savings account. Money put into a savings account is called a *time deposit.* This money is usually not intended to be spent right away. Banks can even ask that you give them 30 to 60 days notice before you take your money from a time deposit account. Most banks, however, will let you withdraw money from a regular savings account whenever you wish.

Time deposits differ from demand deposits in two important ways. First, you cannot write a check to take money out of a time deposit. Second, a bank pays interest on a time deposit. A bank is prevented by law, however, from paying interest on checking (demand deposit) accounts.

MAKING LOANS

Making loans is the main business of commercial banks. These loans often help keep the local economy healthy. The three types of loans banks usually make are (1) personal, (2) commercial, and (3) mortgage loans.

Personal loans are made to individual people for many reasons. For example, loans are made to people so that they can pay their medical expenses, their house repair bills, or the money they owe for their new car. These loans may range in size from one hundred to several thousand dollars. Personal loans may be paid back to the bank in 90 days, or over several years.

Commercial loans are normally made to businesses or farmers. Businesses of all types get commercial loans. Some examples of businesses that might need commercial loans are home builders, manufacturing companies, and local stores. These loans are used to pay for some part of the business operation. Farmers might borrow from banks to buy such things as farm equipment, seeds, and fertilizer. They might also use long-term loans to buy land.

Mortgage loans are made to help people buy homes. These loans are normally paid back over a period of several years, say 20 or 30. When loans are paid back in this way, they are called *installment loans.* Installment loans are discussed in Chapter 22.

An important point to remember is that banks want to make loans. It is their main business. In fact, most of a bank's income comes from the interest paid to it by people and businesses who have taken out loans. *Interest* is the charge paid to the bank for the use of its money.

TRANSFERRING FUNDS

Checkbook money is money placed in a checking account. It is a demand deposit. Checking accounts provide a way to protect money and an easy way to transfer money from one person or business to another.

You transfer checking account money by writing a check. This means that money is moved from your checking account to another account either in the same bank or another bank. More than 80 percent of all payments made in the United States are made by check. One reason is that it is more convenient to pay with checks than with cash. Also, it is safer and quicker.

PROVIDING TRUST SERVICES

A *trust* is a person's money and property that are managed by someone else. Many banks have large trust departments that manage millions of dollars of other people's money and property. Often trusts are owned by children or widows who receive money when the head of a family dies.

Trust departments also advise people how to invest their extra money. To cover the cost of this service, banks charge a fee. This fee is usually a small percentage of the value of the trust.

RENTING SAFE DEPOSIT BOXES

A *safe deposit box* is used to protect a person's valuables and important documents. Items often kept in boxes include stock certificates, contracts, insurance policies, and birth certificates. Banks usually provide safe deposit boxes. Customers rent these boxes for a fee as little as $10 a year.

The boxes are kept in well-guarded steel vaults. Only the person renting the box or someone legally named by the renter can open it. Even a bank does not have the right to open a safe deposit box. It always takes two keys to open a box. One of the keys is the guard key kept by the bank. The other is the renter's key.

KEEPING BANK DEPOSITS SAFE

From 1930 to 1933, about 8,000 banks in the United States failed; that is, they went out of business. At that time they had about $5 billion of their customers' money. These failures wiped out the checking and savings accounts of thousands of people. To keep this from happening again, national and state banks are now regulated by Federal and state governments, This does not mean that any single bank cannot get into financial trouble today. However, to keep bank deposits safe, the Government has taken three important steps.

First, a request to start a new bank must be approved by either the state or Federal government. People wanting to start a new bank must first show that they have enough money to go into business. Also, they have to show that the community needs another bank. If there are too many banks in a community, one of them might fail. Once a bank is formed, it is examined regularly by government officials to make sure it is not in financial trouble.

A second way bank deposits are kept safe is through a government insurance program. After 1933 the United States Government formed the *Federal Deposit Insurance Corporation* (FDIC). By 1973 over 100 million accounts were insured by the FDIC. These accounts represented about 98 percent of all bank depositors in the United States. The FDIC insures a single account up to a maximum of $40,000.

The third way the Government keeps bank deposits safe is through the Federal Reserve System. The Federal Reserve is a bank backed by the Federal Government. In other words, it is the Government's bank.

THE FEDERAL RESERVE SYSTEM

You personally will never use Federal Reserve Banks. They will not accept your deposits, lend you money, or cash your checks. However, the operation of the Federal Reserve System can have an important effect on you.

HOW THE FEDERAL RESERVE SYSTEM IS ORGANIZED

Congress created the *Federal Reserve System*, or *Fed*, in 1913. It is not run by Congress or the President. Instead, it is independent. It is managed by a board of seven governors appointed by the President for fourteen-year terms.

In the Federal Reserve System, the United States is divided into 12 regions. Each region is called a *Federal Reserve District.* Each district has a *Federal Reserve Bank.* Each district bank is managed by a president and a board of nine directors. These districts and banks are shown in Figure 18–1. Notice that each district has one or more branch banks. For example, the St. Louis District, Number 8, has branches in Little Rock, Memphis, and Louisville.

Each Federal Reserve district bank is owned by the commercial banks in the district. These owner banks are called *member banks.* All national banks must be members of the Fed. If a state bank qualifies, it may elect to become a member bank.

Even though member banks own the Federal Reserve district banks, they do not have a responsibility to the public to control banking policies. This is a responsibility of the Federal Reserve System. Other specific jobs of the Fed are discussed in the next section.

Because of its public responsibility, the Fed oversees the operations of member banks. For example, the Fed sets the *reserve requirement.* This determines how much money member banks must keep on reserve (deposit) with the Fed. Also, it explains why the district banks are called

FIGURE 18-1
THE FEDERAL RESERVE SYSTEM

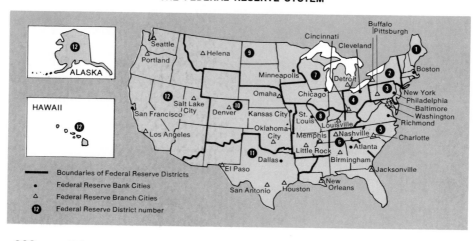

reserve banks. The reserve requirement directly affects three things: (1) the amount of money member banks can lend to consumers, (2) interest rates consumers pay, and (3) the availability of consumer credit.

JOBS OF THE FEDERAL RESERVE

The Fed has several important jobs to do. These jobs include

1. Acting as a bank for banks
2. Acting as the Federal Government's bank
3. Supervising Federal Reserve member banks
4. Managing the nation's money supply.

Because the Fed is a bank for banks, the Fed cashes checks, makes loans, and holds deposits. These are the same types of services a commercial bank does for you individually. When a member bank needs coins or paper money to pay its customers, it goes to the Fed. This explains why most of the paper money in circulation is Federal Reserve notes.

The Fed serves as the Government's bank in two ways. First, it keeps the Government's checking accounts. When the Federal Government writes checks, these checks are backed up by Fed banks. When you pay taxes, the money probably does not go to Washington but goes to the Government's checking account at a Fed bank. The Fed also handles the Government's *IOU's* (debts). If you buy a *savings bond,* you lend money to the United States Government. The Fed puts money in the Government's checking account when people buy bonds.

The Fed supervises commercial banks in two ways. First, it sets rules the banks must follow in their day-to-day business. These rules tell the banks what they can and cannot do. Second, at least once a year the Fed checks member banks that are not national banks. This is to see that they are run properly. National banks are checked by other government agencies.

Finally, the Fed manages the nation's money supply. It tries to keep just the right amount of money in circulation. Too much money can cause inflation; too little may cause a depression. One way the Fed controls the money supply is by the reserve requirement for member banks. Managing the nation's money is a hard job but one of the most important the Fed does.

SUMMARY

A bank is a business that provides financial services at a profit. There are (1) investment banks, (2) savings banks, and (3) commercial banks.

Commercial banks provide many services to businesses and individuals. Most of them provide the following services:

1. Accept cash deposits
2. Make loans
3. Transfer funds
4. Provide trust services
5. Rent safe deposit boxes.

Banks that provide these services are usually called full-service banks.

The Government tries to keep bank deposits safe. This is done by (1) carefully checking applications for new banks, (2) insuring individual accounts up to $40,000, and (3) supervising the operation of banks.

The Federal Reserve System was set up in 1913 by Congress. It is run by a board of seven governors who are appointed by the President. The country is divided into 12 Federal Reserve districts. Each one has a district bank with at least one branch bank. The Federal Reserve regulates most of the activities of member banks.

The main jobs of the Federal Reserve System are to (1) act as a bank for banks, (2) serve as the Federal Government's bank, (3) supervise Federal Reserve member banks, and (4) manage the nation's money supply. These are important jobs. They affect everyone in many ways.

I. REVIEW OF TERMS

Which words complete the statements below?

trust	mortgage
commercial	deposit
savings	demand
national	personal
investment	bank
time	

1. A private business that performs financial services is called a _____.
2. Banks that get a license from the Federal Government to do business are called _____ banks.
3. A person's money and property that are managed by a bank are called a _____.
4. Both _____ and _____ banks accept individual savings accounts.
5. A savings account is called a _____ deposit.
6. Three types of bank loans are _____, _____, and _____.
7. A checking account is a _____ deposit.
8. A _____ bank serves both individual people and businesses.
9. When you put money in a bank, you make a _____.
10. _____ banks are concerned chiefly with helping businesses get money for machinery and other capital goods.

II. REVIEW OF MAIN POINTS

1. What two types of governments can give a bank a license to do business?
2. Name three types of banks in the United States. Explain the main purpose of each type.
3. What is a bank deposit?

4. What is the difference between demand and time deposits?
5. Name five basic services that most commercial banks provide.
6. What is the FDIC? Explain what it does.
7. What types of loans do banks often make?
8. Why are most bills paid in the United States by check?
9. What is the highest dollar amount for which the FDIC will insure a single bank account?
10. What services does the trust department of a bank provide?
11. What is the Federal Reserve System? Who manages it?
12. Describe two important jobs of the Federal Reserve System.

III. THE BANK IN SOCIETY: CONCEPTS

1. Sometimes people call the Federal Reserve Bank "the banker's bank." Explain what is meant by this statement.
2. Read the following newspaper story carefully and answer the questions below:

NEW YORK (AP)—Interest rates, after a record-breaking rise this summer, are likely to go on climbing for some time yet, in the view of several leading economic observers.

And, say a number of those observers, chances are increasing that the end result will be a tight money period like that of several years ago, when consumers and businesses often found it difficult to borrow money at any price. The prime rate—the lending fee which banks post for their biggest and most credit-worthy corporate customers—rose another quarter point early this week to 9.5 percent. That's a full point above its previous high, reached in late 1959.

Why the high interest rates? One reason is the demand for loans has been great. At the same time, the Federal Reserve Board has been tightening up on the money supply. This is to keep order in the economy and to try to stop inflation.

a. What is the meaning of the term *prime rate of interest?*
b. What is the new prime interest rate? What was the old prime rate?

    c. What was the previous high of the prime rate, reached in 1959?

    d. What are two reasons for the high prime rate?

3. Banks have always been interested in seeing that the local community has a healthy economy. Answer the following questions:

    a. Why do banks want the local economy to be healthy?

    b. What can banks do to help a community have a healthy economy?

(Hint: You may want to visit a local bank to get help with these questions.)

4. Any person can start a hardware store or service station. Explain why banks must be approved by either the state or Federal government before they go into business? What matters are checked into before a bank license (charter) is issued?

5. Read and study the bank advertisement that recently appeared in a local newspaper. Answer the questions following it.

Our New Christmas Club plans are now open, and we pay 5% interest on all completed plans, from 25¢ to $20 weekly.

Save this amount each week for 50 weeks	25¢	50¢	$1	$2	$3	$5	$10	$15	$20
Get this amount for Christmas	$12.50	$25	$50	$100	$150	$250	$500	$750	$1000

PLUS 5% INTEREST
on completed plans

NATIONAL BANK AND TRUST COMPANY

PUTTING YOU FIRST MAKES US SECOND
Member FDIC

---

    a. Is this bank a member of the Federal Reserve System? Explain your answer.

    b. Are deposits made by bank customers insured?

    c. What interest rate is paid by the bank on Christmas Club savings?

    d. Is this a commercial bank? Explain your answer.

e. Does the bank offer trust services? How do you know?

f. Was the bank chartered by the Federal Government or a state government? Explain your answer.

IV. THE BANK IN SOCIETY: EXERCISES

1. Make a complete list of all the banks in your town. If you live in a large city, select only five banks. Answer the following questions about each bank:

   a. Is the bank licensed by the Federal or state government?

   b. Is it a member of the Federal Reserve System?

   c. What type of bank is it?

   d. How many workers does it have?

   e. How many branch banks does it have?

2. Pick two local banks, one large and one small. Visit each one and do the following:

   a. Find out what customer services are offered.

   b. Find out which service is the most popular with customers.

   c. Find out if there is a charge for any of the services.

3. Write a short report on commercial banks. Be sure you cover the following points:

   a. Why were banks started?

   b. When did banks first appear in the United States?

   c. Include a short history of banking in the United States. (Hint: Use an encyclopedia to help you.)

4. The Federal Reserve System is very important to banking in the United States. Study the map in Figure 18–1 carefully and answer the following questions:

   a. How many Federal Reserve districts are there in the United States?

   b. List all of the Federal Reserve district banks and place the district number beside each name.

   c. Beside each district, list the number of branch banks it has.

   d. Why do you think there are more Federal Reserve districts in the eastern part of the United States?

   e. In which Federal Reserve district do you live?

YOUR PERSONAL CHECKING ACCOUNT

One of the most important services a bank provides is the checking account. Over 80 percent of all payments made in the United States are made by check. More than 13,000 commercial banks in the United States offer checking accounts. There are many reasons why checking accounts are so popular. All of these different reasons, however, can be summed up in two words: *safety* and *convenience.*

Checks are safer than cash. If they are lost or stolen you do not lose actual cash. By law, a check can be cashed only by the person to whom it is made out. If the check should be lost, a bank can be told not to pay the check. Checks are convenient because you do not have to carry large sums of cash with you. Checks can safely be sent through the mail to pay bills. Checks also serve as permanent records of payment.

Since you are in school, you may not need a checking account right now. However, you probably will want a checking account someday. This chapter will discuss two different types of personal checking accounts and how you can open one. This chapter also will explain why it is important to keep your cancelled checks.

PERSONAL CHECKING ACCOUNTS

A *check* is a written order to a bank to pay a stated amount of money to another person or business. The bank pays the check *on demand.* This is why money in a checking account is called a demand deposit.

Two types of personal checking accounts are offered by most commercial banks. These are (1) regular accounts and (2) special accounts.

245

The type of account you open depends on your particular needs. Someone at the bank can help you choose the best one for you.

A *regular checking account* is best when you are going to write many checks each month. Usually, the bank requires that you keep a minimum balance of a certain amount on deposit. For some banks, this amount may be as little as $5 or $10.

People who write a few checks each month often use a *special checking account.* Usually, only a small balance is needed to maintain it. Banks often use a special name to describe this type of account. One bank calls it a Thrifticheck account. The cost for this type of checking service might be $1.95 for 20 checks. After the checks are used up you can buy another book of 20 checks for the same price.

OPENING A PERSONAL CHECKING ACCOUNT

Opening a personal checking account is quick and easy. Most commercial banks have one or more employees in charge of opening new checking accounts. This person will ask you for information such as your name, address, telephone number, and where and how long you have worked. After getting this information, several things happen.

1. You sign a special card called a signature card.
2. You make a bank deposit.
3. You get a checkbook.
4. You receive a bank statement.

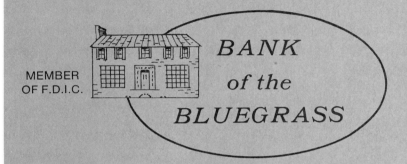
SIGNING THE SIGNATURE CARD

One reason why people put money into a bank is to keep it safe. Once a bank accepts your deposit, it must protect your money. Therefore, the only person who can withdraw money from your account is you. No other person can take money from your account.

To help make sure other people do not remove money from your checking account, the bank depends on the signature card you signed. The *signature card* is the bank's record of how you write your name. A bank will honor (pay) a check only if the signature on the check matches the one on the card.

Almost every bank puts a number on each personal checking account. This helps the bank identify your account from the others it may have. The account number must be used whenever a deposit or withdrawal is made from the account.

YOUR PERSONAL CHECKING ACCOUNT   **247**

The signature card in Figure 19–1 is for the checking account of Ben Peeples. However, when Ben marries Nadine Murphy, they will both want to use the account. If two or more people use the same checking account, it is called a *joint account.* In order for Ben and Nadine to write checks using this account, both must sign the signature card.

FIGURE 19-1

FIRST SECURITY NATIONAL BANK & TRUST COMPANY	

☐ Joint Checking   DATE _1-5-70_

☒ Individual Checking

☐ Joint Savings   BRANCH _____

☐ Individual Savings   ACCOUNT NO. _123-45-6789_

Title of Account: _Ben F. Peeples_

Sign here _Ben F. Peeples_   Social Security No. _555-55-0000_

Sign here _____   Social Security No. _____

Sign here _____   Social Security No. _____

Occupation _____   Former Bank _____

Home Address _1456 Carr Avenue_   Home Phone No. _948-3929_

Said Bank is hereby authorized to:

☐ MAIL all statements and notices to address indicated above.

☐ HOLD all statements, etc, until called for, if not called for after 30 days said Bank may mail statements, etc., to the address indicated above. If the above mailed statements, vouchers and notices are returned undelivered, said Bank is hereby authorized to destroy same (2) years thereafter.

    Bank is relieved of all liability for items lost in delivery by U.S. Mail or otherwise, or not called for by Depositor.

MAKING A BANK DEPOSIT

To open a checking account you must put money in the bank; that is, make a deposit. When the money is put in, a deposit ticket is filled out. A *deposit ticket* is your record of the amounts and types of money (coins, paper bills, or checks) put in the bank.

Although deposit tickets vary from one bank to the next, they all need

1. Your name and address
2. Your checking account number
3. The date of deposit
4. The amount deposited.

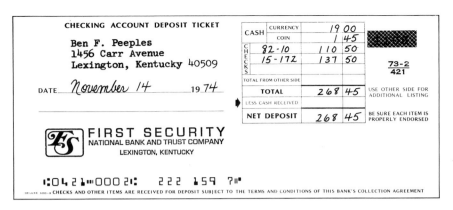

FIGURE 19-2

Figure 19-2 shows that Ben Peeples made a deposit of $268.45 on November 14, 1974. The deposit consisted of $1.45 in coins, $19 in paper money, and $248 in checks. Checks are always listed separately on the deposit ticket. It is the only way to tell exactly which checks were deposited.

The deposit ticket and the checks listed on the ticket are identified by the number given to the bank from which they are drawn. This number is called the *American Banking Association* (ABA) *Code.* On Ben's deposit ticket, notice the number 73-2/421. The number 73 is the city or state code, while 2 is the individual bank code. The 421 code is a code used by the Federal Reserve when the checks are sorted.

When you make a deposit, the bank will usually give you a receipt. At some banks you must ask for one. It is important to always get a deposit receipt. You should keep the receipt until you receive a bank statement showing that the deposit has been added to your account.

YOUR PERSONAL CHECKBOOK

After you open a checking account, you will receive a book of blank checks. This is called a *personal checkbook.* Checkbooks may be given to you free of charge. Most banks, however, charge for personal checks. Personal checks have your name, the bank's name and address, your account number, your check number, and the ABA code printed on them. An example of a personal check written by Ben Peeples is shown in Figure 19–3. Check number 267, made payable to Dick Sutton for $40.10, was written on November 14, 1974.

FIGURE 19-3

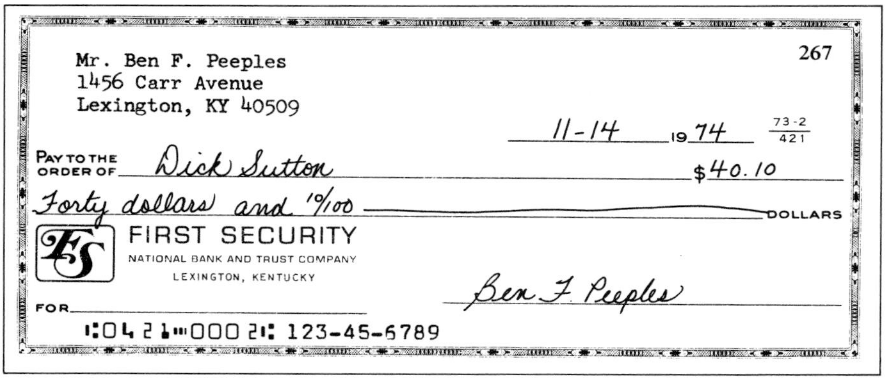
Mr. Ben F. Peeples
1456 Carr Avenue
Lexington, KY 40509

267

11-14 19 74 73-2/421

PAY TO THE ORDER OF Dick Sutton $40.10

Forty dollars and 10/100 DOLLARS

FIRST SECURITY
NATIONAL BANK AND TRUST COMPANY
LEXINGTON, KENTUCKY

FOR

Ben F. Peeples

⑆0421⑈000 21⑆ 123-45-6789

When you have a personal checking account, it is important to keep records. Each time you write a check or make a deposit, the money in the account—the balance—changes. Thus, every transaction in your account must be recorded. There are two ways by which this is normally done: (1) with a check stub or (2) with a check register.

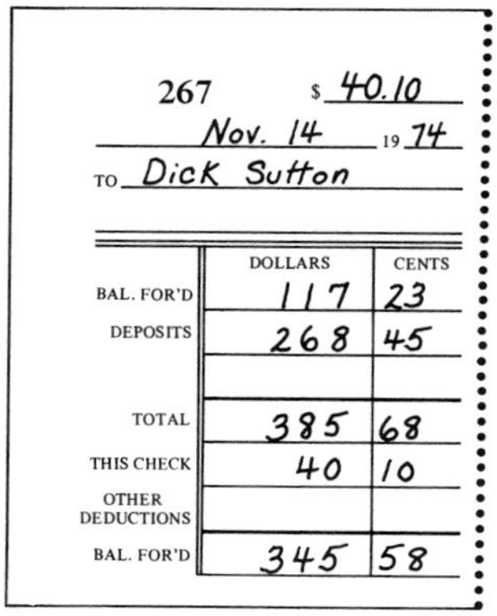
267 $ 40.10
Nov. 14 19 74
TO Dick Sutton

	DOLLARS	CENTS
BAL. FOR'D	117	23
DEPOSITS	268	45
TOTAL	385	68
THIS CHECK	40	10
OTHER DEDUCTIONS		
BAL. FOR'D	345	58

FIGURE 19-4

A *check stub* (Figure 19–4) is bound (attached) in the checkbook. It is separated from the check by a perforated line. The stub has spaces where you fill in such information as the balance brought forward from the previous check, the amount of the deposit, the amount and number of the check, the date, and the new balance.

The second method of keeping records for a personal checking account is the *check register.* The check register (Figure 19–5) contains exactly the same information as the check stub. A check register, however, is not attached to the checks; it is a separate book.

FIGURE 19-5

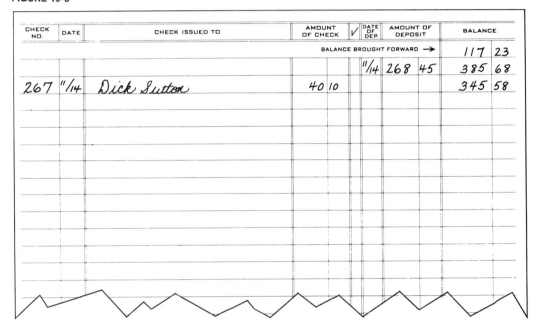

CHECK NO.	DATE	CHECK ISSUED TO	AMOUNT OF CHECK	√	DATE OF DEP	AMOUNT OF DEPOSIT	BALANCE	
						BALANCE BROUGHT FORWARD →	117	23
					11/14	268 45	385	68
267	11/14	Dick Sutton	40 10				345	58

YOUR PERSONAL BANK STATEMENT

Even though you keep a record of your checking account, the bank also keeps one. The bank's account record is usually kept on a computer. The bank sends you a *bank statement* once a month. When you receive a bank statement, your *cancelled checks* are returned with it. These are checks that were written by you and paid to another person or company by the bank. When a check is paid, the bank stamps the word *PAID* on the front of the check and subtracts the money from your account.

A bank statement for Ben Peeples's account is shown in Figure 19-6. It shows only one check written and paid for during the month. Examine the statement carefully. It contains the following information:

FIGURE 19-6

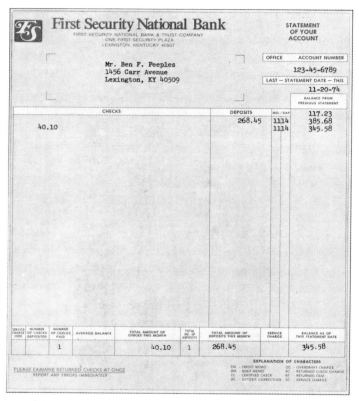

1. The account balance from the month before ($117.23)
2. The number of deposits made during the month (1)
3. The total amount of money deposited during the month ($268.45)
4. The number of checks made out (1)
5. The total amount of money paid by check during the month ($40.10)
6. A service charge, if any
7. The account balance at the end of the month ($345.58).

The upper half of the statement shows the date of deposit and the date that check number 267 was paid.

RECONCILING YOUR BANK STATEMENT

Both you and the bank keep a record of your account. Because of this, you should make sure your records agree with the bank statement. If either you or the bank makes a mistake, the two monthly totals will not agree. Even if no mistake has been made, the totals may not agree. Getting the totals from the two records to match is called *reconciling the bank statement*.

Some reasons why your balance and the bank's balance may be different are

1. Checks written by you have not yet reached the bank. You have deducted the money on your records, but the bank has not subtracted it from its record. These checks are called *outstanding checks*.
2. A service charge has not been subtracted on your records, but the bank has subtracted it on its records.
3. A deposit is not shown on the bank statement. This often happens when a deposit is mailed to the bank just before the statement is prepared.

The reason for reconciling your bank statement is simple: you want to make sure your balance is correct before starting the next bank statement period. There are six steps in reconciling your bank statement.

1. Arrange the cancelled checks in order, usually by check number.
2. Make sure you have *all* the checks charged to your account on the bank statement. (Look carefully to make sure they are *your* checks.)
3. List all of the outstanding checks and total them.
4. Subtract this total from the balance shown on the bank statement.
5. Add any deposits not shown on the statement to the total in Step 4.
6. Subtract any service charges or other charges from the total in Step 5. This new total should agree with the balance in your records.

TO HELP RECONCILE YOUR RECORDS WITH THE BANK'S STATEMENT

1. BALANCE SHOWN ON THIS STATEMENT $ _345.58_

2. LESS OUTSTANDING CHECKS   _31.92_
   (THOSE SHOWN IN YOUR CHECKBOOK
     BUT NOT ON STATEMENT)

   SUB TOTAL _313.66_

3. PLUS DEPOSITS NOT SHOWN ON STATEMENT _50.00_

   TOTAL _363.66_

ABOVE TOTAL SHOULD AGREE WITH THAT SHOWN IN YOUR CHECK-
BOOK, AFTER SUBTRACTING SERVICE CHARGE. DIFFERENCES IF
ANY SHOULD BE REPORTED TO THE BANK WITHIN 10 DAYS AFTER
RECEIPT OF THIS STATEMENT.

CHECKS OUTSTANDING	
NO.	AMOUNT
268	10 75
269	21 17
	31 92

FIGURE 19-7

A form is printed on the back of the bank statement to make it easy for you to complete the different steps. However, if you have a problem, someone at the bank will usually help you.

To show how a bank statement is reconciled, Ben Peeples's account will be used. After completing Steps 1 and 2, Ben found that checks number 268 (for $10.75) and number 269 (for $21.17) had not yet reached the bank for payment. Also, Ben had made a $50 deposit on November 21, but it was not shown on the November 20 statement (Figure 19–6). Subtracting the two checks and adding the deposit to his own records (Figure 19–5) leaves an account balance of $363.66. The steps Ben followed in making the bank statement total (345.58) agree with his check register total ($363.66) are shown in Figure 19–7.

BANK SERVICE CHARGES

Providing checking accounts is a major service of commercial banks. Now that you have learned how a checking account works you may wonder how much this service costs the customer. After all, cashing a check involves many different banking operations. Some of these operations, such as examining the check for the correct signature, are never seen by you. Yet they add to the expenses of providing checking accounts.

To cover these expenses, some banks subtract a *service charge* from your account. The service charge is usually made up of two fees: (1) a *minimum monthly charge* and (2) *a charge for every check written.* The minimum charge might be as low as $1 per month. Charges for individual checks usually vary between 5 cents and 10 cents a check. While this may seem like a small amount, it can quickly add up to several dollars over a year.

If the balance you keep in your account is large enough to offset the cost of check service, there may be no service charge. The money the bank makes by using your money may be enough to pay for the handling of your account. Most banks will not charge a service charge if the account balance stays above a certain amount, say $100 to $300. However, a current trend in banks is to do away with checking account service charges. Many banks now offer free checking service. Because of this, you should shop around when choosing a bank for your checking account.

SAVE YOUR CANCELLED CHECKS

Your cancelled checks should be saved for several years. They are actually valuable receipts; that is, evidence that you have paid certain bills. For example, when you pay a tax to the government, the cancelled check is proof that the tax was paid. A cancelled check is proof of payment because a person or business cashing a check must sign it. This signature is called an *endorsement.*

SUMMARY

Two major reasons for opening a checking account are safety and convenience. Two types of personal checking accounts are (1) regular checking accounts and (2) special checking accounts.

Opening a checking account is easy. You (1) sign a signature card, (2) make a deposit, and (3) receive a checkbook. After using your checking account you should make sure your own records agree with those of the bank. This is called reconciling your bank statement.

Providing checking accounts can be expensive for banks. To cover the costs, some banks charge you a service charge each month. Many banks, however, are now offering free checking accounts.

REVIEW YOUR PERSONAL CHECKING ACCOUNT

I. REVIEW OF TERMS

Which words complete the statements below?

safety	check
signature card	convenience
service charge	cancelled check
joint account	bank statement
outstanding check	deposit ticket

1. The two major reasons for using checking accounts are _____ and _____.

2. To help the bank make sure other people do not remove money from your checking account, you sign a _____.

3. A _____ is your record of the amount and types of money you put in the bank.

4. The bank's record of your account is called a _____.

5. An _____ is one that is not shown on your bank statement.

6. A written order to a bank to pay a certain amount of money to another person or business is called a _____.

7. When two or more people use the same checking account, it is called a _____.

8. A check returned to you along with a bank statement is called a _____.

9. The cost of having a checking account is known as a _____.

II. REVIEW OF MAIN POINTS

1. Why are checks thought to be safe and convenient to use?
2. Explain briefly why money put in a checking account is called a demand deposit.
3. What are the steps in opening a checking account?
4. What are the two major types of personal checking accounts? Explain the difference between them.
5. Why are checking accounts given account numbers?
6. What type of information is on a deposit ticket?
7. If a bank's ABA code is 91–16, what does it mean?
8. What is the purpose of a check stub or a check register?
9. Why should you save and protect your cancelled checks?
10. What is meant by the phrase *reconciling the bank statement?*
11. Give three reasons why your checking account records may not agree with the bank's records.
12. What is the purpose of a checking account service charge?

III. YOUR PERSONAL CHECKING ACCOUNT: CONCEPTS

1. Read the bank ad on p. 247 carefully and answer the questions below:
   a. What bank service does the ad discuss? Explain how the service works.
   b. Does the bank offer free checking accounts? How do you know? Why do you think a bank would offer free service and free checks?
   c. Does the bank charge for personal checks? Is this unusual?
   d. What does the term *full-service bank* mean?
2. Using Figure 19-3 as a guide, draw a blank check. Then do the following:
   a. Write the check for $110.74
   b. Date the check December 21, 1974
   c. Make the check payable to W. C. Royster.
3. Visit two local banks and get all the forms necessary to open a personal checking account.
   a. Examine the forms and compare them carefully.

b. Are there any important differences between them? For example, does one ask for information that the other does not?

c. Try to explain any differences you find.

4. Visit a local bank and find out what happens if you *overdraw* your account.

IV. YOUR PERSONAL CHECKING ACCOUNT: EXERCISES

1. Collect blank bank statement forms from two local banks.

a. Compare these two forms to see if they are different. If different, list the differences.

b. Compare these statement forms with the one in Figure 19-6. Are there any differences? If so, what are they?

2. Suppose John Shute has a personal checking account at the National Bank of Commerce. At the end of last month, he received a statement showing a balance of $141.83. At the beginning of the period, John had an account balance of $310.91. He wrote 26 checks last month, but only 24 were paid from his account. These checks totaled $169.08. Two checks for $10.15 and $53.21 are still outstanding. Also, a deposit of $28 was not shown on the statement. John's checkbook balance is $106.47. Reconcile the bank statement with the checkbook balance.

3. Julie Ann Palazola recently received the following checks:

a. Bank of Tunica, $14.10

b. Jackson National Bank, $110.84

c. First National Bank of Reno, $62

d. People's State Bank of Millington, $10.18.

Julie also has $1.10 in coins and $27 in paper money to deposit. Prepare a bank deposit ticket for her account. Draw your own ticket.

4. Visit a local bank that has a service charge for personal checking accounts. Prepare a short report for the class that explains how this plan works. Explain how the costs vary depending on the number of checks written and the minimum balance kept in the account.

WRITING PERSONAL CHECKS

To benefit from a personal checking account you must use it. This means writing checks. However, personal checks must be written correctly. This chapter discusses the purpose of writing checks, how to write a check correctly, and the different ways to sign checks you receive.

WHY YOU WRITE PERSONAL CHECKS

The main reason for writing a check is to transfer money from your checking account to another person or business. In other words, you make a money payment when you write a check.

More than 80 percent of all payments for goods, services, and debts in the United States are made by check. In fact, most of the money you earn and spend will be in the form of checks. Thus, you should know how to write a personal check correctly and how to handle checks made out to you. Also, you should know some of the problems that can arise when using your checking account.

HOW TO WRITE A PERSONAL CHECK

To show you how to write a check, the check that Ben F. Peeples wrote to Dick Sutton (Figure 20-1) will be used as an example. There are two major transactions when transferring money from a checking account. These are to (1) fill in the check register record or check stub and (2) write the check.

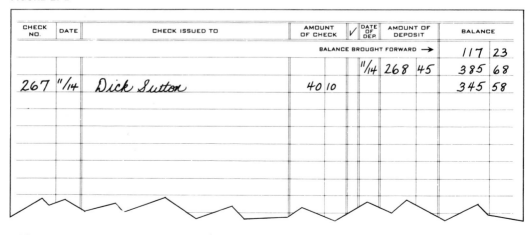

FIGURE 20-1

FILL IN THE CHECK REGISTER

Always start by filling in the check register or stub. Do this before you write the check. This helps you make sure that your account record is correct; that is, it shows how much money you have in the account.

Look at the check register shown in Figure 20–2. It contains important information. For example, check number 267 was written on November 14. It paid $40.10 to Dick Sutton. The balance left in Ben Peeples's account was exactly $345.58. If Ben did not fill in the register correctly, he would not know how much money was in his account.

FIGURE 20-2

CHECK NO.	DATE	CHECK ISSUED TO	AMOUNT OF CHECK		✓	DATE OF DEP	AMOUNT OF DEPOSIT		BALANCE	
							BALANCE BROUGHT FORWARD →		117	23
						11/14	268	45	385	68
267	11/14	Dick Sutton	40	10					345	58

WRITE THE CHECK

Writing a check is easy. However, you must put certain information on the check. You must be careful to do it right.

Every check should have a *number.* In the given example, the check number is 267. Some checks have numbers printed on them. On other types, you write the number on the check. The purpose of numbering checks is to make sure you can identify them if they are lost. Also, it helps you put them in order when reconciling the bank statement.

Every check you write must have a *date* (the month, day, and year). In the given example, the date is November 14, 1974.

Usually, it is not a good idea to postdate a check. *Postdating* means putting a future date on a check. For example, suppose that today is March 2, and you date a check March 15. If someone tries to cash the check before March 15, the bank can refuse to pay it.

Notice the words "Pay to the order of _____" in the example. The name Dick Sutton appears after these words. Dick Sutton is the *payee;* that is, the person to whom the check is written. Always make sure you spell the payee's name correctly. Otherwise, the payee may have trouble cashing the check.

If you want to withdraw money from your own checking account you can do it by writing a check, filling in your own name or the word *Cash* or *Bearer.* If a check is made out to *Cash* or *Bearer,* anyone can cash it. If you lose the check, it is the same as losing cash. If you have a check made out to *Cash* or *Bearer,* always cash it as soon as possible. When cashing a check like this, the bank will make you sign it on the back.

All checks are written for some amount of money. In the example, Ben wrote the check for $40.10. This amount, written in numbers, appears after Dick Sutton's name. A good practice is to always write these numbers close to the dollar sign. This keeps people from adding more numbers in front of those already there.

Notice that the amount also appears in words. All checks must have the amount written out in words. This always appears below the payee's name. The amount should be written as far to the left as possible. This prevents people from adding another word and raising the amount of the check. Any blank space to the right of the written amount should be filled in with a dark line.

The amount written in words should be the same as the amount written in numbers. If the amounts do not agree, the amount written in words is the amount that will be paid. However, many banks simply will not cash a check if the amounts do not agree. Therefore, always compare the two to make sure they agree.

The final item needed to complete the check is the signature of the person writing it. This person is called the *drawer.* The drawer's name always goes at the bottom right of the check. This signature must match the one on the bank signature card.

A word of caution. Never sign a blank check. A *blank check* is one without the amount filled in. If the check is lost, it can be filled in by anyone for any amount and cashed. The bank will cash the check because your signature is real.

A final comment on writing checks. Never erase, cross out, or change a check. A bank will not pay it. If you make a mistake, tear up the check and start a new one. This is called *voiding* a check.

SOME CHECKING ACCOUNT PROBLEMS

Suppose you lose a check or an entire book of checks. Or suppose you discover you made a mistake in writing a check, but the check is already in the mail. In either case, you can tell the bank not to pay the check. This is called *stopping payment* on a check.

Usually, you have to fill out a form like the one in Figure 20-3 to stop payment on a check. This form requires the account number, the check number, the date the check was written, the amount, the drawer's name, and the name of the payee. You also have to sign a stop-payment order.

No matter how well you keep records, you may *overdraw* your checking account. This means that you write checks for more money than is in the account. For example, Ben Peeples's balance was $345.58 on

```
PLEASE SIGN AND RETURN IN 3 DAYS
            STOP PAYMENT REQUEST

FIRST SECURITY NATIONAL BANK AND TRUST CO.
Lexington, Kentucky

                              Date  1-4-75

Gentlemen:

       Please use your best efforts to stop payment on the check described
below which bears the signature of the undersigned.

       The undersigned hereby agrees jointly and severally, to hold you
harmless from any and all liability, loss, expense, or cost resulting from
your non-payment of said check.  Furthermore, the undersigned agrees, in
consideration of his account, to hold you harmless and in no way liable
should the item described below be paid through inadvertence or oversight.

       Kentucky Revised Statute 355.4-405 provides that no stop payment
order shall remain in effect more than 6 months after service thereof on
the Bank unless renewed in writing.

             Yours very truly,

             Signed   Ben F. Peeples
                       (Please note provisions herein)

             Address  1456 Carr Avenue


Special No.          Account No. 123-45-6789  Phone 948-3929

Check Dated  1-3-75   Number  295    For $ 27.45

Payable to   L and W Television Repair Co.

Reason for Stop Payment  Did not fix television set

Date Stopped_____ Hour Stopped_____


Form 13 - Rev. 12/66
```

FIGURE 20-3

November 14. If Ben then wrote a check for $350, his account would be overdrawn by $4.42.

Normally, a bank returns an overdrawn check to the payee. The check is then said to have *bounced*. Banks often charge a fee of $2 to $5 for an overdrawn check. Besides being embarrassing, overdrawn checks are expensive.

HOW TO ENDORSE A CHECK

When you receive a check, you want to cash it. To do this, you must sign your name on the back of the check. This is called an *endorsement*. The person signing the check is called the *endorser*. When a check is endorsed, it can be put in the bank or given to another person.

THE TYPES OF ENDORSEMENTS

There are three main types of endorsements.

1. Endorsement in blank
2. Restrictive endorsement
3. Endorsement in full

To explain these different types of endorsements, the check made out to Dick Sutton (Figure 20-1) will be used.

An *endorsement in blank* is signing your name on the back of the check. This is shown in the first block in Figure 20-4. Any person who holds a check with a blank endorsement can cash it. All the person has to do is sign his or her name under yours. Therefore, a blank endorsement should never be used until you are ready to cash or deposit the check. In other words, when a check is made out to you, never sign the back until you are ready to cash the check or deposit it.

A *restrictive endorsement* limits the use of the check. A restrictive endorsement is shown in the second block of Figure 20-4. With this endorsement, the check can only be put in Dick Sutton's account. If you bank by mail, this is the safest type of endorsement to use. Another person cannot sign his or her name to the check and cash it.

The final type of endorsement is used to transfer a check to another person. It is called *endorsement in full.* It is also called a *special endorsement.* In the third block (Figure 20-4), you see that Dick gave the check to Billy Landers. Now Billy is the only person who can cash the check.

FIGURE 20-4
TYPES OF ENDORSEMENTS

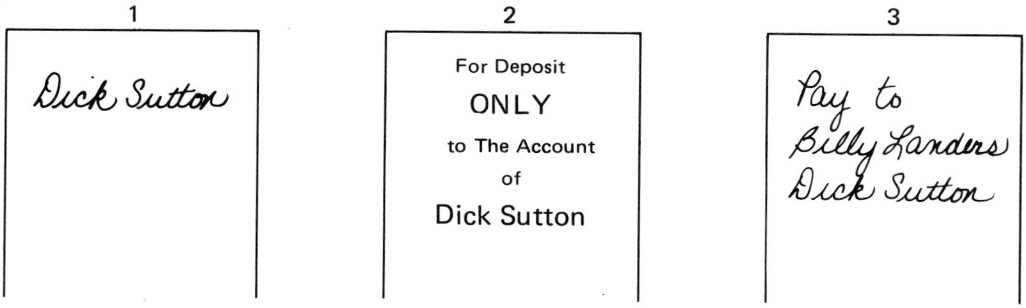

1	2	3
Dick Sutton	For Deposit ONLY to The Account of **Dick Sutton**	*Pay to Billy Landers Dick Sutton*

CASH CHECKS OR DEPOSIT CHECKS QUICKLY

When you get a check, cash it or deposit it as soon as possible. Some people develop a habit of holding checks for several months. This is a bad habit. It can cause trouble for both you and the person who made out the check.

You may lose the check and not know it. This is the same as losing the actual money. Also, most checks will not be paid by a bank if they are over six months old. A good rule is to always cash checks quickly.

CLEARING A CHECK

Clearing a check is the process that takes place from the time a check is deposited until it is paid. Most checks go through two or more banks during this process and may be handled up to 20 times.

To see what happens when a check is cleared, look at Figure 20-5. In this example, the Smiths sent a mail order from Albany, New York, to Chicago, Illinois. If you follow the path of the check from start to finish (Step 1 through Step 6) you will see why the check may take five

FIGURE 20-5
HOW A CHECK IS CLEARED

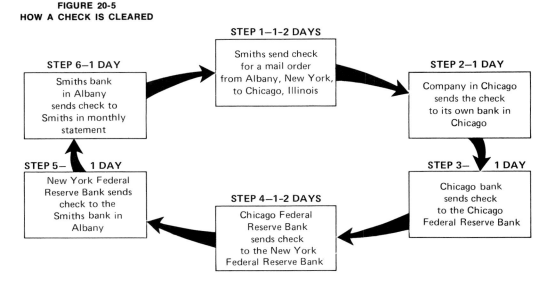

STEP 1—1-2 DAYS
Smiths send check for a mail order from Albany, New York, to Chicago, Illinois

STEP 2—1 DAY
Company in Chicago sends the check to its own bank in Chicago

STEP 3— 1 DAY
Chicago bank sends check to the Chicago Federal Reserve Bank

STEP 4—1-2 DAYS
Chicago Federal Reserve Bank sends check to the New York Federal Reserve Bank

STEP 5— 1 DAY
New York Federal Reserve Bank sends check to the Smiths bank in Albany

STEP 6—1 DAY
Smiths bank in Albany sends check to Smiths in monthly statement

to seven days to clear. Notice how the Federal Reserve System helps in clearing the check.

Clearing checks between banks in the same town does not take as long as it did in the example in Figure 20–5. Clearing checks in the same town is usually done in one or two days.

SUMMARY

Personal checks move money from a checking account to another person or business. The check can be transferred to another checking account, to a savings account, to another person, or be cashed.

Writing a check is easy. However, you must be careful to do it correctly. First, you should fill in the check register or stub. Next, you write the check. There are six items that must be included when writing a check. These are (1) the date, (2) the check number, (3) the payee's name, (4) the check amount in numbers, (5) the check amount in words, and (6) the drawer's signature.

When writing personal checks you may have problems. Sometimes you may overdraw your account. This means you write checks for more money than you have in your account.

When you cash a check made out to you, you must first endorse it. This means you sign your name on the back of the check. There are three basic ways to endorse checks. These are (1) endorsement in blank, (2) restrictive endorsement, and (3) endorsement in full. (See Figure 20–4.) You should always cash or deposit checks quickly. If a check is held too long, a bank may not pay it.

I. REVIEW OF TERMS

Which words complete the statements below?

postdate	drawer
clearing	endorsement
voiding	overdraw
number	payee

1. Signing your name on the back of a check is called an _____ .

2. Destroying a check is called _____ a check.

3. To _____ a checking account means you have written checks for more money than is in the account.

4. Every check should have a _____ to help you keep your records accurate.

5. The person writing a check is called the _____ .

6. To _____ a check means to date the check for a future date.

7. The person to whom a check is made out is called the _____ .

8. _____ a check is the process that takes place from the time a check is deposited until it is paid.

II. REVIEW OF MAIN POINTS

1. Explain the purpose of writing checks.
2. What are the two major transactions involved in transferring money from a checking account?
3. List and explain the steps in writing a check.
4. What is the major problem with postdating a check?
5. Explain the difference between the drawer of a check and the payee of a check.
6. What problems can occur when making a check payable to *Cash* or *Bearer?*

7. What is meant by the phrase *raising a check?*

8. Why should you never sign a blank check?

9. What does *stopping payment on a check* mean? How is it done?

10. Name the three ways in which a check can be endorsed. Explain how the three ways differ.

11. Why should a check be cashed or deposited as soon as possible?

12. What does the phrase *clearing a check* mean?

III. WRITING PERSONAL CHECKS: CONCEPTS

1. Hercules Bowles always wrote a check payable to *Cash* and carried it with him at all times. He did this in case he needed some money quickly while working or shopping. Do you think this is a good practice? Explain your answer.

2. Visit a local commercial bank and find out how it clears checks with other local banks. Write a short report for the class to explain what you found out.

3. Larry Forgy recently bought a pair of shoes for $34.95 from a local shoe shop. He paid for the shoes by check. The first day, one of the shoes split open. Larry complained that same day, but the store owner said he could do nothing about it. Since the shoes were paid for by check, what do you think Larry should do? Explain your answer.

4. Eddie Cook gave Nello Marchetti a check for $16.75. Nello endorsed the check and gave it to Merle Issom. Merle deposited the check, but it was returned to him by the bank with a note saying the checking account was overdrawn.

    a. Whose account was overdrawn?

    b. Who must pay Merle Issom the $16.75? Why?

5. Lynn Abercrombie writes about ten checks per week. He does not keep his check register up to date. Lynn enters the checks he has written about every two or three weeks. Each month, his bank sends a letter telling him his account is overdrawn. If you were the banker, how would you help Lynn solve his problem?

IV. WRITING PERSONAL CHECKS: EXERCISES

1. Listed below are six different dollar amounts. Write each as it would appear in words on a personal check.

   a. $ 10.44
   b. $100.00
   c. $ 2.78
   d. $1,242.90
   e. $5,249.18
   f. $ 59.99

2. Look at the following endorsements and tell what type each is:

   a. For deposit only, John Noe
   b. Pay to the order of Don Shannon, Mike Etzel
   c. Jim and Faye Marshall

3. Frank Argo wrote a check to the Montessi Grocery Store for $41.75 on March 2, 1975. The last check he wrote was number 483. Draw a blank check and fill it in correctly.

4. Visit a local bank and find other ways money payments can be made besides by using personal checks. Be sure to ask about cashier's checks, traveler's checks, certified checks, and bank money orders. Write a short report explaining each of the above items. What special purpose does each one serve?

YOUR PERSONAL SAVINGS ACCOUNT

People often make plans for things they want to buy or do in the future. Woody Forbes, a junior at Southside High School, made such plans. Woody has an evening paper route and wants to buy a second-hand car after he graduates. The car will cost about $900. Woody plans to pay for it out of his savings. *Savings* are the difference between the money he earns and the money he spends. Woody makes $25 a week from his paper route. He spends about $10 for school supplies and lunches. This leaves him about $15 in savings each week.

Over a lifetime, a person's savings can grow to thousands of dollars. It does not take a lot of money to start saving. Of course, if you earn a lot of money, it may be easier to save more. But how much you save depends on how well you manage your money. The important thing

Even in the past, depositing money in a savings account was only one of the many ways to save money.

is to start saving. Get into the habit of saving. It is one habit you will never regret.

This chapter discusses why and how people save. It will explain where and how you can open a savings account. It will also discuss some important points about a savings account.

WHY SAVE MONEY?

People save money for different reasons. Everyone should try to save money each month for *emergencies.* Many emergencies, such as a serious illness or a major car repair, can be very expensive. To be safe, the money you set aside for emergencies—an emergency fund—should be equal to about three months' income.

People also save money to pay for *educational expenses.* The Dick Sutton family (Chapter 12) saved $50 a month for the children's future educational expenses. Some people also save money to pay for *expensive* things they want to buy. These are things such as a new car, a color television, or a special family vacation.

People often save for their *retirement* years. Many people have some retirement income either from the Federal Government (social security) and/or a pension. This income, however, may not be enough. Therefore, some people set aside money during their working years to help out in the future.

PERSONAL SAVINGS ACCOUNTS

There are different ways people can save money. They can invest money in stocks, bonds, investment clubs, mutual funds, or real estate. These investments are explained in Unit VII. Another way to save money is to put it into a savings account. Savings accounts are provided by both commercial banks and savings and loan associations. Savings and loan associations are permitted by law to pay higher interest rates than commercial banks.

REGULAR SAVINGS ACCOUNTS

Personal savings accounts, like checking accounts, are easy to open and use. Someone at the bank will want to know such information as your name, address, telephone number, and social security number. After you sign a signature card, the account is ready to use. A signature card for Ben Peeples's savings account is shown in Figure 21–1. His account number is 97–654.

FIGURE 21-1

FIRST SECURITY NATIONAL BANK & TRUST COMPANY

☐ Joint Checking
☐ Individual Checking
☐ Joint Savings
☒ Individual Savings

DATE ______
BRANCH ______
ACCOUNT NO. 97-654

Title of Account: Ben F. Peeples

Sign here *Ben F. Peeples* Social Security No. 555-55-0000

Sign here ______ Social Security No. ______

Sign here ______ Social Security No. ______

Occupation ______ Former Bank ______

Home Address 1456 Carr Avenue Home Phone No. 948-3929

Said Bank is hereby authorized to:

☐ MAIL all statements and notices to address indicated above.

☐ HOLD all statements, etc, until called for, if not called for after 30 days said Bank may mail statements, etc., to the address indicated above. If the above mailed statements, vouchers and notices are returned undelivered, said Bank is hereby authorized to destroy same (2) years thereafter.

Bank is relieved of all liability for items lost in delivery by U.S. Mail or otherwise, or not called for by Depositor.

You can do two things with a savings account: (1) deposit money and (2) withdraw (take out) money. To deposit money, you must fill out a *deposit ticket.* The deposit ticket in Figure 21–2 shows that Ben deposited $14 in paper bills, 75 cents in coin, and a $119 check to open his account on July 9, 1974. The bank will always keep the deposit ticket as a record of the deposit.

FIGURE 21-2

SAVINGS DEPOSIT ☐ REGULAR ☐ NEST EGG

FIRST SECURITY NATIONAL BANK AND TRUST COMPANY
ONE FIRST SECURITY PLAZA • LEXINGTON, KENTUCKY 40507

DATE *July 9* 19 *74*

DEPOSIT TO THE ACCOUNT OF

Ben F. Peeples

PRESENT ADDRESS

1456 Carr Ave, Lexington, Ky.

SAVINGS ACCOUNT NUMBER ▸ 0 9 7 – 6 5 4 –

CASH	14 75
CHECKS	119 00
TOTAL DEPOSIT	133 75

⑆0421⑈000 2⑆ 64

To keep a record of his account, Ben may receive a special book called a *passbook* (Figure 21-3). The passbook has Ben's name, his account number, and places for recording all of his deposits and withdrawals. Since this is Ben's first deposit, the balance (total) in his account is $133.75.

FIGURE 21-3

No. 97-654	BEN F. PEEPLES

1456 CARR AVENUE

IN ACCOUNT WITH
First Security National Bank & Trust Company
LEXINGTON, KY.

THIS BOOK MUST BE PRESENTED WHEN MONEY IS DEPOSITED OR WITHDRAWN, AND SHOULD BE PRESENTED JANUARY 1ST AND JULY 1ST FOR INTEREST ENTRIES, SUBJECT TO RULES AND REGULATIONS.

DATE	WITHDRAWAL	DEPOSIT	INTEREST	BALANCE	TRANS.
7-9-74		133.75		133.75	

Later in the month, Ben had to take out $40 from his account to pay for an unexpected television repair bill. To do this, he first filled out a *withdrawal ticket* (Figure 21-4). This ticket, like a deposit ticket, is kept by the bank. It serves as a signed receipt to show how much money Ben received. The amount of the withdrawal is also recorded in Ben's passbook (Figure 21-5), leaving a new balance of $93.75.

FIGURE 21-4

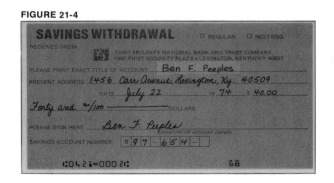

FIGURE 21-5

Notice the initials on the passbook in Figure 21–5. These initials show which person in the bank completed the transaction. For Ben, Rosemary Garrison computed the $40 withdrawal on July 22.

If you have an account that does not use a passbook, you usually must fill in two deposit tickets each time you make a deposit. The bank teller will stamp the second copy and return it to you. This is your record of the deposit. Withdrawals are handled the same way.

At the end of each yearly quarter, that is, every three months, you probably will get a full statement from the bank. Usually, it will show all the deposits, all the withdrawals, the interest you earned, and the latest balance. (See Figure 21–6.) These statements are prepared by electronic computers.

FIGURE 21-6

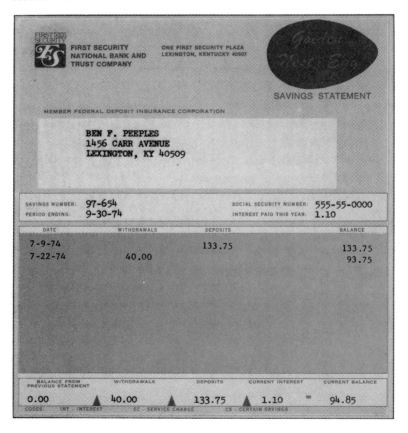

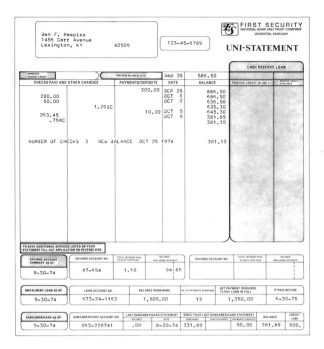

FIGURE 21-7

In recent years, many banks have stopped using passbooks for savings account records. Some banks have started giving their customers uni-statements. A *uni-statement* is a complete account of all of the customer's banking activities. This includes the customer's checking accounts, savings accounts, loans, and any other types of business conducted with the bank. The uni-statement is mailed to each customer once a month. An example of a bank uni-statement is shown in Figure 21–7. This type of statement is convenient because you can get a complete accounting of all your personal financial matters every month.

SPECIAL SAVINGS ACCOUNTS

With a regular savings account, you can usually take out any amount of money at any time. However, there are other types of savings plans that are usually designed for special savings goals. These special savings include:

1. *Savings certificates,* which are accounts that earn higher rates than regular accounts. The money, however, must be left on deposit for a certain period of time. The time may vary between 30 days and five years. This form of savings ties up your money for a specific period of time.

2. *Christmas or Hanukkah clubs* to help people save money to pay for holiday gifts. Often you get no interest unless your money is left on deposit for about one year. However, you may withdraw money at any time.

3. *Monthly income plans,* which give you a check each month. The check is for the interest your savings earned during the month.

4. *Vacation clubs,* which are used to save money for a special vacation. They work much the same way Christmas and Hanukkah clubs do.

5. *Restricted savings accounts,* which require a minimum deposit, say $100, to open. You leave your money on deposit for 90 days. Any interest earned is paid then. You have the next ten days to decide whether or not you want to withdraw the money on deposit. After that, you cannot withdraw your money until the end of another 90 days. These accounts pay a higher rate than regular savings accounts.

If you have a particular savings goal, discuss it with a banker. Local banks may have other types of special savings plans. One may be exactly suited to your needs.

FEATURES OF SAVINGS ACCOUNTS

Savings accounts have several important features: money in them grows, they are protected, and they usually provide you with an easy way of getting ready cash.

SAVINGS ACCOUNTS GROW

The money you put into a savings account actually makes more money. This additional money is the *interest* the bank pays you for the use of your money. Suppose you put $1,000 into a savings account that earns you 4 percent interest. The bank pays interest four times a year. When interest is paid this way, it is said to be paid *quarterly.* At the end of one year, the $1,000 will have grown to $1,040.60.

At the end of the first quarter, the $1,000 will have earned $10 in interest. Thus the new total, or balance, will be $1,010. During the second quarter, interest is paid on this new total—not just on the $1,000 originally put into the savings account. Thus, at the end of the second quarter, the new total is $1,020.10. At the end of the third quarter, the new total is $1,030.30, and at the end of the year you will have $1,040.60.

This is an example of *compound interest;* that is, interest is paid on interest. The interest earned in the first quarter earned interest itself in the second, third, and fourth quarters.

Compound interest is a very important part of any savings account. A compound interest rate of 6 percent will double your money in just over 11 years. To show how money left in savings accounts will grow, look at Table 21–1. In 12 years, a $500 savings account grows to $1,021.75. The original $500 deposit earns $521.75 in interest.

TABLE 21–1 COMPOUND INTEREST MAKES YOUR SAVINGS GROW	
Time	*Savings Account Total*
Original Deposit	$ 500.00
5 years	673.45
10 years	907.00
12 years	1021.75

If more money had been added to the account during the 12 years, the total would have been even greater. Whenever you save, it is important to develop a plan and stick to it. By developing a savings plan and letting the interest build up, your savings account can provide you with a good "nest egg" for the future.

MONEY IS PROTECTED

Savings accounts are insured by the United States Government in the same way as checking accounts. In a commercial bank, the FDIC (Federal Deposit Insurance Corporation) insures each savings account for up to $40,000. In a savings bank, the Federal Savings and Loan Insurance Corporation (FSLIC) is the agency that insures savings accounts. Here, too, the insurance protection does not cover amounts over $40,000. This means that if an account has $50,000, only $40,000 are protected. If the bank fails, the Government will repay your savings up to $40,000.

YOUR SAVINGS ARE READY CASH

Another important feature of a regular savings account is that you can take out money whenever you need it. If you need cash quickly you can get it from a regular savings account.

All savings accounts do not have this feature. Many special savings accounts tie up your money for at least a month. Before putting money into special accounts, it is a good idea to build up a good balance in a regular savings account. You never know when it may be needed.

SUMMARY

A bank is a private business that performs many financial services. It is set up to make a profit. The major types of banks are (1) investment banks, (2) savings banks, and (3) commercial banks. Commercial banks provide many services for businesses and individuals. For example, they accept money deposits, make loans, transfer funds, and provide trust services.

The Federal Reserve System was set up in 1913 by Congress. The main jobs of the Fed are to (1) act as a bank for bankers, (2) serve as the bank for the Federal Government, (3) supervise Federal Reserve member banks, and (4) manage the nation's money supply.

Two bank services that you can use are checking accounts and savings accounts. The main reasons for using a checking account are safety and convenience. There are several reasons for having a savings account. These include saving for emergencies, educational expenses, retirement, and expensive things that you may want to buy.

REVIEW YOUR PERSONAL SAVINGS ACCOUNT

I. REVIEW OF TERMS

Which words complete the statements below?

compound   regular
passbooks   uni-statement
savings

1. The difference between the money you earn and the money you spend is called _____.
2. Some banks use _____ to keep records of savings accounts.
3. Interest paid on interest is called _____ interest.
4. A _____ is a complete accounting of all your banking activities.
5. In a _____ savings account, money can usually be taken out anytime.

II. REVIEW OF MAIN POINTS

1. Give four reasons why people save money. Explain your answers.
2. What is a regular savings account?
3. What is a special savings account? Give three examples.
4. What is the main advantage of a regular savings account as compared to a special savings account?
5. What is the purpose of a savings account passbook?

6. Explain what is meant by the term *uni-statement.*

7. Explain why a savings account grows even when you do not deposit more money.

8. How is the money in a savings account protected?

III. YOUR PERSONAL SAVINGS ACCOUNT: CONCEPTS

1. Study the following ad closely and answer the questions below:

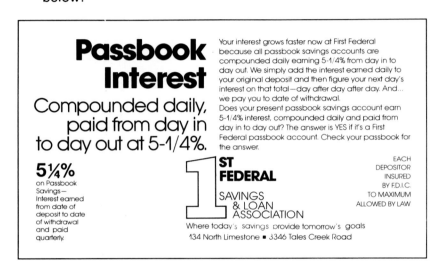

Passbook Interest

Compounded daily, paid from day in to day out at 5-1/4%.

5¼%
on Passbook Savings— Interest earned from date of deposit to date of withdrawal and paid quarterly.

Your interest grows faster now at First Federal because all passbook savings accounts are compounded daily earning 5-1/4% from day in to day out. We simply add the interest earned daily to your original deposit and then figure your next day's interest on that total—day after day after day. And... we pay you to date of withdrawal.

Does your present passbook savings account earn 5-1/4% interest, compounded daily and paid from day in to day out? The answer is YES if it's a First Federal passbook account. Check your passbook for the answer.

1ST FEDERAL

SAVINGS & LOAN ASSOCIATION

Where today's savings provide tomorrow's goals
134 North Limestone ■ 3346 Tales Creek Road

EACH DEPOSITOR INSURED BY F.D.I.C. TO MAXIMUM ALLOWED BY LAW

a. What type of bank is it?

b. What interest rate is paid by the bank on passbook savings accounts?

c. How often is the interest compounded?

d. Explain how daily compounded interest works.

e. Are savings accounts in this bank insured? If so, what is the largest amount that the bank will insure?

2. Make a list of the commercial banks and the savings banks in your community. Find out what interest rates the two types of banks pay on passbook savings accounts. If there is a difference in the interest rates, find out why.

3. Give two reasons why young people should open savings accounts.

4. Read the following savings and loan bank ad closely. Answer the questions following the ad.

NOW an ALL-NEW and even better savings program for every saver!

5¼% per annum	5¾% per annum	6½% per annum	6¾% per annum
Annual yield: (5.47%)	Annual yield: (6.00%)	Annual yield: (6.81%)	Annual yield: (7.08%)
BUSY DOLLAR PASSBOOK	NINETY DAY NOTICE PASSBOOK	ONE YEAR CERTIFICATE	TOP DOLLAR THIRTY MONTH CERTIFICATE
Deposit any amount or withdraw with no loss of interest.	Deposit any amount; withdraw on 90 days notice or during the first 10 days of quarterly period from funds on deposit ninety days.	$1,000.00 minimum account balance. Can be increased with amounts of $100.00.	$5,000.00 minimum account balance. Can be increased with amounts of $100.00.

EXISTING CERTIFICATES WILL CONTINUE TO EARN AT ORIGINAL RATE.
ALL INTEREST COMPOUNDED DAILY AND PAID QUARTERLY.
ASK ABOUT EVEN HIGHER RATES FOR LONGER PERIODS OF TIME.

a. What is the interest rate paid on a 90-day-notice passbook account?

b. How long do you have to keep your money on deposit to earn 6.75 percent interest?

c. How often is the interest compounded?

d. How often is the interest paid?

e. Explain why the bank is willing to pay high interest rates for money left on deposit for long periods of time.

IV. YOUR PERSONAL SAVINGS ACCOUNT: EXERCISES

1. Go to three local commercial banks and get a list of the different types of savings accounts they offer. Compare the lists and note any differences that you can find for the same type of savings accounts.

2. Harry Green has $500 to put into a new savings account. One bank pays 5 percent interest compounded quarterly. Another bank pays 5.5 percent compounded twice a year. Which one would be the best investment for Harry at the end of one year?

3. Herb Buckner has a regular savings account at the Park National Bank. He has $1.49 in coins, $16 in bills, and checks for $14, $83, and $42.81. Prepare a savings deposit ticket so that he can put the money into the bank. His account number is 410–021. (Draw your own deposit ticket.)

4. Bill Curtis has a savings account with Lincoln Savings and Loan. He invested $100 on January 1 when the account was opened. One year later he deposited another $70. The bank pays 5 percent interest compounded quarterly. At the end of two years, how much money will Bill have in his account?

Unit VI
Fundamentals
of Credit

Credit plays an important role in the life of consumers and in the growth of the country's economy. It is important that you learn as much as you can about consumer credit and how you can use it.

Chapter 22 discusses the meaning and importance of credit. It also explains the different forms of consumer credit and how they are used.

In order to use credit, you must first qualify for it. Chapter 23 covers three factors businesses consider before giving credit to their customers. Once you use credit you start to build a credit rating. You will learn how to build a good credit rating and reasons why a good credit rating is important. Chapter 23 looks at some of the problems that arise when credit is not used properly.

There are several sources of consumer credit. Chapter 24 covers the different sources available to most consumers. It also explains why loan costs may vary and why it is necessary to shop for credit. You will also learn how to figure out mathematically the true interest rate for any loan that is made.

UNIT PREVIEW

AS YOU STUDY THIS UNIT YOU WILL BE ENGAGED IN

* PROBING the meaning and uses of credit

* IDENTIFYING the major forms and sources of consumer credit

* DETERMINING the advantages and disadvantages of consumer credit

* UNDERSTANDING what is needed to qualify for credit

* CALCULATING costs of loans and true interest rates

* SELECTING proper terms for loans so that the best credit is obtained.

A FOCUS FOR YOUR STUDY

22 THE MEANING OF CREDIT

Woody Forbes wanted to buy a pair of slacks that cost $15. Woody, however, did not have enough money to pay for the pants. Frank Argo, the clothing store owner, knew that Woody had a job delivering papers after school, so he let Woody take the pants home after Woody agreed to pay for them at the end of the month. In a similar example, Jerry Davis went to see a movie one Saturday without enough money to pay for a ticket. The ticket seller, however, decided to let Jerry have a ticket because Jerry promised to pay for it on the following Monday.

The above situations are both examples of credit. Credit is important to everyone. In fact, the United States economy probably could not work without credit. Woody and Jerry are examples of individual people who used credit to meet certain wants. Families also use credit. Every time you turn on the lights or your mother cooks with natural gas, the family uses credit. Your father uses credit when he fills the car's gas tank and says "Charge it." The family also uses credit when it borrows money from the bank to pay for a new color television set.

Because credit is so important to everyone, it is important that you understand how it is used. In this chapter, you will learn the meaning and the importance of credit, the use and the cost of credit, and the different forms of credit.

THE MEANING AND IMPORTANCE OF CREDIT

The examples of Jerry buying a movie ticket and Woody buying a pair of pants have two things in common. Both boys paid for something after it was used, and both Woody and Jerry were trusted to pay their bills at a future date. The idea of being trusted to pay for something after it is used is common to all forms of credit.

In a barter system, a debt can be repaid at a later date with goods or services rather than with money.

These two examples show that credit, like money, serves as a medium of exchange. People can buy goods and services now in exchange for their promises to pay for the items in the future. They can spend their future income for items bought today. Thus, *credit* is a promise to pay at some future date for the present exchange and use of goods, services, or money. Used wisely, credit can help the nation's economy grow and help individuals and families meet their needs and wants.

It is important to understand that credit does not increase a person's buying power. The debt that is made today through the use of credit still must be paid. Credit, however, allows families to plan for major purchases and build them into their budgets. This is what the Sutton family did when they bought their new car.

The idea of credit is not new. In fact, the idea is probably older than the use of money. Even in a barter system, credit can be used. For example, a carpenter can repair a farmer's house before the crops are harvested. Once the crops are grown, the farmer can pay the debt by giving some of his harvest to the carpenter. Today's wide use of credit, however, is fairly new. Only since about 1945 has the use of consumer credit become widespread.

The use of credit has played an important role in the growth of the United States economy. Through the use of credit, consumers have been able to buy, without delay, many different goods and services.

Expensive items such as houses, cars, televisions, and washing machines could not be bought by most families without the use of credit.

Businesses also benefit from customers who use credit when they make major purchases. Because of credit, most consumers can buy the things they want when they want them. This creates a larger demand for most goods and services. Because of this, businesses must produce goods in large quantities. By doing this, the cost of many different goods can be lower than if they were produced in small quantities.

Thus, the growth of the country's economy is helped by the use of credit. Consumers are now able to buy items that would normally be too expensive if they had to be paid for immediately. Because many consumers can now buy a large variety of goods and services, businesses can produce the items in large quantities. Therefore, businesses can run more efficiently. Thus, credit helps both production and consumption. This results in a healthy, growing, and stable economy.

CREDIT—ITS USE AND COST

Almost every person, business, or government uses credit at one time or another. Goods and services worth billions of dollars are bought every year on credit. Credit is not always used for the same reason. However, the use of credit always has a common purpose—to gain an economic advantage by buying something when it is needed.

Governments use credit to provide citizens with goods and services. Some things governments use credit to provide are schools, highways, airports, sewer systems, water treatment plants, and fire trucks. The

Governments use credit to buy expensive equipment, such as fire engines.

biggest single user of credit is the United States Government. In fact, the credit debt of the Federal Government is several hundred billion dollars. This debt is owed mainly to citizens of the country. Whenever people buy United States savings bonds, they are lending money (giving credit) to the Federal Government. Governments also borrow money from banks to pay their bills and their employees until taxes are collected.

Businesses normally use credit to pay for their everyday operating expenses. These expenses include the cost of raw materials, office supplies, workers' wages, heat, electric power, and telephone service. The money that is borrowed to pay these expenses is called *short-term credit.* It is usually paid back within 30 to 90 days.

Businesses also use credit to build new buildings and to buy land and expensive equipment. These items, called *capital goods,* are used to produce other goods. The money borrowed to pay for capital goods is called *long-term credit.* A business often takes as long as 25 years to repay this type of credit.

THE COST OF CREDIT

Services cost money. When you have a television fixed, you must pay the person who fixed it for the service this person provided. *Providing credit* is also a service. Getting credit is a form of borrowing. When Floyd Gray lends James Jackson $10 for a week, James agrees to pay Floyd $10.50 at the end of the week. This means that the credit cost James 50 cents. The cost of using another person's money is called *interest.*

Families and individuals, as well as businesses and governments, usually have to pay interest when they receive credit. It is important for everyone to learn how to mathematically figure the cost of credit. This is discussed in Chapter 24.

Credit is very important to the economic welfare of governments, businesses, and consumers. Because consumer credit is the type of credit you will probably use, it is important that you have a good understanding of how it works.

FORMS OF CONSUMER CREDIT

There are two basic kinds of consumer credit. They are (1) sales credit and (2) cash credit. *Sales credit* is used when people wish to purchase items. Almost all stores, such as furniture dealers, department stores, and appliance stores, extend some type of sales credit to their customers. *Cash credit* is used for borrowing money. This type of credit is usually offered by banks and finance companies.

Both types of consumer credit can also be classified according to how the money is repaid. Two methods used for repaying debts are (1) installment credit and (2) noninstallment credit. *Installment credit* means that the debt is paid back in more than one payment. This type of credit is usually used for expensive purchases and for cash loans. For example, you might borrow $1,000 from a bank and pay it back in 24 payments over a period of two years. *Noninstallment credit* means that the entire debt is paid back in one payment. This is done for small or regular bills, such as doctor bills, gas and electric bills, credit card bills, and repair bills. The important point is that both sales credit and cash credit can be repaid using either plan.

NONINSTALLMENT CREDIT

Noninstallment credit is usually given through three types of credit accounts. They are (1) open charge accounts, (2) single payment loans, and (3) revolving charge accounts.

Open charge accounts are used for everyday expenses and must be paid back completely within 10 to 20 days after the bill is received. The two most common types of open charge account credit are (1) regular charge accounts and (2) credit card accounts.

Regular charge accounts are used by people who shop regularly at a certain store. Suppose Woody's family buys many medicines and other things at Sanders' Drugstore. Instead of paying for each item when it is bought, the family has a regular charge account. Every 30 days the drugstore sends them a bill for the month's purchases. The entire bill must be paid within 10 days after it is received. This is how a regular charge account works.

There are two advantages to using a regular charge account. One advantage is that it is convenient because you do not have to pay cash for each purchase. Another advantage is that it costs no more than paying cash—provided that the bills are paid on time. If Woody's family do not pay the bills on time, the store charges them interest.

Nearly every large department store and discount store gives special charge cards to its credit customers. Suppose Woody wants to buy a football at a local department store. Without a charge card the clerks at the store would not know that his family has an account there.

This second type of open account is the credit card account. A *credit card* provides the consumer with credit to buy goods and services. Some credit cards can be used at different stores anywhere in the United States and in many foreign countries as well. Other cards can be used only at the stores that issue them. In addition to stores, businesses issuing credit cards include oil companies, car rental agencies, hotel chains, and banks.

Credit cards can be used to buy many different goods and services. The Gulf Oil card can be used to charge gas, oil, and car repairs at Gulf service stations anywhere in the United States. The Sears Roebuck card can be used at all Sears stores in the nation. It is called a *special–purpose* credit card. The BankAmericard and American Express card are *general–purpose* cards. This means that they can be used to charge many types of goods and services in many places. Among the things

Some firms charge as much as 18% interest a year on unpaid bills. Credit is a convenience to be used with great care.

that can be charged with these cards are airplane tickets, food, gas, oil, lodging, clothing, appliance repairs, books, and car repairs. Some states are even considering the use of credit cards for paying traffic fines.

For each credit card you own, you get a bill every month showing how much is owed on the account (Figure 15-3). If the bill is not paid by the date it is due, there is a finance charge which raises the cost of credit. Many firms charge an interest rate of 18 percent a year or 1.5 percent a month.

The BankAmericard is issued free by a bank in your community. The American Express card costs $15 a year for its use.

Credit cards should be guarded as carefully as money. Unwanted credit cards should be destroyed immediately. If a credit card is lost, you should quickly tell the company that gave the card to you. This prevents you from having to pay bills charged to your account by a person who might find the card and use it illegally. Under any circumstances, a federal law protects you from being held responsible for more than $50 worth of charges per lost or stolen card.

A second form of noninstallment credit is the single-payment loan. A *single-payment loan,* usually made by banks, is a loan that is paid back in one lump sum. The loan is normally repaid at the end of 30, 60, or 90 days. This kind of loan is convenient when money is needed for only a short amount of time. However, banks often have a minimum limit of money that can be borrowed this way. This minimum usually ranges between $500 and $1000.

Finally, the *revolving charge account (RCA)* is another popular type of noninstallment credit. This type of account has credit limits that are normally set when the account is opened. Suppose Pete Doyle opens an RCA at a local store in Austin, Texas, and his credit limit is set at $300 by the store. This means that Pete can never owe more than $300 on his account. When this limit is reached, he cannot charge any more goods or services without first making a payment.

At the end of each billing period, Pete receives a statement showing the amount of his bill. He has two choices. If he pays the entire bill, no interest is charged. Used this way, the RCA is a noninstallment credit account. Or, Pete can pay $20, which is only part of the bill. By doing this, the RCA becomes an installment credit account.

INSTALLMENT CREDIT

Installment credit often involves large amounts of credit and long periods of time. If installment credit is used to buy a car that costs $4,000, this money can be paid back in as many as 36 installments, one a month over three years. However, all installment credit is not repaid over long periods of time.

Some stores offer *budget accounts*. These are much like open credit accounts. The difference is that the balance in the budget account may be paid in three equal payments over a 90-day period. Budget accounts often do not have any interest charges. For example, Pete Doyle recently bought a guitar for $114 on a 90-day budget account. Pete must pay the store $38 a month for three months. There is no interest charge.

All budget accounts do not work like the one Pete used. Each store has its own rules. Before using a budget account, be sure you understand exactly how it works. Used properly, budget accounts can be helpful to many shoppers.

The second type of installment credit involves borrowing money. This is called cash credit. *Cash credit* is different from the other forms of consumer credit discussed so far in that those types of credit were for goods and services. Cash credit is for cash. This type of credit is usually extended by banks and finance companies.

As you may recall, the Dick Sutton family planned to use cash credit to pay for part of the cost of their new car. They used $1,500 from their savings account plus the trade-in value ($790) of their old car as a down payment. The rest of the cost, $1,648, was to be paid in monthly installments. This money was to be borrowed from a bank and paid back to the bank over a period of two years. Of course, the Suttons will also have to pay interest to the bank for the money they borrowed. Installment credit is different from noninstallment credit in several ways. Some of the important features of installment credit are:

1. You must sign some type of written agreement covering the exact terms of the credit.
2. A down payment is normally required.
3. You often do not get title to full legal ownership of your purchase until the entire loan is repaid.
4. You have to make regular payments of exact amounts at certain times.
5. In some contracts, if only one payment is missed, the entire balance must be paid right away.

Like any type of credit, installment credit must be used carefully. Otherwise it can cause many financial problems. For example, suppose the Suttons signed a loan contract containing item **5** above. If they missed a payment and could not pay the loan off, they could lose their car and much of the money they had put into it. Remember, always read the credit terms before you sign anything.

SUMMARY

Credit means that you promise to pay for something at a future date, even though you get the goods or services now. Credit, if used wisely, can be a good family money-management tool. In addition, the use of credit can help raise the standard of living of many people.

The users of credit are individuals, businesses, and governments. The largest single user of credit is the United States Government. All credit users have a common goal—to gain an economic advantage by buying goods or services when they are needed.

Credit is not free; it costs money. When you get credit, you are using another person's money and you have to pay the person for it. The cost of using credit is called interest.

There are two basic types of credit. They are (1) sales credit and (2) cash credit. Sales credit is used when goods and services are bought. Cash credit is used when money is loaned. Credit is paid back on either a noninstallment or installment basis. Noninstallment credit is paid back in a lump sum. Installment credit is repaid in several payments.

I. REVIEW OF TERMS

Which words complete the statements below?

installment credit   noninstallment credit

credit card   credit

interest   short-term credit

cash credit   revolving charge accounts

sales credit

1. The cost of using another person's money is called _____ .

2. _____ is usually paid back in 30 to 90 days.

3. A _____ is used to show that a person has credit.

4. A single-payment loan is a form of _____ .

5. _____ is used to buy goods and services.

6. Promising to pay in the future for a service used today is called _____ .

7. _____ can be used as either installment or noninstallment credit.

8. When a bank loans money, that is called _____ .

9. Paying for something in a series of payments is called _____ .

II. REVIEW OF MAIN POINTS

1. What is credit?

2. Is the idea of credit new? Explain.

3. Who are the users of credit?

4. What is the difference between short-term credit and long-term credit?

5. What does the word *interest* mean?

6. Explain the difference between cash credit and sales credit.

7. In what two ways can credit be repaid?

8. What are the two most common types of open charge accounts? Explain how each works.

9. What is a 90-day budget account?
10. What are some of the important features of installment credit?
11. Why should you always read an installment credit contract before signing it?

III. THE MEANING OF CREDIT: CONCEPTS

1. Do you think there should be a difference in the credit limits (amounts) set for different people using revolving charge accounts? Explain the reasons for your answer.

2. People have different ideas about the use of credit. Some, like Don Palmer, say, "If I can't pay cash, I will not buy it." Others, like Jim Gibson, say, "I charge everything possible so I can enjoy life more."
   a. Does either statement agree with your idea about the use of credit? Explain.
   b. What is the problem with having an attitude toward credit like Jim Gibson's?

3. Tony Captino is planning to buy a vacuum cleaner. Tony decides to pay for the vacuum with cash credit; he borrows the money from a bank. He thinks he can get a better buy this way than if he uses sales credit to buy an expensive item such as a vacuum cleaner. Do you agree with Tony? Why?

4. Some stores let high school students open charge accounts. Most students have revolving charge accounts with very low credit limits. High school students usually do not have regular jobs and have never done any installment buying. Why do you think stores permit high school students to have charge accounts?

5. What are some of the possible disadvantages of consumer credit that individuals and families must guard against? Which item on your list do you think is the most serious?

6. Do you think credit helps governments provide more public services than if they had to pay cash? Explain.

7. Explain how credit is
   a. A kind of forced savings
   b. A way to beat inflation.

IV. THE MEANING OF CREDIT: EXERCISES

1. Study the following credit card bill and answer the questions:

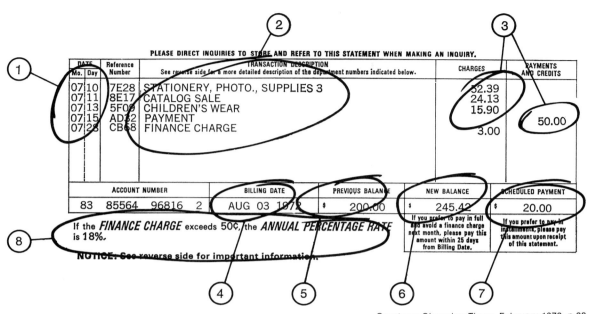

Courtesy: *Changing Times*, February 1973, p.38

    a. How many purchases are reported on the monthly statement? What is the date of the last purchase?

    b. When was the last payment made and how much was it?

    c. What is the new balance to be paid? When must it be paid if no finance charges are to be added?

    d. If the account is to be used as a RCA, what is the minimum installment payment?

2. Read the article "Why Auto Dealers Don't Like Cash Buyers" (*Consumer Reports,* May, 1965, pp. 258–261). Prepare a short report that gives

    a. The general theme of the article

    b. The specific reason why auto dealers want customers to use credit.

3. Visit three businesses in your town that have both regular charge accounts and revolving charge accounts. Find out the following information from each:

a. What name does each store give to its different types of accounts?

b. How do the plans differ among the stores? That is, compare the regular accounts among the three stores. Next, compare the revolving charge accounts.

4. Study the following table closely and answer the questions:

   a. What was the total amount of consumer credit outstanding in 1967? 1973? Write out your answers using zeros.

   b. What was the percentage increase in total consumer credit outstanding from 1967 to 1973?

   c. Did noninstallment credit or installment credit increase by the greatest percentage from 1967 to 1973?

   d. What percentage of the total consumer credit outstanding in 1967 was installment credit? noninstallment credit? What were the figures for 1973?

CONSUMER CREDIT OUTSTANDING, 1967–1973
(In Billions of Dollars)

Year	Total Credit Outstanding	Total Installment Credit	Total Noninstallment Credit
1967	102.1	80.9	21.2
1968	113.1	89.8	23.3
1969	122.5	98.2	24.3
1970	126.8	101.2	25.6
1971	138.4	111.3	27.1
1972	157.6	127.3	30.2
1973 (Est.)	167.1	136.0	31.1

USING CREDIT

Consumer credit has been important for two reasons. First, it has helped the United States develop a strong and growing economy. Because of this, more people have jobs that provide them with the money they need to live well. Second, the use of credit has helped consumers reach the highest standard of living in the world. Money earned from working, plus the use of consumer credit, has made it possible for the people of the United States to buy many goods and services. Expensive things, such as homes, automobiles, and major appliances, could not be bought by many families without using consumer credit.

Because credit can be helpful to you, it is important that you learn how it is used. For example, what do business firms consider important when you apply for credit? What is a credit rating? What are the advantages and disadvantages of using credit? What guidelines should be followed by consumers when using credit? You will find answers to these questions in this chapter.

QUALIFYING FOR CONSUMER CREDIT

Simply because you are a consumer does not mean that you can always get credit. Credit is based on trust. The trust a seller or lender gives you when you buy goods and services or when you borrow money is based on your promise to pay.

Before businesses will give you credit, they will want to know some things about you. Their main concern is finding out if you can make good your promise to pay them back.

You must earn the right to consumer credit. When deciding if a consumer is worthy enough to receive credit, sellers and lenders consider three factors. These factors are sometimes called the *Three C's of Credit.* They are character, capital, and capacity.

CHARACTER

Character is determined by your personal traits and general reputation in your community. Your honesty and your willingness to repay loans or sales credit bills are considered. If you have paid your bills in the past, you are likely to continue to pay them.

If you are applying for credit for the first time, you should expect some personal questions. The businesses involved will want to find out what kind of person you are. They will talk to you and probably ask for personal references to find out what other people think of you.

CAPITAL

Capital refers to your wealth—the money and property you own. It includes things that might be used to pay back a debt if other money is not available. Examples of capital are life insurance policies, household goods, savings accounts, cars, and real estate (land and buildings).

If you have several of these items, it is an indication that you probably manage your money well. In other words, you have something to show for the money you have earned.

CAPACITY

Capacity is your ability to make enough money to repay a debt. Two factors are involved. One factor is your ability to earn money now and in the future. Another factor is how much you presently owe; that is, how deep you are in debt. Many people are willing to repay loans or credit but cannot do it. They already owe too much. For example, the Sutton family could not afford to buy a large and expensive station wagon. They do not make enough money to pay for such an expensive car in addition to other family needs and wants.

A CREDIT APPLICATION

Questions on the Three C's of Credit are usually asked on a credit application form. Filling out such a form (Figure 23-1) is the first step in getting credit. Notice that the information asked for on the application is very detailed.

FIGURE 23-1

TWA Getaway card application

					$ 445	CB	RC
OC	T	#CD
BI	CL	R/A

☐ MR. ☒ MRS. ☐ MISS (print name) FIRST _INEZ_ MID. INITIAL LAST _RAMIREZ_

SEX ☐ MALE ☒ FEMALE — NO. OF DEP. _0_ — MARITAL STATUS ☒ MARRIED ☐ SINGLE ☐ WIDOWED ☐ DIVORCED

PRESENT ADDRESS _5234 Grande Ave._ HOW LONG? _18 yrs._ SPOUSE'S FIRST NAME _Jose_ YOUR AGE _28_

CITY/STATE _Houston, Texas_ ZIP CODE _33201_ ☐ OWN ☒ RENT ☐ WITH PARENTS AREA CODE PHONE NO. _713-612-4380_ SOCIAL SECURITY NO. _709-54-6953_

PREVIOUS ADDRESS _221 San Pablo_ CITY/STATE _Houston, Texas_ HOW LONG? _10 yrs._ OCCUPATION & TITLE _Executive Secretary_

PRESENT EMPLOYER _J.H. Book Publishing Co._ ADDRESS _41-20 South St._ HOW LONG? _8 yrs._ SPOUSE'S EMPLOYER, CITY, STATE & TELEPHONE NO. _Houston Police Dept._ _612-1126_

CITY _Houston, Texas_ STATE TELEPHONE NO. _321-4560_ ANNUAL INCOME _10,000_ PERSONAL REFERENCE _Maria Santos_

PREVIOUS EMPLOYER ADDRESS TELEPHONE NO. HOW LONG? ADDRESS _52 Elm Blvd._ TELEPHONE NO. _321-2100_

NAME, ADDRESS, PHONE OF NEAREST RELATIVE NOT LIVING WITH YOU (parents, if you are under 21) — MAJOR CREDIT CARD _Bank Americard_ ACCOUNT NO. _4113-2103-110-211_

BANK NAME & LOCATION _Houston Savings Bank_ ☐ CHECKING ☒ SAVINGS ☐ LOAN — MAJOR BANK CARD _Master Charge_ ACCOUNT NO. _3120-6321-311-450_

BANK NAME & LOCATION _First National Bank_ ☒ CHECKING ☐ SAVINGS ☐ LOAN — OTHER MAJOR TRAVEL CARD ACCOUNT NO.

*Service mark owned exclusively by TWA. — TWA Getaway Cards are available to U.S.A. residents only.

RETAIL INSTALMENT CREDIT AGREEMENT

You agree with Trans World Airlines (TWA), 605 3rd Ave., N.Y., N.Y., that any "instant credit" purchase by you and all purchases charged under any credit card or supplementary credit card issued to you or at your request by TWA are indebtedness of yours which may be purchased, acquired, assigned or sold by TWA. Within 25 days from each monthly billing date, you shall pay to TWA in U.S. currency either (1) the full amount of your new balance as shown on your monthly statement, in which event no **finance charge** will accrue or (2) an instalment payment equal to the sum of accrued **finance charges** plus, if a new purchase appears on such monthly statement, 1/24th of the amount owed for charge purchases as of such billing date, or, if no new purchase appears, 1/24th of the amount owed for charge purchases as of the date of the last monthly statement on which a new purchase appeared, except that no instalment payment shall be less than $10.00 (or balance if less). **Finance charges** become part of your indebtedness and are applied separately to the airline and non-airline previous balances shown on your monthly statement, less payments and credits during the current billing cycle and unpaid **finance charges** (adjusted previous balances) at the monthly periodic rates of 1½% (18% **annual percentage rate**) on the first $500 of each adjusted previous balance and 1% (12% **annual percentage rate**) on the amount of each adjusted previous balance in excess of $500, except that the rates applicable to your adjusted non-airline previous balance will in no event exceed the rates prevailing from time to time in your state of residence for open-end credit transactions. Airline previous balance includes unpaid purchases of passenger air transportation and tours which include air transportation and **finance charges** thereon; unpaid purchases of all other goods and services, and **finance charges** thereon, are included in non-airline previous balance. **You may at any time pay your total indebtedness.** In case of default in payment or other breach hereof, your entire outstanding balance will then become due and payable at TWA's option. If your account is referred for collection to an attorney not a salaried employee of TWA, you will pay an attorney's fee not to exceed 20% of the amount payable or such lesser attorney's fee, if any, as may be legally permitted. Neither TWA nor any assignee of TWA is responsible if your card is not honored. TWA may revoke your card and you must surrender it on demand. TWA is not responsible for services or goods which are not purchased from and provided by TWA, and all disputes regarding them will be settled by you with the person providing them. **You will notify TWA in writing if any card issued on your account is lost or stolen.** This agreement is not valid or binding until accepted by TWA by mailing to you a copy of this agreement executed by TWA, and shall be governed by New York law except to the extent governed by any law, regulation or order of the United States or any agency or instrumentality thereof. **NOTICE TO THE BUYER: 1. Do not sign this credit agreement before you read it or if it contains any blank space. 2. You are entitled to a completely filled in copy of this credit agreement.**

RETAIL INSTALMENT CREDIT AGREEMENT

THE UNDERSIGNED INDIVIDUALS JOIN IN THIS APPLICATION & ASSUME JOINT & SEVERAL LIABILITY FOR ALL CHARGES INCURRED.

APPLICANT'S SIGNATURE (PLEASE READ AGREEMENT CAREFULLY) — DATE _4/10/75_

X _Inez Ramirez_

ISSUE SUPPLEMENTARY CARD TO: (print name) ☐MR./MRS./MISS _Jose Ramirez_ SIGNATURE AGE _30_ RELATIONSHIP _HUSBAND_

3-74 4-7011-465 Printed in U.S.A.

On almost every application form you will probably be asked

1. Where do you work?
2. How long have you worked there?
3. What kind of job do you have?
4. How much money do you earn?
6. Do you have a checking account? savings account? Where?
7. Do you have any debts? If so, for what and for how much?

When filling out a credit application, always be honest. Never withhold information. The purpose of credit information is to help make sure that you do not get too deeply in debt. Getting deeply in debt could cause you financial worry and losses. It could also ruin your credit rating.

PROTECTING YOUR CREDIT RATING

A *credit rating* is what businesses think of your ability and your willingness to pay back a debt. A person with a high credit rating is called a *good credit risk.* A person with a low credit rating is considered to be a *poor credit risk*. A poor credit risk will usually have trouble getting credit.

Your credit rating starts the very first time you use credit. It stays with you throughout your life. Remember, you make your credit rating. A good rating is one of the most important things you can have. Protect it by paying your bills on time. If you cannot make a payment on time, tell your creditor about it right away.

KEEPING CREDIT RECORDS

There are more than 2,000 credit bureaus in the United States. A *credit bureau* is a business that keeps records on consumers who use credit. These records include personal information taken from the credit applications. They also show how you have used the credit extended to you by businesses and banks.

Most credit bureau information comes from the very businesses that give you credit. Banks, newspapers, and neighbors are also good sources of information. Once a person has a credit record, it can be seen by any business firm that is a member of the local credit bureau.

Credit bureaus can exchange information with one another quickly. Since they are located all over the United States, your credit rating follows you when you move. If you are a good risk, this works to your advantage. You can transfer your credit rating to a new town. By transferring your rating, you can quickly establish credit in the new town.

THE FAIR CREDIT REPORTING ACT

Credit bureaus can be helpful to both consumers and businesses. You can get credit quicker because businesses can easily check with credit bureaus to find out about you. Most businesses cannot afford the time or the money to check every person who applies for credit. By providing this information, credit bureaus save businesses money.

The information collected by credit bureaus is very personal. Consumers must be sure that it is used properly and that the information is accurate and up to date.

To make certain that credit information is not misused, Congress passed the *Fair Credit Reporting Act.* This act went into effect in 1971. It is important to understand it because the act protects you. Some of the important features of the act are

1. Credit information cannot be given to anyone unless it is to be used in connection with a business transaction.
2. If you request it, you must be told about all the information in your file.
3. If you request them, you have a right to know the sources of the information in your file.
4. Credit bureaus must tell you who has requested a credit report on you during the last six months.

Also, if you think your credit file is not correct, you can ask that it be reviewed. If mistakes are found, they must be corrected. This is very important protection for you. Incorrect information can damage your credit rating.

SOME ADVANTAGES OF CONSUMER CREDIT

One major advantage of using consumer credit is that you can buy things when they are needed. You do not have to wait. However, the things must be paid for out of future income.

A SHOPPING CONVENIENCE

Most shoppers use credit when buying certain kinds of goods and services. Things that are bought often are well suited for credit shopping.

People who have charge accounts do not have to carry around large amounts of cash. Also, there are usually fewer bills to pay. For example, by using a BankAmericard, John Malone had only one bill to pay at the end of the month. If he had not used credit, John would have had to pay 26 separate bills.

Credit can also make shopping easier in other ways. Credit customers often get advance notices of sales, they can order things by telephone, and they can buy goods on approval. Also, credit customers can usually return purchases easier than noncredit customers can.

HELP IN FINANCIAL EMERGENCIES

Financial problems can happen at any time. A child can be hurt in an accident, a family may lose its income because the father or mother cannot work, or there may be an unexpected death in the family. When such a situation happens, many families face a financial emergency. They do not have enough money saved to pay for everyday expenses. Both cash credit and sales credit can be helpful in a financial emergency. Money can be borrowed to pay for the rent and other bills. Sales credit can be used to buy other items the family must have.

SAVING MONEY

The proper use of credit can save you money. This is because you can take advantage of sales. Suppose Scott's Bike Shop usually sells a ten-speed bike for $95. This week the bike is on sale for $75. Jerry Davis wants the bike but has saved only $63. In three more weeks he will have earned enough money to buy it. By using credit, Jerry can save $20 and buy the bike now.

SOME PROBLEMS WITH CONSUMER CREDIT

It is important to remember that anytime you use credit, you should ask yourself this question: "Do I really need what I am buying?" Using too much credit can cause serious problems.

CONSUMERS MAY OVERBUY

The most serious problem with credit is that it is too easy to use. It is often hard to say no when told to buy now and pay later. By not saying no, consumers may buy things that they don't need or buy things that are more expensive than they can really afford.

For example, Doug Johnson is usually a smart shopper. He almost always shops with cash. Recently he wanted to buy a pair of shoes and charge them on a credit card. He planned on spending about $25 but ended up buying a pair of shoes that cost $43.95. Had he used cash, Doug probably would have spent only the $25 he had planned on. Remember, credit is just a substitute for cash. It has to be paid back.

FUTURE INCOME IS TIED UP

Credit must be paid back with future income—money you have not yet earned. Some of your future income may already be tied up for other things. You must be careful not to get yourself too deeply in debt.

CREDIT COSTS MONEY

Earlier in this book you read that services cost money. Providing credit is a service. Thus, credit is a service you must pay for. Items bought on credit sometimes cost more than those bought with cash. Suppose a car can be bought for $4,000 cash. If installment credit is used to pay for the car, the cost goes up to $4,300. The difference of $300 between the two prices is the cost of credit.

SOME GUIDES TO USING CONSUMER CREDIT

It is impossible to tell every shopper exactly how to use credit. Every shopper is different. However, there are some basic guides that all consumers should follow when using credit. These include

1. Buying goods and services only when they are needed
2. Buying things that will last longer than the time it takes to pay for them (An example of this is an automobile.)
3. Knowing how much money you will have to spend (Never buy anything on credit hoping that you will make enough money later in the year to pay for it.)
4. Making as large a down payment as possible (This helps keep credit costs down and saves you money.)
5. Reading all credit contracts and understanding them before signing them (Never rush into a credit agreement.)
6. Making credit payments on time
7. Dealing only with reputable, honest businesses.

Following these guidelines does not mean you will not get into credit difficulties. If problems develop, talk to the businessperson to whom you are in debt. Most businesspeople are fair and want to keep you as a customer.

SUMMARY

The use of consumer credit is based on the trust businesspeople have in you. They trust you to pay for goods, services, or money at a future date. When deciding if you are worthy of credit, businesspeople consider three things: character, capital, and capacity.

When you use credit, you build a credit rating. Next to money, a good credit rating is one of your most important assets. You should work to protect it. Information on how you use credit is kept by a credit bureau. There are credit bureaus in more than 2,000 cities in the United States.

There are a number of advantages to using credit. These advantages include (1) the use of goods and services immediately, (2) easier shopping, (3) help for financial emergencies, and (4) saving money by taking advantage of sales.

There are also some problems when using credit. For example, (1) consumers may overbuy, (2) future income may be tied up, and (3) the use of credit may be costly. To avoid these problems, many businesses provide guidelines for using credit. These guidelines suggest that you buy only what is needed and that you deal with honest businesspeople.

REVIEW USING CREDIT

I. REVIEW OF TERMS

Which words complete the statements below?

credit application	capacity
trust	overbuying
capital	shopping convenience
credit bureau	credit rating
costs	character

1. A _____ keeps records on people who use credit.
2. Credit is based on _____.
3. To get credit, you usually have to fill out a _____.
4. _____ refers to your ability to make enough money to pay back a debt.
5. A serious problem when using consumer credit is _____.
6. Credit can be a _____.
7. _____ refers to the money and property you own.
8. Your _____ is what businesspeople think of your ability to repay a debt.

9. _____ is determined by your general reputation in the community.
10. The use of credit usually _____ money.

II. REVIEW OF MAIN POINTS
1. What are the Three C's of Credit?
2. Explain what each of the Three C's of Credit means.
3. List five questions that might be found on a credit application.
4. What is your credit rating?
5. Why is it important to protect your credit rating?
6. What is a credit bureau? How does it help businesses?
7. List four things the Fair Credit Reporting Act does for consumers.
8. Explain the advantages of using credit.
9. What are some problems with using consumer credit?
10. What is the purpose of the guides for using consumer credit?

III. USING CREDIT: CONCEPTS
1. Read the following sentences and answer the questions below:
   a. Bob Spedding always pays his bills on time.
   b. Bob has been a dentist in Gary, Indiana, for 15 years.
   c. Bob and Ann have been married for 20 years.
   d. Except for the washing machine, the Speddings always have paid cash for major household items.
   e. The Speddings are buying their home in Gary and have $4,000 in savings.
   f. The Speddings have two more car payments to make. Then they will have no more installment loans to pay, except on their home.

   Dr. Spedding is thinking about applying for a bank credit card. Which facts above refer to his capital, character, and capacity? Explain your answer.

2. Look at the following list. Tell which items are usually sold on credit and which are normally bought with cash. Explain your answers.

a.	new automobile	**f.**	golf balls
b.	newspaper	**g.**	color television set
c.	gas stove	**h.**	movie tickets
d.	house	**i.**	living room sofa
e.	groceries	**j.**	stereo tape deck

3. Some businesses have claimed that they can make more on the credit extended on an item than on the sale of the item itself. Do you think this is possible? Explain your answer.

4. Explain how the Marshall family, with $10,000 income, can be considered a better credit risk than the O'Neals, with a $45,000 income.

IV. USING CREDIT: EXERCISES

1. Visit a furniture store and ask the manager what is considered important when granting credit to a customer. Compare this answer with the information found in the beginning of this chapter. Then write a short report for the class.

2. Sammy Locastro earns $235 a week. The following amounts are spent weekly to support his wife and two children: food, $65; rent, $40; utilities, $25; personal items and clothes, $20; monthly installment credit, $40; medical, $10; and other items, $15. They have $200 in a savings account. Sammy wants the family to buy a new color television set that costs $495. His wife says they cannot afford it. Sammy says he can get it on credit and only have to pay $7.50 a week. With whom do you agree? Support your answer.

3. Examine the credit card application in Figure 23–1 closely. In a short report, show which questions refer to the applicant's character, capital, and capacity.

4. Make a visit to the local credit bureau and find out how it carries out a consumer credit investigation. Make sure you know what questions are asked during the investigation.

5. It has been said that consumer credit is very important to the nation's economy. Review a daily newspaper and count the number of ads that mention consumer credit. What types of businesses stress using credit the most?

24

CASH CREDIT SOURCES AND COSTS

All credit can be classified as either sales credit or cash credit. Sales credit is used when goods and services are sold. Stores are a major source of sales credit. They include furniture stores, drugstores, hardware stores, and department stores. To extend credit, these stores use many types of noninstallment and installment credit plans.

If sales credit is extended by so many stores, why do people use cash credit? There are several reasons. First, some stores do not give credit. They sell only for cash. Even if retailers do give credit, they may not want to give it to a particular customer. They may not know the customer, or they may think the customer cannot pay them back. Finally, sales credit often turns out to be more expensive than cash credit.

Using cash credit means that consumers are borrowing money. There are several different sources of this type of credit. This chapter dis-

cusses the different sources of cash credit. It covers such issues as how to get cash credit, how the cost of cash credit varies, and how credit costs are determined.

CASH CREDIT SOURCES

Using cash credit is the same as borrowing money. Money can be borrowed from many sources, including banks, savings and loan associations, consumer finance companies, credit unions, life insurance companies, and pawnbrokers. Each of these sources gives different types of cash loans for different purposes.

BANKS

Banks are the largest source of cash credit in the United States. They make loans for a variety of reasons. If a family's wage earner gets sick, many banks will make a loan of several hundred dollars if the borrower is a good credit risk. Banks also make loans for such things as cars, washing machines, and color television sets.

The cost of a bank loan is usually lower than the cost of a loan from any other source. Because they charge lower rates, banks usually do not like to make small loans. Some banks will not make a loan for less than $500. Also, you must have a good credit rating to get a bank loan.

SAVINGS AND LOAN ASSOCIATIONS

A *savings and loan association* is a business that helps people buy or build homes. Most people cannot afford to pay cash for a home. They need a loan. Such loans are paid back over a period of 20 to 30 years. To get a loan, consumers must have a good credit rating. Also, they must have some cash to make a down payment on the house. The down payment can vary between 5 percent and 25 percent of the price of the house and land.

Savings and loan associations make loans for a variety of reasons, including home improvements and education. However, not all states allow the same kinds of loans to be given, so you should check to see what is possible in your own state.

Most savings and loan associations make *passbook loans.* This is like borrowing money from yourself. If you have a savings account, you can usually borrow up to the amount you have in the account. John Johnson, for example, has $750 in his savings account at First Federal Savings and Loan. He can, therefore, borrow up to $750 on a passbook loan. These loans carry a low interest rate and are useful when money is needed for a short period of time. However, you cannot take any money out of your savings account until the loan is paid back.

CONSUMER FINANCE COMPANIES

The main purpose of consumer finance companies is to make cash loans. These businesses are also called *small-loan companies* and *personal finance companies.* They encourage people to take out small loans, usually not over $1,000. However, some states let consumer finance companies make loans as large as $5,000.

It is fairly easy to get loans from consumer finance companies. Generally, finance companies will give loans to people whose credit ratings are so low that banks will not give them loans. Because they take greater risks, finance companies charge more for loans. Depending on where the company is located and the specific conditions of the loans, the interest rate on these loans may be more than 30 percent a year.

CREDIT UNIONS

A *credit union* is a loan-giving business owned by many people with a common interest. Examples of organizations that have credit unions are business firms, hospitals, universities, and governments.

People who put money in credit unions are called *members.* Only members can receive loans. It is usually easy to borrow money from a credit

pay less when you borrow AT your Credit Union

Because credit unions are nonprofit organizations created to serve their members, it is often easier and cheaper to borrow money from them than from a bank.

union. They want to help their members, and they already know something about their members' financial backgrounds.

A credit union is also a savings organization. The money that is loaned to a member comes from the members' savings. The cost of a credit loan may be lower than that of a bank loan. This is because credit unions are nonprofit organizations in business to serve their members.

LIFE INSURANCE COMPANIES

Many families have life insurance policies. Often they overlook these policies as a source of cash credit. The interest rate on a loan from an insurance company is usually between 5 and 6 percent a year. This is a bargain when compared to the interest rates of other organizations.

The main advantages of insurance loans are (1) they cost less than most loans, (2) they are easy to get, and (3) there is not a strict time set for paying back the loans. The last advantage certainly helps when it is hard to make regular payments. This can also be a disadvantage. If the loan is not paid back regularly, the loan cost goes up. This happens because you must pay interest until the loan is repaid. Also, the value of the insurance policy is lowered by the amount of the loan. For example, Stuart Cohen obtained a $1,500 loan on his $10,000 life insurance policy. If he dies before the loan is paid back, the policy will only be worth $8,500.

Most loans from insurance companies can be obtained quickly. All the borrowers have to do is fill out a loan form. When the form is filled out and returned, the loan is usually made.

PAWNBROKERS

Pawnbrokers are not a common source for consumer loans, particularly large loans. The two major features of loans made by pawnbrokers are (1) they are easy to get, and (2) they are very expensive. Most of the loans are small, often only $10 to $25.

Here is how they work. You leave a valuable item—such as a $100 watch —with the pawnbroker. The pawnbroker gives you a small loan. If you

It is not a good idea to borrow money from a pawnbroker or a loan shark.

pay back the loan with interest, you get the watch back. If you do not pay on time, the pawnbroker can sell your watch. Pawnbrokers should be used only if you have no other choices. Even then, you should seriously consider not getting a loan at all.

LOAN SHARKS: PEOPLE TO AVOID

All honest loan companies have state licenses. *Loan sharks* are people who do not have licenses. They cannot get licenses because they charge interest rates higher than the law permits. In other words, loan sharking is illegal. Under the Consumer Credit Protection Act, loan sharking is a federal crime.

Why do people deal with loan sharks? Some people are poor credit risks who need money quickly. Loan sharks charge such high interest rates, often as much as several hundred percent a year, that most people

"You have no idea how tight money is. The best we can do is let you have it at two-and-a-half per cent."

have a lot of trouble repaying their loans. Sometimes it is hard just paying the interest charges. Never borrow money from loan sharks.

BORROWING MONEY

Most lenders will ask you to give a written promise saying that you will pay back the loan by a certain date. This is called a *promissory note*. An example of a promissory note is shown in Figure 24-1. The note for $1,000 was signed by Mike Garcia on July 9, 1975. It is payable to Harry Rosenthal one year later. The interest rate is 7 percent.

FIGURE 24-1

$ _1,000.00_____.   New York July 9 19 75

One year _ _ _ _ _ _ _ _ _after date _I_ promise to pay to

the order of_ Harry Rosenthal_____

One Thousand and 00/100 _ _ _ _ _ _ _ _ _ _ _Dollars

at_ The Harris National Bank_____

Value received, with interest at 7%

No. _103__ Due _July 9, 1976___   ___Mike Garcia_____

AD 41

If you have a good credit rating, you can often borrow money by signing an agreement or contract. This is called a *signature loan.* A lender who trusts you and thinks well of your character may lend thousands of dollars to you this way. You must have an excellent credit rating, however, because the lender has only your promise to repay the loan.

Most borrowers, however, have to *secure* a loan. Different types of property (a house or land), stocks and bonds, jewelry, or a car may be used as security. The items used to secure a loan are called *collateral.* If the loan is not paid back, the collateral can be sold by the lender. Loans secured by collateral often cost less than unsecured loans because there is less risk.

CREDIT COSTS

Credit is usually not free. You pay for it. The reason credit costs is that you are using other people's money. There are other reasons why credit is not free. For example, lenders must get the money to loan. The cost you pay for a loan is related to what the lenders have to pay to the people whose money they are lending. For example, a bank has to pay interest on the money it borrows from the Federal Reserve Bank.

Other lender costs include interviewing loan customers, keeping records, and collecting loans. However, credit costs are not always the same. Different lenders charge different amounts for credit.

There are several specific reasons why credit costs vary. One is the *risk* involved. Companies that loan money to high risk borrowers charge higher rates. A *high risk borrower* is one who is more likely not to repay a loan. These companies, therefore, have higher losses because many of their customers do not repay the loans.

A second factor is the *loan size.* It costs about the same for many credit operations no matter what the loan size is. For example, costs are about the same for checking a credit application, collecting the loan, operating the loan office, and keeping the books. Suppose all of these costs total $75 for a single loan. On a $500 loan they represent a 15 percent cost. However, on a $1,500 loan the same costs fall to 5 percent.

The type of *repayment plan* is another important cost factor. It makes a difference if the credit is paid back on a noninstallment or installment plan. The size of the payment does not matter. It is the number of payments that makes a difference. Suppose a $600 loan is paid back in one payment. If the same loan is repaid in 12 installments, the collection cost is higher.

The cost of a loan is also affected by *state laws.* The laws regulating loan charges vary from one state to the next. Some states permit higher interest rates and loan charges than others. You should be aware of what your state permits before trying to get a loan.

FIGURING OUT THE COST OF A LOAN

Because loan costs vary, you should learn how to figure out the costs mathematically. It is not always simple to compare credit costs, but it is definitely to your advantage to know how.

Lenders are required by the federal *Consumer Protection Act* (Truth in Lending Law) to tell you the credit charges before granting you a loan. They must tell you how much the loan will cost in terms of (1) the dollar amount and (2) the yearly percentage rate. The *dollar amount* tells you how much you are paying for the credit. The *yearly percentage rate* is the cost of the credit in percentage terms.

Knowing the loan cost in dollar and percentage amounts helps you in two ways: (1) you can tell if you can afford the credit, and (2) you can tell who is making the best credit terms available to you.

There are several ways lenders can figure out the cost of a loan. Because of this, you may find it hard to compare the loan costs among different lenders.

To be compared, interest rates must be converted to a *true rate,* or yearly percentage rate. The yearly percentage rate is the cost of the loan divided by the average amount of credit in use during the life of the loan.

The easiest way to figure the yearly percentage rate is to use the following formula:

$$R = \frac{2MC}{P(N+1)}$$

R = yearly percentage rate
M = number of payment periods in one year
C = total loan cost (interest) in dollars
P = the amount of the loan
N = total number of payments to be made

This is called the *constant ratio method* of figuring the yearly percentage rate. This method provides a reasonable yearly percentage rate only when the loan is repaid on schedule.

Suppose Pete Doyle borrows $3,000 from a bank for one year. Pete also agrees to pay back the loan in one payment at a yearly interest rate of 8 percent. This means his interest charges will be $240. Using the above formula, the true yearly percentage rate is 8 percent.

(PLAN 1)

M = 1

C = $240

P = $3,000

N = 1

$$R = \frac{2 \times 1 \times 240}{3,000\ (1+1)}$$

$$R = \frac{480}{6,000}$$

$$R = 8\%$$

Now suppose Pete agrees to repay the loan in 12 equal installments rather than all at once. Using the same formula, the yearly percentage rate is 14.8 percent.

(PLAN 2)

M = 12

C = $240

P = $3,000

N = 12

$$R = \frac{2 \times 12 \times 240}{3,000\ (12+1)}$$

$$R = \frac{5760}{39,000}$$

$$R = 14.8\%$$

Why does Plan 1 cost 8 percent a year, while Plan 2 costs 14.8 percent? The loan size, the interest rate, and the loan cost are the same in both cases. (See Table 24–1.) The answer to the question is that the number of repayments is different. By repaying the loan in one payment, Pete has full use of the loan ($3,000) for one year. But, if he pays it back in 12 installments, this is no longer true. His first payment includes a twelfth of the loan cost plus a twelfth of the loan. By repaying some of the loan each month, he does not have the use of the full $3,000 for the entire year. This means that the average amount of credit *in use* for Plan 2 is less than for Plan 1.

TABLE 24–1
COMPARING PETE DOYLE'S LOAN COSTS

Item	Plan 1	Plan 2
Loan size	$3,000	$3,000
Interest rate	8%	8%
Loan cost	$ 240	$ 240
Loan period	1 year	1 year
Payments	1	12
Yearly percentage rate	8%	14.8%

SHOPPING FOR CREDIT

No matter what you buy, it pays to be a smart shopper. The same holds true when you buy credit. After all, credit is a service for which you must pay.

Once you decide to use consumer credit, shop around. You will find that lenders have different (1) repayment terms, (2) credit costs, and (3) yearly percentage rates.

The repayment terms of a loan can be very important. Your budget may not be able to stand large monthly payments. You may want to repay the loan over a long period of time, say two years. You may choose to use this method of repayment even though the longer repayment period means the loan will cost you more money.

Even if the yearly percentage rates are the same, you may consider one type of loan to be better for you than another. For example, Table 24–2 shows how time can affect the cost of a loan and the size of the monthly payment. As the time period grows longer, two things happen. First, the size of the monthly payment decreases. Second, the total cost of the loan increases. For example, a one-year $360 loan costs $34 with monthly payments of $32.83. Extending the same loan to two years lowers the monthly payment to $17.73 but raises the total loan cost to $65.62.

TABLE 24-2 HOW TIME AFFECTS A CONSUMER LOAN			
Item	Repayment Time 12 Months	Repayment Time 18 Months	Repayment Time 24 Months
Loan size	$360.00	$360.00	$360.00
Loan costs	34.00	49.87	65.62
Amount repaid	394.00	409.87	425.62
Monthly payment size	32.83	22.77	17.73
Yearly percentage rate	17.5%	17.5%	17.5%

(Source: *It's Your Credit, Manage It Wisely*, Household Finance Corp.)

SUMMARY

The main sources of sales credit are the many stores in the United States. When you buy goods or services, the stores give credit directly to you. However, it is often necessary for people to obtain cash credit; that is, to borrow money. Sources of cash credit include banks, savings and loan associations, credit unions, life insurance companies, and consumer finance companies.

When you borrow money, you always have to sign a statement in which you promise to repay the loan. This statement is called a promissory note. If you have to secure a loan, you put up collateral. Collateral can be a home, stocks, bonds, or other things of value that you own.

All loans do not cost the same amount of money. Credit costs vary for several reasons. These reasons include risk, loan size, the repayment plan, and state laws.

Because credit costs vary, you should know how to figure out loan costs mathematically. One way is to calculate the yearly percentage rate of the loan. This tells you the loan's true interest rate. The important thing to remember is to shop for credit. Look at several different credit sources. Shopping around may save you money.

I. REVIEW OF TERMS

Which words complete the sentences below?

loan shark   promissory note
collateral   yearly percentage rate
constant ratio   secured
credit union   risk

1. The _____ is the cost of the credit in percentage terms.
2. Things that are used to secure a loan are called _____.
3. A _____ is a financial business owned by many people.
4. A loan backed by collateral is called a _____ loan.
5. One thing that affects the cost of a loan is _____.
6. Giving your written word to repay a loan is called signing a

    _____ .
7. The _____ method is one way to figure the yearly percentage rate of a loan.
8. A _____ is a person who does not have a license to make loans.

II. REVIEW OF MAIN POINTS

1. What are five sources of sales credit?
2. Name five sources of cash credit.
3. What source of cash credit is usually the least costly? Why?
4. Why do consumer finance companies often charge more for loans than banks do?
5. What are three advantages to borrowing from a life insurance company?
6. Why should you never borrow money from a loan shark?
7. What is a signature loan?
8. What is collateral? Give three examples.
9. Give three reasons why credit costs vary. Explain how they affect loan costs.

10. What two things must a lender tell you before making you a loan? What information do these things give you?
11. Explain the term *yearly percentage rate*.
12. Why is it important to shop around for credit?

III. CASH CREDIT SOURCES AND COSTS: CONCEPTS

1. Time can affect a loan in two ways. The size of the monthly payment changes, and the total cost of the loan changes. Explain the nature of these changes in detail.
2. Explain why the number of payments used to repay a loan can affect the true interest rate.
3. Does the yearly percentage rate help you to decide whether or not you can afford a loan? Why? What is the best way to find out whether or not you can afford a loan?
4. The Third National Bank agreed to lend Frank Florczak $2,000 at two different interest rates. If the loan was secured with Gulf Oil stock, the rate would be 6 percent. An unsecured loan would require an interest rate of 8.5 percent. Explain why the secured loan carried a lower interest rate. What is a disadvantage of using stock to secure a loan?
5. Dick Sutton went to the Union Planters National Bank to borrow the money he needed for a new car. The lending officer wanted to see the Sutton family budget before making a loan. Why do you think the officer asked to see the budget?
6. How can a person's credit rating affect the cost and source of a loan he or she might want to get?

IV. CASH CREDIT SOURCES AND COSTS: EXERCISES

1. Wimberly Royster had to borrow $800 to repair some equipment on his farm. He visited a consumer finance company and a local bank. At the finance company, he could borrow the $800 by signing a note to repay the loan in 12 equal installments of $73.33 each. At the bank, Wimberly could get the loan by signing a note to repay $856 in 12 equal installments.
   a. What is the cost of the loan at the finance company?
   b. What is the true interest rate at the finance company?

c. What is the loan cost at the bank?

d. What is the true interest rate at the bank?

e. Why do you think there is a difference between the rates?

2. Rosemary Carlson recently checked the cost of loans at different sources. She found the following rates to be in effect: (1) banks, 7.5 percent a year; (2) consumer finance companies, 2 percent a month; and (3) credit unions, 1 percent a month. (Monthly rates can be converted to annual rates by multiplying the monthly rate by 12.)

   a. Which is the least expensive source of credit? Which is the most expensive?

   b. Explain why the company that charges the most expensive interest rate can stay in business.

3. Go to a local consumer finance company and meet the manager.

   a. Ask the manager to explain why the finance company charges higher interest rates than a bank.

   b. Find out if the finance company would give the same interest rate as a bank if the customer had a good credit rating.

   c. Compare the manager's answers to what you learned in this chapter. Report the manager's answers to the class.

4. The following table was recently used by a consumer finance company in a local advertisement. Study it closely and answer the questions below:

Amount Financed	Monthly Payment	Total of Payments	Number of Months	Yearly Percentage Rate
$2,500	$ 73.17	$3,512.16	48	—
3,500	—	5,424.60	60	21.63
5,500	124.41	7,464.60	—	14.05
7,500	169.41	10,164.60	60	13.98

   a. What is the yearly percentage rate of the $2,500 loan?

   b. What is the cost for the $7,500 loan?

   c. Figure out the monthly payment for the $3,500 loan.

   d. Tell how many months a borrower has to repay the $5,500 loan.

Unit VII
Investing Money

Investing in stocks, bonds, mutual funds, and real estate is not difficult once you learn some basic principles and terms. Any person who can afford the money can become an investor. The important thing for you to consider is whether you can actually afford to use your money for investments.

To help you decide whether or not you can afford to invest, consider your answers to the following questions:

1. Could I still pay for living expenses, such as food, clothing, education, housing, and recreation?
2. Would I have enough ready cash to meet emergencies, such as an illness or major car repairs?
3. Do I have enough insurance protection for me and my family?
4. Am I ready to spend time thinking about my investment decisions?

If you can answer yes to all of these questions, then you can start thinking about investments. This unit will give you an idea of some investment possibilities.

The first chapter in this unit (Chapter 25) deals with investing money in the stock market, especially common and preferred stock investments. To give you a better understanding of how to buy and sell stocks, you will learn about the New York Stock Exchange and how it operates. Chapter 25 also examines the work of the stockbroker.

Chapter 26 explains how bonds are used and compares stocks with bonds. These comparisons are not meant to promote one type of investment over the other. They are made to show you the difference between the two types of investments.

In Chapter 27, two main subject areas are covered—investment clubs and mutual funds. The similarities between investment clubs and mutual funds are explained. Other topics covered are the different types of mutual funds, how to decide in which mutual funds to invest, and the risks you take when you buy mutual funds.

UNIT PREVIEW

Chapter 28 examines the single family home as an investment. You will study such crucial issues as why people own houses and how much they should invest in houses. Other real estate investments will also be discussed. Some of the advantages and disadvantages are outlined.

The information in the four chapters of Unit VII will show you why people want to invest their extra dollars. Millions of people invest their extra dollars because they would like to make more money. Some succeed and do make more money. Others, however, lose not only their extra dollars but much more. The best advice that can be given to a prospective investor is to be careful. Always try to get professional help when possible before deciding on what type of investment to make and how much money to invest.

AS YOU STUDY THIS UNIT YOU WILL BE ENGAGED IN

* INTERPRETING a financial page listing of daily transactions on the New York Stock Exchange

* EVALUATING the stockbroker's role in buying and selling stocks

* IDENTIFYING the features of bonds as compared and contrasted with those of stocks

* DETERMINING the advantages and disadvantages of an investment club

* DISTINGUISHING between mutual funds and stocks, and isolating the advantages and disadvantages of each

* ANALYZING the advantages and disadvantages of investing in real estate.

A FOCUS FOR YOUR STUDY

25 INVESTING IN STOCKS

Many people have money left over after they have paid such expenses as rent, food, clothing, education, entertainment, and charity. This extra money gives a family or a person a chance to invest. When a person *invests* he or she is putting money into stocks, bonds, mutual funds, real estate, a particular business, or other areas, for the purpose of making more money.

There are many investment opportunities available. A person can buy ownership in a company and become a part-owner. A person can lend money to a corporation or government and receive in return, at regular intervals, a certain amount of interest money. These are only two of the many investments that a person with extra money can make.

If you are interested in investing your extra money you should first answer the following questions:

1. Will I still be able to feed, clothe, and shelter me and my family?
2. Will I still have enough ready cash to meet emergencies?
3. Do I have enough insurance to protect those who depend upon me?

If these basic questions can be answered yes, then you should probably think about investing your extra money.

One possible investment you can make is buying stocks and thus becoming part-owner of a corporation. There are about 31 million people in the United States who own a part of business corporations. These corporations need money in order to expand. They need money to buy more factories and machinery, hire more people, and work on such environmental improvements as cleaner air and water.

INFORMING THE PUBLIC

After receiving its incorporation papers, a corporation writes a special pamphlet called a *prospectus.* The prospectus describes, among other things, the future goals of the company, such as expected company size in five years. It also tells who the directors of the company will be, what the money raised by selling stocks will be used for, and how many shares, or parts of ownership, will be sold to investors. Prospectuses can be obtained from the company or from a brokerage house.

If the dollar amount of the shares to be offered to the public is more than $300,000, the *Securities and Exchange Commission* (S.E.C.) must approve certain features of the prospectus. The S.E.C. is an agency of the Federal Government. It oversees the sales of stock to investors.

Thus, the first step for anyone thinking about buying stock in a company should be to study the prospectus. Because the S.E.C. has approved a prospectus does not necessarily mean that you should invest your money in that particular company. Approval means only that important facts about the company have been made public. It also means that the company has met the requirements of the S.E.C.

KINDS OF STOCK

A share of stock represents a share of ownership in a corporation. If you were to buy stock in the International Business Machines Corporation (IBM) you would become a part-owner of IBM. There are many different kinds of stocks available. Two of the most important types of stock are called *common* and *preferred.*

When you buy a share of common stock you receive a special piece of paper called a *stock certificate.* This certificate shows that a share of stock is registered in your name (or your broker's name) in the books kept by the corporation.

For example, assume that Danny Michael buys one share of common stock from IBM. He pays $350 for it. Danny then becomes one of the thousands of owners of this corporation. As a *shareholder,* Danny has a right to vote for the company's board of directors. The board of directors determines how much of the profits will be used as dividend payments.

A *dividend* is a share of the profit you can receive when you own preferred or common stock. The payment of dividends increases the value of the stock. If a company regularly pays good dividends, it is only natural that many people will want to invest their money in this company. As stated in an earlier chapter, people who invest their money in corporations are liable only for the amount of money they invest. Danny,

This dividend notice was published in the *Wall Street Journal* as general information for the public.

DIVIDEND NOTICE

A quarterly dividend of 38¢ per share has been declared on the common stock outstanding, payable July 15, 1974 to stockholders of record June 28, 1974.

The regular quarterly dividends have been declared on the 9.76%, the 7.95%, the 7.88% and the 8.20% series cumulative preferred stock. Preferred dividends are payable July 15, 1974 to stockholders of record as of the close of business June 28, 1974.

PORTLAND GENERAL (PGE) **ELECTRIC COMPANY**
PORTLAND, OREGON 97205

therefore, is liable only for his $350 investment; that is, if the company fails, he can lose only his $350, not his personal property. This is one example of *limited liability.*

PREFERRED STOCK

Preferred stock entitles its owners to certain special treatment. This usually means that the owners of preferred stock would receive their dividends before the common-stock owners. If a corporation went out of business and the equipment and inventory were sold, the preferred stockholders would get back the value of their investments before the common stockholders. For example, last year George Banks bought one share of preferred stock for $26 and one share of common stock for $18. Today the preferred stock is selling for $14 and the common stock for $6. The company has decided to go out of business and sell its equipment and inventory. The money it gets from this sale will be used to pay back completely the preferred stockholders. What is left over will go to the common stockholders.

THE STOCK MARKET

Wall Street in New York City is the location of the largest and most famous stock exchange in the world—the New York Stock Exchange. About 75 percent of all stock sales in the country take place in this Exchange, which was founded in 1792.

There are about 1,100 corporations who list their stock in the New York Stock Exchange. About 90 percent of these companies pay dividends every year. These corporations are the major companies in the United States.

A SEAT ON THE EXCHANGE

Membership in the New York Stock Exchange is called a *seat.* This term goes back to the time when the members remained seated while the president of the Exchange called out the list of stocks that were for sale. Today the sellers and buyers of stocks scurry about the floor of the Exchange buying and selling stocks for their customers.

The membership of the New York Exchange is limited to 1,366. Anyone who wants a seat must buy it from someone who already owns one. These seats have been sold for as much as $625,000 and for as little as $17,000. Each seat is owned by an individual. Usually, however, these individuals are members of firms that buy and sell stocks for their customers.

THE PRICE AND SALE OF STOCKS

Buying and selling stocks on the New York Stock Exchange is accomplished by means of the *auction method.* Buyers and sellers walk around the Stock Exchange shouting the prices of different stocks and what they are willing to pay for them. One member may offer stock of a company at a certain price and someone else may bid for the stock at a different price. When the buyer and seller agree on a price, a sale is made. These people who buy and sell stocks for their customers are called *brokers.*

The current prices of the more popular stocks are listed in most daily newspapers. One of the best known places to find stock listings is in the *Wall Street Journal,* a daily newspaper.

FIGURE 25-1

THE WALL STREET JOURNAL,
Thursday, June 12, 1975

American Exchange Options Quotations

Wednesday, June 11, 1975

Closing prices of all options. Sales unit is 100 shares Security description includes exercise price.

	– Jul –		– Oct –		– Jan –		Stock
Option & price	Vol.	Last	Vol.	Last	Vol.	Last	Close
Aetna .. 20	a	a	7	8¼	a	a	27
Aetna .. 25	13	3⅛	82	4⅝	3	5⅜	27
Aetna .. 30	b	b	14	1⅞	19	2⅞	27
Am Cya 20	15	7	a	a	b	b	26½
Am Cya 25	33	2⅜	21	3½	18	5	26½
Am Cya 30	162	1 9-16	126	1⅝	39	2⅜	26½
Am Hom 30	21	10¾	3	11⅞	b	b	41
Am Hom 35	31	6⅜	24	7⅜	1	8⅝	41
Am Hom 40	223	2⅜	69	3⅞	21	5	41
Am Hom 45	b	b	32	1¾	a	a	41
Beat F 25	50	⅞	8	1 15-16	25	2⅞	23¾
Burrgh ..60	a	a	2	41	b	b	99⅛
Burrgh 70	3	29½	4	30½	b	b	99⅛
Burrgh ..80	10	20	a	a	b	b	99⅛
Burrgh 90	71	9⅞	5	16	3	20½	99⅛
Burrgh 100	217	3½	24	8¾	4	12	99⅛
Chase .. 30	5	4½	3	5¾	10	7	34
Chase .. 35	154	1 3-16	61	2⅝	33	3⅝	34
Chase .. 40	51	¼	34	1¼	b	b	34
Deere .. 35	34	6½	8	8¾	b	b	41
Deere .. 40	67	2⅞	29	5⅛	18	7	41
Deere .. 45	167	1	61	2¾	4	4¼	41
Dig Eq 50	12	49¼	a	a	b	b	99⅞

– 1975 –			P-E	Sales in				Net
High	Low	Stocks Div.	Ratio	100s	High	Low	Close	Chg.
14⅝	9½	SoJerIn 1.56	7	2	14¼	14¼	14¼ –	⅛
13⅛	8	Southdown	3	8	8⅝	8⅝	8⅝	......
24¼	16½	Sdwn pf1.80	...	7	18¾	18½	18½	......
14¼	9½	SoestBkg .80	8	45	12⅜	12⅛	12⅜ +	⅛
8½	5¾	SoeatPS .64r	5	3	7½	7⅜	7½ +	⅜
20¼	16¾	SoCalE 1.68	5	226	20	19⅝	19⅝	......
12¾	8¾	SouthCo 1.40	8	1671	12¼	12	12 –	⅛
28⅝	23⅝	SoInGE 2.28	7	6	28	27½	28 +	⅝
59½	41	SoNRes 1.65	9	21	55¾	55	55⅜	......
34	28⅛	SoNETI 2.84	9	11	31¼	30⅝	31 +	⅜
31⅞	25¼	Sou Pac 2.24	10	185	26½	26⅛	26⅜ +	⅜
56½	40	Sou Ry 2.12	10	256	56¾	55¾	55¾ +	½
6¼	5⅜	Sou Ry pf.50	...	1	5⅞	5⅞	5⅞ +	⅛
30	19¼	SouUGs 1.60	8	5	29¼	29	29	......
25¼	15¾	Southld .40b	14	27	25	24⅝	25 +	⅜
8⅜	4¼	SwstFor .20	5	8	7⅜	7¼	7⅜	......
18¾	12¾	SwtFI pf1.50	...	6	18¼	18	18 –	¼
11⅜	9⅜	SwstPSv .90	8	98	10⅜	10¼	10⅜	......
9⅝	5	Sparton .24a	4	17	9⅛	8⅞	9⅛ +	½
11⅜	6⅞	SperryHut 1	10	10	11	10⅞	11	......
46¾	25⅜	SperryR .76	12	822	46¼	44⅝	44⅝ –	1¼
12⅜	5⅜	Sprague El	10	36	10¼	9⅞	10 –	⅛
10¾	8⅝	Spring M .75	11	2	10⅝	10⅝	10⅝ +	⅛
19½	14¾	SquarD 1.10	12	142	17⅝	17⅛	17⅜ +	⅜
41½	24⅝	Squibb .84	18	184	38	36½	37 –	⅛
92½	40	StaleyMfg 2	6	60	81	78½	78½ +	¼
43¾	34⅞	StaleyMf wi	...	15	40½	39½	39½ +	½
23⅝	19⅝	StPoor 1.92a	...	27	22¼	22	22⅛ –	⅛
72¼	52½	StdBrands 2	16	113	70	69	69⅛ –	¾
50¼	45	StdBr pf3.50	...	z100	48	47½	47½ –	1⅛
50⅜	28¼	StBPaint .32	28	30	41⅞	41¼	41½ –	⅛
32⅝	22⅛	StdOilCal 2	5	609	31⅞	31½	31¾ +	¼
47⅛	36	StdOilInd 2	7	453	45¼	44½	44⅝ –	⅝
75¼	44½	StOilOh 1.36	21	187	71¾	70⅝	71 –	⅛
8⅛	6⅝	StdPress .40	5	1490	10⅛	7⅞	9½ +	1⅝

– 1975 –			P-E	Sales in		
High	Low	Stocks Div.	Ratio	100s	High	Lo
34	25½	USFidG 2.48	12	48	32⅞	32
17¼	12¼	USFoS 1.50e	...	8	16	15
21¼	14⅛	USGyps 1.60	12	266	16⅝	16
25¼	20	USGy pf1.80	...	2	22¾	22
7½	2⅜	US Home	...	104	6⅛	6
5	2½	US Ind .33r	...	175	4½	4
14	9¼	USLeasg .24	9	167	10⅝	9
4⅞	2½	US RltyInv	...	94	3⅜	3
12¼	7⅜	US Shoe .95	6	16	11¼	11
65⅝	38¼	US Stl 2.80	4	393	57½	56
20⅝	13¾	USTobac .90	11	31	19⅛	19
57⅞	31¼	Unit Tech 2	8	501	54⅜	53
131½	86¼	UnTech pf 8	...	13	124	123
15¾	12½	UniTel 1.08	10	377	14⅞	14
1⅞	7-16	UniTel wt	...	114	1¾	1
20⅜	16⅛	UnTI 2pf1.50	...	14	19⅛	18
9	3½	Unitrode Cp	13	287	9⅛	9
29	16⅞	UnivarCp 1	4	5	25⅞	25
39	25½	UnivLeaf 2	7	12	38¼	38
18	11¼	UOP .90	6	91	14⅜	14
53	30	Upjohn .96	18	513	43	41
17⅛	10	USLIFE .30	7	118	15⅜	14
10½	8½	UslifeF .96a	...	30	9⅝	9
20	12	USM stp1.20	4	49	19⅛	18
26¼	19⅞	USM pf2.10	...	1	25¾	25
74⅞	39½	UtahIntl 1	22	213	72⅞	70
28⅝	23⅛	UtahPL 2.36	9	44	27⅞	27
24¼	17	UV Ind 1b	3	35	22½	21
57½	50¼	UV In pf5.50	...	2	57	56
28	20½	UV In pf1.26	...	1	26⅝	26
		– V–V–V –				
12¼	6½	Varian .20	10	56	11⅜	11
4⅞	3	Vendo Co	...	108	4½	4
5½	2	Venice .20	28	30	5½	5

Figure 25–1 shows how stocks are listed every day in the *Wall Street Journal.* The listing is always for the previous day. The first two columns show the highest and the lowest prices paid for the stocks during the year. For example, the highest price paid for a share of Sperry Rand stock was $46.75, and the lowest price was $25.38. The figures just after the name of the stock show how much of a dividend is paid each year for each share. Sperry Rand is expected to pay 76 cents a share to its stockholders during the year.

The next column shows the *price-earnings ratio.* This is calculated by dividing the price of a share by the average earnings per share of the stock. For Sperry Rand, the ratio is 12 to 1. If a stock is selling for $10 a share and the earnings per share are $1, the company would have a 10-to-1 price-earnings ratio. The earnings per share are the company profits divided by the number of shares of common stock sold to date.

The column to the right of the price-earnings ratio shows the number of shares sold during the day, with the amounts listed in hundreds. Thus, 82,200 shares of Sperry Rand were sold during the day. The next three columns show the highest, the lowest, and the closing prices paid for the stock during the day. The highest amount a buyer paid for a share during the day was $46.25, and the lowest amount was $44.63. The last, or *closing,* price was $44.63. The amount in the column at the extreme right shows the difference between the final price shown and the final price of the day before. A plus sign means the stock went up in price. A minus sign means the stock went down in price.

OTHER EXCHANGES AND UNLISTED STOCKS

In addition to the New York Stock Exchange, there are other stock exchanges in the United States. The second most important exchange is the American Stock Exchange, which is located in Chicago, Illinois. Many people with seats on the New York Stock Exchange also have seats on the American Stock Exchange. Other exchanges that buy and sell stocks of local corporations are the Midwest Stock Exchange, the Philadelphia-Baltimore Stock Exchange, and the San Francisco Mining Exchange.

Brokers trade on the New York Stock Exchange.

Not all the stocks that can be bought are listed on stock exchanges. The stocks of about 15,000 other corporations—most of them smaller than the ones on the major exchanges—are traded by brokers *over the counter.* This market is one that deals with the unlisted stocks of national and local corporations. Any stockbroker can handle an over-the-counter investment for you. The broker would telephone other brokers who specialize in the particular stock you want to buy.

THE BROKER

When you decide to buy stocks you should first get in touch with a broker. Selecting a broker is like choosing a doctor, dentist, or accountant; it is best to find a broker who is qualified and trustworthy.

In Chicago, New York, Boston, Atlanta, San Francisco, or other large cities, finding a good broker is not too difficult. There are many brokerage firms in these large cities. You can visit the firms and discuss your investment plans with one of the many brokers. You can then decide whether or not the broker is trustworthy and knowledgeable. If you feel the broker is not qualified to help you make good investments, you can leave and visit other brokers or brokerage firms.

In a small town there may be no brokerage firm nearby. In that case, you can work with a broker by telephone or mail, or you can have your banker handle your investments. Most banks in small towns have some kind of working relationship with a brokerage firm in a larger city.

Many investors get the advice of friends or relatives when looking for a broker. Other sources of advice would be the Chamber of Commerce, a respected businessperson, or a certified public accountant. Although advice is important, the decision to invest is the individual's final choice to make, and it usually depends upon whether or not he or she trusts the broker. The personal relationship between the investor and the broker is very important.

OPENING AN ACCOUNT WITH A BROKER

Opening an account with a stockbroker is very simple. First, you fill out a form that requires you to list your name, address, social security number, occupation, and some personal references. Since most investments are made without money being paid immediately to the broker, the reliability of the investor to pay is important to the broker.

When your broker buys stock for you, you can pay for the stock in cash or by check. The certificate of ownership issued to you by the company may be sent directly to you or kept at the brokerage firm for safe keeping. If you prefer, the entire investment can be made by telephone. Dividends may go directly to you or to your broker, who will put the money in your account.

THE BROKER'S WORK

Brokers can do many things for their investors. They can buy or sell stock, once given specific instructions. They can give advice to their investors on how to invest their money. For example, if an investor wants to invest $1,000 in stocks, a broker can advise the investor as to which stocks have the best chance of providing the highest yearly dividends.

Some people give their brokers full authority to do what they think is best. In this case, the brokers are the people who make the final investment decisions. The brokers are told how much money the investors have to invest, and this enables the brokers to do what is best. The arrangements that are made with brokers are entirely up to the investors.

THE BROKER'S FEES

Naturally, brokers must be paid for their time, effort, and advice. The amount paid to brokers is set through the rules of various stock exchanges. The fees the brokers receive are called *commissions*. Commissions are set rates and have nothing to do with how much money the investors make or lose. The brokers are paid their commissions when investors buy stocks and again when they sell their stocks.

Investors should get professional advice from a licensed broker.

Commissions are based on the price of the stock and the number of shares that are bought or sold. Table 25-2 outlines some basic commission fees. For example, if you buy 100 shares of a stock selling at $3 a share, the price would be $300. The fee to your broker would be 2 percent of $300 ($6) plus a fixed fee of $3, or a total of $9.

If you were to buy 100 shares of stock selling at $40 a share, the total price would be $4,000. The broker would receive one-half of 1 percent of $4,000 ($20) plus a fixed fee of $19. The total commission fee would be $39. If you were to sell 100 shares of stock at $40 a share, the commission fee would be the same.

TABLE 25-2
BROKER COMMISSION FEES

Amount of Transaction	Commission Rate
Less than $100	Agreed between investor and broker
Between $100 and $399.99	2 percent plus $3 (minimum $6)
Between $400 and $2,399.99	1 percent plus $7
Between $2,400 and $4,999.99	One-half of 1 percent plus $19
$5,000 and above	One-tenth of 1 percent plus $39

THE DIFFERENT KINDS OF STOCK

The stocks listed on an exchange can be grouped in different ways by brokers and investors. One breakdown is based on the risk to the investors; that is, the amount of chance (risk) that investors take when they buy the stock. Such risk factors include the chance of the price of the stock going up or down and the chance that the investors will or will not receive dividends.

BLUE CHIP

The stocks of the largest corporations and those stocks with long, steady records of paying dividends are called *blue chip.* Shares of stock from DuPont, General Motors, and American Telephone and Telegraph (AT&T) are called blue chip.

GROWTH STOCKS

A *growth stock* is issued by corporations whose sales and earnings are growing faster than the economy and faster than the average for the industry. These corporations use their profits to expand their plants and to research and develop new products. Today, companies in such industries as chemicals, drugs, and nuclear power are good candidates for growth.

SPECULATIVE STOCKS

Speculative stocks are stocks that sell at a high price relative to their earnings—that is, the price is high compared to what the company earnings have been. A price of $1 per share of stock is high if the company has no earnings to show for its efforts.

SUMMARY

Approximately 31 million people living in the United States have bought stocks and become part-owners of corporations. They have risked their money by buying these stocks. The two major types of stocks are common and preferred.

The buying and selling of stocks is usually done by brokers who represent investors. Brokers work through one or more of the many stock exchanges. The most widely known stock exchange is the New York Stock Exchange. For representing investors, the brokers receive commission fees.

Investors have different types of stocks from which to choose. There are blue chip, growth, and speculative stocks. To get a better idea of what kinds of stock to buy, investors should get professional advice from licensed stockbrokers.

I. REVIEW OF TERMS

Which words complete the sentences below?

blue chip
New York Stock Exchange
seats
commissions

account
broker
Securities and Exchange Commission
ownership

1. A federal government agency that oversees the sales of stock to investors is the _____.
2. Approximately 75 percent of all stock sales takes place in the _____.
3. A person who buys and sells stocks for his or her customers is called a _____.
4. When you want to buy stock through a broker, you open an _____.
5. _____ are based on the price of the stock and the number of shares bought and sold.
6. DuPont stocks are called _____.
7. A stock represents a share of _____ in a corporation.
8. There are 1,366 _____ on the New York Stock Exchange.

II. REVIEW OF MAIN POINTS

1. How can a broker help in making a stock investment decision?
2. How can one get a seat on the New York Stock Exchange?
3. What is an over-the-counter stock?
4. How can you buy stocks by telephone from your home?
5. How is a stockbroker's fee calculated?
6. Why do you have to pay a commission when you sell stocks?
7. Explain what a growth stock is.
8. Why is a share of General Motors stock considered a blue chip investment?

9. How can an investor use a prospectus?
10. When you invest money in stock, why do you have only limited liability for the amount invested?

III. INVESTING IN STOCKS: CONCEPTS

1. Why is it best to use a qualified stockbroker to help you make investment decisions?
2. Are people interested in receiving cash dividends? Why?
3. Why would a person want to invest in preferred stock instead of in common stock?
4. Explain what is meant by the *high price for a stock during the year.*
5. What are the features of a preferred stock that make it different from a common stock?
6. What does having a seat on the stock exchange allow a person to do?
7. What kind of stocks are sold over the counter?

IV. INVESTING IN STOCKS: EXERCISES

1. Get a copy of a newspaper that has a listing of stocks on the New York Stock Exchange. Answer the following questions:
   a. What is the current selling price of the following stocks?

   General Motors Sperry Rand
   General Foods International Business Machines
   Ford Abbott Laboratories

   b. How many shares of these six stocks were sold during the day?
   c. What has been the high price and the low price for each stock?
2. What are the names of some of the most famous brokerage houses?
3. Look at the newspaper or the *Wall Street Journal.* Determine the common stock selling for the highest price and the one selling for the lowest price on the New York Stock Exchange.
4. By doing some library research, get the names of three blue chip, three growth, and three speculative stocks. Do not use any names that were mentioned in the chapter.
5. What are the current prices of any six preferred stocks on the New York Stock Exchange?

INVESTING IN BONDS 26

Corporations sell shares of stock to investors to raise money. These same corporations as well as governments can also raise money by borrowing. In this chapter you will find out how a corporation or government borrows money by issuing *bonds.*

A BOND

A bond is a promise made by a corporation or a government to pay the investor a certain amount of money, plus interest, at a specific time in the future. When an investor buys a bond, he or she is lending money to the corporation or government.

Let us assume that the Anne Marine Corporation wants to raise $1 million by issuing 1,000 bonds selling at $1,000 each. On each bond, it would be indicated as to how much money would be paid back to the investor at a specific date. In addition, the corporation would pay the investor interest. In this case, the Anne Marine Corporation agrees to pay back $1,000 for each bond ten years after the bonds are bought. They also agree to pay 8 percent annual interest over those ten years. Thus, if Lori McLaughlin buys a bond for $1,000, she would be paid $80 a year in interest for the next ten years. At the end of ten years, she would receive her $1,000 back from the corporation. Lori's investment of $1,000 would get her a total of $800 interest plus her original $1,000. She would get her $1,000 at the end of the tenth year on a date called the *maturity date.*

TYPES OF BONDS

To assure investors that they will get back their money and get their interest payments, a company has to *secure,* or promise to repay, the loans. In some cases, a mortgage on the company property secures the loans. Property, such as machines or buildings, is the guarantee that the investors will be repaid. This type of bond is called a *mortgage bond.*

If Lori held a mortgage bond and did not receive her $1,000 back at the end of the tenth year, she could start legal action to force the company to sell some of its property so that she could get back her $1,000. This is similar to a mortgage on a home when a bank or mortgage company lends the homeowner money. The bank or mortgage company can take over the house if the owner fails to meet the payments.

If a bond is not secured by a mortgage but is secured only by the company earnings, it is known as a *debenture bond.* In most cases, debenture bonds are only issued by well-established business firms. These firms have good earnings records and are likely to keep making profits.

FEDERAL GOVERNMENT BONDS

The United States Government sells a number of bonds. The most popular with investors is the *Series E savings bond,* which can be bought

at various prices. After two months from the time it is bought, a Series E bond can be cashed at the *issue* (original) price. After six months it can be cashed at a higher price, which would include the issue price plus interest. The money you can get for the bond increases at the end

Take Stock in America

BUY U.S. SAVINGS BONDS

of each six-month period until the date of maturity. At present, the date of maturity is five years and ten months after the date of purchase.

The difference between what you pay for the bond and what you receive at the maturity date is the interest that is earned on the investment. If Lori bought a $1,000 Series E bond for $750, she would earn $250 interest if she held it for five years and ten months.

TABLE 26-1
FEDERAL GOVERNMENT
SERIES E BOND PRICES AND VALUES
AT MATURITY DATE

Purchase Price	Maturity Value Five Years and Ten Months Later	Interest Earned
$ 18.75	$ 25	$ 6.25
37.50	50	12.50
56.25	75	19.75
75.00	100	25.00
150.00	200	50.00
375.00	500	125.00
750.00	1,000	250.00

LOCAL GOVERNMENT BONDS

Assume that a community wants to build a civic center to house plays, sports events, concerts, and other forms of entertainment. To pay for the center, extra taxes would have to be collected. The tax money would then have to be saved until enough dollars were available to begin building. This means that the civic center could not be built for a number of years.

If the center is wanted right away, the money could be raised by issuing bonds. The center could be started now, and the bonds could be paid off out of tax dollars over a period of years. This type of bond issued by a city is called a *municipal bond.* Such bonds are also used to raise money for new schools, new sewer systems, new streets, and new water treatment plants.

WALL STREET JOURNAL

"What if EVERYONE puts his money in tax-free municipal bonds?"

BONDS VERSUS STOCKS

The investor must often choose between a number of investment opportunities. Lori, for example, must decide whether to buy stocks or bonds.

OWNERSHIP

When Lori buys a bond, she is lending money to a corporation or government for a specific period of time. When she buys stock she becomes a part-owner of a business. As a bondholder she is simply a lender, or *creditor*. So long as she receives her interest and her original investment, she has no voice in the business.

INVESTING IN BONDS   **345**

As a stockholder, however, Lori is an owner. If she owns common stock, she can vote for the board of directors and possibly receive dividends.

CLAIMS ON INCOME

The three major ways to invest in a corporation are to buy bonds, preferred stocks, and common stocks. If the corporation fails, the bond-holders have first claim on getting their money back. Bonds are a loan of money to the corporation. Preferred stockholders have second claim after bondholders. Common stockholders have third claim.

SAFETY OF INVESTMENT

The bonds of a well-established company are generally a safe invest-ment. In some cases they are backed by something like a mortgage. In addition, if the interest is not paid on time the corporation can be sued. In the case of common and preferred stocks, there is no guarantee that you will get your investment back.

VALUE OF YOUR INVESTMENT

One basic theme of investing is that if you are willing to take risks, you should also have a chance to make money. In the case of bonds, the risks are small when compared to certain types of stocks. When a bond is paid off at maturity, say 20 years in the future, the cash you receive at that time may have less value than it did when you paid for the bond. If Lori bought a $1,000 bond 20 years ago and got her money back today, her $1,000 would not buy as much as it would have 20 years ago. This is due to inflation and the resulting change in the value of money. She would have received interest money, however, during the time she had the bond.

FIXED-RETURN INVESTMENT

A bond is called a *fixed-return investment*. This means that the amount of interest the investor receives stays the same for the life of the bond. If

Lori bought a 4.25 percent $1,000 bond, she would receive $42.50 a year for the life of the bond. She could count on always receiving this amount of money.

Common and preferred stock returns are not as predictable or fixed. The return you get in the form of dividends may vary a great deal. The amount of the dividend, if any, would depend on such factors as profit, capital spending, and decisions of the board of directors.

SELLING AN INVESTMENT

An investor can always sell a bond before its maturity date. How much he or she receives depends on the current interest rates on bonds. Suppose Lori bought the 4.25 percent $1,000 bond that had a 20-year life. During the twelfth year Lori decides to sell her bond. If the going interest rate on this type of bond is lower than 4.25 percent, she will probably get more than the $1,000 face value of the bond because other investors would rather buy her bond than new ones. If the interest rate is higher than 4.25 percent, she will probably get less than her original $1,000.

SUMMARY

A bond is a promise made by a borrower to an investor. Bonds are issued by both corporations and governments.

When they are issued, bonds are sold at a set price. If a bond is held by the investor until it reaches maturity, the investor will receive its full value and interest. This means that a bond is a fixed-return investment.

There are specific things which wise investors should think about when deciding how to try to make their available extra money grow. When trying to decide on whether to invest in bonds or stocks, such factors as ownership, claims, income, safety, value, return, and selling procedures are usually considered.

I. REVIEW OF TERMS

Which words complete the numbered statements?

fixed rate of return   creditor

property   life

Series E bond   maturity

1. The _____ is issued by the United States Government.
2. In the case of a mortgage bond, a piece of _____ is a guarantee that the investor will be paid back.
3. A bondholder is a _____.
4. A bondholder receives a _____.
5. The face value of a bond is paid on the _____ date.
6. If an investor bought a 5.33 percent $1,000 bond, he or she would receive $53.30 a year for the _____ of the bond.

II. REVIEW OF MAIN POINTS

1. Explain what a debenture bond is.
2. What does *a claim on the income of a corporation* mean?
3. Describe the meaning of *the date of maturity for a bond.*
4. Why do local governments issue bonds to investors?
5. What does a *fixed-return investment* mean?
6. Explain what the interest payment to bondholders is.

III. INVESTING IN BONDS: CONCEPTS

1. If you wanted to become a part-owner of a corporation by investing, would you purchase bonds? Why or why not?
2. How do interest rates affect the value of your bond between the date you bought the bond and its maturity date?
3. Why would an investor be interested in Series E savings bonds?

4. What are the major advantages of owning a bond as opposed to owning common stock in a corporation?
5. Should an investor consider the time value of money when considering the purchase of a bond? Why? Think about whether or not $1 today will be worth $1 ten years from now.

IV. INVESTING IN BONDS: EXERCISES

1. Find out from a stockbroker or banker how and where an investor can buy bonds.
2. Review the financial pages of the newspapers and various articles in your library and complete the following projects:
   a. List the maturity dates and interest rates for two over-the-counter corporation bonds, two state government bonds, and two municipal, or local, bonds.
   b. What are the current predictions about bond interest rates in the newspapers and other sources you have read?

27

There are many people who want to invest but who have too few dollars to pay for the professional services of a broker or investment analyst. Sometimes these people pool their dollars and form an *investment club.* Others may invest in a *mutual fund.* There are a number of similarities between investment clubs and mutual funds. Both ways of investing should be considered when deciding how to invest your extra dollars.

INVESTMENT CLUBS

For an understanding of how investment clubs work, one case history will be described. Daniel Pipp, twenty-two years old and a high school graduate, worked as an apprentice bricklayer. Dan rented an apartment and tried to save about $50 a month. Dan was interested in investing his extra dollars, so he read financial newspapers, magazines, and books to help him decide what type of investment to make. He decided to invest in common stocks because he thought that in the long run he would get more money for his dollars. In other words, he hoped that for each dollar he invested, he would earn more than a dollar in the years ahead. For example, if he invested $100 in stock in 1975, he would want to be able to sell this stock for more than $200 in 1980.

Dan planned to invest $30 a month in what he believed to be good common stocks. Although he had only $30 a month to invest, he did qualify for a plan that allows small investors to invest as little as $40 over a three month period. This plan is called the New York Stock Exchange *Monthly Investment Plan* (MIP). It was started in January 1954, and it allows

350

These people are forming an investment club.

investors to buy stock by the dollar. A person can buy any amount, say $5 worth of stock or $15 worth. Before the plan began, the investor had to have enough money to buy a full share of stock, which in many instances is much more than $5 to $15.

Dan was cautious about doing things on his own. He knew very little about which stocks to buy, what a blue chip stock was, what a growth stock was, and other similar but important issues. Dan's interest in making a small monthly investment was shared by a number of his friends. One friend, Tony Matts, knew a lot about investment clubs. He convinced the others to look into starting such a club, and he sent away for written materials from the *National Association of Investment Clubs,* a nonprofit organization in Royal Oak, Michigan, that has helped many investment clubs get started. This material explained how to organize and run an investment club. (For information on how to start an investment club, write to the National Association of Investment Clubs, 1515 East Eleven Mile Road, Royal Oak, Michigan, 48067.)

Dan and his friends carefully reviewed the material on investment clubs. After considering every aspect of investing their money they officially formed a club. They decided to join the National Association of Investment Clubs and paid the annual dues. They also established activities and operating plans for the club.

Reports, such as these above, guide the investment club in purchasing stocks.

THE ACTIVITIES

Dan and his friends decided to call their club the Futurama Investment Club. They all signed a written agreement stating that

1. The club would be named the Futurama Investment Club.
2. The club would be run as a partnership.
3. Each partner would invest $25 a month in the club.
4. All dividends received from investments would be used to purchase more shares of stock.
5. The members would meet once a month to talk about investments.

6. If a partner had to withdraw, he or she must give the club two months' advance notice. After two months, he or she would be paid the value of the amount of his or her investment. For example, if he or she invested $150 over six months and notified the members during the fourth month that he or she was going to withdraw, he or she would receive the value of his or her investment at the end of the sixth month. Assuming that the $150 investment was then worth $200, he or she would receive this amount.

7. The president in charge of setting up meetings and making the investments for the next year would be Daniel Pipp. He would also open the account for the club with a stockbroker.

In addition to these specific points, the club members agreed to use the following National Association of Investment Clubs guiding principles: (1) to invest a set sum of money each month no matter what the condition of the stock market, (2) to buy growth stocks whenever possible, and (3) to invest in growth stocks in different industries so that the club would have diversified investments. This is done so that if one industry does poorly because of economic conditions, one that is growing will help offset the loss. For example, many investors buy stocks in the food, auto, steel, and transportation industries. If there is a problem in the steel industry because of foreign competition, the price of steel stocks may suffer. Good news about the food industry, however, would offset the loss in steel by gains in food.

THE OPERATION OF FUTURAMA

At the first meeting of the Futurama Investment Club, it was discovered that there were many different opinions about which stocks to buy. To solve this problem Dan assigned each member, including himself, two growth stocks to study. He wanted the members to study the price changes in the stocks during the past year, their dividend policies for the last five years, and the future plans of the corporations. Each member reported his or her findings at the monthly meetings. The reports helped the club members decide on which stocks to buy.

SOME ADVANTAGES OF INVESTMENT CLUBS

Each member of an investment club enjoys certain advantages. First, each one is investing a relatively small amount of money, only $25 a month. (In some clubs, members can even skip a month if necessary. This is not unfair to the other members because the club's earnings are shared according to each member's investment.) The smart investor only invests money that is left over after buying food, clothes, insurance, and education.

Second, each member takes part in the club's decisions on which stocks to buy. This type of involvement in a worthwhile project can give each member a feeling of satisfaction and accomplishment.

Third, by being assigned specific stocks to study, each member becomes more aware of the stock market and the corporations that sell stock. This knowledge makes the club members more informed.

Fourth, the members have a common goal to invest their money wisely. This encourages them to work hard together. Finally, any member can withdraw after giving enough advance notice. This allows a member to withdraw and be paid his or her investment in the club within a fairly short period of time.

MUTUAL FUNDS

Another type of investment is buying stock in a *mutual fund,* also called an *investment company* or *investment fund.* A mutual fund sells its stock to the public and buys stocks and/or bonds of other corporations.

An investor's money goes into a common pool along with the dollars of other investors. The money in this pool is then invested by the managers of the fund. Thus, the mutual fund is similar to an investment club. Like the club, it takes the money of investors and invests it in the stocks and/or bonds of corporations.

The money that the mutual fund makes is in the form of dividends and interest. It is used to pay the expenses and the salaries of the managers who make the investments. The money that is left over is paid to the stockholders.

A major difference between the Futurama Investment Club and a typical mutual fund is that the mutual fund hires outside people to invest the pooled money. In Futurama, Dan and his partners were the investors. In a mutual fund, the experts are paid for their advice, while in the club the amateurs are not paid.

Mutual funds are also generally much larger than investment clubs. Many funds have more than 10,000 stockholders and more than $100 million in investments.

TYPES OF MUTUAL FUNDS

The two basic types of mutual funds are the *open-end fund* and the *closed-end fund.* The open-end fund has an unlimited number of shares of stock to sell. It will continue to sell its shares as long as there are buyers. The money that comes in is used to make more investments. The people who buy open-end mutual fund stocks can invest at any time. They can also withdraw all or part of their investments at any time.

Like other corporations, a closed-end mutual fund has a certain number of shares to sell. The money is used to invest in other stocks and/or bonds. The shares of stock in a closed-end mutual fund are traded on major stock exchanges and over the counter.

Just as stocks of corporations do not have the same value and risk, neither do the stocks of mutual funds. Mutual funds are classified according to how they invest their money. *Bond funds* put most of their dollars in bonds that pay high interest. *Balanced funds* put part of their dollars (about one-third) in bonds or preferred stocks and the rest in common stock. This is done so that the fund will earn some money, no matter how economic conditions may change. *Income funds* put their dollars in current income-producing corporations. *Growth funds* invest their money in companies that have a promising future.

Fortunately, when investors are thinking about investing in a mutual fund, they can find clear statements in the prospectus of the fund describing the type of fund it is. This will help investors make up their mind about which fund in which to invest.

THE MUTUAL FUND FEE

The mutual fund, like any large corporation, has many expenses. One of the biggest expenses is the salaries it pays its money managers. When you buy shares in a closed-end mutual fund, you pay the same brokerage fees you would pay for any other stock, such as IBM or General Mills. This fee is for the services provided by the broker.

In some open-end mutual funds a fee is charged when a stock is sold. The price at which the stock sells is generally 8.5 percent higher than the price at which the fund will buy back a share of the fund stock. In the open-end fund the person buying stock can sell his or her stock at any time. Table 27–1 shows the prices of a number of mutual funds listed in the *Wall Street Journal*. For each fund, the *asked price* is the price at which the mutual fund will sell one share of its stock. The *bid price* is the price at which the fund will buy back a share of its stock. The difference between the asked price and the bid price is about 8.5 percent. This is called a *loading charge*. Mutual funds with these charges are called *load funds*.

There are also a number of *no-load funds*. These funds sell their shares directly to the public without adding the sales charge. You can see the

TABLE 27–1

Mutual Funds

Thursday, June 12, 1975

Price ranges for investment companies, as quoted by the National Association of Securities Dealers. NAV stands for net asset value per share; the offering includes net asset value plus maximum sales charge, if any.

	NAV	Offer NAV Price Chg.
Adm Gwth	3.58	3.92— .01
Adm Incm	3.28	3.59+ .01
Adm Insur	6.86	7.52— .04
Adviser Fd	3.39	3.70— .01
Aetna Fnd	6.78	7.41— .03
Aetna InSh	11.68	12.77— .03
Afuture Fd	7.51	N.L.— .07
AGE Fund	4.22	4.31— .03
Allstate	9.57	10.29— .07
Alpha Fnd	9.98	N.L.— .05
Am Birthrt	10.24	11.25— .04
Am Equity	4.37	4.79— .03
American Express Funds:		
Capital	5.89	6.44— .04
Income	7.69	8.40 ..
Invest	6.79	7.42— .01
Spec Fnd	5.92	6.47— .01
Stock Fd	6.38	6.97— .04
American Funds Group:		
Amcap F	4.58	5.01— .02

	NAV	Offer NAV Price Chg.
Dreyfus Group:		
Dreyf Fd	10.38	11.38— .03
Eqty Fd	3.73	3.99— .02
Dreyf Lv	13.09	14.35— .07
Dryf LAs	(z)	(z) (z)
Spl Incm	6.50	7.12— .02
Third Cn	10.25	11.23— .03
E &E Mutl	3.03	N.L.— .01
Eagle Gth	7.66	8.37— .05
Eaton Howard:		
Balncd F	8.08	8.83— .03
Growth	9.04	9.88— .06
Income	5.36	5.86+ .01
Spec Fnd	5.71	6.24— .07
Stock Fd	9.28	10.14— .03
EDIE SpG	17.44	N.L.— .06
EGRET F	10.00	10.87— .60
Elfun Trst	13.13	— .13
Energy Fd	12.10	N.L.— .06
Fairfld Fd	7.80	8.52— .02
Farm Bru	7.72	N.L.— .05

	NAV	Offer NAV Price Chg
Signatr	7.37	8.01+ .01
Keystone Custodian Funds:		
Cust B 1	16.99	17.78— .03
Cust B2	17.47	19.14+ .06
Disct B 4	7.23	7.93+ .02
Cust K 1	6.58	7.21— .01
Cust K 2	5.03	5.51— .05
Cust S 1	18.31	20.06— .18
Cust S 2	8.67	9.50— .03
Cust S 3	7.22	7.92— .04
Cust S 4	3.10	3.39— .02
Apollo	3.77	4.14— .04
Polaris	3.09	3.38— .03
Lndmk Gw	6.44	7.07— .04
LD EdieCa	13.02	13.93— .05
Lexington Group:		
Cp Ledrs	13.39	14.74+ .02
Growth	6.17	6.74— .04
Income	10.29	11.25— .02
Resrch	12.23	13.37— .02
LifeIns Inv	6.03	6.55+ .02
Lincoln National Funds:		
Linc Cap	5.87	6.42— .03
Selct Am	6.39	N.L.— .02
Selct Op	9.01	N.L.— .04
Selct Spl	13.06	N.L.— .07
Loomis Sayles Funds:		

	NAV	Offer NAV Price Chg
Voyage	9.77	10.68— .11
Reserv Fd	1.00	N.L. ...
Revere Fd	4.78	5.22
Safeco Equ	7.14	7.80— .03
Safeco Gth	5.65	6.17— .04
Scudder Funds:		
Intl Invst	12.95	N.L. ...
Mang Rs	10.05	N.L.
StvC Bal	13.36	N.L.— .02
Stv Com	8.24	N.L. ..
Specl Fd	20.91	N.L.
Seabd Lev	4.61	5.05— .02
Security Funds:		
Equity	3.19	3.50— .02
Invest	5.83	6.39+ .01
Ultra Fd	6.86	7.52— .20
Sentinl Gw	8.61	9.36— .03
Sentry Fd	11.74	12.76— .02
Shareholders Group:		
Comstk	4.20	4.59— .01
Entrprs	4.96	5.42 —.04
Fletc Fd	4.09	4.47— .01
Harbor	7.23	7.90— .01
Legal Lt	6.18	6.75— .02
Pace Fd	7.59	8.30— .09
Shearson Funds:		
Apprec	15.78	17.25— .60

no-load funds in Table 27–1 because the asked price is the same as the bid price. The no-load funds often must use more of the money they earn to pay their expenses than the load funds use. This means that the dividends no-load funds pay to stockholders may be smaller.

DECIDING ON A MUTUAL FUND

There are no set guidelines for deciding which mutual fund stock to buy. There are, however, a number of questions you can ask yourself to help you determine what your mutual fund investment aims are.

1. Am I investing for a long period of time or do I want cash on short notice?
2. How great is my need for current dollars?
3. Do I want the job of investing done for me by professionals?
4. Can I stand to lose money for a short period of time?

PURCHASING PLANS

Mutual fund managers have developed a number of purchasing plans that are attractive to different kinds of investors. If you want to buy mutual fund shares, but at no set time, a Direct Outright Purchase (DOP) plan is best. Under this plan you receive a certificate for each purchase.

Another investment plan is one in which you pay and your money is immediately invested. You tell the fund managers the number of dollars you will send monthly or every few months. As soon as the fund managers receive your money they will purchase stocks. Thus, your dollars are immediately invested. You may at any time invest more money than what you had agreed to invest. If you miss a payment, there is no penalty. This plan is called a Voluntary Accounts plan (VA).

THE RISKS OF MUTUAL FUNDS

No mutual fund, no matter how large and well managed, will or can protect investors from losing money if the stock market is falling. No expert can predict how stable a fund will be during a time of economic trouble.

The belief that mutual funds always make money is not always true. Some mutual funds have earned money, while others have performed poorly. This indicates that some money managers make bad investments. It is important to examine the past record of a mutual fund that interests you. This will give you an idea of how good the money managers are. The value of the stocks and bonds owned by the mutual fund will probably rise if the fund is carefully managed.

Mutual funds are not always successful investments. Sometimes they are better investments than other stocks and bonds. However, at other times it would be best to keep your extra dollars in the bank. The money you put in a savings account does not vary with market conditions. Wise investors must fully understand the advantages and disadvantages of mutual funds. In addition, investors should know what they want their investments to do for them.

SUMMARY

There are many people who have extra dollars to invest but who have little knowledge about how to buy stocks and/or bonds. Many of these people have formed groups—investment clubs—and pooled their dollars. These clubs enable members to exchange ideas and learn more about investing money properly.

Another type of investment opportunity that combines the money of investors is the mutual fund. There are two basic types of funds—open-end and closed-end. Funds are also classified according to how they invest the pooled dollars. No matter which fund stock you buy you should be aware of the risks involved. Some investors think only of the advantages of mutual funds and do not consider the risks. There are definite risks, however, and they may cost you valuable, hard-earned dollars.

I. REVIEW OF TERMS

Which words complete the numbered statements?

fee
Direct Outright Purchase
bid

National Association of Investment
   Clubs
small
professional

1. The _____ publishes materials that provide information on how to start an investment club.

2. The price at which a mutual fund will buy back a share of stock is called the _____ price.

3. A plan that allows a person to buy mutual fund shares whenever he or she wants to is called a _____ plan.

4. _____ managers are in charge of the investment of mutual fund dollars.

5. In some open-end mutual funds a _____ is charged when a stock is sold.

6. The Monthly Investment Plan is designed for _____ investors.

II. REVIEW OF MAIN POINTS

1. What is a no-load mutual fund?
2. What is a balanced mutual fund?
3. What is a professional expert working for a mutual fund paid for?
4. How does an investment club open a stock account?
5. What is a Voluntary Accounts plan?
6. Describe the Monthly Investment Plan (MIP).
7. What is a mutual fund?

III. INVESTMENT CLUBS AND MUTUAL FUNDS: CONCEPTS

1. What are some of the advantages of being a member of an investment club?
2. Describe the steps in forming an investment club.
3. What factors should you think about when trying to decide whether or not to invest in mutual funds?
4. How can a mutual fund fail?
5. How can an investment club fail?
6. Who can purchase mutual fund stocks?
7. Where can you get information on the bid price and asked price of mutual funds?

IV. INVESTMENT CLUBS AND MUTUAL FUNDS: EXERCISES

1. Find out if there are any investment clubs in your community. Who belongs to the clubs? Who can become a member?
2. Look at the financial pages and determine the current highest asked price and lowest asked price for
   a. Load mutual funds
   b. No-load mutual funds.
3. Name two growth mutual funds and two bond mutual funds.
4. Assume that Daniel Pipp paid $2,325 for 100 shares of mutual fund stock. Today the bid price per share is $15.75. If Dan sold his interest in the fund today, what would be his loss or gain?
5. Look at the asked price of one mutual fund for the last 20 days. What percentage of increase or decrease in the value of the fund has occurred?
6. Check your library and see if it has the National Association of Investment Clubs kit. If it does, write a report about what is in the kit.

INVESTING IN REAL ESTATE

28

Millions of people in the United States own single-family dwellings. In other words, they own their own homes. For most of these people, buying a home is the largest and most important financial decision they ever make, and many families live in more than one house during their lifetime. On the average, a family lives in one home from 7 to 10 years.

WHY OWN A HOUSE?

Most of the people who invest in homes buy the houses for their own personal use. But there are other advantages to owning a home besides having a place to live. First, the money invested in a home is a form of savings. Instead of putting money into a vacation trip and having only memories of a good time, the homeowner has a house. The payments the owner makes on a mortgage are actually forced savings. A *mortgage* is money that the homeowner borrows to buy the home. For example, Robin Raye wanted to buy a $40,000 home and had only $12,500 in cash. Because she had a steady job and a good credit rating, she was able to borrow the remaining $27,500 from her local bank. She had 25 years to pay off the loan. Each month, she paid a certain amount to the bank plus an interest charge. When she paid off the mortgage completely the home was entirely hers.

Second, owning a home gives the investor certain advantages when figuring his or her income tax. The amount of money paid for property taxes as well as the interest paid on the mortgage is deducted from the owner's total income. Property taxes are paid to the local government. On the average, they are about 2 percent of the value of the property. If the house Robin Raye wanted to buy was valued by the local government at $40,000, she could expect to pay property taxes of about $800 a year.

Finally, when the homeowner sells his or her home for more than he or she paid for it, he or she is not subject to a capital gains tax provided that he or she buys another home of at least equal value within a year. If after two years Robin sells her home for $46,000, she would make a $6,000 profit. This is called a capital gain of $6,000. If she then bought a home for at least $46,000 within a year, she would not have to pay a capital gains tax on the $6,000.

Capital gains are profits received from the sale of certain assets not typically used in the regular course of business. These assets may be stocks, bonds, real estate, or a patent. Robin has a capital gain of $6,000 on the sale of real estate—her home. The amount of tax she has to pay on this amount depends on what she does with the money. If she buys another home for $46,000 or more during the year after selling her house, she would not have to pay a capital gains tax right away. This tax could be put off until she bought a less expensive house.

HOW MUCH TO INVEST IN A HOME

There is no one answer to the question of how much a family or person should invest in a home. Yet very often people are told to spend no more than 25 percent of their income. Actually, the only good answer to the question depends on how many other payments the person has to make. How much money does he or she owe other people? How much money does he or she normally spend to live at the standard he or she likes?

Anyone interested in buying a home should think carefully about the following three things:

1. *Earning power* What are the possibilities of increasing my paycheck? What are the chances of being laid-off from work?
2. *Assets* What do I own that can be sold for cash?
3. *Financial obligations* What are my normal expenses? How much money do I owe?

PROTECTING THE HOME

Homes are subject to a number of risks. Some of these risks are

1. Destruction by fire, flood, or windstorm
2. Deterioration and aging, making the house less valuable
3. Owner not being able to meet the monthly mortgage payments (This could cause the mortgage holder—the bank, in Robin Raye's case—to take over, or repossess, the home.)
4. Death of the major income-earner.

Most homeowners are insured against many of these hazards. Wise investors should have insurance protecting them against all types of hazards.

The need to properly maintain and repair a home is obvious. Letting a house go to ruin will certainly decrease its value.

Meeting mortgage and tax payments is a serious issue for home investors. There are various types of insurance policies that protect an injured person or the family of a deceased owner by making mortgage payments.

The person who is working and cannot meet his or her mortgage and tax payments has a number of possibilities. He or she can try to find a job that pays more. He or she can sell the house and find a less expensive one. The important thing to consider is that owning a home involves a financial risk. If the owner does not make the payments, the person or company holding the mortgage will usually take over the house.

DISADVANTAGES OF OWNING A HOUSE

Although "your home is your castle" it can also be a nuisance. If you want the value of your home to increase you must maintain it. This means that you or someone you hire must occasionally paint it, cut the lawn, repair plumbing, and plant trees and shrubbery. Some people believe that these chores are too time-consuming. If these chores are not done, however, the value of the home will suffer, and the owner could have difficulty selling the house.

Another potential disadvantage of owning a home involves changes in zoning laws. *Zoning* is the regulation of land use by a local government group. For example, land that is zoned for single-family housing cannot by law be used for a shopping mall. There is, however, the possibility that land can be rezoned. If you buy a home and the surrounding area is originally zoned for the building of a recreational park, you would probably be happy. By rezoning, the government can change its plans and allow a company to build a steel mill on that same land. This would probably decrease the value of your home.

ANOTHER TYPE OF HOUSING: CONDOMINIUMS

Until several years ago, most people either rented a place to live or bought their own house. What you rented belonged to the landlord. What you bought was your own. You had to take care of it inside and out, but if you wanted to paint it bright red no one could stop you.

Recently, more people have wanted to own their own place but have wanted the repair and upkeep to be done by others. This type of ownership is called a *condominium form of ownership*. In condominium living, each owner has full ownership rights to the area inside his or her apartment. He or she also has exclusive use of a patio or balcony and a parking space. He or she and his or her neighbors share the ownership of the grounds and other common areas, such as a swimming pool. Of all new types of housing for sale in 1972, about 30 percent were condominiums. The percentage of apartments sold as condominiums continues to grow rapidly. A form of ownership similar to the condominium is *cooperative ownership*.

The reasons for the rapid growth of this type of living arrangement include the following:

1. Much of the land in and near large cities is too expensive to be used for single-family houses.
2. Many people prefer not to do their own upkeep and repair work.

Condominium living is popular because many people like having their own place but want the repair and upkeep done by others.

INVESTING IN REAL ESTATE

Real estate is land and those things that are permanently attached to the land. Land has always been valuable because it has provided the essentials for life. Our ancestors knew that some real estate had more value than others because it produced more food, wood, minerals, or other things of value. Today, real estate is a popular form of investment. Like other investments, it has advantages and disadvantages.

ADVANTAGES

There is a general tendency for the value of real estate to increase. Parts of California and Florida are good examples. The climate and style of living in southern California have made this area very popular. The great demand for land there has increased the value of real estate. Similarly, the value of land in certain Florida areas has increased greatly. Near Orlando, Florida, for example, is Buena Vista, where the Walt Disney Corporation decided to construct Disney World. This caused a tremendous demand for land in that area to be used for houses, stores, motels, and shopping centers. Thus, the value of that land increased.

These examples point out a definite advantage of investing in real estate: there is a limited supply of real estate. The amount of available land is going to stay the same. There will never be much more land than there is now.

The Ford Foundation has predicted what economic conditions will be like in the United States in the year 2000. One of the shortages will be usable land. It is definitely becoming more important to utilize the available land effectively. The State of California, for example, is using land for buildings, shopping centers, schools, and other uses at a rate of about 300 acres a day.

Another advantage of real estate is that it is salable; that is, you can always sell it at some price. The price may not always be what you hope for, but at least you can get some money back.

DISADVANTAGES

One of the obvious disadvantages of investing in real estate is that you generally need many extra dollars. To invest in the stock market, mutual funds, and Series E savings bonds, it is possible to spend only small amounts of dollars. For example, a Series E savings bond can be bought for $18.75. Not much real estate can be purchased for this small amount. In fact, in the early 1970's, one acre of land in Lakeland, Florida, cost $5,000, and one-third of an acre in a suburb of Chicago cost $55,000.

Another disadvantage is that real estate is fixed and cannot be moved. If you own a house in Palos Hills, Illinois, and there is a shortage of houses in Miami, Florida, you cannot take advantage of the situation. You cannot move the house to Florida and sell it.

Just because you own real estate does not mean that you will be able to sell your land quickly and turn it into cash. For example, you may own land worth $100,000, but selling it often takes time because of a lot of legal "red tape." Although you own valuable land you still must go through the selling process to get your money.

In the stock market, each share represents an ownership in a corporation and each share is exactly the same amount of ownership. In real estate this is not true. Each acre of land, each office building, and each shopping center is special. Each has its own value. This creates a problem when buying and selling real estate. In the case of land, many investors want to see the land before buying it. The land in Boulder, Colorado, is very different from the land in Key West, Florida.

"DEPENDING ON HOW MUCH YOU WANT TO SPEND, I CAN ALSO SHOW YOU A HOUSE OF STRAW AND A HOUSE OF BRICKS."

REAL ESTATE INVESTMENT RISKS

After studying the advantages and disadvantages of investing in real estate, the investor must think about the risks involved. Many people believe that they cannot lose money on real estate investments.

Many investors, however, lose money in real estate because they do not take into account the hidden charges of investing. When they decide to buy, they are interested only in the price, the down payment, and the terms of paying off the rest of the money. When the time comes to close the sale, they realize they must pay insurance, taxes, legal recording fees, and other costs. These *closing costs* add up, and the amount of cash needed to close a deal is often more than the investors expected.

Before investing in real estate, you must check with various county and city offices to find out about zoning restrictions, sewers, and highway routes. Suppose you bought a plot of land for building a home for your family. After paying for the land you may find that only office buildings can be placed on your land. Thus, it is necessary to check out the real estate zoning laws before buying the land, not after.

In many cases, the investor tries to buy real estate without first getting professional help. Real estate investment can be tricky and complicated. The best thing to do is to work with qualified real estate salespeople so that you can avoid the risks of this type of investment.

TYPES OF REAL ESTATE INVESTMENTS

There are a number of real estate investments available. A few of the more popular real estate investments are:

LAND

Land is a very popular type of investment. Usually people who buy land believe that it will increase in value. They can then sell it and make a profit. There are a number of factors that affect the value of land. First is the location. If the land is located in the swamps of Florida it would have little value to people.

Other factors that should be considered are climate, public services, and available jobs. For example, some people want the seasonal changes of Maine, while others want the constant dry heat of Arizona.

APARTMENT HOUSES

A major type of real estate investment is the apartment house. Sky-rocketing housing and land costs are causing more and more people to live in apartments.

Some of the factors to be considered in purchasing an apartment house are location, convenience to shopping and transportation, and the work involved. Owning an apartment house involves collecting rents, paying bills, and taking care of complaints about such things as icy driveways. The investor must do the work alone or hire someone to do it.

OFFICE BUILDINGS

The office building is another form of investment in real estate. There are different types of office buildings. Some are only one story and have only one tenant. Others are tall office buildings with many tenants.

A number of factors are important in making an office building a good money-making investment. Just as is the case with land and apartment houses, location is important. The office building must be in a place that is convenient for the people who work there. In addition, the building must have a nice appearance and certain modern features, such as air conditioning.

Other features that an investor should consider are the parking facilities and the availability of transportation. Some people would use their own cars, and others would use public transportation to get to work.

SUMMARY

There is no one best way to invest money. For some people stocks are best. In other cases, bonds, mutual funds, a home, or real estate is best. The most important thing to consider is your own investment goal, which should be measured by the opportunities available. You should decide on what you want your investment to do for you.

People make investments for a number of reasons. Some of the reasons are

1. *To increase income* Most investors want to increase their regular income with dollars from interest payments, dividends, or rents.
2. *To force savings* By having an investment in real estate or by joining an investment club, you are forced to save and put your dollars aside.
3. *To increase value* Another important goal of the average investor is to have the value of his or her investment increase.

The reasons listed above are some of the common objectives of all investors. Yet each investor is unique and has some specific reason for risking his or her extra dollars.

REVIEW   INVESTING IN REAL ESTATE

I. REVIEW OF TERMS
Which words complete the numbered statements?

moves	mortgage
location	supply
equal	demand
increase	closing costs

1. A factor that should be considered when buying land, apartment houses, and office buildings is _____ .

2. Real estate in California and Florida has had a tendency to _____ in value.
3. It is generally recognized that there is a limited _____ of land in the world.
4. If a homeowner sells his or her home for more than he or she paid for it, he or she is not subject to a capital gains tax if he or she purchases another home of at least _____ value within a year.
5. On the average, a family living in the United States _____ every 7 to 10 years.
6. The _____ for apartment houses seems to be growing more rapidly than that for single-family dwellings.
7. The _____ represents the money borrowed to purchase a home.
8. In completing a real estate purchase deal, the purchaser must usually pay insurance premiums, taxes, legal fees, and other costs called _____ .

II. REVIEW OF MAIN POINTS

1. What is meant by *a mortgage payment on a home?*
2. Is there a limited supply of land in the United States? Why or why not?
3. What are some of the features of valuable land?
4. Describe the importance of knowing what your objectives are before making an investment.
5. Why do people want to own their own house?
6. What kind of work is involved in owning an apartment house?
7. What are some of the common mistakes made by real estate investors?
8. Can land be easily converted into dollars? Why or why not?
9. What are some of the disadvantages of investing in real estate?
10. How does land increase in value? In other words, what causes land to become more valuable?

III. INVESTING IN REAL ESTATE: CONCEPTS

1. How would you compare and contrast two different plots of land to be used for office buildings?
2. What is real estate?
3. If California is consuming 300 acres of land a day, how many acres are being consumed or developed in 365 days?
4. Why is earning power an important consideration to make before taking out a mortgage for the purchase of a home?
5. What type of protection does a home investor need?
6. Why did the value of land increase in the Orlando, Florida, area?
7. What is the major difference between owning land and owning an apartment house?
8. What is meant by the term *forced savings*?

IV. INVESTING IN REAL ESTATE: EXERCISES

1. Look at a local newspaper and find the following:
   a. The highest-priced home for sale
   b. The highest-priced land for sale.
2. What are the zoning restrictions in your community? Are there zoning restrictions for the area in which your school is located?
3. Find out the names of two licensed real estate experts in your community. Interview these people and find out their opinions about the advantages and disadvantages of real estate investment. Prepare a brief report for your class.
4. Find out the value of one acre of land in southern California, western Florida, and downtown Chicago. The library should have this information.
5. Write a report that would inform your class of your real estate investment objectives. In this report, list your goals and your plans for reaching them.

Unit VIII
Insurance
Protection

Every day you face many risks. You cross streets and play ball in the playground. These are only a few of the many risks you can be exposed to during a typical day. Insurance can enable you to protect yourself against some of these risks. The types of insurance covered in this unit will include life, health, home, automobile, and social insurance.

Chapter 29 introduces the topic of insurance and explains some of the special terms. A major problem for many people is not knowing how to read an insurance policy. Three guidelines for buying insurance—identifying risks, evaluating risks, and obtaining proper protection—are also explained in this chapter.

In Chapter 30, the characteristics of life insurance are reviewed. The importance of mortality tables in insurance programs is explained, as well as the issue of death and its inevitability. Basic types of life insurance are also discussed.

Some of the different types of combination life insurance policies are described in Chapter 31. Specific contract features, such as dividend options, loan options, grace periods, and beneficiary clauses, are presented. Understanding these features helps the insured person know what to expect from his or her policy.

Chapter 32 shows how a life insurance plan for the Pete Doyle family is developed. The use of insurance programing by an insurance agent is traced.

Some of the various types of health insurance are covered in Chapter 33. Two major protection categories covered are expenses and income. The health plans that cover expenses include hospital insurance, medical insurance, and major medical insurance. The income plans of insurance include disability income and commercial income. Blue Cross and Blue Shield are also discussed.

Chapter 34 reviews insurance protection for the home and the automobile. Liability protection, uninsured motorist protection, comprehensive protection, and collision protection are described. No-fault insurance is also covered.

UNIT PREVIEW

Chapter 35 covers social insurance. The reasons for social insurance and the Social Security Act of 1935 are explained. The types of benefits covered by the Social Security Act are discussed. Other types of social insurance covered include unemployment insurance, Medicare, Medicaid, and black lung disease benefits. Finally, the importance of the social security card is discussed.

AS YOU STUDY THIS UNIT YOU WILL BE ENGAGED IN

* ANALYZING the concept of risk and the pooling of risks

* INTERPRETING a mortality table

* DEFINING term insurance, whole life insurance, endowment insurance, annuity contracts, family insurance, family income insurance, and modified life insurance

* UNDERSTANDING insurance practice with regard to beneficiaries, loan options, grace periods, dividends, dividend options, insurance dividends, face amounts, the insured, the insurer, contracts, and policies

* PROBING the difference between health insurance expense protection and health insurance income protection

* ANALYZING Blue Cross and Blue Shield plans, Medicare, and Medicaid

* DETERMINING the nature of bodily injury liability, property damage liability, uninsured motorist protection, comprehensive protection, collision protection, deductible features, and no-fault insurance

* ANALYZING automobile insurance premiums

* UNDERSTANDING the national social security system.

A FOCUS FOR YOUR STUDY

29 FUNDAMENTALS OF INSURANCE

Risk is part of your everyday life. You are surrounded by risks from birth to death. A home that has cost many dollars may be destroyed in minutes by a fire or a tornado. An automobile that is a family's source of transportation may be stolen. The income of a family may stop because of an accident to the wage earner.

Families, individuals, and businesses are exposed to many risks. Insurance protects a person, a whole family, or a business from *economic risks*. These are risks that involve the loss of property or earning power. If the family station wagon is stolen or the wage earner suffers a broken leg, there is a loss involved. No matter how careful or lucky you are, economic risks cannot be completely eliminated.

It is possible, however, to minimize a large financial loss by sharing the risks with a group of people. Assume that you and 49 other young people belong to a social club. One evening there is a fire in the club-room of the community center where the group holds weekly meetings.

Insurance protects people from economic risks.

The fire causes $300 damage to the club's furniture. If you were the only person responsible for the club's furniture, you would have lost $300 worth of property. But if all the club members had agreed to share any unexpected losses, each of the 50 members would have to contribute only $6 to replace or repair the damaged furniture. By sharing the economic risk with every other club member, the burden of loss is much less. This *sharing of economic risk* is a major principal of insurance.

MEANING OF INSURANCE

Because our society is so complex, it is not possible to form small clubs for people to share economic losses. There are simply too many risks and too many people to be protected by thousands of small clubs. Protection from many risks is provided by insurance companies. These companies provide protection by developing plans that enable large numbers of people to share economic risks.

In the United States there are approximately 5,000 insurance companies that provide various types of insurance protection. These companies are experts in providing insurance. *Insurance* is defined as a way of pooling funds so that a group of people share the risks of losing their property and earning power. The aim of insurance, as defined here, is to spread the economic burden of losses by using the pooled dollars of a group of insured people. Each insured person pays a certain number of dollars to minimize the blow of being faced with a large loss of property or earning power.

INSURANCE AND CHANCE

Insurance is a form of gambling. In both insurance and gambling, money changes hands on the basis of a chance event happening. For example, you pay dollars to insure against the loss of your car or motorbike. If they are not stolen, the insurance company keeps your money. If, on the other hand, your property is stolen, the insurance company pays you for your loss. Similarly, if you bet a friend $10 that the San Francisco Giants will win the National League Pennant, money will change hands on the basis of the Giants' chances.

It is important to see that in gambling you create the risk of loss by making the bet. You are not subject to losing your $10 until you make the bet. In the case of insurance, however, whether you buy the insurance or not, you are faced with the possibility of losing your property or earning power. This is an important difference between insurance and gambling.

INSURANCE LANGUAGE

The insurance field has a language of its own. Some of the more widely used (and misused) terms are presented here.

Basically, insurance is a promise by an *insurer* (the company) to an *insured* person of protection and/or service. *Protection* means repaying the insured for financial losses. *Service* means helping the insured before and after any losses occur.

To show that a legal agreement has been reached between the insurer and the insured, an *insurance policy* is drawn up. This is a kind of contract. Insurance contracts are pretty standard because of laws and customs. For example, a homeowners policy states exactly what home and property are protected from loss. Damage caused by such things as fire, lightning, smoke, windstorm and hail, explosion, riot and civil commotion, vandalism, theft, snow, sleet, electrical damage, overflow of water, or collapse is protected against in the contract.

People who sell insurance are either independent *insurance brokers* or *insurance agents,* who are representatives of insurance companies. Insurance companies also have *adjusters.* These are people who work on claims against insurers. When a *claim* (statement of loss) is made, it is the adjuster's job to handle it.

A person who wants to become insured must pay money for his or her insurance protection. The money he or she pays is called a *premium.* The company takes the premiums paid by the insured people and uses the money to pay for any losses that may occur. The money is also invested in stocks, bonds, real estate, and mutual funds.

Deciding what the premium should be is a hard decision that must be made by the insurance company. If the premiums are too high, people may decide to buy the insurance of another company. However, if the premium rates are too low, the collected money may not be enough to cover losses and pay the claims of the insured people.

THE INSURANCE POLICY

Many people are puzzled by insurance policies. An insurance policy is similar to a dictionary. When using a dictionary, a person must know what word he or she is looking up. An insured person should know what he or she is looking for before trying to understand an insurance policy.

The first step that should be taken when reading a policy is to decide what you want to know. The second step is to get an overall view of the policy and to find out where certain information is. The third step is to read the important sections carefully.

In order to get the most out of reading an insurance policy, it is helpful to seek answers to the following questions:

1. Who is the insured?
2. What kinds of risks are covered in the policy?
3. What property, if any, is protected?
4. What risks or losses are not protected by the policy?
5. What period of time does the policy cover?
6. What conditions can lead to the cancellation of the policy?
7. What must the insured pay for the protection?

These questions are not suited for every type of insurance policy. They do, however, help you read a policy and understand what you are protected against.

THE INSURANCE PROCESS

The two important parties to the insurance process are the company (the insurer) and the insured.

Federal and state governments regulate the insurance industry to protect the insured. This regulation sets premium prices and encourages competition among the various insurance companies.

Sample insurance policy

SCHEDULE OF BENEFITS

INSURED	JOHN DOE		$10,000	AMOUNT INSURED
CONTRACT NUMBER	SPECIMEN		JANUARY 1, 1974	CONTRACT DATE
ISSUE AGE	35		JANUARY 1, 1974	DATE OF ISSUE

* *

BENEFIT DESCRIPTION	PREMIUM PAYABLE FROM	PREMIUM PAYABLE TO	ANNUAL PREMIUM
WHOLE LIFE.	1 JAN1974	1 JAN1989	$ 186.70
	1 JAN1989	1 JAN2004	$ 289.70
PROVISION FOR —			
PREMIUM WAIVER.	1 JAN1974	1 JAN1999	$ 5.00
$10,000 ADDITIONAL INDEMNITY.	1 JAN1974	1 JAN2004	$ 11.00
$200.00 MONTHLY INCOME TO EXPIRY DATE, 1 JAN1989, OR 48 MONTHS IF LONGER. CONVERSION EXPIRY DATE, 1 JAN1984.	1 JAN1974	1 JAN1989	$ 106.20
FAMILY INSURANCE. 10.000 UNITS. INITIAL AMOUNT ON WIFE $10,000. AMOUNT DECREASES AS SPECIFIED. $2,000 ON EACH CHILD INCLUDED.	1 JAN1974	1 JAN2004	$ 49.30
GUARANTEED INSURABILITY OPTION. OPTIONAL ADDITIONAL AMOUNT $10,000.	1 JAN1974	1 JAN1979	$ 25.00

TOTAL INITIAL ANNUAL PREMIUM IS $383.20.

PREMIUM IS PAYABLE FOR THE PERIOD SPECIFIED ABOVE OR UNTIL PRIOR DEATH OF THE INSURED. EACH PREMIUM IS DUE AND PAYABLE IN ADVANCE ON THE FIRST DAY OF ITS INTERVAL OF PREMIUM PAYMENT. WHICH FOR THE FIRST PREMIUM IS THE CONTRACT DATE.

L-01*S1*L-01B*L-V1 MOD LP 65/3/*L1-P2*L1-P1*L-P6-1*L-P10-1*L-P8-3*L-OP1*LE-1
S1

TIC Ed. 1-64

FIGURE 29-1
THE INSURANCE PROCESS: A GENERAL OVERVIEW

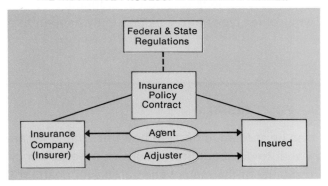

As Figure 29–1 shows, federal and state regulations must be followed in the policy contract. The contract should be agreed to by both the insurer and the insured. The agent or broker should explain the contract and the premium payments. If there is a claim to be paid, it should be handled by the adjuster who represents the company. Other people, such as lawyers, are also involved in the insurance process, but the diagram shows only some of the people most insured individuals meet when they buy and use insurance.

BUYING INSURANCE

Insurance premiums have come to be more and more a major part of the budgets of individual people, families, and businesses. Two important factors that affect an insurance purchase plan are 1) the money available to buy insurance and 2) the particular risk that should be insured against. Each person must study the possible risks, find out what to do about them, and get protection from the best company at the most reasonable premium that can be paid.

IDENTIFYING YOUR RISKS

Everyone is exposed to many risks. If the head of the family is ill or injured, the family's income may be stopped. The family's medical bills will also increase. It is very important to think about what will happen if the wage earner's income is reduced or stopped. It is also important to find out what other types of risks commonly happen to a person or family.

WEIGHING YOUR RISKS

Risks must also be studied to find out how important they are. Then you must decide what to do about them. Risks, in order of importance, may be (1) total disability of the main wage earner, (2) death of the head of the family, (3) property loss, and (4) property damage. The important point is that the risks must be ranked in order of importance and then studied realistically.

GETTING THE RIGHT INSURANCE PROTECTION

Many people cannot identify the name of the company from which they have bought their insurance. This is unfortunate because it is important for the people buying insurance to learn as much as possible about their insurance companies. They should study the management and overall quality of the companies. Information on insurance companies can be found in *Best's Life Reports and Best's Insurance Reports,* which is published every year by Alfred M. Best Company. It is in most libraries and gives information on the history of insurance companies, their management and financial strength, and an evaluation of their performance.

Another thing of interest to the insured person is the company's policy about claims. It is very important to find insurance companies that do not fight all claims. This would be very frustrating. How a company pays its claims cannot be found in a book. Instead, you have to check with friends, businesspeople, and insurance agents who might know this kind of information. Perhaps the best and most reliable sources of information are the people who are already insured by the company.

Another important thing to consider is what the company does once it has paid a claim. Does the company tend to cancel a policy as soon as a loss occurs? This information can also be found by asking those people who have had to make claims.

Finally, the insurance buyer should check to be sure that the company can operate in his or her state. Buying insurance from a company that is not licensed to operate in the state in which the insured person lives can create much legal red tape if the insured person has to report a loss.

THE INSURANCE SALESPERSON

As with a stockbroker, it is important to find a good insurance agent or broker. An *agent* sometimes works for one particular insurance company. A *broker* handles insurance policies of several companies.

A good agent is interested in his or her customers and also knows the company's insurance plans. How interested an agent is in his or her customers can be found out by asking some of the agent's clients.

A good agent or broker will identify the person's risks, evaluate them, and develop the right insurance plan for him or her. An agent will explain, in as much detail as necessary, what the policy does and does not cover. An agent will also carefully explain the exact costs of the various plans he or she has discussed. In some cases, insured people have not understood how much they had to pay or the length of time over which the premiums had to be paid.

Finding the right agent or broker is easier said than done. The only sure test is to do business with an agent and find out for yourself how reliable, knowledgeable, and trustworthy the agent is. Also find out if the agent has a C.L.U. and/or C.P.C.U. diploma. These show that the agent has met ethical and experience requirements and passed a series of special tests administered by the insurance industry. The C.L.U. (Chartered Life Underwriter) is granted by the American College of Life Underwriters. The C.P.C.U. (Chartered Property Casualty Underwriter) is granted by the American Institute for Property and Liability Underwriters. The agent with these diplomas has passed a series of examinations in insurance, law, economics, social legislation, finance, accounting, and management.

TYPES OF INSURANCE PROTECTION

Almost anything can be protected by insurance. Policies have been written to protect an artist's hands, a piano player's fingers, and the beautiful legs of a movie starlet. Most insurance policies, however, can be divided into two groups: commercial and social.

COMMERCIAL INSURANCE

Commercial insurance is provided by both private firms and the government. Private firms give insurance covering life and health risks (personal insurance) and fire, marine, liability, and similar risks (property insurance).

Government commercial insurance is provided by the Federal or state government. It can be divided into personal and property insurance. For example, Wisconsin provides commercial life insurance on a voluntary basis for its residents. The Federal Government offers life insurance to veterans. The Federal Housing Administration insures home loans for lenders. The Department of Agriculture offers crop insurance to farmers.

SOCIAL INSURANCE

Social insurance provides protection against the financial risks of old age, disability, death, sickness, unemployment, and job-related injury and death. This protection is provided by state and federal programs. The Federal Government, under the Social Security Act of 1935, operates the old age, survivors, disability, and health insurance programs. With the exception of the health insurance program, these programs are financed by taxes paid by both employers and employees. The health insurance program, called *Medical Care* (Medicare), covers people who receive social security old age benefits. These people pay a monthly premium; the amount varies according to the type of coverage they choose.

The risk of losing one's job is covered by the federal State Unemployment Insurance program, which was also established by the Social Security Act of 1935. Each state operates its own program under federal regulations. Weekly payments are made to workers who meet certain qualifications and who lost their jobs through no fault of their own. These payments may be made for six months or longer.

The workmen's compensation program, the oldest type of social insurance in the United States, is operated by each state. Wisconsin, in 1911, was the first state to enact such legislation. Workmen's compensation provides weekly benefits to workers who have been injured while on the job and are unable to work as a result. Death benefits are also provided for survivors of those workers accidentally killed while on the job. Rehabilitation is also provided for injured workers to help them get back to work.

Social insurance is described in more detail in Chapter 35.

SUMMARY

Everyone is exposed to certain risks. Sometimes a person or family is faced with a loss of property or earning power. To help a person or family to overcome this loss is an important function of insurance. The person who buys insurance actually pools his or her funds with others so that the risks are shared as a group.

To better understand what insurance is about and how the insurance process operates, you first have to learn some special terms. Such important terms include *protection, insurance policy, agent, claim,* and *adjusters.* When buying insurance, it is important to identify your risks, evaluate them, and get the proper insurance protection.

There are many kinds of insurance policies written by companies. Two broad categories of insurance protection are commercial and social. The following chapters cover specific types of insurance that millions of people have bought to protect themselves and their families from such occurrences as death, injury, illness, tornadoes, hailstorms, and theft.

I. REVIEW OF TERMS

Which words complete the numbered statements?

social insurance	*Best's Life Reports and Best's*
Federal and state	*Insurance Reports*
economic	agent
identifying risks	insured

1. The loss of property or earning power is referred to as _____ risk.

2. _____ is insurance required by law.

3. The representative of a company who handles the preparation of the insurance policy is called an _____.

4. The person who buys the insurance is commonly referred to as the _____.

5. It is recommended that the first step in buying insurance is _____.

6. The insurance field is regulated by both _____ governments.

7. Information on insurance companies can be found in _____.

II. REVIEW OF MAIN POINTS

1. What kinds of economic risks does a family often face?
2. Why must the government regulate the insurance field?
3. What are some of the characteristics of a good insurance agent?
4. How is an insurance policy paid for?
5. What kinds of questions should be asked before trying to read an insurance policy?
6. What is an insurance claim?
7. Explain the difference between insurance and gambling.
8. What is an insurance contract?
9. What is social insurance?

10. Assume that a person carries automobile-theft insurance for years and never has his or her car stolen. What has the person received for all of his or her years of paying premiums?

III. FUNDAMENTALS OF INSURANCE: CONCEPTS

1. Do you think that it makes sense to buy automobile insurance? Why?
2. Why is the agent an important individual in the insurance process?
3. Do you think that the Federal Government should be involved in social insurance programs? Why?
4. Do you think that earthquake insurance should be bought by people in California? Why?
5. Why is it important to understand that insurance involves the pooling of funds from a group of people?
6. Why is it important to find out about the financial status and competence of an insurance company before purchasing a policy?
7. What steps should be taken when deciding whether to purchase a particular kind of insurance protection?
8. Some people believe that buying insurance is gambling. Do you agree? Why?

IV. FUNDAMENTALS OF INSURANCE: EXERCISES

1. Max Uzelatz believes that insurance premiums are too high for the type of automobile insurance protection he wants. During the time that he owns a car, he deposits $10 a month in the bank. When he sells the car he takes the money out of the bank and takes a vacation trip. He starts the process again when a new or used car is purchased. Do you believe that this is a good plan? Why?
2. Find out from your library or other sources what the ten biggest life insurance companies are. Base your conclusions on the amount of life insurance protection the company had outstanding during the past year.
3. Determine what the state regulations are on insurance prac-

tices in your state. Do you believe that stricter regulations are necessary? Why?

4. Assume that Maria Garcia earns $19,000 a year as a computer programing specialist. Her insurance premiums total $6,500 a year. Do you feel that this is too much protection? Why?

5. Write a short report on the history of insurance protection in the United States. Where and how did it start?

LIFE INSURANCE PROTECTION 30

As you know, death is inevitable. This means that life insurance provides protection against something that is certain to happen. The purpose of life insurance is to make up for any loss of income resulting from the death of an insured person. The person who receives the money is called a *beneficiary.*

RISKS TO INCOME

When a family's main wage earner dies, his or her income stops immediately. For most people who live long enough to retire, there is another kind of risk. These people run the risk of living beyond retirement age but not having enough money for living expenses.

Suppose that Vince Rizzo is thirty years old and earns $14,000 a year. One day Vince suddenly dies. Immediately, his widow and two children would have no income because Vince was the only wage earner in the family. This certainly would be an uncomfortable and difficult position for Vince's survivors.

The risk of living beyond retirement poses another kind of problem. Suppose Rich Anderson, a machine-lathe operator, decides to retire at the age of sixty-two. Rich has a wife, and a son in medical school, and they both depend on him for financial support. Rich is earning $21,000 a year when he decides to retire. After retirement, his earnings would stop. He then would begin to receive a monthly pension check from his former company and a social security check from the Government. These checks would help support his family, but Rich would also have to use his savings or other investments. How long his savings would last is uncertain.

389

DEATH AND RETIREMENT RISKS

An important issue that must be faced is how to handle the risk of death before retirement and the risk of a reduced income after retirement. Steps can be taken to soften their crushing impact on a family. Proper medical care and regular medical examinations can help reduce the probability of early death. And a well-planned savings and investment program can provide needed dollars when a person retires. Another way is to buy life insurance that protects against loss of income caused by early death.

POOLING RISKS

Life insurance, like other forms of insurance, is based on the idea of pooling risks. The premiums collected from a group of insured people are pooled, and the losses of a few are paid from the fund.

Suppose that Romain Cool has bought an insurance policy that promises to pay her beneficiary $1,000 if she dies. The company must collect enough dollars to pay off this type of policy. If the statistical experts of the insurance company predict that 1 percent of the insured group will die during a particular year, there will be 10 deaths for every 1,000 insured people. If a group of 500,000 is insured, there will be 5,000 deaths expected. If each person has a $1,000 policy, this means that $5,000,000 in death claims will have to be paid during the year. Thus, $10 from each person would probably cover the death claim payments.

This is a simple example to show the idea of insurance pooling. In a more realistic example, the premium collected would have to cover the expenses as well as the death claims faced by the company. A company also must pay its employees' salaries, advertising expenses, transportation costs, and other expenses. These expenses must be considered when setting insurance premium rates.

PROBABILITY AND MORTALITY TABLES

When a sports fan says "there is a great chance that this team will win the National League Pennant" or "there is little chance that this horse will win the Kentucky Derby," he or she is thinking in terms of probability. *Probability* is simply the chance of something happening. When there is no chance of an occurrence, the probability is 0. For example, the probability of a person living forever is 0. When an occurrence is definitely going to happen, the probability is 1. The probability of finding four kings in a normal deck of 52 cards is 1.

Probabilities are often expressed as fractions or percentages. If there are two possible outcomes and each has the same chance of occurring, the probability of either is ½, or 50 percent. In a fraction, the numerator is the number of actual outcomes and the denominator is the number of possible outcomes.

In an earlier example, it was stated that 10 people out of each 1,000 in the insured group would die during the year. This figure is called the *death,* or *mortality, rate.* It is often expressed in terms of the number of deaths per thousand. Thus, the death, or mortality, rate is 10 per 1,000, or 1 in 100, or 0.01, or 1 percent.

It is generally known that a person's chance of dying increases as he or she gets older. This is an important consideration for insurance companies when figuring premiums for people of different ages.

Insurance companies think in terms of probability just as racing fans do at the track.

TABLE 30-1
MORTALITY TABLE

Age	Deaths Per 1,000	Expectation of Life (Years)	Age	Deaths Per 1,000	Expectation of Life (Years)
0	7.08	68.30	50	8.32	23.63
1	1.76	67.78	51	9.11	22.82
2	1.52	66.90	52	9.96	22.03
3	1.46	66.00	53	10.89	21.25
4	1.40	65.10	54	11.90	20.47
5	1.35	64.19	55	13.00	19.71
6	1.30	63.27	56	14.21	18.97
7	1.26	62.35	57	15.54	18.23
8	1.23	61.43	58	17.00	17.51
9	1.21	60.51	59	18.59	16.81
10	1.21	59.58	60	20.34	16.12
11	1.23	58.65	61	22.24	15.44
12	1.26	57.72	62	24.31	14.78
13	1.32	56.80	63	26.57	14.14
14	1.39	55.87	64	29.04	13.51
15	1.46	54.95	65	31.75	12.90
16	1.54	54.03	66	34.74	12.31
17	1.62	53.11	67	38.04	11.73
18	1.69	52.19	68	41.68	11.17
19	1.74	51.28	69	45.61	10.64
20	1.79	50.37	70	49.79	10.12
21	1.83	49.46	71	54.15	9.63
22	1.86	48.55	72	58.65	9.15
23	1.89	47.64	73	63.26	8.69
24	1.91	46.73	74	68.12	8.24
25	1.93	45.82	75	73.37	7.81
26	1.96	44.90	76	79.18	7.39
27	1.99	43.99	77	85.70	6.98
28	2.03	43.08	78	93.06	6.59
29	2.08	42.16	79	101.19	6.21
30	2.13	41.25	80	109.98	5.85
31	2.19	40.34	81	119.35	5.51
32	2.25	39.43	82	129.17	5.19
33	2.32	38.51	83	139.38	4.89
34	2.40	37.60	84	150.01	4.60
35	2.51	36.69	85	161.14	4.32
36	2.64	35.78	86	172.82	4.06
37	2.80	34.88	87	185.13	3.80
38	3.01	33.97	88	198.25	3.55
39	3.25	33.07	89	212.46	3.31
40	3.53	32.18	90	228.14	3.06
41	3.84	31.29	91	245.77	2.82
42	4.17	30.41	92	265.93	2.58
43	4.53	29.54	93	289.30	2.33
44	4.92	28.67	94	316.66	2.07
45	5.35	27.81	95	351.24	1.80
46	5.83	26.95	96	400.56	1.51
47	6.36	26.11	97	488.42	1.18
48	6.95	25.27	98	668.15	.83
49	7.60	24.45	99	1,000.00	.50

Insurance companies use mortality tables to give them some idea of the probability of death at various ages. A table developed by the Society of Actuaries and the National Association of Insurance Commissioners is widely used. A portion of this table is shown in Table 30-1. The major parts of the table are the columns showing the age, deaths per thousand, and the expectation of how many more years a person will live when he or she reaches a particular age. For example, among fifteen year olds, the death rate is 1.46 per thousand. Also, the fifteen year old is expected to live 54.95 more years.

PREMIUMS

Mortality tables are used to figure life insurance premiums. Suppose that 100,000 high school students from New York, Chicago, and Boston, all fifteen years old, decide to form an insurance company. Each student agrees to purchase a $1,000 policy covering one year. According to the mortality table, only 1.46 persons out of every 1,000 in this age group are expected to die during one year. Thus, the total payments for the year will be $146,000. Each student will have to pay at least $1.46 for his or her one-year policy. However, the company will have other expenses, such as salaries, advertising, and rent. Assume that these costs will add up to $54,000. Each student will then have to pay $2 a year for his or her policy.

The $2 price may be lowered because the company will invest its premium money before claims are paid. Just how much the price is lowered will depend on how successful the managers are in earning interest on their investments.

BASIC TYPES OF LIFE INSURANCE

Insurance companies sell four basic types of life insurance policies: (1) term, (2) whole life, (3) endowment, and (4) annuities. Other types of contracts combine these four in some way. The aim of the first three types is to pay a sum of money when a particular event, such as reaching sixty-five years of age or death, occurs. The annuity makes payments to the insured person. The payments start on a particular date and continue for a specified number of years.

TERM INSURANCE

Term life insurance protection is for a specific period of time. If a company gave Vince Rizzo a one-year term life policy, it would promise to pay his beneficiary the face amount of the policy if Vince died during that year. If Vince did not die during the year, his beneficiary would receive nothing.

The length of the term varies from 1 year to 20 years. Some policies have a renewal clause. If Vince's policy did not have this clause, he would have to apply to the company all over again when his policy expired. He would have to show that he was still a good insurance risk. This means that he might have to have a medical examination. If his health were considered poor, he might not be able to renew his insurance. This problem can be avoided by buying term insurance that allows the insured person to renew the policy without having to prove sound health.

The insured person may buy term insurance with a *convertibility option.* This gives the insured person the right to convert the term policy to whole life or endowment insurance without proving sound health. For

TABLE 30–2
ANNUAL PREMIUMS FOR
$1,000 OF LIFE INSURANCE PROTECTION
(BASED ON 1973 RATES FOR A LEADING INSURANCE COMPANY)

Age at which Insurance is bought	(Five-Year) Term (Renewable & Convertible)	Whole Life (Ordinary)	(Twenty-year) Endowment
15	$6.40	$13.40	$16.70
16	6.40	13.50	17.00
20	6.50	15.10	19.30
25	6.60	16.80	21.50
30	7.30	20.00	27.00
40	10.30	26.90	41.20
50	19.20	40.10	73.10

example, a person who at the age of nineteen buys a one-year convertible term policy renewable to age fifty-five may renew the policy
each year. Then, when he or she is thirty-four years old, he or she can
then decide on another form of life insurance. This is important because
some people become too ill to be insured.

Term insurance is best when the insured person needs only temporary
protection or when he or she cannot afford to pay the higher premiums
for other forms of life insurance. If a person buys term insurance at a
young age, the premium rates are fairly low because the probability of
death is low.

Normally, term life insurance is not available to people over the age of
sixty-five or seventy. If term protection were available at age seventy,
the premium rates would be very high.

WHOLE LIFE INSURANCE

Whole life insurance pays money when the insured person dies, no matter when it happens. As long as the premiums are paid the insurance
protection continues. This is why whole life insurance is called *permanent insurance.*

There are two major types of whole life insurance: (1) ordinary, or
straight life, insurance and (2) limited-payment life insurance. The
premiums for an *ordinary life insurance* policy are based on the idea
that as long as the insured person is living, the premiums will be paid.
The insured person is buying a policy in which the payments are spread
out over his or her lifetime.

The *limited-payment life insurance* plan offers protection for the person's whole life, but the person has to pay premiums for only a certain
period of time. After the premiums have been paid, the policy still continues for the rest of the person's life. This kind of policy is also called
paid-up life insurance. A 20-year-payment life insurance policy is paid
up after premiums have been paid for 20 years.

This type of installment buying of insurance protection is different in
one major way from buying a home on installment. In the case of a

home, if the buyer dies before the home is paid for, the rest of the money must still be paid. If a person insured by a limited-payment insurance policy dies before the end of the payment period, the policy is considered paid up.

Whole life insurance gives permanent protection for the insured. It is also a form of savings, since it can be cashed in.

ENDOWMENT INSURANCE

Endowment life insurance is similar to whole life insurance in that it gives both protection and an investment. The protection lasts until a specific date. The investment value is greater than that of ordinary or limited-payment life insurance. If the insured person dies during a certain period of time, his or her family receives money totaling the face value of the policy. If he or she does not die during that time, he or she gets the money when the time is up.

Custer was in a high-risk profession.

Assume that Al Olympia is thirty-two years old and buys a $10,000, 20-year endowment policy. If he lives to the age of fifty-two, he will get $10,000 from the insurance company. If he dies any time before then, his beneficiary will receive the face value of the policy ($10,000) from the insurance company. This type of policy certainly gives the insured person protection and an investment. The premiums are therefore much higher than for other types of life insurance.

An endowment policy can be written for any number of years. It is a popular type of insurance for people who want to save money for education and retirement. If the family wage earner can afford this type of insurance, his or her family can be provided with money to help pay for the children's college education. If Al Olympia had a daughter, Susan Marie, he could start an endowment for her education. If he bought a 15-year endowment plan, the endowment funds would be available when Susan was sixteen years old. When she graduated from high school the money could be used for her college education.

Al, like other income earners, must decide whether protecting the family through a term, whole life, or limited-payment life insurance plan is more important than an endowment policy that would also provide educational funds for Susan. This choice is an important family matter that should be considered when buying life insurance.

Endowment insurance can provide money for education or retirement.

THE ANNUITY CONTRACT

Under an annuity arrangement, the company agrees to pay the insured person an income for a specific period of time. When the period is a definite number of years, the contract is called an *annuity contract.*

The purpose of an annuity contract is to protect the income of the insured person. Suppose a woman reaches retirement age with only $40,000 in savings, and she has no other income. Can she live on her savings? If she invests her savings at a 5 percent return, her income will be about $167 per month. This is definitely not enough to live on, and she would have to start using up her savings. But, as she uses up her savings, she receives smaller and smaller interest payments.

What she can do is buy an annuity contract for $40,000. This could increase her monthly payments to $300 or $400. The insurance company can guarantee her payments for as long as she lives. The company can make these promises for the same reasons it can promise to pay for premature death. That is, there are groups of people pooling their funds for annuity contract protection.

LIFE INSURANCE AND CASH VALUE

All basic life insurance policies, except for term insurance, include some aspect of savings or investments. As long as the person keeps his or her protection, whole life and endowment policies have a growing cash value. If the insured person gives up his or her policy, he or she is paid the cash value. The longer the policy is kept, the higher its cash surrender value will be. The *cash surrender value* is the money the insured person can get for his or her policy when it is cashed in.

The cash value may be either more or less than the premiums that have been paid. It depends on the person's age, the type of policy, and the length of time the person has had the policy.

Suppose that Pete Parker, a fifteen-year-old high school student in Salt Lake City, Utah, bought four different policies—term, ordinary life,

TABLE 30-3
FOUR POLICIES AND THEIR CASH
VALUES AT THE END OF 20 YEARS
(BASED ON 1973 RATES FOR A LEADING INSURANCE COMPANY)

	5-Year Term Renewable and Convertible	Whole Life (Ordinary)	20-Year Limited Payment	20-Year Endowment
Yearly premiums	$ 6.40	$ 9.50	$ 17.90	$ 42.50
Total premiums paid after 20 years	128.00	190.00	358.00	850.00
Cash value after 20 years	NONE	188.20	374.00	1000.00
Cash value minus premiums		−1.80	16.00	150.00

20-year limited-payment life, and 20-year endowment. Each of the policies had a face value of $1,000. Table 30-3 shows the annual premiums for each policy, the total amount Pete would pay over 20 years, the cash value at the end of 20 years, and the difference between the last two amounts.

The figures in the table show that whole life and 20-year limited-payment policies have cash values that are almost the same as the premiums paid over 20 years. The term policy has no cash value at all. In the case of the 20-year endowment, the cash value is $150 more than the premiums that were paid. This is because the insurance company invests the money and thus makes it earn even more money. Also, the premiums for the endowment plan are larger than those for the other policies, so they earn more money when invested by the company. Life insurance companies invest in bonds, stocks, and real estate to make their money grow.

SUMMARY

The aim of life insurance is to make up for income that is lost when the insured person dies. However, it can also help provide money after retirement. Thus, life insurance is concerned with both death and retirement.

Life insurance premium rates are determined largely by the mortality rate. Table 30–1 lists mortality rates for people from birth to the age of ninety-nine. It is clear that after the age of eleven the risk of death gradually increases as the person grows older.

The four basic types of life insurance are term, whole life, endowment, and annuity. Term insurance provides protection for a specific period of time. Whole life policies give permanent protection. They also provide for payment upon the death of the insured, no matter when it occurs. Endowment insurance provides for payment of a certain amount of money during a specified period of time or at the end of the protection period. An annuity contract means that an insurance company will pay the insured a specific income for a definite number of years.

"Would you run through that once again, please, Walter?"
Drawing by Stan Hunt; © 1974 The New Yorker Magazine, Inc.

I. REVIEW OF TERMS

Which words complete the numbered statements?

probability   endowment
term   specified
income   premature
premiums   cash value

1. If a car racing fan said that there is a one in ten, or 10 percent, chance that car number 18 will win the Indianapolis 500 race, he or she would be thinking in terms of _____ .
2. The basic purpose of using mortality tables is to compute life insurance _____ .
3. The life insurance policy that provides protection for a specified period of time is _____ .
4. Generally, the premiums for an _____ policy are the highest.
5. Under a limited-payment life insurance policy, the insured only has to pay premiums for a _____ period of time.
6. Life insurance protects a family or an insured person against loss of income due to _____ death.
7. The major objective of an annuity contract is to protect the _____ of the insured.
8. As long as life insurance protection is kept, whole life and endowment policies accumulate a _____ .

II. REVIEW OF MAIN POINTS

1. How does endowment insurance differ from whole life insurance?
2. What kind of certainty is important to consider when thinking about life insurance protection?
3. What are the advantages of buying life insurance at a young age, such as fourteen or fifteen?
4. Why does term insurance have no cash surrender value?

5. How are life insurance premiums determined?
6. Why is it important to think about the fact that life insurance companies invest the money they receive?
7. How can endowment insurance be used for an educational fund for a family?
8. What is a renewable term insurance policy?
9. What is an annuity contract?
10. What kind of information is in a mortality table?
11. What is the objective of a limited-payment life insurance policy?
12. Explain what is meant by the statement "whole life and endowment insurance policies can be viewed as a savings or investment plan."

III. LIFE INSURANCE PROTECTION: CONCEPTS

1. Briefly explain why a person would want to buy an annuity contract?
2. Why is it generally accepted that the risks of death increase for each person every year?
3. Suppose that George Rogers bought, at the age of twenty-five, a $50,000, 20-year endowment policy. When George was thirty-one years old, he suddenly died. What was his beneficiary entitled to under this type of plan?
4. John Kurawoski, who is nineteen years old, is considering buying an insurance policy. Here are some of his choices:

	Premium at 19 Years of Age	Cash Surrender Value at End of 20 Years
Ordinary Life	$16.50	$ 312.00
20-Year Limited Payment	23.40	500.00
20-Year Endowment	41.50	1000.00

   a. What would John have to pay over the 20-year period for each type of policy?
   b. Why should John think about the cash surrender value?
   c. How does the management of the insurance company influence the cash surrender value?

5. Why would a person want to purchase term life insurance that has a convertibility option?

6. What factors should be considered by a person who expects to live several years after retirement?

7. Why are the premiums on a term insurance policy generally lower than those on other types of life insurance?

8. How is probability a part of life insurance?

IV. LIFE INSURANCE PROTECTION: EXERCISES

1. Talk with a life insurance agent and find out the premiums his or her company would charge for a person your age for the four types of life insurance policies: term, whole life, endowment, and annuity.

2. Do you believe the following statement: As a family's income increases a larger amount should be spent on life insurance? Prepare a short report to support your belief.

3. When choosing a life insurance policy for a young career woman, twenty-eight years old, single, and earning $18,000 per year, what factors would you look for in the contract?

4. Take a poll of five of your older friends and relatives and find out the following information:
   a. How many have life insurance policies?
   b. Which companies insure them?
   c. What kinds of policies do they have?
   d. When did they first purchase life insurance?
   e. Do they recommend life insurance?

5. Prepare a short report showing how and where insurance companies invest their premium dollars. Show their investment patterns for the last five years. Have these patterns changed?

3

LIFE INSURANCE CONTRACTS AND OPTIONS

The kinds of life insurance protection described in the last chapter are the most common types. There are, however, many contracts that combine various kinds of protection. In addition to standard and combination contracts, a person buying life insurance should also consider various features, or options, in contracts.

COMBINATION LIFE INSURANCE

Some of the more popular combination contracts are family life insurance, family income insurance, modified life insurance, and double indemnity insurance.

An example of a high-risk business.

A FAMILY LIFE INSURANCE POLICY

A *family life insurance* policy covers all members of the family. Suppose that Al Olympia buys $10,000 whole life protection for himself, $2,000 term insurance to age sixty for his wife Alice, $1,500 term insurance to age twenty-two for his daughter Susan, and $1,500 term insurance for any child born after this policy goes into effect. In addition, Al has the company write $10,000 term protection on him which is payable only if he dies after Alice and before he reaches age sixty-five. The important point in this example is that various combinations of protection can be written into a single contract.

A FAMILY INCOME POLICY

A *family income* policy says that if the insured person dies within a certain period, usually 10, 15, or 20 years, his or her beneficiary will get payments every month. Each payment will be a certain percentage of the face value of the policy. These payments will continue for the rest of the specified period. At the end of this period, the entire value will be paid to the beneficiary. For example, suppose Ulysses Green bought a 3 percent, $20,000, 20-year family income policy at age twenty-five. If Ulysses died within that period, the benefits in Table 31–1 could be collected by his wife Cindy.

TABLE 31–1
BENEFITS TO CINDY GREEN ON HUSBAND'S 3 PERCENT, $20,000, TWENTY–YEAR INCOME POLICY

If Ulysses Green Died On:	Benefits For Cindy Green
Day Policy Started	$600 a month for 20 years, $20,000 at end of 20 years
Five Years Later	$600 a month for 15 years, $20,000 at end of 20 years
Ten Years Later	$600 a month for 10 years, $20,000 at end of 20 years
Fifteen Years Later	$600 a month for 5 years, $20,000 at end of 20 years
Twenty or More Years Later	$20,000 to be paid immediately

The reason why Ulysses and many other people like this kind of protection is that it gives their family a large sum of money if they die while the family is young. The $20,000 protection is provided by the whole life portion of the contract combination. The $600 a month comes from two places: 1) the interest earned by the company on the premium payments and 2) the decreasing term insurance. *Decreasing term insurance* means that over the 20 years, the term protection decreases. It becomes zero at the end of 20 years.

A MODIFIED LIFE POLICY

A *modified life* policy is one for which the cost is lower during the first few years and higher later on. The face value of the insurance policy, however, remains the same. This type of policy is meant for people who need whole life protection but who cannot start paying the regular high premium right away. For example, assume that the regular premium for every $1,000 of 20-year whole life insurance is $10 a year. Joe Mendoza, who is only nineteen, does not want to pay this premium. The company designs a whole life contract that lets Joe pay $7.50 a year for five years. Then, Joe would start to pay a premium of $12. If Joe waited five years to buy this type of policy, he would have to pay a premium of $13. He gets the lower rate because of his young age. The modified contract lets Joe pay a lower premium for five years and a higher premium after that. His premium after five years was still lower than that which he

Because it is less probable that death will occur by accident, premiums for double indemnity insurance are not much higher than for a typical life policy.

Certain causes of death, such as a skydiving accident, are not accepted in double indemnity claims.

would have had to pay if he had waited until then to buy this kind of insurance.

DOUBLE INDEMNITY

The *double indemnity insurance* policy says that if the insured person's death is caused by accident, his or her beneficiary will get double the amount of the face value of the policy. (There is also a triple indemnity contract that pays a beneficiary three times the face amount of the contract if the insured's death is the result of an accident.) This type of policy is popular, and the premiums are not much higher than for a typical whole life policy. The double indemnity feature can be attached and often is a *rider,* or special feature, in a normal whole life contract.

There are certain causes of death that are not accepted in double indemnity claims. These include suicide, violations of the law, war, skydiving, and certain flying activities other than flying on a regularly scheduled airline.

SOME LIFE INSURANCE CONTRACT FEATURES

Life insurance policies are written contract agreements between the insurer and the insured. The contract specifies the rights and duties of both parties—the insurer and insured. Everyone interested in life insurance should know about the important features that are described under the topics listed on the following pages.

BENEFICIARY CLAUSE

The *beneficiary clause* lets the insured person tell the company to whom the payments should be made. Because a beneficiary must live longer than the insured, it is customary to name a second and third beneficiary. The beneficiaries are listed in the contract in order of priority.

DIVIDENDS

Life insurance is bought on either a participating or nonparticipating basis. *Participating* policies share in the good fortune of the company when its investments make more money than expected. The sharing can be in the form of a refund, or *dividend*.

Nonparticipating policies do not share in dividends. Generally, premiums for participating insurance are higher than those for nonparticipating. The dividends are certainly not guaranteed. Participating policyholders run the risk of the company not earning more than expected on their investments.

The participating policyholder has a number of options available concerning the dividends. He or she can receive them in cash or use them to pay premiums. Or he or she may let them build up and let the company pay interest on the growing sum of money. If the participating policyholder dies, the beneficiary receives the face value of the policy plus the dividends.

The exact arrangement the insured person makes for his or her dividends depends on his or her insurance budget and goals. Also, even after a particular dividend arrangement is written into the contract, it can be changed.

SETTLEMENT PLANS

Life insurance is designed to create a sum of money that can be used to replace some of the income lost by a family when the insured person dies or retires. Just how this money will be paid can often be chosen by the beneficiary or the insured person. Two of the most popular settlement choices are the interest option and the fixed amount option.

With an *interest option,* the beneficiary does not get the full amount but gets only the interest earned by the money. In some policies, the beneficiary can also gradually take money from the principal amount. Both of these options are similar to having the money in a savings account. For example, if the face value of the policy is $10,000, the insurance company may guarantee interest payments of 5 percent. Thus, the beneficiary would get $500 a year.

In a *fixed amount option,* a specific sum is paid to the beneficiary until the entire fund is used up. How long it takes depends on the size of the original sum, the interest rate agreed to, and the size of the payments.

LOAN OPTION

Under a *loan option,* the insured person can borrow any amount up to the cash surrender value of the policy. The interest he or she has to pay on this loan is written into the contract. It is usually 5 or 6 percent. In some cases, the insured can get an *automatic premium loan* clause in the policy. This means that if he or she fails to pay a premium, a loan in the amount of the premium will automatically be made to the insured. Thus, the premium will be paid, and he or she does not run the risk of the policy being cancelled.

GRACE PERIOD

If the insured person fails to pay a premium after the day it is due, he or she is allowed a *period of grace*—a period of time in which to pay it. The grace period is usually 31 days. During this time, the insured person is still protected. If he or she dies within the grace period, the price of the premium is subtracted from the amount given to the beneficiary.

REINSTATEMENT

After failing to pay a premium within the grace period, the contract can usually be *reinstated,* or renewed, within three or five years. First, however, the insured must provide satisfactory information on his or her insurability. This is usually done by giving the company the results of a thorough medical examination. Usually, reinstatement is not allowed if the policy has been cashed in.

CHANGE OF BENEFICIARY

In most contracts, the insured has the right to change the beneficiary. In some cases, however, the insured may want a *binding contract.* In this contract, the insured may not change the beneficiary without the beneficiary first agreeing to the change.

SUMMARY

There is more to life insurance protection than the standard term or whole life type of protection. Various contract provisions are part of different types of policies. Combination life insurance policies include a family policy, a family income policy, a modified life policy, and the double indemnity type of policy.

Important features of life insurance contracts include beneficiary clauses, various dividend arrangements, settlement plans, loan options, grace periods, reinstatement provisions, and rights to change beneficiaries. Any person or family buying life insurance should learn as much as possible about the many types of contracts and contract features that are available.

I. REVIEW OF TERMS

Which words complete the numbered statements?

cash surrender value   contract

nonparticipating   modified life

grace period   beneficiary

insurability   suicide

fixed amount option

1. In a _____ policy the early premiums are generally low, although the face amount of protection remains constant over the life of the policy.

2. Life insurance policies should be considered written _____ agreements between the insurer and the insured.

3. _____ policyholders do not share in dividends.

4. A _____ type of settlement allows for a fixed amount of dollars to be paid a _____ until the fund is exhausted.

5. The _____ is usually 31 days.

6. A _____ would not be considered a valid double indemnity death claim.

7. Under a loan option the insured person can borrow an amount up to the _____ of a policy.

8. Under a reinstatement option the insured must provide satisfactory information on his or her _____ .

II. REVIEW OF MAIN POINTS

1. Why would a family insurance policy appeal to a family?

2. Briefly explain *double indemnity insurance.*

3. Why is it necessary to name more than one beneficiary?

4. What is an insurance dividend?

5. Why is it important to have a grace period option written into a life insurance contract?

6. Explain the premium payment arrangement under a modified life policy.

III. LIFE INSURANCE CONTRACTS AND OPTIONS: CONCEPTS

1. What is meant by the statement that insurance dividends for participating policyholders are not guaranteed?
2. What is the advantage of having the dividend option in a life insurance policy?
3. What is the purpose of the interest option?
4. What is the automatic premium loan clause in a life insurance policy?
5. Why would a husband want to have term insurance protection for his wife?
6. Why would young people be attracted to the family income plan?
7. Explain how the family income insurance policy works.
8. Why would the change-of-beneficiary feature be important in some situations?

IV. LIFE INSURANCE CONTRACTS AND OPTIONS: EXERCISES

1. Recently, life insurance companies paid over $15 billion in benefits to beneficiaries and policyholders. Beneficiaries received 47.4 percent of this total.
   a. How much money did policyholders receive?
   b. Would the 47.4 percent figure be the same year after year? Why?
2. From a large life insurance company or an agent find out about their modified life insurance premium plans for a person your age. Prepare a short report on what you learn.
3. Examine Table 31–1 and decide whether this would be enough protection for you when you reach age twenty-five. Why?
4. By going to the library or some other source find out how much in dividends the three largest insurance companies paid out this past year.

DEVELOPING A LIFE INSURANCE PLAN

32

This chapter describes the programing approach to selling life insurance. This approach is used in developing a life insurance plan for someone interested in buying life insurance. In the case study about the Doyle family, the numbers are not the important facts to study. Instead, you should learn how the programing approach is put into action.

THE INGREDIENTS OF PROGRAMING

All organized activities, whether they are Girl Scout troops, art classes, Little League baseball teams, or social clubs, have to have organization plans. Little League baseball teams, for example, have managers, assistant managers, ballplayers, and fans. The plan of action is to have each ballplayer take part in the team activities. The plan also involves deciding when to have practice, who will bat in the line-up, and who will be substituted into a game at a particular point. If the plan is programed properly, each ballplayer will enjoy the Little League experience. If there is no plan or it is poorly run, the players will be unhappy.

The programing approach to selling life insurance is similar to the organization of any activity.

Programing life insurance is as necessary and important as Little League managers' plans. There are a number of steps for programing life insurance. If followed properly, they can make life insurance protection more understandable.

The *first step* is to make a complete study of the needs of the insured person and to develop some kind of ranking; that is, what is the most important protection today, what is the next most important, and so forth. The *second step* is to find out information regarding the insurance protection the insured person already has. This is often hard to do because of the various kinds of insurance a person may already have. The social security benefits the person will be entitled to in the future also have to be considered. The person's present coverage is then matched against the needs and priorities listed in step one. The *final step* in programing is determining how to get the best insurance protection at the lowest cost.

A CASE STUDY: THE DOYLE FAMILY

Pete Doyle is a research engineer for IBM in Austin, Texas. He is twenty-seven years old and he earns $14,500 a year. After taxes and other payments are subtracted from his paycheck, he takes home about $950 a month. He is covered by social security.

The IBM Corporation, as part of its benefits, provides him with term life insurance in the amount of $20,000. When Pete reaches the retirement age of sixty-two, he will get a pension equal to 60 percent of the average monthly salary he earned during the last five years that he worked. The amount he will receive from social security will be subtracted from his pension checks. This plan may change at any time. It is believed that the plan will soon be changed to make pensions equal to 70 percent of the average monthly salary.

Pete's wife, Terri, is twenty-six. They have two children: Margaret, who is four, and Rita, who is one and one-half. They own a home valued at $32,000 and pay a mortgage payment of $250 every month. The mortgage, which is held by the bank, has a balance of $27,000; that is, Pete

TABLE 32-1
THE DOYLE FAMILY INCOME, INSURANCE PROTECTION, AND HOME MORTGAGE

Item	Amount
Present Salary	$14,500/year
Take-home Pay	$950/month
IBM Group Term Insurance	$20,000
Pension	60% of Average Monthly Salary For Five Years Before Retirement Minus Social Security Retirement Benefits
Home	$32,000 value
Mortgage Payment	$250/month

has $27,000 left to pay the bank. The family now has very little money in its savings account. In this case study, money in savings will not be considered because Pete and Terri always seem to spend their savings account money during the holiday season.

THE RISKS TO THE DOYLES

Right now, all the Doyles are in excellent health. However, the risks that face the family include the death of Pete, Terri, Margaret, and Rita. Also, one or more of them may become disabled by an accident or because of poor health. Pete is the family's only wage earner. If he dies or becomes disabled, the family's income would be greatly reduced or cut off completely. If any family member had to be hospitalized, the family would have large medical bills to pay.

Pete and Terri have often talked about setting up an education fund for the girls. They also want to move to the coast of North Carolina when Pete retires. They want to plan for these costs as soon as possible.

THE FAMILY NEEDS

When considering their short-term and long-term plans, Pete and Terri have discussed what would happen to the family if Pete were to die early. Death is an unpleasant subject to discuss, but they both agree that it must be talked about since the future is so uncertain. One thing they have to do is figure out what would be needed if Pete were to die suddenly. One definite need would be income. Pete and Terri estimate that if Pete were to die that night, the family would need an income of $850 a month. This amount would be necessary in order to support Terri, Margaret, and Rita at their present standard of living. Right now, the family has $950 to spend every month. If Pete were not present, the family expenses would be about 10 percent lower. Pete and Terri assume that the family budget will drop to $700 a month when the girls are at college. The girls will probably have jobs and pay for their tuition and some of their living expenses. When the girls complete college, Terri could probably live on $550 a month.

Pete and Terri have also thought about setting up what they call a *clean-up fund*. This money would be used to pay funeral expenses, bills, and taxes. They feel that $4,000 would be needed in this fund. Pete also feels that Terri would need some ready cash for herself immediately after his death. They consider $2,000 reasonable for her needs. The family estimates of dollar needs if Pete were to suddenly die are presented in Table 32–2.

TABLE 32–2
PETE AND TERRI'S ESTIMATE OF FAMILY DOLLAR NEEDS IF PETE WERE TO DIE SUDDENLY

Situation	Amount
Family Living Requirement	$850/month
When Terri Is Forty-three, Forty-four, & Forty-five Years Old	700/month
When Terri Is Between Forty-five And the Rest of Her Life	550/month
Clean-up Money Immediately Needed After Pete's Death	4000
Ready Cash Immediately Needed After Pete's Death	2000

If Terri were to die suddenly instead of Pete, there would also be a need for extra money. This money would be needed for hiring people to take care of the house and care for the children. Pete and Terri feel that $350 a month would be a fair amount to have available in the event of Terri's death. In this case study, however, only the risk of Pete's death will be studied.

PRESENT LIFE INSURANCE PROTECTION

If Pete were to suddenly become disabled or die, the family would be entitled to social security benefits of $434 a month. These payments would continue until Margaret is eighteen. They would then be cut to $327 a month until Rita reaches age eighteen. At that time, when Rita is eighteen years old, Terri will be forty-two. She will then stop receiving social security benefits until she is sixty. After age sixty, she will be entitled to $156 per month for the rest of her life.

A survivor is entitled to a lump-sum benefit of $255 from the social security program. If Pete were to die, Terri would get $20,000 from the IBM group term life insurance. Thus, Terri would have $20,255 in cash and would need only $6,000 ($4,000 to clean up bills and expenses and another $2,000 for immediate needs). This would leave a balance of $14,255.

If this $14,255 were placed in a savings account and earned 4 percent interest, it could provide Terri with some money while the girls grow up. She could earn about $470 interest the first year and use this and some of the savings account as additional money. Over a period of 17 years she could possibly receive about $100 per month. This would include the interest and part of the savings account, which would get smaller

TABLE 32–3
THE DOYLE FAMILY INCOME PICTURE IF PETE WERE TO DIE SUDDENLY

	Terri, Margaret, Rita	Terri (Girls both off at college or away from home)	Terri	Terri
Terri's Age	26 to 43	43 to 45	45 to 60	60 to death
Family's Plan of Monthly Income to Sustain Acceptable Standard of Living	$850	$700	$550	$550
Social Security Benefits	$434	$434	0	$156
Group Life Insurance Money	$100	0	0	0
Unfilled Money Need	$316	$266	$550	$344
Length of Time	17 years	2 years	15 years	Indefinite

every year. This money, plus her social security benefits, would give her $535 a month until Margaret reaches age eighteen. This would be $316 less than the family wanted Terri to have if Pete were to die suddenly.

Unfortunately, Terri would constantly have a shortage of dollars. She would not be able to live as well as when Pete was alive.

THE DOYLE FAMILY INSURANCE PROGRAM

There is no one answer to the amount of insurance the Doyles should get to help Terri keep her family together and support them if Pete were to die suddenly. To help them decide what kind of insurance is best they asked a reputable insurance agent, Bill Nokomaru, to prepare a plan for them. Bill divided the dollar needs of the family, if Pete were to die, into three periods of time. The first part is the *child-rearing* segment. It would be 19 years long and extend from when Terri is twenty-six to forty-five. For 17 years of this period she would need an extra $316. For the next two years she would need $266 a month. This could be provided with an annuity of $316 a month for 16 years and a second annuity of only $266 for the remaining two years. This amount of income could be provided by an annuity policy of $35,000 with 3 percent interest.

Next, Bill decided that a temporary life annuity of $550 a month would be needed for Terri during the next time period, from the age of forty-five to sixty. This would mean that a policy with a face value of $120,000 would have to be bought. But it would not have to be bought for 19 years. If the plan were purchased today for later protection, it would have to have a value of about $72,000. For the third time period, which

TABLE 32–4
PLAN PREPARED BY BILL NOKOMARU FOR DOYLE FAMILY

Amount For Period	Insurance Required
$316 for 17 Years at Terri's Age Twenty-six $50 Less, or $266, for 2 Years at Terri's Age Forty-three	$ 35,000
$550 for 15 Years at Terri's Age Forty-five	72,000
$344 for Rest of Life at Terri's Age Sixty	60,000
Total Needed	$167,000

starts when Terri is sixty, a remaining life annuity of $344 a month would be needed. It would be valued at over $60,000.

A SUGGESTED PLAN FOR THE DOYLES

There is no one single plan that every insurance agent would suggest for the Doyle family. Any plan that allows the family to buy $167,000 of protection is going to cost a lot of money. The least expensive method of purchasing $167,000 worth of insurance would cost about $5 per thousand dollars for a yearly renewable term policy. This would mean a yearly cost of $835 (167 × $5) for a nonparticipating term policy. This cost would increase every year because the premium is based on Pete's age. If the Doyles wanted ordinary permanent life insurance protection in the form of a $167,000 policy, it would cost them about $1,975 a year, or almost two-and-one-half times the amount for the term protection.

The family agrees with Bill Nokomaru that $1,975 a year is more than the family can afford. They decided to disregard, for the time being, Terri's needs after age forty-five. This means that they want to protect Terri specifically during the time the girls are growing up. The Doyles then decided to buy a $35,000 whole life, nonparticipating policy. This policy will cost about $480 a year. They could add a $40,000, 20-year decreasing term clause to the ordinary life policy for about $3.30 per thousand dollars, or $132 a year. This would provide some of the money needed when the girls are growing up. This means that the family will have to pay a yearly premium of about $612.

There is certainly nothing magical about the program outlined for the Doyles. It is realistic in that it meets the family's needs for particular insurance protection during the child-raising years. A good insurance

TABLE 32-5
THE DOYLE FAMILY PLAN

Type of Insurance	Cost
$35,000 of Whole Life (Nonparticipating)	$480/per year
$40,000, 20-year Decreasing Term Insurance	132/per year
Annual Life Insurance Premium for Now	$612

agent would certainly go through the programing steps that Bill Noko-maru used.

SUMMARY

The case study in this chapter showed a programing approach for life insurance protection. You should not memorize any of the figures but should instead think about the problems this family had in developing a plan. What is good for the Doyles may be completely wrong for the Parkers, Johnsons, Tarkanians, Mannetis, Goldbergs, or any other family with four people.

Also, our example concentrated only on life insurance. A typical family usually also pays for health, home, and automobile insurance. Thus, a complete programing approach would have to take these insurance needs into consideration.

REVIEW DEVELOPING A LIFE INSURANCE PLAN

I. REVIEW OF TERMS

Which words complete the numbered statements?

child-raising   clean-up
two-and-one-half   second step

1. The Doyle family thought that a _____ fund would be necessary to pay expenses, bills, and taxes if Pete were to suddenly die.

2. The _____ in programing life insurance is to find out the insured's present coverage.

3. The Doyle family finally decided that the _____ period would be the most difficult time for Terri in providing for the family.

4. It was estimated that $167,000 of ordinary life insurance, if purchased now, would cost about _____ times the amount for term protection for this amount.

II. REVIEW OF MAIN POINTS

1. What are the three steps in programing life insurance?
2. What is the child-rearing segment in the Doyles' plan?
3. When is the greatest need for income for Pete's survivors?
4. How can an agent help a family that is developing a plan for life insurance protection?

III. DEVELOPING A LIFE INSURANCE PLAN: CONCEPTS

1. Why are dollars in the budget for insurance limited?
2. If the Doyle family had to pay a yearly life insurance premium of $1,975, how much would have to be set aside each month for insurance?
3. Should the Doyle family consider buying educational endowment funds for the girls? Why?
4. What do you think would be the family's three largest expenses in a month?

IV. DEVELOPING A LIFE INSURANCE PLAN: EXERCISES

1. Contact a life insurance agent in your community and ask the agent if he or she uses a programing approach. Write a short report on the approach the agent describes.
2. Do you believe that with the dollar decreasing in value every year that the estimates for the Doyle family's income after the death of Pete are realistic? Please explain your answer.
3. You hear the following conversation take place between two adults:

   John: "Bill, did you know that 8 out of 10 Americans own life insurance? But few families can buy all of the protection they really need."

   Bill: "Why can't families buy all the protection they really need?"

   Use the discussion of the Doyle family's problem of insurance budget dollars to provide Bill with an answer. Prepare a short report answering Bill's question.

33 HEALTH INSURANCE PROTECTION

In addition to life insurance, families also think about health insurance. The health risk that everyone faces is the chance that an injury or sickness will suddenly occur. It is estimated that every year, four out of five people are disabled for at least one day because of some illness. One in every eighteen people is disabled due to accidental injury. In addition, one person in every seven is hospitalized.

When a person such as Pete Doyle is disabled, his family has to pay increased medical bills while often receiving less income. On the average,

"Here I am—Johnny on the spot, your friendly insurance agent."
Drawing by Geo. Price; © 1958 The New Yorker Magazine, Inc.

a person under forty-five years of age loses 4.5 days of work every year. Illness and accidents, like death, are inevitable and highly unpredictable. A regular program of medical care, including examinations, proper diet, and exercise, can lead to better health.

THE RISK POOL

The possibility of illness and disability always exists. Instead of a family saving money for a day when illness strikes, insurance companies pool the money of insured individuals. Table 33-1 shows average medical costs per year for people in three different age groups.

TABLE 33-1
HIGH COST OF AGING—ANNUAL EXPENSE BY AGE GROUP

	Under 19	19–64	65 and over
Hospital	$ 33	$141	$372
Doctors	41	64	136
Dentists	14	25	17
Other professional services	5	7	15
Drugs and sundries	16	34	84
Eyeglasses, medical appliances	4	10	19
Nursing homes	—	2	129
Other	10	13	17
TOTAL Annual Expense	$123	$296	$789

NOTE: *The figures quoted are for 1972.*

TYPES OF HEALTH PROTECTION THAT PAY EXPENSES

The variety of health insurance contracts is endless. There are a number of popular policies that help cover the expenses caused by illness.

HOSPITAL INSURANCE

A popular policy to help pay for room and board in a hospital plus certain extras is the *hospital insurance contract.* Some policies also pay some of the nursing expenses.

A regular program of health care is important. This mother waits in a hospital for checkups for herself and her children.

Usually, the insurance company pays the patient's room and board expenses up to a certain amount per day. The money is paid directly to the insured person, not the hospital. One plan pays the full room and board bill for 60 days of hospitalization and one-half of the bill for an additional 30 days. Hospital extras include such items as X-rays, drugs, and laboratory tests. Usually, hospital insurance pays for at least some portion of these extra expenses.

For a family such as the Doyles it would be necessary to have Pete's policy cover his dependents—Terri and the two girls. In a hospital insurance policy, dependent coverage includes the wife and unmarried children under the age of eighteen. If the children are full-time students they are covered until they reach the age of twenty-one or, under some policies, age twenty-five.

SURGICAL INSURANCE

Any kind of surgical operation is very expensive. *Surgical insurance contracts* pay various amounts for different operations. In most policies these payments range from $200 to $1,000.

MEDICAL INSURANCE

Medical insurance is often called *basic medical* or *regular medical* insurance. It aims to cover all or part of the expense of ordinary doctors' fees for hospital, office or home visits other than for surgical procedures.

Benefits are paid on three bases: 1) in-hospital, 2) total disability, and 3) nondisability. *In-hospital* insurance pays only while the person is in the hospital. *Total disability* insurance pays doctors' fees whether or not the patient is in the hospital. However, the patient has to be completely disabled to collect. *Nondisability* coverage pays doctors' fees for home, office, or hospital visits.

MAJOR MEDICAL INSURANCE

Major medical insurance covers almost every type of medical expense. It pays almost all hospital and doctor costs. It provides hospital, surgical, and medical coverage and includes such expenses as X-rays and drugs. Some policies require that the patient be admitted to a hospital at some time during treatment. Other policies cover whatever is prescribed by a doctor no matter where the service is performed.

Major medical insurance policies have a *deductible payment feature*. The deductible payment feature is a certain amount of money, say $250, that the insured person has to pay before the insurance company starts its payments. Then, the company pays 75 to 80 percent of the remaining expenses up to a certain amount.

As an example, assume that Pete Doyle has an accident and has to be hospitalized. He would have to pay the first $250 of his medical bills. His major medical insurance policy would then pay 75 percent of the rest of his expenses up to $8,500. If Pete's expenses came to $3,000, his payment and insurance coverage would look like this:

A) Pete pays $250—the deductible amount.
B) The total expense after the deductible amount is subtracted is $2,750.
C) Pete pays 25 percent of the $2,750, or $687.50.

Many insurance companies now include coverage for a variety of important health services.

D) Thus, Pete pays $250 plus $687.50, or $937.50.

E) The insurance company pays $2,062.50.

Pete thus would pay almost one-third ($937.50) of the bill. If his expenses were over $8,500, he would have to pay every cent of the amount over $8,500. The premiums on a major medical policy depend on such factors as family size and the amount of the deductible.

NURSING HOME, DENTAL SERVICES, AND MENTAL ILLNESS INSURANCE

Insurance companies have increased their coverage to include many kinds of services. Many people who are hospitalized could be properly cared for at less cost in a nursing home. Thus, nursing home insurance protection has become fairly common.

Dental insurance covering the cost of examinations, X-rays, fillings, extractions, and other dental procedures has become more popular in the past ten years or so. Many businesses have added dental insurance to their insurance programs for their employees. Most dental policies, like major medical insurance, require a deductible amount to be paid by the insured person. The insurance company then pays a certain percentage of the remaining amount.

Until recently, mental illness was almost never covered by health insurance contracts. Many contracts still exclude these illnesses. There are some contracts, however, that provide limited coverage for mental illness. For example, hospital room-and-board coverage up to 60 days for mental illnesses is found in an increasing number of contracts.

TYPES OF HEALTH PROTECTION THAT PROVIDE INCOME

If a major income earner in a family is disabled by an illness or injury, family expenses go up while family income goes down. The family must struggle to pay for groceries, clothing, education, and other needs. There are, however, several types of insurance that provide some financial help when disability or illness strikes.

DISABILITY INCOME

Disability income insurance is sometimes a special feature, or *rider,* that is included in life insurance contracts. This type of insurance can give a family $10 a month for every $1,000 of the face amount of the life insurance contract. These payments are made only when the insured person is completely disabled. They do not start until the person has been disabled for six months. Also, the disability must occur before the person reaches age fifty-five.

COMMERCIAL CONTRACTS

The commercial contract is similar to the ordinary life insurance contract. It is issued for income benefits only and for a term of only one year.

Accidental injury and sickness may both be covered by one commercial contract. Accident benefits include weekly payments for both total and partial disability. They also include special benefits for such things as medical expenses, accidental death, and loss of sight. Sickness benefits include weekly payments for total disability and some hospital and medical expenses.

MAJOR SOURCES OF HEALTH INSURANCE

Health insurance protection is offered by both government and non-government groups. The largest government health insurance plan is the disability income and medical benefits portion of the social security program. State governments also have workmen's compensation laws. These laws provide medical and income benefits for workers who are disabled by work-related injury or disease. This kind of protection is very important. More than two million workers suffer disabling injuries each year, and approximately 14,000 people die as a result of work-related accidents.

Nongovernment sources of health insurance protection include insurance companies, Blue Cross and Blue Shield, and independent company plans. Independent plans are usually sponsored by a company for its workers and their families. Two such plans are the Kaiser Foundation Health Plan for Kaiser employees in California, and the United Mine Workers of America Welfare and Retirement Fund for union members and their families. Blue Cross and Blue Shield, because of their widespread use, will be discussed in detail in the following section.

BLUE CROSS AND BLUE SHIELD

Blue Cross and Blue Shield are nonprofit organizations. They were formed to provide hospital and surgical insurance protection for their members. For this protection, the members have to pay a fee—the premium.

This type of insurance is bought on a group basis. The group is usually made up of the employees of a company. In most group insurance contracts, the insurer makes an agreement with the company, and each insured employee gets a certificate showing that the employee and the employee's dependents are protected.

The Victerite Packaging Corporation of Chicago has a typical group insurance plan. Any employee can join the plan. When the employee joins, he or she pays 50 percent of the monthly premium. The company pays the other 50 percent. The premiums are the same for all employees, regardless of age. In some plans, however, the premium varies according to age.

The Blue Cross Association plan is for hospital expenses. It has been approved by the American Hospital Association. A popular type of contract is one that provides full coverage for hospital room and board—usually for a semi-private room. It also covers hospital extras. Maternity benefits are also included. The coverage for a child usually begins at birth and lasts until the child reaches age nineteen.

There are many variations in the coverage provided by a Blue Cross contract. It is important for the insured person to know exactly what his or her particular plan covers.

Blue Shield plans cover doctors' fees and are controlled by doctors in the organization. Note that the Blue Cross plan is controlled by member hospitals, while the Blue Shield plan is controlled by member doctors.

Doctors in the Blue Shield plan agree to provide services to those who are insured. However, very often the doctor's fee is higher than the amount of coverage stated in the contract. Thus, not all of the doctor's fee will be covered by the plan.

SUGGESTED GUIDELINES FOR BUYING HEALTH INSURANCE

With the many kinds of health insurance protection available, you should always take care to study the policy so that you can get the kind of protection you want.

WHAT DOES THE POLICY COVER?

No policy pays for all of a person's or family's medical expenses. Every contract covers only specific kinds of expenses. Thus, you have to find out what the coverage of the policy is. This can only be done with careful study.

WHAT WILL THE POLICY PAY?

Perhaps $500 a week seems like a lot of money for health expenses. But on the average, room and board in a hospital cost about $85 a day. In addition, there are doctors' fees, drugs, X-rays, and other extras. Thus, an insurance plan that pays $500 a week may not be enough. You should always find out exactly what the policy pays during disability and sickness.

WHEN DO BENEFITS START?

Read the benefit coverage clauses in your contract carefully. They will tell you when and for how long the benefits will be paid. A long waiting period may cause a tremendous financial burden for a family.

IS THE COMPANY DEPENDABLE?

Every insured person wants his or her insurance company to pay claims quickly, without arguing over amounts. This means that you should check with friends or people who have made claims through the company. It is also important to find out if the company is licensed to do business in the state where the insured person lives. Not being licensed may mean that an insured person may not receive his or her benefits. It may also mean that the insured person may have difficulty in getting help to sue an insurance company, should this become necessary.

SUMMARY

Accidents and illnesses are facts of life that every person must face at one time or another. There are many health insurance protection policies that can reduce the financial burden caused by disability. Many plans cover hospital expenses, doctors' fees, nursing home costs, and dental services. Health protection plans are divided into plans that cover expenses and plans that provide income.

Both government and nongovernment sources offer health insurance protection. The three major nongovernment sources are insurance companies, Blue Cross and Blue Shield, and independent plans.

REVIEW   HEALTH INSURANCE PROTECTION

I.   REVIEW OF TERMS

Which words complete the numbered statements?

regular medical insurance	mental illness
Blue Shield	disability income
extra	deductible
forty-five	employees
health	sixty-five and older

1. Costs for such items as drugs, laboratory tests, and X-rays are _____ hospital expenses.

2. Until recently _____ was usually not covered in health insurance contracts.

3. A popular feature added to life insurance contracts is the _____ insurance.

4. It is generally accepted that both the life risk and _____ risk are inevitable facts of living.

5. Recent statistics show that the average cost of hospital care a year for people _____ is $372.

6. Medical insurance is often called _____.
7. Major medical insurance has a _____ payment feature.
8. Many business organizations have added dental insurance for their _____.
9. Blue Cross and _____ are nongovernment sources of health insurance.
10. A person under _____ years of age loses approximately 4.5 days of work a year.

II. REVIEW OF MAIN POINTS

1. What kind of questions should be considered when thinking about buying health insurance?
2. Who controls Blue Shield plans?
3. Explain how disability income insurance works.
4. What is the difference between medical insurance and major medical insurance?
5. What kind of accident benefits are paid by commercial health contracts?
6. What kind of expenses would a dental insurance policy cover?
7. Briefly define *surgical health insurance.*

III. HEALTH INSURANCE PROTECTION: CONCEPTS

1. Is it a good idea to get insurance protection for illness? Why?
2. How can a person buy health insurance?
3. Mr. Robert Smart stated that because of the improvements in medical services in this country, it is not good sense to purchase medical insurance. Do you agree? Explain.
4. Are there any similarities between life insurance and health insurance protection?
5. Explain what steps can be taken to minimize disabilities. Which of these steps do you follow?
6. In major medical insurance policies the insurance company pays only up to a maximum amount. What does this mean?
7. What is an independent health insurance plan?
8. What does a regular Blue Cross policy cover?

IV. HEALTH INSURANCE PROTECTION: EXERCISES

1. Ask five older people that are employed by business organizations if they have Blue Cross-Blue Shield protection. How many of them do?

2. Assume that Pete Doyle has a hospital bill for $8,900. His major medical policy will pay 75 percent of this bill over $300 and up to $8,000. How much will Pete have to pay?

3. In the State of California, no health insurance policy will be approved for sale in the State if any of the benefits it provides fail to meet a specified dollar amount. Why do you think the State has passed this requirement?

4. Briefly explain why it would be important for a four-member family, such as the Doyles, to have their health insurance benefits start as soon as illness or injury strikes.

5. Prepare a short report that traces the history of how Blue Cross and Blue Shield started in this country. Use the library or ask the Blue Cross-Blue Shield representatives in your community for information.

HOME AND AUTOMOBILE INSURANCE

For most people, their homes and their cars are the most expensive things they ever buy. Most homes and cars in the United States are insured against loss caused by fire, theft, and other types of damage. This type of protection is definitely needed.

It is also important to be protected against other people's losses when they occur on your property. When someone owns a home, he or she is responsible for the safety of those people who use or visit that home. This means that the homeowner must be responsible for guests, neighbors, baby-sitters, mail carriers, people who do repairs, and others. Homeowners insurance has this type of coverage.

Car owners have the same responsibility to their passengers, other drivers, pedestrians, and property. Car owners, too, can buy insurance against losses to themselves and others.

RISKS OF OWNING A HOME

The single-family home is exposed to many different risks. Those that can be covered by insurance are listed below:

Direct Damage Direct damage to a home can be caused by fire, lightning, vandalism, earthquake, glass breakage, and explosion. Some insurance companies offer protection against all of these risks. Others only provide coverage for some of these risks.

Liability The owner of a home or a car may become liable to people who are injured or killed while on or in the property. To be *liable* means that the property owner is legally required to make good any loss or damage

434

that occurs on or in his or her property. However, the injured person must prove that the injury was caused by the carelessness of the owner. For example, a mail carrier who is bitten by a dog may sue the dog's owner. But the mail carrier must prove that his or her injured leg and ripped clothing were caused by the owner's negligence. Like direct damage, liability can be protected against by insurance.

Declining Value of Home—Depreciation of a home is a gradual decrease in value that occurs because of normal wear and tear. *Obsolescence* refers to a home becoming no longer useful. Depreciation and obsolescence are two reasons why a home decreases in value. These losses cannot be insured against, but they are serious risks and always have to be considered.

HOMEOWNERS INSURANCE

A homeowner may want to buy insurance for only his or her real property, such as the home and garage. Every home, however, has furniture, clothing, and other personal items. These things have value and can be lost, stolen, damaged, or destroyed. Thus, personal property protection is also needed. Today, most homeowners buy a combination in-

Houses are major investments and are exposed to many costly risks.

435

surance policy that provides a wide range of coverage for real and personal property. This combination policy is called a *homeowners policy.*

In this policy all the property and liability needs of the homeowner are covered. It usually includes fire insurance and coverage against loss of personal property. There are various forms of protection that can be included in the homeowner policy. Each form provides specific kinds of protection. For example, the basic form of homeowners protection provides limited protection. The *elite form* provides broad coverage.

The elite, or *Cadillac,* form of one nationally-known homeowners policy protects against the following losses:

Fire and lightning	Damage by aircraft
Damage by smoke, windstorm, and hail	Vandalism
	Loss due to theft
Damage by explosion	Collapse
Riot or civil commotion	Damage by electrical accidents
Damage by vehicles	Damage by weight of snow, ice, or sleet
Water escape and rupture of hot-water heating systems	Damage by freezing
	Specified damage to trees, shrubs, plants, lawn

This policy also insures against loss from negligence. This is called protection against *personal liability.* The insurance company must pay up to a certain amount for any injury, disease, or death of a person resulting from his or her being present on the insured person's property.

The elite homeowners policy would also pay all reasonable expenses for medical, dental, surgical, ambulance, hospital, nursing, and funeral services for each guest whose injury or death occurred while on the owner's property. These expenses would be paid for an entire year after the accident.

Another feature of the elite homeowners policy is that it insures against any loss caused by the theft of the owner's credit cards. Someone who steals a credit card can sometimes run up a large bill. Insurance against credit card theft is important for people who have a lot of credit cards. It should be noted that each of the types of protection discussed here can be purchased separately. For example, a homeowner may want only personal liability protection. He or she would buy only this type of protection and not the elite homeowners policy.

COST OF HOME INSURANCE

The two most important things that determine the cost of home insurance are 1) the kind of coverage and 2) the amount. The premium for a policy covering only fire insurance is usually lower than the elite homeowners policy, which covers many more risks.

The way in which premiums are determined differs for specific coverage, such as fire insurance or the elite homeowners policy. The premium for fire insurance is affected by the construction of the house (brick or frame), how good the local fire department is, how far the house is from a fire hydrant, and the amount of insurance bought.

The premium for an elite homeowners policy is much more than that of an individual fire or theft insurance policy. But it usually costs less than buying the protection in separate policies. Once the homeowner decides how much insurance he or she needs, the premium for a homeowners policy is looked up in special tables made for different types of homes according to their construction and location.

The American Insurance Association inspects cities and develops a rating scale that is used to determine homeowners' premiums. The better the fire protection, water supply, building materials, and other factors are, the lower the rating and the premiums are.

TABLE 34-1
PREMIUMS FOR THE ELITE HOMEOWNERS POLICY

Class Rating of Cities by the American Insurance Association	Annual Premium for a $32,000 Home
1-6	$159
7-8	$168
9	$183
10	$195

NOTE: *The premium also covers $12,000 of the contents of the home. That is, the furniture, lamps, clothing, etc. are covered up to $12,000 worth of damage, loss, or theft.*

Suppose that Pete Doyle's home, which is in Austin, Texas, is insured for $32,000. Since Austin has a paid fire department the Doyle home would probably be rated in the 3, 4, 5, or 6 class. Assume that Austin is a class 4 city. Pete would then have to pay $159 a year for his homeowners policy. (See Table 34–1.) This policy would give him property loss, property damage, fire, theft, personal liability, and credit card forgery protection. Of course, the more protection he has, the higher the premium would be.

GETTING MONEY FROM THE INSURANCE COMPANY

Whenever property is destroyed, stolen, or damaged, the owner is concerned about how much the insurance company will pay him or her for the loss. If the Doyle family home was insured for $32,000, the insurance company would pay Pete $32,000 if the house was burned to the ground.

TABLE 34–2
AN INVENTORY OF THE CONTENTS OF THE DOYLE HOME

Item	Purchase Date	Cost	Item	Purchase Date	Cost
Desk	1971	$ 348	Bed Furniture	1974	$ 182
				1972	112
Couch	1972	652		1972	114
TV	1970	340	Dressers	1969	180
				1973	195
Lamps	1970	81		1974	353
	1971	80		1974	512
	1971	42			
	1971	52	Matresses & Springs	1972	655
Radios	1973	49			
	1973	68	Chairs & Table	1974	385
Movie Camera	1969	150			
			Drapes	1973	650
Clothing (estimate)	1969	2,500			
	1974		China Cabinet	1973	800
		$4,362			$4,138

Total Estimate: $4,362 + $4,138 = $8,500.

Even if the house was valued at $41,000, Pete would receive only $32,000. The destroyed contents of the house, however, would pose a problem. Insurance companies, in their home insurance contracts, usually state that the insured person must show some *proof of loss* of the destroyed items. This means that it is the owner's responsibility to show how many items there were and what these items cost when they were bought. In order to show proof of loss, many careful homeowners make an *inventory list.* This is a list of the major items in the house, the dates they were bought, and how much they cost. A list of most of the major items in the Doyle home is shown in Table 34–2. This list is the kind of proof that the insurance company can use to repay the Doyles for their losses. In addition, some insurance companies suggest taking photos of furniture and other property. These photos can be used to support claims.

AUTOMOBILE INSURANCE

On the average, one person is killed or injured in an automobile accident every eleven seconds. According to the National Safety Council, there are more traffic deaths and injuries every year than our armed services suffered during World War II, the Korean War, and the Vietnam War. In addition to the human suffering and loss of life caused by automobile accidents there is almost always some financial loss.

An interesting fact is that the average American family spends more on automobile insurance than on home insurance. This may be because the automobile exposes many people to risk. For example, cars may be destroyed, damaged, or stolen. They may damage private property and injure or kill other people as well as the owner. Almost everybody is exposed to the many risks of car travel.

THE RANGE OF INSURANCE PROTECTION

There is an endless range of automobile policies. Also, the types of protection available always seem to be changing. From year to year new items are covered and other items are dropped.

Another reason why there is a variety of policies is that there are so many insurance companies trying to attract customers. This competition leads to many different forms of insurance from which the buyer can choose.

TYPES OF AUTOMOBILE COVERAGE

Most individual and family automobile policies cover a number of risks. Exactly what a policy covers depends on what the car owner wants or what the insurance company provides. Common kinds of coverage are described under the following topics:

LIABILITY PROTECTION

Liability insurance protects the car owner against claims for injuries or property damage caused by the owner's car or by someone else's car when he or she was driving it. There are two types of liability insurance: (1) bodily injury liability and (2) property damage liability.

Bodily injury liability insurance covers people riding in the insured person's car, people riding in other cars, and pedestrians. It does not, however, cover the insured person. The amounts of coverage are expressed as 10/20, 25/50, 75/150, 100/300, and so forth. The first number is the basic limit in thousands of dollars that the company will pay for bodily injury to each person. The second number is the maximum number in thousands of dollars that will be paid to *all* of the people who are injured in one accident.

The insurance company will pay all reasonable medical expenses within one year of the accident for injuries caused by the accident. Usually, bodily injury insurance covers the injuries of other persons, not the insured. To get protection for himself or herself and his or her family, the insured person must get medical insurance as well as bodily injury insurance.

Property damage liability protection is another type of liability insurance. If you were to cause a car wreck, or wreck your brother's or sister's car while driving it, or knock down a telephone pole owned by the city, you could be responsible for the property damage you caused. Many people buy $5,000 worth of property damage protection. This means that if the insured person causes the wreck of another automobile, the company will pay up to $5,000 for losses caused by the accident. Note that this protection does not include damage to the insured person's car.

UNINSURED MOTORIST PROTECTION

Sometimes automobile accidents are caused by people who do not have insurance. If the motorist is not insured, the insured person may have to pay for the damage to his or her own car as well as his or her own medical expenses. This is certainly unfair to the insured person. The uninsured person is a menace to every insured person. In most states it is illegal to drive an uninsured car.

By buying uninsured motorist protection, the insured person would be covered for damages resulting from an accident caused by an uninsured motorist.

The question of who caused the accident and the amount to be paid to the insured is generally determined by agreement between the insurance company and the insured. If they cannot agree, the amount is decided by a neutral party, someone they both agree will make a fair decision.

COMPREHENSIVE PROTECTION

In a comprehensive insurance policy, the insurance company agrees to pay for losses other than those caused by collision. This type of protection is for the breakage of glass, losses caused by falling objects, theft, explosions, earthquakes, windstorms, tornadoes, vandalism, and similar risks. Sometimes comprehensive insurance also covers the loss of things from inside the car.

These losses are based upon estimates of the value of the car and the things in it. Suppose a fairly new car owned by Frances Murphy was destroyed by fire. The car was bought in January for $3,950. In the car were her brand new $350 golf clubs and two tennis rackets, each costing $50. The fire occurred in November, nearly eleven months after the car was bought. The insurance company would pay Frances $3,300 for the car, $330 for the golf clubs, and $45 for each of the tennis rackets.

COLLISION PROTECTION

Collision insurance protection covers the car against damages that occur when it collides with other objects. It doesn't matter if the other objects are moving or standing still. A car that turns over without having hit another object is also covered by collision insurance.

There are a number of reasons why collision insurance is bought separately from comprehensive protection. Some people buying comprehensive coverage do not want to spend the extra money to buy collision insurance, which is rather expensive. Also, collision insurance usually includes a deductible statement. This means that for each accident, the car owner agrees to pay the deductible amount, and the insurance company agrees to pay the rest of the bill. For example, a $100 deductible means that if Gene Kupeli's car was involved in an accident and the repairs cost $575, Gene would pay $100 and the company would pay $475.

Since many cars are bought on installment plans, it is important to know that most banks and other creditors require both comprehensive and collision protection. These kinds of insurance plans offer some protection to the creditor until the car is completely paid for.

TABLE 34-3 CAR INSURANCE SUMMARY		
	Who Is Covered?	
Type of Insurance Protection	The Insured	Other People
Bodily Injury Protection		
Bodily Injury Liability	NO	YES
Medical Payments	YES	YES
Uninsured Motorists	YES	YES
Property Damage Protection		
Property Damage Liability	NO	YES
Comprehensive Coverage	YES	NO
Collision	YES	NO

COSTS OF AUTOMOBILE INSURANCE

Most of the money used by insurance companies to pay claims is the money paid to them by insured motorists. The premium each insured person pays is influenced by a number of factors. Three of the most important are the following factors:

EXPOSURE TO RISKS

The type of risks a motorist is exposed to affects his or her premium rate. One important consideration is where the insured person lives. The city driver is faced with the dangers of heavy traffic, narrow city streets, and a fairly high rate of car theft. These risks might be much lower in other places.

Another risk factor involves distance, namely, how far the car will be driven every day. The more a car is on the road, the greater its chances of being in an accident.

DRIVER'S EXPERIENCE

The cost of the premium is also affected by the driver's experience: how long he or she has driven and whether he or she is considered a safe driver. The driver's safety record can be determined by the number of accidents he or she has had and the traffic tickets he or she has received. This information is usually asked for on an insurance application form.

DRIVER'S AGE

Younger drivers usually pay higher premiums than older drivers. However, lower rates are given to drivers under the age of twenty-one who have successfully completed a recognized driver education course. A number of companies also give lower rates to students with good school grades. They seem to believe that students with good grades are safer drivers.

To get a more complete picture of premiums you should examine the rates for an adult male over twenty-five years old. (The rates for men sixteen to twenty-five change so much from one year to the next that they would not provide a meaningful example.) In the given example, large, medium, and small communities are used to show differences

Often lower rates are given to young drivers who have completed driver education courses.

TABLE 34-4
PREMIUMS FOR A NEW $4,000 CAR

Insurance Protection	(Large) Chicago	(Medium) Columbus, Ohio	(Small) Iowa City, Iowa
Bodily Injury Liability [10/20]	$ 64	$ 52	$ 34
Property Damage Liability [$5,000 per accident]	42	40	20
Comprehensive	25	20	20
Collision [$50 deductible]	62	42	40
TOTAL	$193	$154	$114

in the rates. The premiums are for bodily injury liability, property damage liability, comprehensive, and collision insurance with a $50 deductible. The rates shown in Table 34-4 suggest that the Chicago motorist is faced with more risks than the car owner in Columbus, Ohio, or Iowa City, Iowa.

NO-FAULT INSURANCE

In 1968, the American Insurance Association proposed an insurance plan that would pay all insured people in a car accident no matter whose fault it was. This insurance would cover the car owner and the owner's family as well as other passengers who are not otherwise insured. This plan has been tried in various parts of the country and has met with great success.

In 1970, Massachusetts became the first state to enact a no-fault insurance law. Under this law the insurance company must pay, regardless of fault, the first $2,000 of bodily injury losses suffered by the insured. Injured persons can still bring claims against the insured driver for negligence.

Whether no-fault insurance will be widely adopted in the future is unknown at this time. There is much controversy over whether no-fault plans should be made compulsory or voluntary. Some people propose that no-fault automobile insurance should replace the traditional types of insurance. With no-fault insurance it is no longer important to find out who is at fault; legal battles—and lawyers' fees—can be avoided. Also, the elimination of lawsuits means that the payments of benefits to victims are speeded up. Some opponents of no-fault insurance argue that if all accident victims are covered there will be a drop in the total benefits paid. They believe that no-fault insurance will lead to paying smaller claims only.

SUMMARY

Homes are exposed to various risks, including direct damage, liability, and a decrease in value. These hazards must be considered when thinking about protecting real property, such as the home, and personal property, such as jewelry. In the elite homeowners policy, the homeowner is insured against property damage, liability claims, medical payments, and even credit card theft.

Automobile insurance policies protect car owners against liability, uninsured drivers, and collision damages. Insurance premiums are determined largely by the driver's exposure to risks, his or her experience, and his or her age. A new type of car insurance is the no-fault policy, which pays insured persons no matter who is at fault.

I. REVIEW OF TERMS

Which words complete the numbered statements?

eleven

American Insurance Association

personal

real

collision

liability

proof of loss

higher

insured

ten

1. A home is called _____ property.
2. The _____ develops a rating system for homeowners policy premiums.
3. Showing _____ means that the insured person is responsible for making a list of items either damaged or destroyed according to their value on date of purchase.
4. A shocking statistic is that every _____ seconds someone in the United States is either injured or killed in an automobile accident.
5. _____ insurance protects the insured against claims for injury or property damage.
6. Furniture and clothing are classified as _____ property.
7. The highest premium for an elite homeowners policy would be paid in a city with a class _____ rating.
8. Property damage automobile liability insurance does not cover the _____.
9. On the average, young drivers pay _____ premiums for automobile insurance.
10. If a driver overturned his or her car, he or she would be covered for this type of accident if he or she had _____ insurance.

II. REVIEW OF MAIN POINTS

1. Briefly describe no-fault insurance.

2. Why is depreciation an important issue in home insurance coverage?
3. What are three important factors in setting car insurance premium rates?
4. Why is property damage liability coverage important to motorists?
5. What is an inventory list?
6. What is a homeowners policy?
7. Why are automobile insurance premiums higher for a driver in a big city than for a driver in a small town?
8. Should a homeowner insure his or her home for $50,000 if it is valued at $25,000? Why?
9. What does 100/300 mean when bodily injury liability insurance is being discussed?

III. HOME AND AUTOMOBILE INSURANCE: CONCEPTS

1. Explain why the value of a home may decline over the years.
2. Should the contents of a traveling salesperson's automobile be covered by insurance protection? Why?
3. Sally Frain's car is now seven years old and has been driven over 99,000 miles. Sally's friend Betty suggests that there is no need for collision insurance. This leads Sally to call her insurance agent and drop her collision coverage. Would you have made this decision? Why?
4. Dick Gallant purchased a two-year-old car that cost $2,950. He is financing the car through a loan from the National Security Bank. What type of automobile insurance is he required to have by the bank? Do you believe that this is enough protection? Why?
5. If the Wilcox family own a home that is valued at $23,000 and has an estimated $6,500 worth of personal property in it, how much should they insure the real and personal property for?
6. What kinds of liability risks do most homeowners face in a typical year?
7. What is the argument against a mandatory no-fault insurance plan?

8. Do you think that home and automobile theft insurance are necessary? Why?

9. Do you believe that uninsured motorist protection is necessary? Why?

10. Explain what is meant by *deductible*.

IV. HOME AND AUTOMOBILE INSURANCE: EXERCISES

1. The following is a list of annual collision insurance premiums for one large national firm.

Coverage	Yearly Cost of Premiums
$ 50 deductible	$62.50
$100 deductible	50.50
$200 deductible	29.00

   Why do you think the annual premium for $200 deductible is $33.50 less than the premium for $50 deductible?

2. Contact an insurance company in your community and find out the following:
   a. What would the annual premium be for their elite home-owners policy on a $32,000 home with $12,000 personal property?
   b. If property is destroyed, what must be shown as proof of loss?

3. Carl Brunswick prepared a proof-of-loss inventory list for his home office.

Item	Date Purchased	Cost
Carpet	1974	$300
Desk	1974	425
Chair	1974	95
Lamp	1974	100
Bookcases	1974	250

   A tornado completely destroyed all of the items shown on Carl's proof-of-loss list. The insurance company agreed to pay 80 percent of the original cost of the items.
   a. How much did the company pay Carl for his destroyed office contents?
   b. How many dollars did Carl lose because of the tornado damage?

HOME AND AUTOMOBILE INSURANCE   449

4. Contact a local car insurance company and find out the following information:
   a. What is the premium cost for an eighteen-year-old single male driver for
      1. 10/20 bodily injury liability
      2. Comprehensive coverage for a $4,000 car
      3. $100 deductible collision?
   b. What is the premium cost for an eighteen-year-old single female driver for the same coverage?
5. Prepare a short report on the current status of no-fault automobile insurance. In your report cover the following areas:
   a. The history of no-fault insurance
   b. The states that currently have no-fault insurance
   c. The opinion of your community politicians about no-fault insurance.

SOCIAL INSURANCE PROTECTION

35

The United States has a system of insurance programs that is largely financed by employers and employees and operated by the Government. These programs are called *social insurance.* Each citizen is entitled to certain benefits, including social security benefits, unemployment insurance, old-age, survivors, and disability insurance, Medicare, and workmen's compensation.

SOME REASONS FOR SOCIAL INSURANCE

Any discussion of social insurance eventually gets around to why a nation such as the United States needs social insurance. The Government believes that it has an obligation to provide its citizens with at least a minimum standard of living. The purpose of social insurance is

Medicare is just one of the programs designed to provide older people with health insurance protection.

to provide everyone with some protection against the risks of job-related death, disability, job loss, and poor health.

If a family's main income earner could not work, the family would suffer because they would lose most, if not all, of their income. Social insurance is meant to help reduce the financial burdens of people who suffer when an income earner is disabled or cannot find work.

Also, more people are living longer today. Almost 10 percent of the population is sixty-five or older, compared to only about 4.3 percent in 1900. The Government believes that it should provide some benefits for these senior citizens during the years they are retired.

THE SOCIAL SECURITY ACT

The first large effort in the United States to develop a national social insurance program was in 1935. At this time the *Social Security Act* was passed. This act provided financial help for the elderly and for unemployed workers. It also provided health and welfare aid to the dependents (families) of needy citizens. In 1965, the act was changed to provide health insurance protection through Medicare.

SOCIAL SECURITY BENEFITS

A worker and his or her family are entitled to benefits only if he or she has worked a certain length of time. The work year, according to the Social Security Administration, is divided into quarters. For example, April, May, and June make up one quarter. After working a certain number of quarters, a worker is entitled to various benefits. About 90 percent of all workers reaching sixty-five are eligible for retirement benefits.

Under the nation's social security system, five types of benefits are paid: 1) disability, 2) survivors, 3) retirement, 4) hospital, and 5) medical.

Disability After a six-month waiting period, a worker who is completely disabled can receive payments every month. The maximum (largest) payment will be made if the worker is fully insured by social security; that is, if he or she has worked 20 quarters out of the last 40 quarters.

Survivors If a worker covered by social security dies, his or her survivors are entitled to monthly benefits. If he or she were married and fully insured, his or her widow or widower, aged sixty or over, would receive the payments.

Retirement When a worker has worked long enough to be fully insured and has reached the age of sixty-two, he or she and certain members of his or her family can receive monthly payments. The amount he or she would receive would depend upon his or her average monthly salary before retirement.

Hospital The hospital protection plan provides benefits for individuals aged sixty-five and over. This plan pays for any reasonable cost of hospitalization up to 90 days. It also provides benefits for medical care and services up to 100 days after hospitalization.

Medical The Government medical insurance and hospital insurance plans work together and are called *Medicare*. People over sixty-five years of age who want to participate must pay half of the monthly premiums.

THE AMOUNT OF BENEFITS

Since the Social Security Act went into effect, benefits have increased regularly. In 1937, for example, the smallest benefit payment was $10 a month. In 1972, it was $65 a month. Table 35-1 shows some examples of monthly benefits based on a worker's average monthly income.

As an example, the Doyle family will once again be used to show some of the benefits they would receive through social security. If Pete were to suddenly die at age twenty-seven, Terri and the two girls would receive a lump-sum death benefit of $255. They would also get $434.40 a month. If Pete were to live and decide to retire at the age of sixty-two, he would receive $250.70 a month for the rest of his life.

Social security retirement benefits are affected by what a person earns from various sources after retirement. As of 1974, a retired person seventy-two years old is not entitled to full benefits if he or she earns more than $2,400 a year. After age seventy-two, a retired person receives

TABLE 35–1
SOCIAL SECURITY BENEFIT PAYMENTS:
DISABILITY, SURVIVORS, AND RETIREMENT*

Average Yearly Earnings After 1950[1]	$75/month or $899 or Less/Year	$150/month or $1800/Year	$250/month or $3000/Year
Disability			
Worker	$64.00	$101.70	$132.30
Wife with Child in her care	32.00	50.90	66.20
One Child	32.00	50.90	66.20
Disabled Widow at 50, No Child	38.90	51.00	66.30
Survivors			
Widow at 62 or Older	64.00	84.00	109.20
Widow at 60, No Child	55.50	72.80	94.70
Widow under 62, One Child	96.00	152.60	198.60
Widow under 62, Two Children	96.00	152.60	202.40
Lump-Sum Death Benefit	165.00	255.00	255.00
Retirement			
Worker at 65 or Older	64.00	101.70	132.30
Worker at 62	51.20	81.40	105.90
Wife at 65 or Older	32.00	50.90	66.20
Wife at 62	24.00	38.20	49.70
Maximum Family Benefit	96.00	152.60	202.40

the full social security benefit no matter how much money he or she earns.

If Pete were to become disabled because of an illness or an accident and the disability lasted a year or more, he would be entitled to benefits.

TABLE 35-1 (continued)

$350/month or $4200/Year	$450/month or $5400/Year	$550/month or $6600/Year	$660/month or $7800/Year
$161.50	$189.80	$218.40	$250.70
80.80	94.90	109.20	125.40
80.80	94.90	109.20	125.40
80.90	95.00	109.30	125.50
133.30	156.60	180.20	209.90
115.60	135.80	156.20	179.40
242.40	284.80	327.60	376.20
280.80	354.50	395.60	434.40
255.00	255.00	255.00	255.00
161.50	189.80	218.40	250.70
129.20	151.90	174.80	200.60
80.80	94.90	109.20	125.40
60.60	71.20	81.90	94.10
280.80	354.40	395.60	434.40

*These benefits are periodically changed and at the time of using this Table, they may be a little more than what is currently being paid.
[1]Average earnings are figured over the period from 1950 until the worker becomes disabled, dies, or retires. Up to five years of the lowest annual earnings are not included in calculating benefits.

As shown in Table 35-1, a disabled worker whose average earnings are $660 a month would receive $250.70 a month for as long as he or she could not return to work. He or she could get these benefits 12 months after the disability.

HOW THE GOVERNMENT PAYS
FOR SOCIAL SECURITY BENEFITS

The money that the Government uses to pay social security benefits comes from the taxpayers. The disability, survivors, retirement, and hospital payments come from taxes collected from employers and insured employees. For example, Pete Doyle pays half the government tax and his employer, IBM, pays the other half. Table 35–2 shows how much money employers and insured workers must pay into the tax fund that is used for disability, survivors, retirement, and hospital benefit programs.

TABLE 35–2
PETE DOYLE AND IBM
TAX RATES ON INCOME
FOR SOCIAL SECURITY INSURANCE

Year	Disability, Survivors, and Retirement Tax		Hospital Insurance		Total
	Pete	IBM	Pete	IBM	
1972	4.6 %	4.6 %	0.6 %	0.6 %	10.4 %
1973–77	4.85	4.85	1.00	1.00	10.7
1978–80	4.80	4.80	1.25	1.25	11.1
1981–85	4.80	4.80	1.35	1.35	12.3
1986–92	4.80	4.80	1.45	1.45	12.5
1993–97	4.80	4.80	1.45	1.45	12.5
1998–2010	4.80	4.80	1.45	1.45	12.5
2011+	5.85	5.85	1.45	1.45	14.6

NOTE: *If Pete earned $12,000 in 1974, he would pay $582 and IBM would pay $582 in social security taxes.*

Under the *Federal Insurance Contributions Act* (F.I.C.A.), the Internal Revenue Service has the right to collect the taxes used for social security payments. The tax rates, like the social security benefit payments, are often increased to take into consideration the rising cost of living.

Benefits paid under the Medicare plan are paid for by the premium payments of the people in the plan plus matching amounts paid by the

Federal Government. The monthly premium in 1975 was $6.70. Thus, in 1975 a sixty-five-year-old person paid $80.40 a year and the Government paid $80.40 a year.

UNEMPLOYMENT INSURANCE

An important part of the Social Security Act deals with *unemployment insurance* protection. Every state has an unemployment insurance program which operates under Federal Government regulations. State unemployment insurance programs are designed to

1. Provide some income for a limited period of time for workers who lose their jobs through no fault of their own
2. Protect the general work population by partly guaranteeing them some of the income lost to them by unemployment.

Each state determines how much it will pay unemployed workers and for how long. In most states there is a one-week waiting period between the time the unemployed worker files a claim and the time he or she starts to receive benefits. In addition, the unemployed worker must register for work at a public employment office. Once the waiting period is over and the unemployed worker has applied for work, he or she can, in some states, expect to receive payments for as long as 26 weeks.

MEDICARE, MEDICAID, AND BLACK LUNG BENEFITS

In 1965, Congress changed the social security laws to provide most of the country's senior citizens with national health insurance. This program is popularly known as Medicare. Each person protected by Medicare receives a health insurance card. The card is used whenever a person is admitted to a hospital or nursing home or visits a doctor's office.

The hospital insurance part of Medicare is called Part A. It entitles cardholders to the following benefits:

1. Except for the first $72, all costs are paid for the first 60 days in a hospital.
2. For the 61st through the 90th day, all costs over $18 a day are paid.
3. All costs are paid for the first 20 days in a nursing home. For the next 80 days, all but $9 a day is paid.

The medical insurance portion of Medicare is called Part B. This insurance helps pay for

1. Doctors' fees
2. Medical services and supplies
3. Home health services.

Under Part B, the person must pay the first $60 of the total bill. (This is the deductible feature of the medical insurance under Medicare.) Eighty percent of the rest of the year's medical bill is paid by Medicare. The senior citizen pays the other 20 percent. For example, seventy-year-old May Brown had a medical bill of $1,400 for the year. Since she is protected by Medicare, she paid the first $60 and 20 percent of the remaining $1,340. Thus, she had to pay a total of $328 for the year.

State governments also provide citizens with health insurance protection. The state plans are called *Medicaid*. In 1965, the Federal Government agreed to help state governments support poor families who needed medical help but could not afford it. Poor families could not possibly pay $85 a day for a hospital room, nor $1,000 for an operation.

Medicaid aids needy citizens by paying for 1) hospital care, 2) doctors' services, 3) X-rays, 4) laboratory tests, and 5) nursing-home care. Without Medicaid, many of the nation's poor and underprivileged citizens would not be able to get any kind of medical care.

Black lung disease is a serious condition in the lungs that affects many coal miners and often causes early death. The *Black Lung Benefits Act of 1972* makes it possible for afflicted miners to receive benefits. A miner can get these benefits if he is totally disabled by black lung disease. Being disabled means that the black lung disease keeps the miner from doing the work he regularly did before he got the disease.

Should the miner die, the 1972 act also provides benefits to widows and their children until they reach the age of eighteen, or twenty-three if they are full-time students. If the miner is not survived by a widow or children, the benefits can be paid to his parents.

Medicare assures senior citizens of getting medical care at a time when they are highly prone to illness and may not have much money for proper health care.

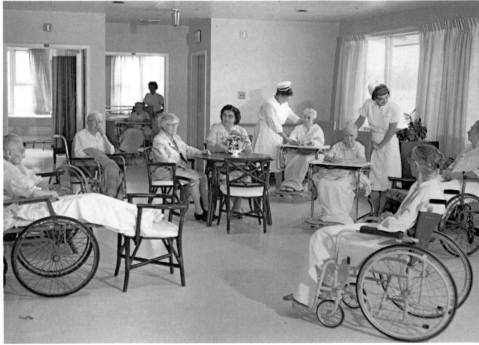

The amount of payment depends on the number of dependents the miner has. The basic benefits are

1. $169.80 a month for a disabled miner, or for the widow of a deceased miner, or for the parent of a deceased miner
2. $339.50 a month for a disabled miner or for the widow of a deceased miner providing they have three or more dependent children.

THE SOCIAL SECURITY CARD

The first time you get a job that is covered by social security you must get a social security card with your own social security number. This number will be assigned to only you and you will keep it for life. This number helps the Government keep a record of your earnings, which is so important in figuring what benefits you are entitled to under the Social Security Act.

You can apply for a social security number by filling out a special form. Once the form is sent to the Social Security Administration, a card will be sent to you. A sample of a social security card is presented in Figure 35-2.

Whenever you change your job you have to give your new employer your social security number. You also need to use your social security number when filling out your federal income tax form. Even a three-year-old child who has a savings account in his or her name and is receiving interest payments must have a social security number.

FIGURE 35-2

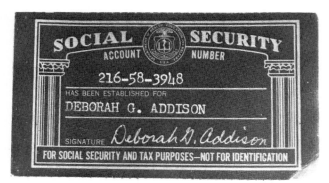

The social security card and number are very important. If your card is lost you should immediately apply for another one from the nearest Social Security Administration office. It is also important to check on your record of social security earnings. Remember that your benefits depend on your average yearly earnings. You can check on your account by filling out a special form at your nearest social security office.

SUMMARY

A major purpose of life, health, home, automobile, and social insurance is to provide some financial protection against various risks. A costly illness, for example, can force a family to change their standard of living. The death of the major income earner can even force a family to break up.

Everyone faces risks every day. You cannot cross the street without some risk that you will be injured or even killed by a car. You cannot own property without taking the chance that it may be damaged or lost or that someone will be injured on or in it. It is not possible to eliminate every risk. The basic principle of each kind of insurance is that it pools the risks of many different people. The pooling principle allows individuals to share risks.

Life insurance helps replace income that has been cut off by the death of a wage earner. Home insurance can help provide the money to rebuild a damaged or destroyed home. Health insurance can help pay for medical expenses as well as replace some of the income that is lost when a wage earner is sick. Automobile insurance can help pay for repairing a damaged car. Social insurance can help support people who are retired.

I. REVIEW OF TERMS

Which words complete the numbered statements?

ninety   Medicare
Social Security Act   services
unemployment insurance   social security
number   Black Lung Disease Act

1. The _____ was passed in 1935.
2. A self-employed person must also pay _____ taxes.
3. The hospital insurance part of _____ is called Part A.
4. The _____ provides for benefits to afflicted coal miners and their dependents.
5. Each state has an _____ program which it operates in cooperation with the Federal Government.
6. Medical insurance would provide benefits for a doctor's _____ .
7. The Government estimates that about _____ percent of all workers reaching age sixty-five are eligible for retirement benefits.
8. A person starting his or her first job must get a social security _____ by applying to the Social Security Administration.

II. REVIEW OF MAIN POINTS

1. What is unemployment insurance?
2. Why do people need a social security number?
3. What is the maximum family benefit for a worker that averaged $550 a month?
4. Define *social insurance*.
5. How are Medicare premiums paid?
6. Explain the major difference between Medicare and Medicaid.
7. How can you apply for a social security number?

8. What is a disability benefit?

9. Why must insurance protection be planned?

10. What are the basic benefits under the Black Lung Disease Act?

III. SOCIAL INSURANCE PROTECTION: CONCEPTS

1. Do you feel that poor people should be helped in meeting medical expenses? Why?

2. Do you feel that the cost of Medicare premiums will increase in the next few years? Why?

3. What do you think are the reasons for the 1972 Black Lung Disease Act?

4. Check on the unemployment insurance benefits in your community by contacting a public employment office. Answer the following questions:

   a. What is the waiting period before a person can begin receiving benefits?

   b. How much can a person with no dependents, one dependent, or two dependents collect?

   c. For how long a period can a person collect benefits?

5. What planning steps are necessary when trying to develop your own insurance protection plan?

6. If Tony Morty died suddenly he would leave a widow, thirty-seven-year-old Joyce, and three children. Assume that he is covered by social security and that his survivors will be paid on the basis of his average yearly income of $5,400.

   a. What would the lump-sum benefit payment be?

   b. How much would Joyce receive for the next 25 years?

   c. How much would she receive 26 years from now?

7. Suppose that George Trotter is fired by the Spider Glass Manufacturing Corporation because the organization is moving 800 miles from their present location. What kind of benefits would George qualify for in his home state of Louisiana?

8. A retired worker may receive his or her full social security benefits no matter how much income he or she has from such sources as savings accounts, insurance annuities, and real estate investments. Is this fair to the people that have not been lucky with their investments? Why?

9. Do you expect the minimum social security benefit to increase from its present level in the next five years? Why?

IV. SOCIAL INSURANCE PROTECTION: EXERCISES

1. Contact your local Social Security Administration office and find out what kinds of free materials interested citizens can receive from them. Send away for these materials and distribute them to your classmates.

2. Prepare a report which traces historically the changes that have been made in the United States social security program. Some of your information can be obtained from the library, encyclopedias, and local social security offices.

3. Do you believe that any changes are needed in the social security program? Discuss and be prepared to defend your proposed changes.

4. What types of social insurance not discussed in this chapter does your state provide?

5. Do you believe that any changes in social security benefit payments are made because of politics? Explain your answer.

6. Do you believe that a twenty-five-year-old widower with two children should be entitled to social security benefits? Why?

Unit IX
Government, Labor Unions, and Business

There are two important things that directly affect businesses: governments and labor unions. When a government raises taxes or forces businesses to work within the law, some businesspeople feel that the government is interfering with their business. When a union demands higher wages or improvements in working conditions, some businesspeople complain that they cannot afford to meet these demands. This unit will not discuss the questions of whether or not the government actually interferes with business or whether or not a union has the right to make demands. Instead, it will try to show that each business must be aware of and become involved with government and labor unions.

Chapter 36 discusses government and business. The public has demanded that the government provide people with such things as public schools, public parks, and social insurance. Governments also have programs that aid businesspeople.

The money used by governments to provide services and programs comes from the people in the form of taxes. Chapter 37 discusses many of the different types of taxes. These include income taxes, sales taxes, and estate taxes.

Governments are concerned with the public interest. To protect the public, it is necessary to have some control over business. In Chapter 38, some methods of government control are discussed.

Chapter 39 discusses the important role that labor unions play in business organizations. The aims of unions and the aims of businesses often conflict.

UNIT PREVIEW

466

AS YOU STUDY THIS UNIT YOU WILL BE ENGAGED IN

* IDENTIFYING the demands that the public makes on governments with regard to the economy

* IDENTIFYING likenesses and differences in a monopolistic and a competitive organization

* UNDERSTANDING the nature of taxation in the United States

* ANALYZING progressive and regressive taxes

* PROBING the features of the Sherman Antitrust Act, the Clayton Act, and the Federal Trade Commission Act

* ANALYZING the major provisions of a union contract

* UNDERSTANDING the objectives of labor unions and management.

A FOCUS FOR YOUR STUDY

36 GOVERNMENT AND BUSINESS

One important job of the government is to serve as a watchdog and to protect the public. It is generally believed that the public wants government to

1. Provide parks and support education and scientific research not conducted by private corporations
2. Protect the public from such practices as false advertising and work stoppages
3. Provide health insurance protection
4. Provide social insurance protection
5. Make sure that Blacks and other minorities are not discriminated against in getting jobs, education, and housing
6. Work on reducing such important problems as crime and air pollution, and improving mass transportation systems.

This chapter examines some of the ways in which government tries to satisfy these public wants. The government has the power to oversee the activities of private corporations, such as IBM and General Mills, partnerships, such as *The Jill and Amy Fashion Store,* and proprietorships, such as *Jill's Women's Fashion Store.* Without the support of the public, the government would be only a very weak watchdog of the public interest.

GOVERNMENT SERVICES

All governments—Federal, state, and local—work towards protecting the public. Thus, governments provide various services that help keep the economy healthy and satisfy the wants and desires of the people.

REGULATING PRIVATE BUSINESSES

The government regulates business by enforcing laws. If a business firm violates a government regulation, the firm can be fined, and depending on the violation, its executives can be jailed.

The government also tries to keep businesses from forming monopolies. A *monopoly* is a single company that has full control of a product or service. Monopolies are allowed only in the area of public utilities. A *public utility* is a private company that provides a very important service, such as gas, electricity, water, or telephone service. However, even though the government allows monopolies to provide gas, electricity, water, and telephone service, it still has the right to regulate the prices charged by these companies. Also, any increases in their prices must be granted by the government. For example, if a telephone company in southeastern Ohio wants to increase the rates for in-state long distance calls, it must first obtain approval from the state public utility commission.

Governments work to fight crime, air pollution, and other problems.

SPECIAL SERVICES

Governments help build highways, schools, parks, libraries, and hospitals. These are things that people want and need. These things, however, cost a lot of money. For example, a large Veterans hospital near Denver, Colorado, cost the Federal Government $13 million. A highway in the suburbs of Washington, D.C., cost the Federal Government and the state government of Maryland $1.1 million for each mile. A state park in Kentucky cost the state government over $500,000.

Local governments also provide police and fire protection for their residents. These services are costly but very necessary. The Federal Government pays the costs for the armed forces.

Governments help finance bridges.

GUARDING AGAINST UNFAIR BUSINESS PRACTICES

In our society of over 210 million citizens, there are some people who engage in unfair business practices. Some butchers, for example, try to sell spoiled meat. A manufacturer of cosmetics recently failed to warn customers of the harmful ingredients in a face cream. A drug company tried to sell a harmful drug. The Government stopped these practices. Because individuals do not have the know-how, the money, or the time to uncover unfair practices, they depend on the Government to protect them against misleading advertising and harmful products.

PROTECTING PROPERTY RIGHTS

If you buy a plot of land in LaCrosse, Wisconsin, it becomes your *private property*. Everyone has a right to own property. Within certain limits, you have a right to do what you want with the property. The government protects your right to this property.

The government, however, can also take your property when it is necessary to do so for public welfare. When this happens, the property owner is paid a fair price for the property. The government is then said to be exercising its right of *eminent domain*.

The eminent domain issue is sometimes very controversial. In the 1960's, the government of the State of Illinois decided to build the Chicago campus of the University of Illinois on the South Side of the city. The people living in the neighborhood were against the plan because many of them would lose their homes. For about five years the issue of eminent domain was argued in the courts. Finally, the courts allowed the government to build the school. Since then, some of the neighborhood children have even attended the school. Thus, some people believe that the public was served by the school, while others believe that the government destroyed a neighborhood.

PROTECTING HUMAN RIGHTS

Governments have passed laws that forbid discriminating against people because of their race, religion, sex, or other factors. These laws were passed because some businesses would not hire a woman executive or a Black accountant or a Jewish salesperson or a Chicano lawyer because of their sex, race, or ethnic background. Although these people were qualified to do certain jobs, they were not hired. In recent years, however, job opportunities for minority groups and women have improved.

The government also has passed laws that prohibit discrimination in the renting or selling of homes. These laws are called *open housing laws.* If George Jones, who is Black, has the $38,000 needed to buy a home in an all-White area, he is entitled by law to buy this house if he makes the first offer.

The Federal and state governments also do not allow most businesses to pay wages that are considered too low to meet the basic human needs for food, clothing, and shelter. These laws are called *minimum wage laws.* They clearly state that no person employed by a business covered by the law can be paid less than a certain rate per hour. Even though these laws are generally followed, some businesses find loopholes (excuses) that will let them pay less than the minimum wage. For example, assume that Jessie Mendez works as a dishwasher in Pueblo, Colorado. The law states that if Jessie works 35 hours a week, he must be paid $2 an hour. The owner of the restaurant, Mr. Joe Richards, lets Jessie work only 34 hours a week so that he can pay Jessie $1.25 an hour. Since Jessie works less than 35 hours, the owner is able to pay the less-than-minimum-wage of $1.25 per hour. Mr. Richards has found a loophole—the amount of time Jessie works—and has taken advantage of the law. Thus, although the law is meant to improve wages of unskilled workers, it is still sidestepped by some businesspeople.

The Department of Agriculture offers information to farmers.

HELPING PRIVATE BUSINESSES

What you have read so far might lead you to think that the government only watches out for shady business deals or crooked businesspeople. This is definitely not so. Governments at every level—local, state, and Federal—have many programs to help businesspeople. The Federal Government provides aid for businesses in the form of *subsidies.*

The Government also protects many businesses by placing a tariff on goods that are shipped from a foreign country into the United States. A *tariff* is a tax that is paid by the company that manufactures the product. Suppose a Japanese camera manufacturer can produce and ship a camera to New York and sell it for $100. This camera competes directly with a similar American-made camera that sells for $115. If there were no tariff on the Japanese camera, it would probably outsell the American camera. To protect the American manufacturer, the Government places a tariff of $15 on the Japanese camera. If the Government did not charge the tariff, the American company could not compete with the Japanese firm for the dollars of Americans who want this kind of camera.

The Federal Government also collects a lot of information on various subjects and publishes reports. This information is used by many business firms to help them with their marketing and other programs. The Bureau of Labor Statistics, the United States Weather Bureau, the Department of Commerce, and the Department of Agriculture all provide information for private businesses.

The Government also makes loans to small business firms, home contractors, and farmers. This kind of money helps our economy grow. Without this money, many small businesses could not be started, some home builders could not construct homes, and some farmers could go out of business.

In every state there are employment agencies that help workers find jobs. These agencies, unlike commercial employment agencies, do not charge a fee.

SHOULD THE GOVERNMENT BE MORE ACTIVE IN BUSINESS?

Ask ten people in any community how they feel about the role of government in business and you will probably get ten different answers. Most people believe that the armed forces, public schools, public recreation facilities, police and fire protection, and good roads are necessary. However, there are some complaints about these government-operated facilities or services. If these complaints were translated into votes the government officials might be voted out of office.

Thus, some people believe that the voters determine the role of government in business. If the majority wants a government that is active, then this will be the role of the government. However, if the majority wants the government to play a limited role in business affairs, then this will be the government's role.

The role of the Federal Government in regulating businesses has grown steadily since the disastrous depression in the 1930's. Most of the people who live in the United States believe that although the government can make decisions that can lead to a depression, it is the only organized body that can also make decisions to prevent one.

It is safe to conclude that the government's role in regulating business, encouraging employment, and supporting various kinds of productive and service industries will continue to grow. There appears to be no sign that the public wants the government to stop its present role in the business world.

SUMMARY

Governments provide many kinds of services at the Federal, state, and local levels. The country's military forces are directed by the Federal Government. State governments build miles of public highways, and local fire departments protect lives and property against fire. Government is everywhere, and there seems to be a general acceptance of the services it provides. This is not to say that people do not complain about government services.

I. REVIEW OF TERMS

Which words complete the statements below?

regulate   tariff
open housing laws   eminent domain
depression   public utility

1. It appears that the government's role in regulating business has grown since the disastrous _____ in the 1930's.
2. One duty of the government is to _____ the prices charged by monopolies, such as water and electrical companies.
3. A _____ is a private company that provides citizens with a very important service.
4. When the government takes the property that is owned by a citizen and pays the citizen a fair price for public use of this property, the government is exercising the right of _____.
5. _____ prohibit discrimination in the rental or sale of homes.
6. A _____ is a tax that is paid by a foreign manufacturer when the foreign manufacturer exports goods to the United States.

II. REVIEW OF MAIN POINTS

1. Why does the government usually prevent the formation of a business monopoly?
2. What business practices are considered unfair by the government?
3. Under what conditions can the government force a person to sell his or her property?
4. What is the minimum wage law?
5. Why does the government become involved in the armed forces, public education, and recreation facilities?

III. GOVERNMENT AND BUSINESS: CONCEPTS

1. Is it right for the government to become involved in the hiring practices of a private organization? Why?
2. Do you believe that fear plays a role in the general public's attitude about the role of government in business?
3. How is the government involved in business practices in your community?
4. What is the public interest?
5. What can happen to a nation that places a very high tariff on imported goods? In other words, can another country retaliate against the high tariffs placed by the United States? Explain your answer.
6. Do you believe that scandals, such as the Watergate incident of the early 1970's, influence public opinion of the role of Government in business? Why or why not?

IV. GOVERNMENT AND BUSINESS: EXERCISES

1. Interview five adult friends and ask them if they feel the government's role in business is too large. Then ask them what the role of government should be. Prepare a short report on the interviews.
2. What are the open housing laws in your community? Contact your community government or use your library for sources.
3. Prepare a short report on the Watergate scandal of the early 1970's. Specifically report on how businesspeople were involved in the scandal. Use your library to help you.
4. Find out how much money your state government and the Federal Government have spent in the last year on the following:
   a. Roads in your community
   b. Schools in your town or city
   c. Recreation facilities in your neighborhood or community.
   Use your library for source materials.
5. Prepare a table showing the names and political parties of the current President and Vice President of the United States, your state senators in Congress, your governor, and your three top community leaders.

UNDERSTANDING THE TAX SYSTEM

Many people complain that for every dollar they earn, only about 75 cents finds its way into their pockets. The other 25 cents is taken by governments for taxes. Taxes are often thought of as a one-way flow of money from the public to the government. Although this view is certainly popular, it is not an accurate view of taxes in the United States.

Everyone in the United States can share in the goods and services provided by Federal, state, and local governments. Everyone can visit the Smithsonian Institution in Washington, D. C., a public employment office, and a neighborhood park. These facilities are paid for by government dollars. These government dollars come from taxes and are called *government revenue.* Without government revenue, there would be fewer museums, employment offices, and parks.

This chapter covers the tax system of the United States. A number of different taxes are discussed, along with their benefits and disadvantages.

THE NEED FOR TAXES

The public school system is one example of why tax dollars are needed. The government, by providing schools, has enabled all children to attend school. Most children go to public schools because their families cannot pay the high costs of private schools. Thus, without tax dollars, there would be very few schools that could provide a reasonably inexpensive education.

The government also helps the less fortunate and poverty-stricken people in our society. It is estimated that 9 million Blacks and 16 million Whites have a standard of living at what is called the *poverty level.* This is a level where only minimum needs for food, shelter, clothing, and education are met. Without tax dollars these people would be even worse off. Certainly there is no private corporation that would be willing to help most of these poverty-stricken people.

TAXES GOING UP, UP, AND UP

The Federal Government today collects about $250 billion a year in taxes. In 1935 this figure was only about $10 billion. Thus, taxes have risen and will continue to rise. A few of the reasons for rising taxes are presented here.

THE GROWING POPULATION

In 1935 the United States' population numbered approximately 122 million. Today, there are over 210 million Americans. This is a gain of

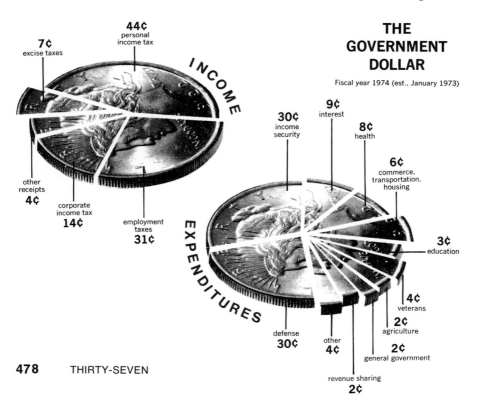

7¢
excise taxes

44¢
personal
income tax

INCOME

THE GOVERNMENT DOLLAR

Fiscal year 1974 (est., January 1973)

other
receipts
4¢

corporate
income tax
14¢

employment
taxes
31¢

EXPENDITURES

30¢
income
security

9¢
interest

8¢
health

6¢
commerce,
transportation,
housing

3¢
education

4¢
veterans

2¢
agriculture

2¢
general government

defense
30¢

other
4¢

revenue sharing
2¢

about 72 percent. This kind of increase in the population means that more government goods and services are needed. There are more schools needed, more state parks needed, more public libraries needed, more teachers needed, more police needed, more firefighting equipment needed, and more highways needed. More of everything is needed, and this means that more tax dollars must be collected.

INFLATION—RISING PRICES

Since 1935 the prices of all goods and services have risen significantly. In 1972 prices were about three times higher than they were in 1935. This type of price increase means that buyers, businesses, and even the government must pay more to buy the same goods and services they bought before for less.

THE PUBLIC DEMAND FOR MORE

In 1965 the Federal Government began to pay part of the cost of Medicare. This means that this form of social insurance protection required additional government dollars.

Not only do Americans want increased social insurance protection, they also want more highways, better schools, more libraries, more parks, and other goods and services. These demands for more of everything are aimed at governments at every level.

EXPENSIVE PROGRAMS

In 1972 the national defense of the United States cost about $78.2 billion. Clearly this is a great expense in the national budget. These dollars are spent for tanks, airplanes, wages, and military aid to foreign nations.

Another expensive item in the national budget is the space research program. Placing space stations, such as Skylab 2, in orbit costs the Federal Government millions of dollars.

The Government is also doing research on the energy crisis in the nation. The Federal Government is concerned about shortages of fuel. It has poured money into programs to find out how the nation can best survive the dwindling supplies of crude oil, natural gas, and other resources.

These four factors—increasing population, inflation, increased demand, and expensive programs—are some of the reasons why taxes have been increasing. In addition to these reasons, the Federal Government is now involved in *revenue sharing* programs with the 50 state governments.

In 1972 a law entitled *State and Local Fiscal Assistant Act* was passed which established the Secretary of the Treasury as a trustee for the *Office of Revenue Sharing.* Under the guidance of the Secretary, this act allows the Federal Government to give funds to local and city governments. These funds have been collected through the federal income tax. The local and city governments can use these funds for public safety (law enforcement, fire protection), environmental protection (sewage disposal, sanitation, and pollution reduction), public transportation, recreation, and other similar activities. The idea behind *revenue sharing* is that the Federal Government has collected tax dollars that can be turned back to local and city governments for their own use. It allows local and city governments to use some of their citizens' tax dollars in the community.

Do not get the impression that the Federal Government just turns over revenue to local governments. The chief executive officer of the local government (for example, the mayor) has to file a certificate, which clearly indicates how the money will be used, with the Secretary of the Treasury. The certificate is carefully reviewed and if the funds are provided, the Office of Revenue Sharing will check on the use of the money.

TYPES OF TAXES

Governments collect money by putting a tax on an item, such as a new automobile, or some activity, such as getting married. When the government collects money this way, it is said to have *levied* a tax. The cost of the item or the service is the basis for the tax. The amount of tax to be paid is called the *tax rate.* It is often expressed as a percentage, such as a 5 percent tax on a new car. This means that a new car costing $4,000 would actually cost the owner $4,200. The extra $200 is the 5 percent tax.

CLASSIFYING TAXES

One way of classifying taxes is based on how the tax money is paid to the government. *Direct taxes* are paid by the taxpayer directly to the government. The federal income tax is an example of a direct tax. Another kind of tax is called an *indirect tax.* This tax is paid to someone other than the government. That person then gives it to the government. For example, in some areas you pay a tax on groceries. The tax money goes to the store owner who then gives it to the government.

The second way of classifying taxes is based on how they relate to the taxpayer's income. A tax is called *progressive* if the tax rate increases as the taxpayer's income increases. For example, a person earning $18,000 a year would pay a higher tax rate than a person earning $10,000 a year.

A tax is called *regressive* if the tax rate is the same for all people. This tax takes a greater percentage of lower incomes than it does of higher incomes. For example, a tax that is the same for the person making $18,000 and the one earning $10,000 is a regressive tax. Suppose that two men buy the same necklace for their wives. The jewelry tax on the necklaces is $25 each. The person earning $18,000 is paying less tax in relation to his income than the man earning $10,000.

So far, only general terms have been used to discuss taxes. Now look at the taxes that generally result in the majority of the money being paid to the Federal Government.

FEDERAL INCOME TAX

Of every dollar the Federal Government receives from taxpayers, about 65 cents comes from federal income taxes. Each citizen and business corporation is required by law to pay an income tax. Sole proprietor-ships and partnerships are taxed the same way as individuals.

There are also nearly 40 states with state income taxes. These taxes are paid directly to the state governments.

FIGURE 37-1

Form 1040 US Department of the Treasury—Internal Revenue Service Individual Income Tax Return 1974

For the year January 1–December 31, 1974, or other taxable year beginning ...., 1974, ending ...., 19........

Name (If joint return, give first names and initials of both) **Pete and Terri**	Last name **Doyle**	COUNTY OF RESIDENCE Travis	Your social security number 000	00	000
Present home address (Number and street, including apartment number, or rural route) **1498 Palos Drive**			Spouse's social security no. 000	00	000
City, town or post office, State and ZIP code **Austin, Texas**		Occu-pation Yours ▶ **Research Engineer** Spouse's ▶ **Housewife**	

Filing Status (check only one)
1 ☐ Single
2 ☒ Married filing joint return (even if only one had income)
3 ☐ Married filing separately. If spouse is also filing give spouse's social security number in designated space above and enter full name here ▶
4 ☐ Unmarried Head of Household (See Instructions on page 5)
5 ☐ Widow(er) with dependent child (Year spouse died ▶ 19   )

Exemptions   Regular / 65 or over / Blind
6a Yourself . . . ☒ ☐ ☐   Enter number of boxes checked ▶ **2**
 b Spouse . . . ☒ ☐ ☐
 c First names of your dependent children who lived with you _____ Margaret _____ Rita _____   Enter number ▶ **2**
 d Number of other dependents (from line 27) . . . ▶
7 Total exemptions claimed . . . . ▶ **4**

8 Presidential Election Campaign Fund . . ▶   Do you wish to designate $1 of your taxes for this fund? . . | Yes | No
If joint return, does your spouse wish to designate $1? . . | Yes | No
Note: If you check the "Yes" box(es) it will not increase your tax or reduce your refund.

Income (Please attach Copy B of Forms W–2 here)

9	Wages, salaries, tips, and other employee compensation (Attach Forms W–2. If unavailable, see Instructions on page 3.)	9	14,500 00
10a	Dividends (See Instructions on pages 6 and 13) $................, 10b Less exclusion $.............., Balance ▶ (If gross dividends and other distributions are over $400, list in Part I of Schedule B.)	10c	0
11	Interest income. [If $400 or less, enter total without listing in Schedule B] [If over $400, enter total and list in Part II of Schedule B.]	11	100 00
12	Income other than wages, dividends, and interest (from line 38)	12	0
13	Total (add lines 9, 10c, 11, and 12)	13	14,600 00
14	Adjustments to income (such as "sick pay," moving expenses, etc. from line 43)	14	0
15	Subtract line 14 from line 13 (adjusted gross income)	15	14,600 00

● If you do not itemize deductions and line 15 is under $10,000, find tax in Tables and enter on line 16.
● If you itemize deductions or line 15 is $10,000 or more, go to line 44 to figure tax.
● CAUTION. If you have unearned income and can be claimed as a dependent on your parent's return, check here ▶ ☐ and see Instructions on page 7.

Tax, Payments and Credits

16	Tax, check if from: ☐ Tax Tables 1–12 ☐ Schedule D ☐ Tax Rate Schedule X, Y, or Z ☐ Schedule G OR ☐ Form 4726			16	1,424 00
17	Total credits (from line 54)			17	0
18	Income tax (subtract line 17 from line 16)			18	1,424 00
19	Other taxes (from line 61)			19	0
20	Total (add lines 18 and 19)			20	1,424 00
21a	Total Federal income tax withheld (attach Forms W–2 or W–2P to front)	21a	1,434 00		
b	1974 estimated tax payments (include amount allowed as credit from 1973 return)	b			
c	Amount paid with Form 4868, Application for Automatic Extension of Time to File U.S. Individual Income Tax Return	c			
d	Other payments (from line 65)	d	1,434 00		
22	Total (add lines 21a, b, c, and d)			22	1,434 00

Pay amount on line 23 in full with this return. Write social security number on check or money order and make payable to Internal Revenue Service.

Balance Due or Refund (Please attach Check or Money Order here)

23	If line 20 is larger than line 22, enter **BALANCE DUE IRS** . . . . . . ▶	23	
	(Check only one) ☐ , if Form 2210, Form 2210F, or statement is attached. See Instructions on page 7.)		
24	If line 22 is larger than line 20, enter amount **OVERPAID** . . . . . . ▶	24	
25	Amount of line 24 to be **REFUNDED TO YOU** . . . . . . ▶	25	10 00
26	Amount of line 24 to be credited on 1975 estimated tax. ▶	26	If all of overpayment (line 24) is to be refunded (line 25), make no entry on line 26.

Sign here
Under penalties of perjury, I declare that I have examined this return, including accompanying schedules and statements, and to the best of my knowledge and belief it is true, correct, and complete. Declaration of preparer (other than taxpayer) is based on all information of which he has any knowledge.

Pete Doyle 3/14/75
Your signature   Date

Terri Doyle
Spouse's signature (if filing jointly, BOTH must sign even if only one had income)

▶ Preparer's signature (other than taxpayer)   Date

Address (and ZIP Code)   Preparer's Emp. Ident. or Soc. Sec. No.

Every person and corporation paying federal income tax fills out a form called an *income tax return.* An income tax return for the Doyle family of Austin, Texas, is shown in Figure 37–1. This form covers the year 1974 and had to be turned in by April 15, 1975. In some cases, as when a wage earner is sick, the Internal Revenue Service (IRS) may allow a taxpayer to turn his or her form in later than April 15.

Some of the major sections on the Doyles' tax return, called *Form 1040,* include the listing of exemptions. An *exemption* is an amount of money that cannot be taxed. Pete, Terri, Margaret, and Rita are entitled to a total tax exemption of $3,000, or $750 a person.

Pete pays income tax only on income that is left after he subtracts his exemptions and deductions. *Deductions* are certain expenses and gifts that are not taxed. The Doyles have $3,400 of deductions.

Some of the expenses and gifts a person can deduct are payments for medicines, drugs, vaccines, and vitamins prescribed by a doctor, gifts to religious and charitable organizations, state and local income taxes, gasoline tax, and interest paid on loans or bank credit card plans, such as BankAmericard.

After subtracting the exemptions and deductions, the Doyles have a taxable income of $8,200 (line 55). They then consult a tax table provided by the Government and figure out how much income tax they have to pay. An example of a federal tax table is shown in Table 37–1. Notice that two families of four with the same incomes can pay different taxes because they have different amounts of deductions.

A look at federal income tax rates clearly shows that the tax is progressive. Pete and his family pay a tax of $1,424 on their taxable income of $8,200. This is a tax rate of approximately 18 percent. If a married person's taxable income were $32,000, the tax rate would be approximately 27 percent, while a person with a taxable income of $100,000 would pay a tax rate of about 45 percent.

The federal income tax is collected by withholding dollars that are earned. Money to be paid to the Government is taken out of each taxpayer's paycheck. In Pete's case, IBM takes out a portion of Pete's earnings and pays it to the Government. The company is responsible for sending Pete's tax dollars directly to the Government every time he is paid.

The federal income tax laws are said to have certain *loopholes,* or weaknesses. Some people hire tax experts who help them search for ways to legally pay less taxes than the laws intend for them to pay. Around April 15 of every year, magazine and newspaper articles tell about a number of millionaires who paid no federal income tax at all during the past year. The sad fact is that by finding loopholes these people accomplished this tax evasion legally.

TABLE 37-1

1973 TAX RATE SCHEDULES

If you do not use one of the Tax Tables, figure your tax on the amount of Form 1040, line 48, by using the appropriate Tax Rate Schedule on this page. Enter Tax on Form 1040, line 16.

SCHEDULE X—Single Taxpayers Not Qualifying for Rates in Schedule Y or Z				SCHEDULE Y— Married taxpayers filing separate returns.			
				Married Filing Joint Returns and Certain Widows and Widowers			
If the amount on Form 1040, line 48, is:		Enter on Form 1040, line 16:		If the amount on Form 1040, line 48, is:		Enter on Form 1040, line 16:	
Not over $500 . . . 14% of the amount on line 48.				Not over $1,000 . . . 14% of the amount on line 48.			
Over—	But not over—		of excess over—	Over—	But not over—		of excess over—
$500	$1,000	$70+15%	$500	$1,000	$2,000	$140+15%	$1,000
$1,000	$1,500	$145+16%	$1,000	$2,000	$3,000	$290+16%	$2,000
$1,500	$2,000	$225+17%	$1,500	$3,000	$4,000	$450+17%	$3,000
$2,000	$4,000	$310+19%	$2,000	$4,000	$8,000	$620+19%	$4,000
$4,000	$6,000	$690+21%	$4,000	$8,000	$12,000	$1,380+22%	$8,000
$6,000	$8,000	$1,110+24%	$6,000	$12,000	$16,000	$2,260+25%	$12,000
$8,000	$10,000	$1,590+25%	$8,000	$16,000	$20,000	$3,260+28%	$16,000
$10,000	$12,000	$2,090+27%	$10,000	$20,000	$24,000	$4,380+32%	$20,000
$12,000	$14,000	$2,630+29%	$12,000	$24,000	$28,000	$5,660+36%	$24,000
$14,000	$16,000	$3,210+31%	$14,000	$28,000	$32,000	$7,100+39%	$28,000
$16,000	$18,000	$3,830+34%	$16,000	$32,000	$36,000	$8,660+42%	$32,000
$18,000	$20,000	$4,510+36%	$18,000	$36,000	$40,000	$10,340+45%	$36,000
$20,000	$22,000	$5,230+38%	$20,000	$40,000	$44,000	$12,140+48%	$40,000
$22,000	$26,000	$5,990+40%	$22,000	$44,000	$52,000	$14,060+50%	$44,000
$26,000	$32,000	$7,590+45%	$26,000	$52,000	$64,000	$18,060+53%	$52,000
$32,000	$38,000	$10,290+50%	$32,000	$64,000	$76,000	$24,420+55%	$64,000
$38,000	$44,000	$13,290+55%	$38,000	$76,000	$88,000	$31,020+58%	$76,000
$44,000	$50,000	$16,590+60%	$44,000	$88,000	$100,000	$37,980+60%	$88,000
$50,000	$60,000	$20,190+62%	$50,000	$100,000	$120,000	$45,180+62%	$100,000
$60,000	$70,000	$26,390+64%	$60,000	$120,000	$140,000	$57,580+64%	$120,000
$70,000	$80,000	$32,790+66%	$70,000	$140,000	$160,000	$70,380+66%	$140,000
$80,000	$90,000	$39,390+68%	$80,000	$160,000	$180,000	$83,580+68%	$160,000
$90,000	$100,000	$46,190+69%	$90,000	$180,000	$200,000	$97,180+69%	$180,000
$100,000	....	$53,090+70%	$100,000	$200,000	....	$110,980+70%	$200,000

The federal income tax also allows people to deduct interest payments. This means that favored treatment is given to people who are heavily in debt and are paying a lot of interest. Is this fair to those people who are not heavily in debt? Of course not, but a way to build into the federal income tax system a rate that is equally fair to everyone still has not been found.

PROPERTY TAXES

Property taxes are levied by both state and local governments. This tax money is often used for improvements in a particular area and for

SCHEDULE Y (contd) Married Filing Separate Returns				SCHEDULE Z—Unmarried (or legally separated) Taxpayers Who Qualify as Heads of Household			
If the amount on Form 1040, line 48, is:		Enter on line 4, Form 1040, line 16:		If the amount on Form 1040, line 48, is:		Enter on Form 1040, line 16:	
Not over $500 . . . 14% of the amount on line 48.				Not over $1,000 . . . 14% of the amount on line 48.			
Over—	But not over—		of excess over—	Over—	But not over—		of excess over—
$500	$1,000	$70+15%	$500	$1,000	$2,000	$140+16%	$1,000
$1,000	$1,500	$145+16%	$1,000	$2,000	$4,000	$300+18%	$2,000
$1,500	$2,000	$225+17%	$1,500	$4,000	$6,000	$660+19%	$4,000
$2,000	$4,000	$310+19%	$2,000	$6,000	$8,000	$1,040+22%	$6,000
$4,000	$6,000	$690+22%	$4,000	$8,000	$10,000	$1,480+23%	$8,000
$6,000	$8,000	$1,130+25%	$6,000	$10,000	$12,000	$1,940+25%	$10,000
$8,000	$10,000	$1,630+28%	$8,000	$12,000	$14,000	$2,440+27%	$12,000
$10,000	$12,000	$2,190+32%	$10,000	$14,000	$16,000	$2,980+28%	$14,000
$12,000	$14,000	$2,830+36%	$12,000	$16,000	$18,000	$3,540+31%	$16,000
$14,000	$16,000	$3,550+39%	$14,000	$18,000	$20,000	$4,160+32%	$18,000
$16,000	$18,000	$4,330+42%	$16,000	$20,000	$22,000	$4,800+35%	$20,000
$18,000	$20,000	$5,170+45%	$18,000	$22,000	$24,000	$5,500+36%	$22,000
$20,000	$22,000	$6,070+48%	$20,000	$24,000	$26,000	$6,220+38%	$24,000
$22,000	$26,000	$7,030+50%	$22,000	$26,000	$28,000	$6,980+41%	$26,000
$26,000	$32,000	$9,030+53%	$26,000	$28,000	$32,000	$7,800+42%	$28,000
$32,000	$38,000	$12,210+55%	$32,000	$32,000	$36,000	$9,480+45%	$32,000
$38,000	$44,000	$15,510+58%	$38,000	$36,000	$38,000	$11,280+48%	$36,000
$44,000	$50,000	$18,990+60%	$44,000	$38,000	$40,000	$12,240+51%	$38,000
$50,000	$60,000	$22,590+62%	$50,000	$40,000	$44,000	$13,260+52%	$40,000
$60,000	$70,000	$28,790+64%	$60,000	$44,000	$50,000	$15,340+55%	$44,000
$70,000	$80,000	$35,190+66%	$70,000	$50,000	$52,000	$18,640+56%	$50,000
$80,000	$90,000	$41,790+68%	$80,000	$52,000	$64,000	$19,760+58%	$52,000
$90,000	$100,000	$48,590+69%	$90,000	$64,000	$70,000	$26,720+59%	$64,000
$100,000	....	$55,490+70%	$100,000	$70,000	$76,000	$30,260+61%	$70,000
				$76,000	$80,000	$33,920+62%	$76,000
				$80,000	$88,000	$36,400+63%	$80,000
				$88,000	$100,000	$41,440+54%	$88,000
				$100,000	$120,000	$49,120+66%	$100,000
				$120,000	$140,000	$62,320+67%	$120,000
				$140,000	$160,000	$75,720+68%	$140,000
				$160,000	$180,000	$89,320+69%	$160,000
				$180,000	....	$103,120+70%	$180,000

schools. Property taxes are based on the value of real estate, such as land and buildings, and on personal property, such as furniture, stocks, jewelry, and cars.

Real estate taxes are based on the estimated value placed on a plot of land, a building, or other taxable property. These taxes differ from community to community. An important issue is how the value of the property is *assessed,* or estimated. Suppose Pete Doyle's home in Austin, Texas, is assessed at $32,000. If the local tax rate for every $1,000 of assessed value were $28, Pete would have to pay $896 in property taxes. If Pete's home were in Houston, it might be taxed at a rate of $14 per $1,000 of assessed value. He would then pay only $576.

Real estate property taxes make up over 75 cents of every dollar received by local governments. It is the major source of money for community improvements, police and fire protection, and schools.

SALES TAXES

Sales taxes exist in over 35 states and in the District of Columbia. They usually range from 2 to 7 percent of the purchase price.

There are a number of different kinds of sales taxes. A *general sales tax* is one that a buyer pays when he or she makes a purchase. For example, if a state has a 4 percent general sales tax on clothes dryers, a buyer would pay this tax rate. Suppose that Ms. Janelle Wilton buys a $170 electric clothes dryer. She would pay a tax of $6.80. Some cities have a sales tax that generally ranges from .5 to 8 percent of the purchase price. If Janelle lived in a city that also levied a sales tax, say a 1 percent tax, she would pay an extra $1.70. Thus, she would pay the state $6.80 and the city $1.70.

Sales taxes are considered regressive because people at all income levels pay the same tax. The person earning $100,000 a year pays the same rate as the person earning $6,000 a year. Thus, the person earning a lower income has a greater tax burden than the person earning the higher income.

There is also a tax called an *excise tax.* This is a tax that the Federal, state, and local governments may levy on the purchase of a particular product or service. In 1972 the Federal Government had to take special security measures to reduce skyjacking. They hired and trained a special security force. This cost a lot of money. To help pay for this security force, the Government levied an excise tax on airplane tickets. These tax dollars were paid by those people buying tickets.

Tariff taxes on imported goods were briefly discussed earlier. Recall that the Japanese camera company had to pay a tariff of $15 on each camera imported by the United States. Only the Federal Government can levy and collect this type of tax.

SOCIAL SECURITY TAX

The *social security tax* is used to pay for a variety of benefits, including retirement and disability. Some people think of the social security tax as an insurance premium that is paid for social insurance benefits. However, because it is money paid to the Government for various benefits, it qualifies as a tax.

ESTATE TAX

An *estate tax* is a tax levied by the Federal Government on property left by a person who has died. Anything a person owns makes up his or her estate. Most people who inherit money or property do not have to pay this tax because an exemption of $60,000 is allowed; that is, there is no tax if the belongings of the deceased are valued at less than $60,000. The estate tax rate starts at 3 percent and increases to 77 percent tax on estates worth more than $10 million.

GIFT TAX

Many wealthy people are against having their survivors pay estate taxes. If it were possible, they would probably try to give away most of their belongings before they died, avoiding the estate tax. To prevent this, the Government levied a *gift tax* which must be paid on gifts of property, money, stocks, or bonds. Here, too, the gift must be valued over a certain dollar amount if it is to be taxed.

The various types of taxes discussed here are either progressive or regressive and either direct or indirect. Remember that the progressive tax increases as the taxpayer's income increases, while a regressive tax takes a greater percentage of lower incomes than it does of higher incomes. The direct tax is paid directly to the government, while the indirect tax is paid to another person who then gives it to the government. Table 37–2 summarizes these taxes.

TABLE 37–2
CLASSIFICATION OF TAXES

| Progressive | Regressive | |
Direct	Direct	Indirect
Income Taxes Federal State Local	**Property Taxes** State Local	**Sales Taxes** State Local
Social Security Taxes Federal		**Excise Taxes** Federal State Local
Estate and Gift Taxes Federal		**Import Taxes** Federal
Corporation Taxes Federal State		

Notice in the table that there are no progressive indirect taxes. When a shopper makes a purchase or buys an imported product, he or she pays the same tax rate regardless of how much he or she earns.

Taxes allow governments to provide various services. Figure 37–2 shows where the Federal Government's money comes from. As much as 78 cents of every federal dollar comes directly to the Government from the taxpayers. In 1972, individuals paid $94.8 billion in income taxes, corporations paid $32 billion, social insurance taxes were $53.9 billion, and excise taxes were $15.5 billion.

These dollars were spent on a variety of things. Thirty-four cents of every tax dollar received by the Federal Government ($78.2 billion) was spent on national defense. A total of $11.1 billion was used for building highways and mass transportation. The Government also spent $17 billion on health expenses, such as Medicare and medical research.

FIGURE 37-2
THE TAX SOURCE OF THE
FEDERAL DOLLAR

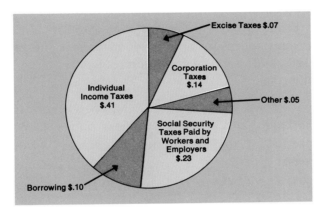

ARE TAXES REALLY NECESSARY?

April 15 is a familiar date to all taxpayers. All people filing federal income tax returns must do so by this date. The Government provides the necessary forms. They are sent in the mail to each taxpayer. They can also be picked up at post offices, Internal Revenue Service offices, and banks.

Although the forms are easy enough to get, tax laws and requirements often change from year to year. This tends to confuse and frustrate many taxpayers. It is unrealistic to say that people enjoy paying their federal income tax. In the first place, it costs money. In the second place, it seems to become more and more complicated.

UNDERSTANDING THE TAX SYSTEM   **489**

However, the basic issue is Are taxes necessary? The answer is a loud yes. If the government is to provide needed and wanted services, it must collect tax dollars. If there are to be paved highways, modern schools, public hospitals and other medical facilities, and other goods and services provided by Federal, state, and local governments, everybody must carry his or her share of the tax burden.

SUMMARY

The taxes everyone pays provide the money for the goods and services that citizens expect from the Federal, state, and local governments. Taxes are certainly necessary, and everyone looks to the government to use its tax dollars for highways, schools, space research, military defense, and other needs.

Every taxpayer knows that taxes are going up. Because of increasing population, inflation, and an almost endless public demand for more goods and services, taxes have gone up. It seems that they will continue to increase.

I. REVIEW OF TERMS

Which words complete the statements below?

property taxes   Internal Revenue Service

$94.8   estate tax

April 15   general sales tax

indirect   real estate

regressive   tariff

1. Federal income tax returns must be filed by midnight of _____ .

2. The _____ is the federal agency that receives income tax returns.

3. A tax is called _____ when it takes a greater percentage from a person with a lower income than it does from an individual with a higher income.

4. _____ are levied on the value of land and buildings.

5. A _____ is one which purchasers of goods, such as clothes dryers, pay when they buy the product.

6. The _____ property tax is estimated to provide over 75 cents of every dollar of the revenue of local governments

7. A tax on imported goods is called a _____ .

8. In 1972, individuals paid _____ billion in federal income taxes.

9. All _____ taxes are regressive.

10. A tax levied by the Federal Government on property left by people who have died is called an _____ .

II. REVIEW OF MAIN POINTS

1. Briefly discuss the main reasons why taxes are increasing.

2. What are some of the services provided by the government?

3. What are the reasons for a tariff tax?

4. What is a progressive income tax?

5. Why is the assessed value of property an important figure for calculating property taxes?
6. What deductions are shown on an income tax Form 1040?
7. Why is there a gift tax?
8. What is the major difference between a state sales tax and the federal income tax?

III. UNDERSTANDING THE TAX SYSTEM: CONCEPTS

1. In your own words give your opinion on whether taxes are necessary.
2. If someone stated that the federal income tax should be regressive, what would your position be?
3. Are there any political reasons for having high tariffs on the goods of a particular country?
4. Do you believe that social security payments should be viewed as a tax or an insurance premium? Why?
5. Explain the concept of revenue sharing.
6. Should the government listen to the public's demand for more goods and services? Why?

IV. UNDERSTANDING THE TAX SYSTEM: EXERCISES

1. Nan Lowery bought a house in Lafayette, Indiana, for $24,500. When she got her property tax statement, she found that the house was assessed at $23,000.
   a. If the Lafayette property tax were $2 for every $100 of value, how much property tax would she pay?
   b. If the property tax were increased to $2.50 per $100, how much would she pay with the new tax rate?
2. Determine the following tax rates in your community:
   a. Sales tax   b. Gasoline tax   c. Property tax
3. Use Table 37–1 for the following questions:
   a. Judy and Randy Schweitzer filed a joint return in 1974. They used the schedule Y tax rates to figure their tax. Suppose their taxable income was $22,000. How much tax would they have to pay?

b. Kelly Johnson filed a single return in 1974. She used the schedule X calculations. Kelly had a taxable income of $22,000. How much federal income tax would she have to pay?

4. Assume that Tony Santo had an adjusted gross income of $18,200 shown in line 41 of the Form 1040. Tony is single and claims only himself as an exemption. His deductible items are shown below:

Sinai Religious Association	$300
Y.M.C.A.	100
Red Cross	50
Disabled Veterans	25
Real estate taxes	150
State gasoline taxes	100
Interest on home	180
Professional literature	200

Considering his single exemption and the deductions, figure out Tony's federal income tax (Table 37−1).

5. Write a report on the state tax systems of Colorado, New York, and Nevada.

38 GOVERNMENT CONTROLS OF BUSINESS

Business in the United States is affected by Federal, state, and local governments. Many businesspeople believe that the government tells them when and how to do what things. This chapter examines some ways that government affects business. It explains why there are government controls, the methods of government controls, and the laws used to carry them out. The discussion does not support either businesspeople or government officials in their debate over how much control of business is needed. Its purpose is to provide you with a fair picture of the government controls of business.

WHY GOVERNMENT CONTROLS ARE NEEDED

A large company, such as General Motors or General Mills, uses the dollars of thousands of investors, employs thousands of people, and provides products, such as cars or food, for thousands of people. If the cars or food products were not safe, many people would suffer. Generally, the way business firms do their business affects the entire society.

It is not always safe to assume that businesses are concerned about protecting the public interest. There have been a number of times, however, when the government has been concerned about businesses taking advantage of the public.

1. People have been swindled out of their hard-earned dollars by people selling them stock that had no real value.
2. Men, women, and children have had to work at dangerous jobs with low pay and no job security.
3. People were not allowed to work because of their race, religion, sex, or background, even though they had all the necessary qualifications.

4. People were sold groceries that were impure.
5. The wastes of factories have polluted the air and water in many places.
6. Large amounts of electricity and oil have been wasted by some businesses (as well as by individuals).

There have been enough of these and other abuses that the government and many private citizens have become interested in protecting the public. The government maintains that some regulation and control of business is needed to protect the investors, the workers, the consumers, and society in general from the abuses of the corrupt members of the business world. The honest businesspeople must also be protected from the dishonest businesspeople.

Business controls have largely been the result of public pressure. Investors have demanded protection from swindlers. The public has demanded social insurance protection. Consumers have demanded an end to impure foods and harmful products.

A century ago there were very few government controls. There were only a few large, powerful corporations at that time. Today, however, there are many large corporations, and they can make decisions that can affect large groups of people. With the growth of large business corporations has come the growth of government regulation and controls.

METHODS OF GOVERNMENT CONTROL

There are several ways that the government can exert some control over business. They include passing and enforcing laws, granting licenses and certificates, and collecting taxes or giving subsidies.

LAWS

Many of the regulations that affect business are based on laws passed by Federal, state, or local governments. If these laws are broken, the violators can be fined or put in jail.

CERTIFICATES AND LICENSES

A business that provides transportation or utility services (such as telephone service) must get a *certificate* from federal or state authorities before it is permitted to operate. Both the service and the rates charged by these businesses are regulated by a special board or a commission.

Doctors, dentists, druggists, barbers, stockbrokers, distributors of liquor, tobacco, and milk, and operators of restaurants, hotels, pool halls, and taxicabs are only some of the businesspeople that must have a permit, or *license,* to do business. Licensing is designed to protect the public against unqualified people, such as a barber who has not taken the proper courses in haircutting. The license grants the holder a right to practice. It is usually temporary; it has to be renewed at regular intervals and can be taken away if the holder is convicted of a crime or if the government can prove that he or she is incompetent.

TAXES AND SUBSIDIES

Taxes are the government's main source of obtaining money for building schools, highways, parks, and museums. Taxes on liquor and tobacco, in addition to raising money for the government, are also designed to discourage drinking and smoking. These taxes are a form of control used by the government.

The government also uses subsidies as controls. A *subsidy* is a payment by the government to a businessperson or a firm. Subsidy payments are made by the government to operators of merchant ships in order to keep the shipyards busy building ships. Because the government encourages shipbuilding, more ships are built and more people are employed to build them.

GOVERNMENT OWNERSHIP

When a government owns a business it definitely has control over it. Water systems are owned by many city governments. In some states liquor stores are owned and run by the state.

COMMISSIONS

The control of business by the Federal Government is carried out largely by various commissions. These commissions are appointed by the President with the approval of the Senate. The most widely publicized commissions are the Interstate Commerce Commission, the Federal Aviation Commission, the Federal Communications Commission, the Nuclear Regulatory Commission, and the Securities and Exchange Commission.

The *Interstate Commerce Commission* (ICC) is involved in controlling such industries as the railroads, trucking, water carriers, and oil pipelines. One of its most important jobs is the approving or disapproving of rates charged by these industries. The commission is headed by a chairperson, and it handles as many as 5,000 complaints from consumers, competitors, and politicians about the areas over which it has control.

Dixy Lee Ray was head of the now disbanded Atomic Energy Commission.

Air traffic controllers' work is supervised by the FAC.

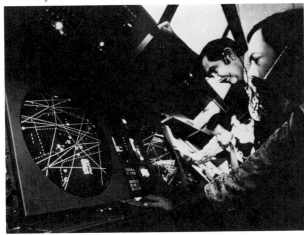

The *Federal Aviation Commission* (FAC) is concerned with making air travel safe and efficient. It sets safety standards for the airlines and also grants money for the building of city airports.

The *Federal Communications Commission* (FCC) issues licenses to radio and television stations. These stations cannot operate without the commission's license. The commission also regulates telephone and telegraph rates and services. If American Telephone and Telegraph Company wants to raise telephone rates between states, it must first receive permission from this commission.

In January 1975, the *Nuclear Regulatory Commission* assumed some of the functions of the disbanded Atomic Energy Commission. Its main responsibility is seeing that the use of nuclear materials does not endanger public safety, the environment, or national security. The research functions of the AEC were transferred to the Energy Research and Development Administration.

The *Securities and Exchange Commission* (SEC) tries to prevent the fraudulent sale of stocks and bonds. It requires that all new securities be registered and approved. It is responsible for the issuing of licenses to brokers who sell stocks and bonds to the public. To get a license, a broker must be qualified to help investors in buying stocks and bonds.

ANTITRUST LAWS

A *monopoly* is one giant firm that has so much control over an industry that it can set prices and prevent other firms from competing with it. If the Government allowed monopolies to exist, would prices go up? The past history of business in the United States shows that prices would rise and the public interest and pocketbook would suffer. To prevent the creation of powerful monopolies, a series of *antitrust* laws have been developed.

THE SHERMAN ANTITRUST ACT

In 1890, the Sherman Antitrust Act was passed to control the growth of monopolies and conspiracies. A *conspiracy* is the grouping together of two or more firms to control certain features of a particular market. Such a feature could be the price of goods. *Section 1* of this law prohibits conspiracies specifically. Examples of conspiracies include

1. *Price Fixing* Suppose all the restaurants near a high school agreed to price all of their food exactly the same. This would mean that their hot dogs, hamburgers, bacon-lettuce-tomato sandwiches, and other popular lunch meals would cost the same in all the restaurants. If these restaurants charged higher prices than other restaurants that were too far away, the students would have no choice but to pay the higher prices.

2. *Market Sharing* Suppose the bottlers of soft drinks got together and divided up the Chicago market for selling their product. Each one agreed to sell to only those stores in his or her assigned area.

3. *Bid Tampering* Suppose various plumbing companies met to decide how each one would bid on certain contracts for copper tubing. Although the companies were supposed to be competing with each other, they decided beforehand who would have the low bid.

In each case, the Government must prove that the law has been violated. This is often difficult, but if it is proven, the people responsible can be fined or imprisoned.

Section 2 of the act makes a monopoly of an industry illegal. In general, a firm that has more than 60 percent of a market is considered by the courts to be a monopoly. This is not a definite rule, however, since there are firms that have more than 60 percent of the market and have not been prosecuted.

THE CLAYTON ACT

The Clayton Act was passed in 1914 to strengthen the Sherman Antitrust Act. It was meant to prevent monopolies from forming. This act was changed in 1936 by the *Robinson-Patman Act*. This act prohibits price discrimination that reduces competition. *Price discrimination* occurs when a business charges customers different prices for things that are the same in grade and quality. An example would be charging a large gasoline station 42 cents a gallon and a small independent gasoline station 81 cents a gallon. The oil company is probably discriminating against the small station.

The Clayton Act also prohibits a firm from getting control of another firm if the combining of the two companies reduces competition in a market area. For example, if a large firm plans to buy control of a smaller firm and the two together control 80 percent of a market, the Clayton Act might be enforced to prevent this. The *merger,* or combination, of the two business firms into a single firm would create a monopoly.

THE FEDERAL TRADE COMMISSION ACT

The Federal Trade Commission Act was passed in 1914 to deal with unfair competition not covered in the Clayton Act. It also established the Federal Trade Commission (FTC) which has power to enforce the act. The FTC has the power to take action against business practices that are considered harmful to competition or to the public.

If a businessperson is charged with a violation of the act, the FTC makes a formal complaint. The businessperson must answer the complaint within 30 days. If the FTC is not satisfied with the businessperson's answer to the complaint, the FTC can issue a *cease and desist order.* This means that the violation must be stopped. The businessperson can then stop violating the law, appeal the order through the courts, or continue the violation and risk being fined up to $50,000 a day.

THE OCCUPATIONAL HEALTH AND SAFETY ACT (OHSA)

In 1973 more than 2 million disabling injuries and over 14,000 deaths occurred in United States business firms. The Government is well aware of the need to improve plant safety practices. A step in this direction was the passage in 1970 of the Occupational Health and Safety Act (OHSA). This law is intended "to assure so far as possible every working man and woman in the Nation safe and healthful working conditions and to preserve our human resources." Employers must maintain certain safety and health standards. Workers have the duty to obey the health and safety rules.

OHSA has created a new right for workers in the United States—the right to a safe and healthful place of employment. If an employer violates this right, the company can be fined or shut down. If an employee complains, federal inspectors can visit the plant and review the health and safety practices there.

SUMMARY

Business firms in the United States are influenced in what they do by regulations and controls at the Federal, state, and local levels of government. The pricing, marketing, and servicing of products that a firm sells must be carried out within the limits set by the government.

The history of business abuses includes such practices as stock frauds, hiring discrimination, selling impure foods, and polluting the water and air. The government's answer to these illegal practices is to exert some control over business. Such controls include laws, certificates, licenses, taxes, subsidies, and government ownership.

To help control business, a number of regulatory commissions are needed. These commissions include the Interstate Commerce Commission and the Federal Aviation Commission.

Also, antitrust laws have been established to (1) prevent monopolies from forming, (2) eliminate business conspiracies, and (3) protect the public from the few businesspeople who mislead and trick buyers. These laws, however, are hard to enforce. The Government commissions that can enforce the laws are swamped with complaints. This means that the process of stopping violations is slow. The commissions and the courts are overburdened with work. Despite these and other difficulties, the control and regulation of businesses by the Government has resulted in fewer monopolies in the United States than in any other industrialized nation.

I. REVIEW OF TERMS

Which words complete the statements below?

monopolies	brokers
license	taxes
radio and television	Robinson-Patman Act
President	cities
	Sherman Antitrust Act

1. The Clayton Act was amended in 1936 by the _____.
2. In 1890 the _____ was passed to curb the growth of monopolies and conspiracies.
3. Water systems are generally owned by _____.
4. Doctors and druggists must have a _____ to do business in most states and local communities.
5. _____ are considered a control device of government in that people must pay them when buying liquor and tobacco.
6. The Federal Communications Commission is responsible for issuing licenses to _____ stations.
7. The Securities and Exchange Commission is responsible for issuing licenses to _____ who sell stocks and bonds.
8. One objective of antitrust laws is to prevent _____ from forming.
9. The federal commission members are generally appointed by the _____.

II. REVIEW OF MAIN POINTS

1. What is meant by the term *public interest*?
2. Briefly define *price discrimination*.
3. What is a monopoly business corporation and a monopoly public utility?

4. Why does the government believe that licensing people in various occupations is necessary?
5. What is price fixing?
6. What is a cease and desist order?
7. What is a merger?

III. GOVERNMENT CONTROLS OF BUSINESS: CONCEPTS

1. Is it necessary for the Government to still be concerned about price fixing?
2. What companies that are not classified as public utilities do you consider monopolies? Why?
3. Do you feel that the government should be involved in trying to deal with an energy crisis? Why?
4. Do you believe that taxes should be considered a control? Why?
5. Give recent examples which lead you to believe that government controls are either decreasing or increasing.
6. What is the difference between the Sherman Antitrust Act and the Clayton Act?
7. Should the Government be involved in controlling telephone long-distance rates? Why?
8. How can people influence the controls that government uses on business corporations?

IV. GOVERNMENT CONTROLS OF BUSINESS: EXERCISES

1. Prepare a report which answers the following questions:
   a. How many members are there on the Securities and Exchange Commission?
   b. What kinds of previous experience do commissioners have?
   Use your library or contact a stock brokerage for help.
2. Have any business executives been put in jail for violating the antitrust laws? To answer this question, use encyclopedias and library materials.

3. What has the government in your community done about air, water, and noise pollution? Is it enough? Why or why not?

4. Make a short report that describes three recent business abuses which affected the public interest. Use newspapers, magazines, and other similar sources to write your report.

5. Write a short report on the history of the development of antitrust laws in the United States. What led to their development? Have they been successful in doing what they were designed to do?

LABOR UNIONS AND BUSINESS

39

Unemployment, strikes, demands for higher wages—these are all important issues that affect everyone. Higher unemployment rates for minority groups, such as Chicanos, Blacks, and American Indians, pose an explosive problem that faces business corporations as well as the Federal Government. Strikes by teachers, city workers, nurses, and engineers—as well as industrial workers—raise the issue of whether or not certain people have the right to strike when many people depend on them. Continuing pressure from workers for higher wages adds to the problem of inflation. These are all labor problems that affect everyone. This chapter discusses these problems and the important role that organized labor plays in society.

ORGANIZED LABOR: UNIONS

A *labor union* is a group of workers who have banded together to improve their wages and working conditions. One goal of a union may be to have the company pay for the workers' life insurance premiums. In the United States, slightly more than 19 million workers belong to unions. This is about 24 percent of the total number of workers.

Unions are divided into two major groups: craft unions and industrial unions. A *craft union* is made up of workers representing a single occupation, such as glass blowers or machinists. An *industrial union* includes all the workers of a plant, no matter what their occupation is. An industrial union, such as the United Automobile Workers (UAW), includes skilled, semiskilled, and unskilled employees in the industry.

TABLE 39–1
LABOR UNION MEMBERSHIP

Year	Union Membership (in thousands)	Total Number of Workers (in thousands)	Percentage
1950	14,262	64,749	22.0
1960	17,049	73,126	23.3
1968	17,900	79,000	22.6
1972	19,400	80,500	24.0

THE UNION ORGANIZATION

Large unions in the United States, like the government, operate at local, regional, and national levels.

THE LOCAL LEVEL

The labor union organization at the local level is called a *local union.* Local unions hold meetings to elect officers, hear speakers, conduct union business, and sponsor local affairs or activities, such as Little League baseball teams. Each union member has a voice in union business and can vote for local officers. Each one also pays *union dues.* This money is used to cover the cost of meetings and to pay the salaries of elected local union officials.

At the local level, an important union official is the *shop steward.* He or she collects union dues, handles workers' complaints, and represents the union. Shop stewards are elected by the local union or by a smaller group of workers they represent.

THE REGIONAL LEVEL

At the state or regional level, unions are represented by district offices, regional councils, and joint boards. State or regional officials are elected either by the entire union or by all the local unions in the region. These union officials coordinate the activities of the local

TABLE 39–2
ESTIMATES OF THE MEMBERSHIP OF THE FIVE LARGEST UNIONS (1970)

Rank	Union	Total Members
1	Teamsters, Chauffeurs, Warehouse Workers and Helpers	1,829,000
2	Automotive, Aircraft, and Agricultural Implement Workers	1,486,000
3	Steelworkers	1,200,000
4	Electrical Workers	922,000
5	Machinists	865,000

unions. An activity such as endorsing political candidates is usually coordinated at the regional level by elected union officials.

THE NATIONAL LEVEL

At the national (or international) level of unions, the elected officials of the local unions are required to meet in a convention at least once every five years. In most unions, a president and other key officials are elected at the convention.

When a union such as the United Automobile Workers negotiates with General Motors or Ford, the most important discussions occur at the national level. The local unions discuss problems with business managers of a plant only when the problems involve a particular plant.

Craft and industrial unions often band together at the local, regional, and national levels to achieve their goals. The major body stressing joint goals is the AFL-CIO (American Federation of Labor—Congress of Industrial Organizations), a union that represents over 300 separate local, regional, and national union groups. Before joining together, the AFL was the national federation of craft unions, and the CIO was a group of industrial unions.

SOME UNION GOALS

Labor unions present business executives and company owners with demands for increased wages, better working conditions, job security, and other similar things. School boards, hospital administrators, and government managers are also faced by these demands from unions.

MORE WAGES AND FRINGE BENEFITS

Unions often press for higher wages. They generally point out that business profits are improving and since labor is an important reason for this rise, the employees should share in the increased profits.

Labor unions also place more stress on improving fringe benefits, such as pension plans, health care, vacation time, and sick leave. Some business firms report that fringe benefits cost their company as much as 50 percent of the total wage and salary cost.

BETTER WORKING CONDITIONS

Unions have steadily prodded business firms to improve their working conditions. They have stressed the need to increase rest periods and reduce the number of working hours.

UNION SECURITY

Many unions in the construction trades and longshore workers trade attempt to operate a *closed shop,* which is illegal by law. A closed shop means that only union members will be hired. In a *union shop,* an em-

These people wait long hours to apply for a small number of jobs open to nonunion members.

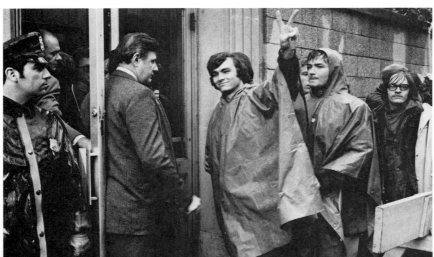

ployer is free to hire whomever he or she chooses, but all new workers must join the union within a certain period of time, such as 30 days. In an *open shop,* each worker can decide whether or not to join the union. Unions are generally opposed to open shops.

Improving wages, fringe benefits, and working conditions, and providing union security are not crucial goals for business corporations. Companies believe that they must 1) pay wages and fringe benefits that are reasonable, 2) provide reasonable and safe working conditions but focus primarily on achieving acceptable levels of production, and 3) hire employees that are motivated to produce. These three goals of management are somewhat different from the goals of unions and their members. These differences sometimes lead to problems and conflict.

UNIONS VERSUS MANAGEMENT

Conflicts over wages, fringe benefits, working conditions, and union security often lead to the union and/or management using various techniques to get their way. The chief threat of the union is the *strike.* A strike occurs when union members as a group refuse to work until some kind of an agreement is reached between the company and the union.

A *wildcat strike* is one in which workers walk off the job without their union's authorization. This is an illegal strike. In a *sit-down strike,* which is also illegal, workers remain in the plant or office but refuse to work.

A strike usually involves *picketing,* the placing of union members at entrances to the business. The picketers, usually carrying signs, publicize the strike. They show nonunion people that the union is behind the strike, and they try to discourage nonstriking workers from entering the plant.

To counteract a strike, management can use what is called a *lockout.* In a lockout, management shuts the doors of a plant and does not allow workers to enter. The workers receive no wages during either a strike or a lockout. Sometimes during a lockout, management may continue to run the business using upper-level managers to do the work.

Because strikes are so costly to both union members and the struck company, it is to everyone's advantage to avoid them. Management and union representatives are often able to negotiate a labor contract without a strike.

The eventual result of collective bargaining is the *union contract.* This is a written agreement between the union and management. It describes in detail the rules and procedures to be followed by both parties during the period covered by the contract. Some of the items included in a union contract are

1. The length of time the contract covers
2. Wage rates and fringe benefits for employees
3. Certain working conditions—length of coffee breaks, length of vacation, and amount of sick leave
4. Union security—the hiring of new workers
5. Procedures for firing employees
6. Ways of handling complaints (These are complaints in which one side accuses the other side of not living up to the rules and procedures in the contract.)
7. Use of an arbitrator (If the company and the union cannot settle a grievance by themselves, they may ask an outsider to decide who is right. This outsider is called an *arbitrator.* His or her decision is usually binding for both the union and the company.)

In some cases, contracts are 300 to 400 pages long. Violations of contract rules by either the union or management can result in a lawsuit.

UNIONS AND THE LAW

Discussions between management and employees on such issues as wage levels and fringe benefits would be completely one-sided if the workers had no legal power. To get legal power, the labor unions usually have to go through the courts so that the laws ensuring them of certain rights are followed by management. Some laws that have had a lasting influence on union-management relations are discussed in the following paragraphs:

THE NORRIS-LAGUARDIA ACT

The Norris-LaGuardia Act of 1932 provides workers with the right to engage in collective bargaining through the unions that they choose. Before this act was passed, management had to get a court injunction to prevent workers from striking. This act also prevents management from using a *yellow dog contract.* This is a signed pledge by a new employee to not join a union.

THE NATIONAL LABOR RELATIONS ACT

The National Labor Relations Act of 1935, which is more commonly called the *Wagner Act,* forces employers to bargain with unions. It also requires that management not engage in such practices as firing union leaders unfairly, spying on unions, and hampering union attempts to organize a group of employees.

THE TAFT-HARTLEY ACT

The labor union has become a well-established bargaining group in the United States. In 1947, Congress passed the Taft-Hartley Act to bring about a better and more fair balance of power between labor unions and management. Many people at this time thought that unions had become too well established and more powerful than management.

Some of the unfair union practices forbidden by the law are

1. Requiring an employer or self-employed person to join a union
2. Pressuring an employer to discriminate against an employee in order to encourage or discourage union membership
3. Mass picketing and violence in strikes.

THE LABOR-MANAGEMENT DISCLOSURE ACT

After the passage of the Taft-Hartley Act, which unions referred to as the *slave labor act,* attempts were made by both unions and management to change certain parts of the act. During this time, congressional hearings were held, and it became clear that racketeers had worked their way into the local, regional, and national levels of some unions.

These discoveries led to the passage in 1959 of the *Landrum-Griffin Act*, which is legally called the *Labor-Management Disclosure Act.* This act requires that unions and employers file reports, such as annual financial reports, with the Secretary of Labor. The act also states that union members shall have the right to attend and vote in union meetings and elections, vote on increases in dues and fees, and receive notice and a fair hearing before any major union disciplinary action can be taken.

THE CIVIL RIGHTS ACT

The Civil Rights Act of 1964, as changed in 1972, makes it unlawful for a union to refuse membership to a person because of race, sex, or national origin. This act is also having an influence on women's rights. It supports the *Equal Pay Act,* which states that it is against the law to pay women less than men for doing the same work. It also states that it is unlawful for a union to attempt to cause an employer to discriminate on the basis of sex.

SUMMARY

A quick look at a newspaper, a television news program, or a weekly magazine shows that unions are an important force in the United States. Business organizations must collectively bargain with the union that represents its employees.

The size of unions has increased by about 5 million members since 1950, but only 24 percent of the labor force is organized today. Although about only one in four workers is a union member, organized labor plays an important role in getting better wages and working conditions for all workers.

A union organization includes officials at the local, regional, and national levels. At the local level, the important union official is the shop steward. This person represents the union members. The local, regional, and national officials try to communicate the goals of the members to the management of business firms.

Some of the goals sought by unions include higher wages, better fringe benefits, better working conditions, job security, and union security. Management often has a slightly different set of goals, which includes reducing costs and encouraging workers to produce more. Thus, union goals and management goals can conflict with each other.

There are several laws at the Federal Government level that affect labor-management relations. Such laws include the Norris-LaGuardia Act of 1932, the National Labor Relations Act of 1935, the Taft-Hartley Act of 1947, the Labor-Management Disclosure Act of 1959, and the Civil Rights Act of 1964.

REVIEW   LABOR UNIONS AND BUSINESS

I. REVIEW OF TERMS
Which words complete the statements below?

yellow dog contract	craft union
AFL-CIO	Teamsters
lockout	union contract
Taft-Hartley Act	open shop

1. A _____ is made up of workers that represent a single profession, such as machinists.
2. The largest union in terms of total membership is the _____.
3. A union body representing over 300 separate local, regional, and national union groups is the _____.
4. In an _____, workers may decide whether or not to join a union.
5. A management weapon used to fight union demands is called a _____.
6. The hoped-for result of collective bargaining is the _____.

7. The _____ was made illegal by the Norris-LaGuardia Act of 1932.

8. According to the _____, a union cannot force workers to join that union.

II. REVIEW OF MAIN POINTS

1. What are some of the major goals of business management?

2. What is an industrial union?

3. Describe the duties of a shop steward.

4. What are fringe benefits?

5. Describe what is meant by a *closed shop.*

6. What is a wildcat strike?

7. What are some of the things covered in a union contract?

III. LABOR UNIONS AND BUSINESS: CONCEPTS

1. Do you believe that it is necessary for unions and management to prepare contracts on issues such as pay and fringe benefits? Why?

2. Can the Teamsters Union try to organize nurses?

3. Do you feel that it is fair to society to make wildcat strikes illegal? Why?

4. Should a high school student working in a supermarket be required to join a union if the store is a union shop? Why?

5. Why do you think that unions have not increased their size significantly with regard to the total labor force?

6. Have unions become too powerful? Why?

IV. LABOR UNIONS AND BUSINESS: EXERCISES

1. Do a library report and study in detail the organizational structure of one of the five largest unions at the local, regional, and national level.

2. Discuss the history of union violence in this country. Use your library and encyclopedias for help.

3. Should the closed shop be allowed to exist? Why?

4. Should police officers be allowed to strike? Why?

Unit X
The Challenge
of the Future

Most high school students today will sooner or later become employees in the business world. The business world contains millions of Americans of all ages, backgrounds, and educational levels. There is no magic formula that will guarantee a person a successful career. There do appear to be, however, a few keys that can help a young person have a better chance at succeeding in the business world.

One key is education. Unless you graduate from high school, the career road is bound to be bumpy. Look in your community, on your television set, and in your newspapers. Few high school dropouts are living a comfortable life. A comfortable life does not necessarily mean being rich but does mean eating enough nutritional food, being warmly clothed, and having a clean and safe place in which to live.

Another key appears to be fairness by business firms in hiring people. If business firms discriminate against a man or woman because of age, color, religion, sex, or background, many career paths could be difficult. This type of discrimination, in fact, is against the law.

Another key concerns social responsibility. Unless business leaders work on problems such as pollution and discrimination, the careers of all Americans could be threatened. This is true because businesspeople are important providers of jobs.

This final unit provides no sure answers, only guidelines and some predictions about careers and problems of tomorrow. It is not the final word on career planning, but it should be seen as a starting point.

Chapter 40 begins by trying to explain why people work. In simple terms, people work to survive. However, people also work because it is necessary for them to express themselves and gain status. This chapter also points out some of the differences in various jobs. These differences should be considered when planning a career.

Chapter 41 deals with the world of work. There are thousands of different occupations which require different levels of training and education. This chapter reviews occupational trends so that the reader can see what jobs are increasing in number and which jobs are decreasing.

UNIT PREVIEW

The chapter closes by discussing various sources of information that can help students learn more about different occupations.

Chapter 42 provides a number of job search guidelines. Résumés, letters of application, ads, the use of employment agencies, and other guidelines for finding jobs are discussed.

The final chapter talks about present and future problems that business-people must handle if the United States is to continue to grow economically. Some of these problems are pollution, energy crises, discrimination against women and minorities, and lack of social responsibility. Because the United States operates in a dynamic and ever-changing world, and because the population continues to grow, these and other problems will be magnified in the future unless action is taken today.

Of course, it is not only up to businesspeople to clean up the air, earth, and water, reduce discrimination, and eliminate dishonesty. Everyone must help out. This chapter highlights some of the challenges with which every man, woman, and child will be faced in the next ten years.

AS YOU STUDY THIS UNIT YOU WILL BE ENGAGED IN

* **UNDERSTANDING** the factors underlying work

* **IDENTIFYING** what is required in various occupations

* **ANALYZING** the trends in employment in different occupations

* **PROBING** what business is doing for women and minorities in the work world

* **PRACTICING** personal business procedures, such as writing letters of application and personal résumés

* **EVALUATING** the responsibilities of business to meet the challenges of energy shortages, pollution, and other environmental factors.

A FOCUS FOR YOUR STUDY

40 WHY PEOPLE WORK

Why do people work? One answer is that people work to earn a living. People must have money to buy the things they need and want, such as food, clothing, education, a home, and a car. For most people, the way to get money is to work. This chapter examines some of the more important economic and noneconomic reasons why people work. It will become clear that there can be more to working than just earning money.

People do work so that they can earn money. In addition to this important and most popular reason, there are other reasons why people work, such as those described in the following sections:

SELF-EXPRESSION

It is important that people find work that allows them to develop their abilities and skills. A job can be seen as the chance to express oneself. The chance to develop skills for cutting hair, building homes, or drawing pictures helps to make work interesting. It is interesting because

Modeling and photography are creative professions.

workers can use their talents or skills. Builders of homes can construct outstanding homes and feel proud of their work.

SECURITY

Many people believe that security is the most important reason to work. These people want to earn enough money so that they do not need financial help from the government or their family. These people need to feel that they will never have to depend on anyone else for money.

STATUS

When you meet someone for the first time, it is a common practice to ask what he or she does for a living. When the person answers, "I am an accountant," or "I am an electrical engineer," or "I am a bricklayer," you can usually get a quick picture of the person's work status. The work status of a person often says something about his or her wealth and income, his or her standard of living, and his or her interests. Many people work so that they can reach a higher level of status in their community, in the place where they work, and in their own mind.

People in the United States often classify occupations on the basis of status. One such classification system for business organizations includes

Professional manager—a top executive, such as a president or vice president of a company

Technical workers—engineers

Managerial workers—office managers (or leaders of small groups) in a company or store

Clerks and sales personnel

Skilled workers—mechanics

Semiskilled workers—mechanics' apprentices

Unskilled workers—janitors.

HUMANITARIAN REASONS

Many people work for humanitarian reasons; that is, so that they can help others. Such people as physical therapists, teachers, and nurses often feel that their jobs enable them to help sick people, young children, and the aged. This feeling of helping others allows these workers to feel that they have really contributed to society. They are involved in what are called the *helping occupations.*

DIFFERENCES IN OCCUPATIONS

Jobs differ in the money that can be earned, the chances to display talents and skills, job security, status, and the opportunity to serve others. They also differ in the amounts of education and training they require, in the types of physical skills they require, and in the types of business organizations and settings in which they are found.

Some occupations, such as being a lawyer, an accountant, or a doctor, require a college education. Some occupations require a great deal of physical ability. Not everyone can hit home runs like Hank Aaron or score goals like Bobby Orr. In business, there are some occupations that require special physical skills. Such jobs include machinists and lathe operators. Other occupations, such as being a manager, require physical endurance but not necessarily physical skills.

Working conditions also differ in various organizations. For example, the industrial engineer working in a Republic Steel plant in Chicago works in a different setting than an industrial engineer working in Chicago's Jackson Park Hospital. These engineers may have had similar training, but they do their work in different settings.

Occupational preferences must be understood in light of what a young person expects to get from his or her work. Before deciding on a career —whether as a doctor, mechanic, or industrial engineer—it would be best for a person to consider answers to the following questions:

1.   What kind of special training or study is required?

2. What physical skills are needed?

3. In what setting would I work?

Only if you understand these different factors can you get what you want from work. The person who does not have the physical skill to be a lathe operator would find little chance of satisfying his or her work needs.

SUMMARY

Most people work to earn money. But there are also important psychological reasons for working. Such reasons include self-expression, security, status, and the wish to help others.

It is in your best interest to understand the requirements of various occupations. Knowing the requirements of different occupations should help you decide whether or not you have the mental and physical skills to derive satisfaction from doing the work of a particular occupation.

If you look at what adults do during the day, it becomes clear that their jobs take more of their time than any other activity. Thus, choosing the right work is a serious matter that has important significance.

REVIEW WHY PEOPLE WORK

I. REVIEW OF TERMS

Which words complete the statements below?

physical   professional manager
independence

1. It is generally believed that the highest status occupation in a business firm is that of _____.

2. Athletes have certain _____ skills that enable them to perform their work.

3. The job-security need felt by some people could be called a need for financial _____.

II. REVIEW OF MAIN POINTS
1. What is status?
2. Is earning a satisfactory income a "security" reason for working? Why?
3. What is an important difference between the requirements for being a lawyer and those for being a mechanic?
4. Why is it important to some people to be able to express themselves in their work?

III. WHY PEOPLE WORK: CONCEPTS
1. How could truck operators express themselves in their job?
2. Do you feel that teachers should have a desire to help others? Why?
3. Name two other noneconomic reasons why people work that were not discussed in this chapter.
4. Do you feel that women have the same work needs as men? Explain your answer.
5. Do you think that there is too much emphasis in the United States on the economic reasons why people work? Why?

IV. WHY PEOPLE WORK: EXERCISES
1. Make a list of the six occupations that you feel work hardest at serving others. Explain your reasons for choosing the six.
2. Do you believe that education is related to the status attached to various occupations? Explain your answer.
3. Find out some of the tasks performed in the following occupations:

   a. A corporation lawyer   **d.** A chemist
   b. A certified public accountant   **e.** A salesperson
   c. A bank teller

   Visit people in your community who are in these occupations and ask them what tasks they do as part of their work.

THE JOB WORLD

It is important for people to know about themselves and the world in which they will try to find a job and begin a career. To learn something about the jobs that are available, you have to seek out information. This chapter will try to provide facts, figures, and ideas about some, but certainly not all, of the jobs that exist. If you want more information on jobs, look at the *Encyclopedia of Careers and Vocational Guidance* in your public library.

OUR EARLY LIFE EXPERIENCES

Even as a young child you were exposed to many different kinds of workers: the plumber, the bus operator, the mail carrier, the teacher, the police officer, and the grocery store owner. In addition, you probably became familiar, through television, radio, and the newspapers, with professional athletes, news commentators, artists, actors, and many others.

Many young people themselves have jobs. They work in stores, bakeries, ice cream parlors, and gasoline stations. They deliver newspapers, cut lawns, and baby-sit.

It is also a part of every young person's life to see dentists, doctors, and nurses. These professional jobs become very real when you have a toothache or a cut that needs stitches.

Thus, you are exposed to many, but certainly not all, kinds of jobs. Many students never think about the work of a lawyer, a chemist, an FBI agent, a farmer, an interior decorator, a rabbi, a stockbroker, an

523

economist, a mathematician, a foreign service officer, an astronomer, or a computer programer. A person who is not exposed to information about jobs, or one who has no contact with a person doing a particular job, cannot be expected to develop an interest in that kind of work.

JOB TRENDS IN THE UNITED STATES

It is important to high school students to have a general knowledge of the job trends and job needs of the society in which they live. In Figure 41−1, workers are listed by occupational category. The occupational categories are

Professional and Technical—doctors, lawyers, druggists, chemists

Agricultural—farmers

Managerial—workers who own their own business or work in a management job for others

Clerical—clerks and stenographers

Skilled—highly trained experts, such as glass blowers, wood lathe operators, or pottery makers

Operative—apprentice plumbers, apprentice ironworkers, or apprentice bricklayers

Service—social workers or librarians

Labor—sanitation workers, steelworkers

Sales—door-to-door salespeople, cosmetics salespeople, or machine salespeople.

Figure 41−1 shows a large increase in the number of professional and technical workers, along with a drastic decrease in the number of agricultural workers. This means that there is a greater demand for the work skills of the professional and technical workers and much less of a need for farmers. Farming today produces more than in the 1940's because of new machinery, new breeding techniques, and other improvements. Thus, although more farm goods are being consumed, fewer farmers are needed.

FIGURE 41-1
MAJOR OCCUPATIONAL GROUPS IN PERCENTAGES OF
APPROXIMATELY 80 MILLION WORKERS

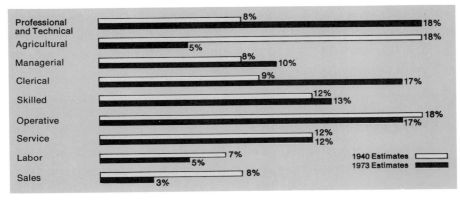

THE JOB MARKET

Many high school students today can look forward to spending about 40 years as a worker. Thus, it becomes very important to the high school student to look at basic trends, or patterns, in the business world. Studying trends can help answer such questions as what work is being done now, how many people are working, and what areas appear to have a shortage of workers. Some of the important trends to consider in preparing for a career include the following:

Two unusual professions: wood carving and color correcting in an advertising agency.

MORE NEW WORKERS

In the United States the average age at which people graduate from high school is eighteen. Around 1950 about 2 million people a year reached age eighteen. By 1960 that figure was up to 2.6 million, in 1965 it was 3.8 million, and in 1972 it was 4.0 million. These figures indicate that every year there will be more high school graduates competing for jobs. It is estimated that in 1976 almost one out of every four workers will be under twenty-four years of age.

EDUCATION AND TRAINING

The competition young people will face in the years ahead is important to consider when choosing a career. The amount of education and training required for various jobs has been rising and is expected to continue to go up. The young people are responding by getting more education before starting their careers.

Table 41-2 shows how unemployment varies with the level of education a person has. Note how much lower the unemployment rate is for high school graduates than it is for those who do not finish high school.

It is interesting to see that for all workers eighteen years old and over, the average educational level is 12.3 years of schooling. This is clear

TABLE 41-2
UNEMPLOYMENT RATES BY EDUCATIONAL LEVELS
For People 18 Years Old and Over (1970)

Average Years of Education	Unemployment Rate
(All persons 18 years old and over)	6.0%
0 Years of school	13.5
1-4 Years of school	8.9
5-7 Years of school	8.8
8 Years of school	6.9
9-11 Years of school	7.1
12 Years of school	4.9
(High school graduate)	
13-15 Years of school	4.2
16 Years of school	2.0
17+ Years of school	1.3

evidence why the high school dropout finds it so hard to find a job. About half of all high school dropouts end up in unskilled, low-paying jobs.

Table 41-3 shows how educational levels vary with different occupational groups. Note how every one of the so-called white-collar jobs requires at least a high school diploma.

TABLE 41-3
EDUCATIONAL LEVELS FOR VARIOUS OCCUPATIONS
For People 18 Years Old and Over (1970)

Occupations	Average Years of Education
Professional and Technical	16.5
Managerial	13.0
Clerical	13.0
Sales	12.5
Skilled	12.5
Service	11.0
Semiskilled	10.5
Unskilled	9.3
Agricultural	8.8
Labor (Farm)	8.2

SHIFTS IN NEEDS

Throughout history, the great majority of American workers worked at producing the goods that everyone used to live. The farmers produced the fuel, food, and fibers; the miners provided coal, zinc, copper, and other resources; and the construction workers built homes, factories, and offices.

There are other occupations that are service oriented. The workers at airports, railroads, and gas companies provide services.

Teachers, bankers, police officers, and insurance agents also provide services. It is expected that the largest area of growth for workers will come in the jobs that provide services. People are demanding such services as education, medical treatment, travel, police protection, and recreation at the highest rate ever. This means that in the years to come, there will be a growing demand for workers who deal in these services.

WHITE-COLLAR AND BLUE-COLLAR JOBS

There are more workers classified as white-collar workers than there are workers classified as blue-collar workers. The white-collar group includes professional, technical, managerial, clerical, and sales workers. The blue-collar group includes skilled, semiskilled, and unskilled workers.

In the white-collar group, the number of managers has increased over 30 percent from 1960 to 1972. The need for managers is expected to increase another 30 percent by the early 1980's. In fact, each white-collar category increased by over 25 percent between the early 1960's and the early 1970's.

There was a time when there were more blue-collar jobs than white-collar jobs. But they dropped behind the white-collar jobs around 1965. The biggest decreases of this century were in farm and unskilled jobs. New equipment and production methods have replaced much of the manual labor of the farmer and unskilled worker.

WOMEN IN THE WORLD OF WORK

During the past 100 years there has been a great change in the employment of women. In 1890 there were about 4 million working women in

Women have made great strides in the area of management. Pictured are an architect and a social service worker.

the United States. Today, there are about 30 million working women.

Many women who work are in the clerical, service, and professional job categories. However, it is expected that there will be an increase in women entering such areas as management, law, and medicine in the next ten years. In 1965 one million women were employed as proprietors, managers, or officials. This group is expected to double by 1980. Thus, it appears that the job future is bright for educated women.

MINORITIES

Laws forbidding discrimination have been important in decreasing discrimination in job hiring of such people as Blacks, Mexican-Americans, Chinese, and American Indians. There seems to be a growing interest among businesspeople to hire the most qualified job applicants, no matter what their race or color.

It seems that things will be even better in the future. This is not to say that all barriers of discrimination or racism will be completely removed in the near future. What seems to be happening, slowly, is that businesspeople as well as the rest of society are beginning to finally recognize that people's talents, skills, and education should be the key to securing jobs, not their background or the color of their skin.

WHERE TO GET INFORMATION ABOUT JOBS

Very often you hear about various jobs or read a brief note on jobs in the newspaper but do not know where to get more information. One good source is the *Dictionary of Occupational Titles.* This book is published by the Department of Labor. It describes most of the kinds of occupations in the United States. It describes the job of a surgeon as well as that of a waitress in a fast-food restaurant. In fact, more than 26,000 occupations are listed. For each job, you can see what requirements, in terms of job duties, training, and education, are involved. The book also shows you what jobs are grouped together. If you are trained for a group of jobs you have a better chance of getting a job.

Another good way to find out about an occupation is to talk with people who do that kind of work. Dentists can give you the best understanding of their job duties, working conditions, training, and education. A woman lawyer can best explain what it is like being a female in a profession that is made up mostly of men. Talk with these people and you will soon find out that most people want to encourage young people to enter their occupation.

You can also write to companies and ask for information about the jobs they have. Most businesspeople are happy to inform young people about job opportunities with their companies.

Other sources of information about jobs include

1. Discussing your interest in various occupations with your teachers or guidance counselors
2. Reading such magazines as *Business Week*, *Forbes*, and *Sales Management*
3. Reading the want ads in newspapers
4. Visiting businesses in your community and talking with workers
5. Contacting your state employment agency or a private employment firm.

SUMMARY

Although you may have some knowledge about various occupations, there are many jobs that you may know little about. Most high school students will eventually enter the work world. It is therefore to your advantage to find out as much as you can about various types of jobs. For example, it is important to know that the fastest-growing occupational group is the professional and technical, and the fastest-declining group is the agricultural.

It is also important to know some of the specifics about the job market. Such specifics include the increase in young workers, the needed education and training, the types of workers wanted, white-collar and blue-collar trends, the increasing number of women in the work world, and the job opportunities for minorities.

I. REVIEW OF TERMS

Which words complete the statements below?

clerical	*Forbes*
30	4
service	*Dictionary of Occupational Titles*
managerial	12.3
professional	labor

1. A steelworker's job is considered part of the _____ occupational category.
2. As of 1972 approximately _____ million young people reached the age of eighteen.
3. For workers eighteen years old and over, the average educational level is _____ years.
4. Such jobs as professional, technical, clerical, sales, and _____ are considered white-collar positions.
5. Today, the occupational groups with the most women are _____ , _____ , and _____ .
6. There are approximately _____ million working women.
7. A valuable source for learning something about the thousands of occupations available in the United States is the _____ .
8. *Business Week* and _____ are magazines that may provide information about jobs.

II. REVIEW OF MAIN POINTS

1. What kinds of jobs are considered professional and technical?
2. Is there increased competition among young people for jobs? Why?
3. What kind of jobs are involved with producing goods?
4. Discuss three ways in which a young student can get information about an occupation.

5. What kinds of information can be found in the *Dictionary of Occupational Titles?*

6. Why is a good education so important when trying to find a job?

7. What are the chances of a person without a high school education becoming a manager?

8. What does the future look like for Blacks, Mexican-Americans, Chinese, and American Indians who want professional and technical jobs?

III. THE JOB WORLD: CONCEPTS

1. Should women be given preference for jobs when they have the same qualifications as men? Why?

2. With what trends in the job market are you most concerned? Why?

3. When should a high school student start finding out about an occupation? Why?

4. Why is it necessary for a doctor and lawyer to have a high school education?

5. Make up a list of occupations that includes the job titles of five skilled, five semiskilled, and five unskilled jobs.

6. Do you feel that business corporations are beginning to provide minority groups and women with more higher-paying jobs? What evidence do you have to support your answer?

7. What jobs can a recent high school graduate get? What occupations require more than just a high school education?

8. What kind of occupational information can a student receive from the Federal Government?

IV. THE JOB WORLD: EXERCISES

1. Visit the library and get the *Dictionary of Occupational Titles.* Using this book, do the following:

   a. List three occupational jobs for each of the classifica-cations shown in Figure 41-1.

b. Name some of the duties of the following jobs:
1. computer programer
2. state senator
3. newspaper editor
4. biologist
5. geologist

c. What are the training requirements for a college professor, police officer, waitress, and electrical engineer?

2. Make a list of three occupations in which you are interested. Describe why these occupations appeal to you. Also tell why you feel that you have the ability to be a success in each occupation.

3. Analyze your teacher's job. What parts of the job do you like and which do you dislike? Why?

4. Look at your local newspaper. What kind of job openings are there? Do you think these same kinds of jobs are available in other parts of the country?

5. In what parts of the United States do you believe there will be greater job opportunities in the next ten years. Why?

6. Using newspapers, magazines, and radio and television news, write a report showing the efforts that are being made by business organizations to hire minority members, women, the handicapped, veterans, and similar kinds of workers. What has to be done to continue the trend toward hiring these kinds of workers?

42 FINDING A JOB

People looking for jobs should first try to understand the work world. They should then develop a suitable plan for finding a job. This chapter discusses the process of finding a job. There are four stages in this process: (1) finding job vacancies (openings), (2) contacting companies with vacancies, (3) being interviewed for the vacancies, and (4) getting the right job.

THE MATURE JOB APPLICANT

Most companies look for maturity in a job applicant. *Maturity* in the job market means that the candidate knows what he or she wants from a job and is realistic about such factors as the amount of education required, the preparation needed, the experience needed, and the duties of the job.

A candidate must have a general idea of his or her career objectives. An example of a career objective statement is

> My objective is to work for an organization that will allow me to improve my selling abilities. I want to sell the company's products to customers. Eventually I want to learn about all aspects of selling so that when I am qualified, I can become a district sales manager.

This statement says that the candidate wants to prepare for a management position by learning about various aspects of selling. It shows that the person has some understanding about the job of selling. It shows that the candidate knows that there are a number of duties a salesperson must do.

534

Although maturity is hard to understand, it appears that employers look for it when screening candidates. The mature person gets to the point, is thorough, and is realistic. By reviewing the objective statement, the employer can see whether or not the young person is thorough and realistic.

THE JOB SEARCH PROCESS

There are four specific stages in finding a job. Each one is important.

FINDING JOB VACANCIES

The first step is to find companies that have suitable job openings. You can do this by checking with school placement bureaus, public employment agencies, and Civil Service offices, reading want ads and directories, and talking with people you know.

STATE EMPLOYMENT OFFICES

State employment offices are found in most medium-sized and large communities. They serve both job candidates and employers and do not charge a fee. Young job candidates entering the work world often receive help from specialists in youth employment. Most public employment offices have valuable information on local trends and employment conditions.

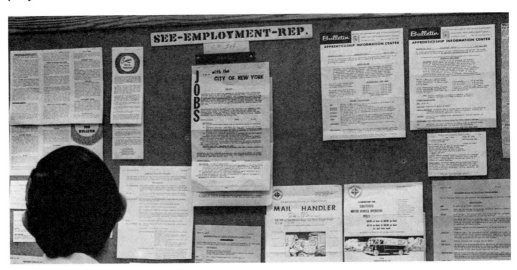

PRIVATE EMPLOYMENT AGENCIES

The private employment agency is in business to make money. It charges a fee for finding people jobs. In some cases employers pay the fee, which is about 5 percent or more of the first year's salary. In most cases, however, the candidate must pay a fee if he or she accepts a job found by the agency. The fee can be deducted on your income tax return.

CIVIL SERVICE OFFICES

The Federal Government lists job vacancies with Civil Service offices. These offices are located in such cities as Boston, New York, San Francisco, Dallas, Chicago, Denver, and Seattle. The announcements of Civil Service vacancies usually mention the title of the position, the duties, the educational background needed, and the deadline for filing applications. Almost all government positions are filled through open competition. Veterans and disabled veterans receive a special priority when competing for vacancies.

WANT ADS

The want ad section of a newspaper provides information on job vacancies. A newspaper in a large city, such as New York, Chicago, or San Francisco, will have all kinds of jobs listed. A sample want ad is shown in Figure 42–1. If you happen to live in a smaller community, there will probably be fewer ads listed in your local newspapers.

FIGURE 42-1

DIRECTORIES

Some organizations list their job openings in directories. High school guidance counselors often keep a directory of local job openings. Another informative source is the *College Placement Annual*. This book is kept by college placement offices and lists companies and positions. Other directories that include names of companies, but not necessarily job openings, include the classified section of telephone directories and membership lists of trade and professional organizations.

PERSONAL CONTACTS

Sometimes personal contacts are used to get information about job vacancies. These contacts may be people who work for a business that has openings or people who know of openings at other companies.

CONTACTING EMPLOYERS

The way to get in touch with an employer varies with the source of information you have. A private employment agency is usually contacted by telephone, while a public employment agency is usually visited in person. An important part of finding a job is to be interviewed by the company or agency.

TELEPHONE

People with a particular skill might find telephoning the best way to start the job search process. They can present their qualifications and ask about vacancies. A problem with telephoning is that some people have difficulty communicating this way. The speed of finding vacancies must be weighed against the ability to present your qualifications clearly. The telephone can be impersonal, while a visit to the place of business offers a more personal touch.

For many jobs, a personally written letter is the most effective way to contact employers. It is best to type the letter carefully and follow a standard business letter style, such as the one shown in Figure 42-2.

**FIGURE 42-2
LETTER OF
APPLICATION**

2936 East 89th Street
Chicago, Illinois 60617
January 15, 1975

Mr. John Richardson
Vice President of Personnel
International Stylist Corporation
10001 Commercial Avenue
Chicago, Illinois 60617

Dear Mr. Richardson:

    Ms. June Riley, the career counselor at Bowen High School, felt that my record and qualifications are suited for a position in your company. At this time I would like to apply for your managerial training program.

    I have worked the past two summers and during the Christmas season at Gassman's as a sales clerk. I had to supervise three other high school students and service customers in the women's clothing department. This valuable experience has convinced me that I would like to eventually become a manager in a large national corporation.

    I will be graduating from Bowen High School on June 7 and would like to start my career on June 14. I have enclosed my resume which will provide you with more personal information.

    I am looking forward to hearing from you about possible opportunities in your managerial training program. Thank you for finding time to review my letter and resume.

Sincerely yours,

Jill Marie Stanley

Jill Marie Stanley

Enclosed: Resume

In the sample letter, the first paragraph explains that Jill is looking for a job in managerial training. The middle part of the letter tells Mr. Richardson about Jill's training. The final section asks him to reply and also thanks him. The three major parts of the letter are—what Jill wants, what her background is, and that she would appreciate a response.

The résumé that Jill encloses with her letter is a summary of her background and qualifications. It is shown in Figure 42-3.

**FIGURE 42-3
RÉSUMÉ**

```
                              RESUME OF

                          JILL MARIE STANLEY

                          2936 East 89th Street
                          Chicago, Illinois 60617
                          (Telephone 374-4382)

PERSONAL:   Born:     December 1, 1958 (Washington, D.C.)
            Height:   5'7"
            Weight:   110 pounds
            Health:   Excellent
            Hobbies:  Swimming, Tennis, Reading, Piano

EDUCATION:  Bowen High School (Chicago)
                 1971-present
            Expect Diploma - June 1975

            Courses:  Business, Accounting, Typewriting, Shorthand,
                      Physics, Chemistry, Mathematics

            Grades:  In upper 20 percent of class

            Activities:  Business Honorary President
                         Vice President of General Business Club
                         Member of Speakers Panel
                         Cheerleader

WORK EXPERIENCE:  Summers and Christmas Season 1973 and 1974 - Sales
                  clerk and supervisor of women's clothing department.
                  Responsible for receipts and handling customer com-
                  plaints.

REFERENCES:  June Riley
             Career Counselor
             Bowen High School
             2947 East 87th Street
             Chicago, Illinois 60617

             Robert Hearn
             Principal
             Bowen High School
             2947 East 87th Street
             Chicago, Illinois 60617

             Anthony Mirosso
             Personnel Manager
             Gassman's
             9141 Commercial Avenue
             Chicago, Illinois 60617
```

The key sections of a high school graduate's résumé should be

1. Identifying Information—name, address
2. Personal Information—age, health
3. Education—high school, class standing, activities
4. Work Experience—jobs held and their duties
5. References—names, titles, and addresses of people who know something about your qualifications.

THE JOB INTERVIEW

The interview is an important step when trying to get a job. It involves face-to-face contact between the candidate and a representative of the company. The letter of application, a telephone call, the company's application form, and a résumé can all help a person get an interview. Very few job vacancies are filled without an interview.

Before going for the interview, learn what you can about the company. Get information about the company's products, size, location, types of employees, and job requirements. This information can be found in publications and reports that you can get from the public relations department of the firm. Most employers assume that a mature applicant will be prepared to discuss himself or herself and why he or she wants to work at that company.

There are a number of typical questions a job candidate should be prepared to answer. These include:

The job interview is important for both the candidate and the company.

1. Why do you want to work for the company?
2. What is your career objective?
3. What kind of schooling and work experience have you had?
4. For what job are you applying? Why?
5. What would you like to be doing ten years from now?
6. What are your future education plans?
7. What courses did you like best in school?
8. Do you like working with people?

The candidate should also prepare questions to ask the company representative. Hopefully, these questions will show the representative that the applicant is mature and interested in the company.

A number of other things are also important. The candidate should be on time, neat, and courteous. The candidate who is late, sloppy, and impolite will almost certainly not get the job.

There is no reason to be nervous about an interview. Even if the candidate is nervous at first, the nervousness will most likely subside shortly after the interview begins. Throughout the interview, the applicant should remain alert and ask questions if something is not understood. The applicant might also want to ask about certain job-related matters, such as vacation time, sick pay, and health insurance plans.

After the interview, it is polite to send the interviewer a note thanking him or her for the interview. If a company is interested in a candidate after the interview, the applicant may be asked to take employment tests and to see other company representatives. The candidate may also be asked to fill out a job application form. This form is similar to the résumé but is usually a little more detailed.

Exactly when the applicant takes tests, sees other respresentatives, and fills out an application blank depends on the particular system used by the firm. There really is no correct sequence; it is up to the company.

THE END OF THE PROCESS

Once an applicant agrees to take a particular job, he or she should stop following all other leads. For example, once Jill Stanley accepts a job at International Stylist Corporation she should immediately tell other firms that she is out of the job market. Then Jill must start concentrating on beginning work for International. She may get more information from the person who will be her boss on how she can best get ready to start work.

Although the job-hunting process has ended, it may begin again in the future. Thus, it is important to keep some record of how the job was found. It is also important to keep carbon copies of letters of application, résumés, and any other correspondence written to prospective employers. These records could possibly be used again when looking for another job. Most people work for a number of different companies during their work career.

SUMMARY

Finding a job can be easy when specific guidelines are followed. First, it is important to show maturity. A candidate's maturity is a crucial issue in finding a job. Maturity can be shown by the sincerity and interest of the candidate.

The job-finding process itself includes finding job vacancies, getting in touch with employers, going for interviews, and finally getting a job.

It is the smart student who prepares himself or herself for the job interview. The interview is a two-way street. The company learns about the applicant, and the applicant gets information about the company and what is expected of its employees.

I. REVIEW OF TERMS

Which words complete the statements below?

Civil Service offices   résumé

application   interview

job   private employment agency

1. A _____ charges a fee for finding jobs for people.

2. The Federal Government lists job vacancies with _____ .

3. A _____ is a summary of personal information about a job candidate.

4. An _____ involves face-to-face contact between a job candidate and a representative of the company.

5. There appear to be four distinct stages in the process of finding a _____ .

6. The personal letter of _____ is one way of finding out about job openings.

II. REVIEW OF MAIN POINTS

1. Why is it sometimes necessary to use a private employment agency?

2. In the job market, what is meant by *maturity*?

3. What is included in a résumé?

4. What is a state employment office?

5. What is the difference between a Civil Service office and a private employment agency?

6. What should be included in a letter of application?

7. Why would it be foolish to include false information about yourself on a résumé?

8. Why is it important to have a clear view of your job objective?

III. FINDING A JOB: CONCEPTS

1. Look at some newspaper want ads. What kinds of jobs are listed? Who would you have to contact if you were interested in any of these jobs?
2. Why is the interview such an important part of the job search process?
3. Look at your telephone directory and contact a private employment agency. Ask them what their fee is for finding a job.
4. Develop a list of three possible jobs that appeal to you. How would you first contact employers about these jobs?
5. Is a letter of application the same as a company's job application blank? If not, explain the differences.

IV. FINDING A JOB: EXERCISES

1. Write your own personal résumé using Figure 42-3 as an example.
2. How would you write a letter to Mr. Richardson of International (Figure 42-2)?
3. Contact a personnel manager of a company in your community and ask him or her about preparing for an interview.
   a. What preparation does he or she recommend?
   b. What are the most important qualities that he or she looks for in a candidate during the interview?
4. If you were a personnel manager of a company in charge of hiring high school students for clerical jobs during the summer, what qualities would you look for among the applicants?
5. Write a paper about the possible problems of finding a job through a private employment agency. Have there been any articles or publicized stories about problems when using private agencies?

THE BUSINESS CHALLENGE 43

While reading this book, you have been introduced to many different ideas. The economy, the structure of business organizations, managing money, buying goods and services, using banks and consumer credit, investing money, insuring yourself, the roles of government and unions, and the work world were all discussed. If anything at all is learned from your reading and study it should be that business is an important force in society.

It is important for you to look forward and think about some of the challenges that lie ahead. If the people in the United States are to enjoy a comfortable standard of living, they must plan for changes that will take place in the population growth, economy, ecology, and ways of thinking. This chapter highlights some of the changes that will challenge everyone.

THE FORCES FOR CHANGE

In various parts of this book you learned about a number of forces that lead to making changes. For example, it was shown that advertising has a tendency to pressure people into changing their buying habits. A razor blade ad is so convincing that many people think seriously about switching to the new brand. As another example, American business has and will continue to sell goods overseas. This means that businesspeople must not only know what buyers in the United States want but must also find out what buyers in Japan and other countries want.

These two examples show the ever-changing side of the business world. There are, however, more obvious examples.

THE POPULATION BOOM

It is believed that the growth rate of the country will continue to slow down over the next 15 years or so. Some experts predict that the total population will grow by nearly 20 percent between 1970 and 1985. However, they say the number of people under twenty years of age will grow by only 3.5 percent. This is not good news for toy manufacturers or processors of baby foods.

It is also expected that there will be about one million new households formed every year. This means a growing demand for housing, home appliances, and furniture.

Experts also believe that by the start of the twenty-first century, there will be three major areas where the population will be concentrated. These will be Boston-Washington, Chicago-Pittsburgh, and San Francisco-San Diego. About 100 million people will probably live in these areas. This means that crowding and pollution may be much more serious than they are now. Programs to ease these problems will most certainly be needed.

In summary, 15 years from now the average American will be older, living in a crowded city or suburb, and demanding more products. Businesspeople will have to change the kinds of goods they produce and the ways they distribute them. In addition, the average person will be better educated and probably less likely to be swayed by advertising.

THE ECONOMY

By the year 2000, it is believed that over 75 percent of all United States families will be earning $20,000 or more. If this happens, Americans will have more money to spend. The more money that is spent, the greater the demand for goods and services. More food will be bought, more automobiles will be bought, more people will be going to school, and more services, such as help from accountants, will be needed.

Experts believe that the economy will grow rapidly in three areas: (1) industries selling services rather than goods, (2) industries in which new changes in technology or equipment occur rapidly, such as in computers, and (3) the medical industry. These growth areas will mean more jobs in both white-collar and blue-collar areas.

In addition to changes in population and the economy, a number of other areas need to be examined by businesspeople. These areas include pollution, energy shortages, consumerism, and the treatment of minorities.

THE POLLUTION PROBLEM

Concern about pollution is not new in the United States. Only recently, however, have large groups of citizens complained about dirty air, airplane noise around airports, and filthy beaches. Business firms are largely responsible for many of these problems.

Every year, the United States has more people, cars, power plants, and blast furnaces. Unless pollution can be controlled, there can be only one result—more pollution.

In addition to pollution, people are surrounding themselves with garbage. The average adult now creates 5.3 pounds of garbage a day. In heavily populated areas, the garbage is collected and carried to less populated areas. It is then dumped. The dumps have been building up, and there is garbage almost everywhere.

There is no doubt that everybody and every business is an air, earth, and water polluter. Some businesspeople today continue to resist the demands of citizens to clean up the environment. Other businesspeople have taken the lead and are cleaning up the air, earth, and water. Unless more businesspeople work on this problem, however, the entire human race is in trouble.

THE ENERGY PROBLEM

The United States energy problems became a real issue late in 1973. Car owners were forced to use less gasoline; homeowners who used oil had to use less; *brownouts* and *blackouts* occurred because power plants were in need of oil, coal, and gas to keep steam boilers going; transportation among farmers, truckers, and bus lines had to be cut; and speed limits on highways had to be reduced to save gasoline. This experience showed that everyone must work together to minimize the energy problems during the next decade.

THE CONSUMER MOVEMENT

Consumerism is a movement that demands that consumers be protected, if possible, against dishonest businesspeople and dangerous products. It is a movement that is supported by consumers, government, and responsible businesspeople.

The terrible safety record of some automobiles, the defects found in automobile tires, the sale of flammable children's clothes, and the sale of medicines before they are fully tested have caught the public eye. The public interest in and criticism of these practices appear to be growing stronger. Today, consumer organizations are weak when compared to business, labor, and government. But they do appear to be gaining more and more public support and encouragement.

The problems of unsafe, defective, or impure products, misleading advertisements, false contests, worthless guarantees, and expensive repair services seem to indicate that businesses will not stop these practices by themselves. Thus, the future will probably see more laws protecting consumers, an increase in organized groups, and more public support of people such as Ralph Nader. Until consumers have the power to stand up to business firms, they will be abused in the marketplace.

MINORITIES AND WOMEN

Two of the major issues of today (and probably tomorrow) are the role in society of Blacks, Mexican-Americans, American Indians, and women, and the share of the nation's wealth they receive. In the past, other minorities, such as the Italians, Irish, and Jews, have been discriminated against in the work world and were at a disadvantage.

The role of business is important in improving the status of minorities and women. Business can provide job opportunities and equal promotion chances for all workers. Neither business nor government alone can solve the work problems of minorities and women. They have to work together.

Recently, business firms have started hiring qualified minority members and women. However, companies often fail to help the discriminated in such areas as providing transportation to new jobs, housing near new jobs, and training programs. This is unfortunate, since transportation, housing, and training are closely related to getting jobs.

BUSINESS RESPONSIBILITY

In recent years, television programs and newspapers have carried stories about oil spills killing animals and ruining beaches, about housing contractors building homes on radioactive landfill, and about steel mills dumping waste into drinking water reservoirs. Such irresponsibility is making news because citizens are now questioning and criticizing such actions of business firms.

The socially responsible firm is one that tries to meet the needs of the public before society demands that it do something about economic, social, and pollution problems. The areas of social responsibility are determined by the values of the society. It seems that society does want a cleaner environment, enough energy, safe products, and no discrimination. The firm that pollutes the air, wastes energy, produces unsafe products, and does not hire qualified women and minority members is not in touch with what society wants. Society's values change, but it seems that the four factors discussed in this section will certainly be important in the near future.

SUMMARY

The future growth of society depends largely on the efforts of every citizen. Businesspeople are an important group of people who will determine what the future will be like. The business firm that is out of touch with what society wants is not a major contributor to the chance for people to survive in a complex world.

The theme of this entire book is that there are many ideas, values, and skills in business about which a young person should know. Of course, at this time in your life you cannot be an expert in each area. However, you will surely be better off and probably enjoy a more comfortable standard of living if you (1) understand the economy, (2) understand the structure of organizations, (3) manage your money well, (4) buy goods effectively, (5) use banks and credit wisely, (6) invest your money wisely, (7) buy insurance carefully, (8) see how the government, unions, and business are related, and (9) understand what a career is and how to find a job.

I. REVIEW OF TERMS

Which words complete the statements below?

Blacks   noise

one hundred   twenty

socially responsible

1. It is estimated that between 1970 and 1985 the population in the United States will grow by nearly _____ percent.

2. Three major areas of population concentration will have _____ million people by the start of the twenty-first century.

3. Airplane sound is classified as _____ pollution.

4. _____ are considered a minority group in our society.

5. The _____ firm is one that attempts to meet the demands of the public before society demands that it do something about economic, social, and pollution problems.

II. REVIEW OF MAIN POINTS

1. As the population changes, why do businesspeople have to change the kinds of goods they produce?

2. What is meant by the terms *air*, *earth*, and *water pollution*?

3. What is the current energy problem in the United States?

4. Explain *consumerism*.

5. What must be done before consumer abuse can be reduced in the United States?

6. What have businesses done about hiring more women?

7. Does the public have a right to cleaner air? Why?

8. In what industries will there be growth in the near future?

III. THE BUSINESS CHALLENGE: CONCEPTS

1. How can each citizen help in reducing pollution problems?
2. Should citizens cut back on their use of energy? Why?
3. Does society want businesspeople to be socially responsible? Why?
4. Businesses continue to put unsafe products on the market. Do you think more laws are necessary to protect consumers? Why or why not?
5. Do business and government have to work together in reducing job discrimination? Why?
6. Should women be considered a minority group in society? In the work world? Explain.

IV. THE BUSINESS CHALLENGE: EXERCISES

1. What kinds of pollution control are used by business firms in your community?
2. Should businesspeople be expected to be any more socially responsible than other people? Are businesspeople qualified to be socially responsible? Explain your answers.
3. Write a brief report on the history of the energy problem in the 1970's. Use your library and encyclopedia sources for help.
4. Should people support groups that promote consumerism? Why?

Glossary

AAAAAAAAAAAAAAAAAAAAAAAAAAAAAAAAA

ABSOLUTE COST ADVANTAGE—when one nation can produce a product more cheaply than another nation because of its available resources.

ADJUSTER—a person who works on claims filed against the insurer.

ADVERTISING—a form of communication used to create or increase the demand for goods or services.

ANNUITY CONTRACT—a contract between the insurer and the insured that guarantees the insured of an income for a specific period of time.

ANTITRUST LAWS—laws established by the Federal Government to prevent monopolies, eliminate business conspiracies, and protect the public from dishonest businesspeople.

ARBITRATOR—an outsider who is called in to settle a grievance between a company and a union that cannot do so on their own.

ARTICLES OF PARTNERSHIP—a legal written agreement that explains the duties and responsibilities of business partners.

AUTOMATIC PREMIUM LOAN—a clause that entitles the insured to an automatic loan in the amount of the policy premium in the event that he or she fails at some time to pay an insurance policy premium.

BBBBBBBBBBBBBBBBBBBBBBBBBBBBBBB

BALANCE OF PAYMENTS—the dollar value of all the economic activities that take place between a country and the rest of the world during one year.

BANK—a profit-making corporation that performs many different financial services.

BANK STATEMENT—the bank's record of a customer's checking account.

BARTERING—the exchange of goods and services without the use of money.

BASIC MEDICAL INSURANCE—protection that covers all or part of the expense of ordinary doctors' fees for hospital, office, or home visits other than for surgical procedures.

BENEFICIARY—the person named in an insurance policy to receive the insurance benefits.

BLANK CHECK—a check written without the amount filled in.

BLANK ENDORSEMENT—an endorsement that consists of a name only and permits a check to be cashed by anyone.

BLUE CHIP STOCKS—stocks of the largest corporations and those stocks with a long, steady record of paying dividends.

BLUE-COLLAR WORKERS—workers who are skilled, semiskilled, or unskilled.

BLUE CROSS—a nonprofit organization that is controlled by member hospitals and covers hospital expenses.

BLUE SHIELD—a nonprofit organization that is controlled by member doctors and covers doctors' fees.

BOARD OF DIRECTORS—corporation members elected to pick the officers to manage the organization.

BODILY INJURY LIABILITY INSURANCE—insurance that protects against loss due to the injury of passengers riding in the insured person's car, people riding in other cars, and pedestrians.

BOND—a written promise made by a corporation or government to pay the investor a certain amount of money, plus interest, at a specific time in the future.

BROKER—a person who represents investors in the buying and selling of stocks and bonds on a commission basis.

BUDGET—a plan for personal spending and saving.

BUDGET ACCOUNTS—credit accounts that may be repaid in three equal payments over a 90-day period. Usually there is no interest charge.

BUSINESS—all of the activities that take place between people when money changes hands.

BUYING INCOME—the money that is left for needs and wants after taxes have been taken out.

CCCCCCCCCCCCCCCCCCCCCCCCCCCCC

CANCELLED CHECK—a check that is written by a customer and paid to another person or business by the bank.

CAPITAL—can mean money that has been invested or a person's wealth; that is, money and owned property.

CAPITAL GAINS—profits received from the sale of assets not typically used in the regular course of business.

CAPITAL GOODS—goods used to produce other goods.

CAPITAL RESOURCES—man-made items used in the production of goods and services.

CAPITALISM—a type of economic system that offers the right to private ownership of property, private enterprise, and economic choice.

CASH CREDIT—credit used for borrowing money.

CASH SURRENDER VALUE—the amount of money the insured can get for his or her insurance policy when it is cashed in.

CENTRAL PROCESSING UNIT—consists of the arithmetic logic, control, and storage units of a computer, and controls the entire system.

CHANNEL OF DISTRIBUTION—the route that goods take in moving from the producer to the consumer.

CHECK—a written order to a bank to pay a stated amount of money to another person or business.

CHECK REGISTER—a separate book in which to record checking account transactions.

CHECK STUB—the form, bound (attached) in a checkbook, on which to keep a record of checking account transactions.

CHECKBOOK MONEY—money placed in checking accounts at banks.

CHECKING ACCOUNT—a bank account in which all types of money can be deposited, but money can be taken out only by writing a check.

CIVIL SERVICE OFFICES—establishments where job vacancies in the Federal Government are listed.

CLEARING A CHECK—the process that takes place from the time a check is deposited in a bank until it is paid.

CLOSED SHOP—the illegal practice of a shop or workplace in which only union members will be hired.

CLOSED-END MUTUAL FUND—a fund that has a limited number of shares of stock to sell.

CLOSING COSTS—extra costs involved in closing a real estate sale, such as insurance, taxes, and legal recording fees.

COLLATERAL—items of value used to secure a loan.

COLLISION INSURANCE—insurance that protects the insured car against damages that occur when the car collides with other objects.

COMMERCIAL BANKS—banks that offer a wide variety of services to both individual people and businesses.

COMMERCIAL INSURANCE—insurance provided by both private firms and the government. If the government provides it, it is on a volunteer basis.

COMMERCIAL LOANS—loans made to businesses or farmers.

COMMISSION—a percentage of a sale made or a service performed, paid to the worker responsible for it.

COMMON STOCK—stock that carries no particular preference over other stock in a corporation.

COMMUNISM—a type of economic system in which the government tightly controls all of the country's economic resources.

COMPOUND INTEREST—interest paid on interest.

COMPREHENSIVE INSURANCE—insurance that protects the insured car against losses or damages, except those caused by collision.

COMPUTER—a series of machines that process (handle) data according to a set of stored instructions.

COMPUTER PROGRAM—a set of instructions that a computer follows to do a specific job.

CONGLOMERATE—an organization that develops when one business firm gets control of a number of other firms.

CONSPIRACY—the grouping together of two or more firms to control certain features of a particular market.

CONSUMER—a person who purchases a product or service for final use, not for resale.

CONSUMER GOODS—goods used to satisfy personal needs and wants.

CONSUMER PRICE INDEX—an index that measures changes in the general price level for all goods and services.

CONSUMERISM—the effort on the part of individuals, governments, and businesses to protect consumers from bad business practices.

CONVENIENCE GOODS—inexpensive goods bought with little or no shopping effort.

CONVERTIBILITY OPTION—a feature in an insurance contract that gives the insured the right to convert a term policy to another form of insurance without having to prove good health.

COOPERATIVE—a business owned by its customers.

CORPORATION—a business organization made up of a number of owners who have the right to do business as a single legal unit.

CORPORATION LAWS—state laws that concern the formation and regulation of corporations.

CRAFT UNION—a union that is made up of workers who represent a single occupation, such as glass blowers or machinists.

CREDIT—a promise to pay at a future date for the immediate exchange and use of goods, services, or money.

CREDIT BUREAU—an agency that keeps records on consumers who use credit.

CREDIT CARDS—cards that are issued by many stores, banks, and other businesses and provide the consumer with credit to buy goods or services.

CREDIT RATING—what businesses think of a person's ability and willingness to repay a debt.

CREDITOR—a person to whom money is due.

CURRENCY—paper, or folding, money and coins.

DDDDDDDDDDDDDDDDDDDDDDDDDDDD

DATA PROCESSING—the collecting, classifying, summarizing, reporting, and storing of information.

DATA PROCESSING SYSTEMS—the people and machines used to process data.

DEBENTURE BOND—a bond that is secured only by the earnings of the issuing company.

DEDUCTIBLE PAYMENT FEATURE—a specific portion of expenses that the insured must pay before the insurer will start payments.

DEDUCTION—a certain gift or expense that cannot be taxed.

DEFICIT BUDGET—a budget in which expenses are greater than income.

DEFLATION—a fall in the average level of prices of all goods and services.

DEMAND DEPOSIT—money put into a checking account.

DEMAND-PULL INFLATION—inflation that occurs when the total demand for goods and services is more than can be supplied.

DEPOSIT TICKET—the printed form that a customer fills out showing the amounts and types of money (coins, paper bills, or checks) to be deposited in a bank account.

DIRECT TAX—a tax that is paid directly to the government agency that levied the tax.

DISABILITY INCOME INSURANCE—insurance designed to help replace lost income due to permanent injury or illness.

DISTRIBUTION—the process of moving goods and services from producers to consumers.

DISTRIBUTOR—a person or business that moves goods between the producer and consumer.

DIVIDEND—the share of a corporation's profits paid to stockholders.

DOMESTIC TRADE—trade conducted within one country.

DOUBLE INDEMNITY INSURANCE—a life insurance feature that pays the beneficiary double the amount of the face value of the policy if the insured person's death is caused by accident.

DRAWER—the person who writes a check.

EEEEEEEEEEEEEEEEEEEEEEEEEEEEEE

ECONOMIC GROWTH—the increase in a nation's production of goods and services.

ECONOMIC SYSTEM—the way in which a nation uses its economic resources.

ECONOMIC VOTE—the vote consumers cast each time they buy a certain product or service, thereby influencing the nation's economic decisions.

ELECTRONIC DATA PROCESSING (EDP)—a method that uses electronic computers to process data quickly.

EMERGENCY EXPENSES—expenses that cannot be predicted.

EMINENT DOMAIN—the right of the government to take property and then pay the owner a fair price, when the property is to be used in the public interest.

END-OF-SEASON SALES—sales used to clear out certain merchandise at different times of the year.

ENDORSEMENT—the signing of one's name on the back of a check in order to cash the check.

ENDORSEMENT IN FULL—an endorsement used to transfer a check to another person.

ENDOWMENT LIFE INSURANCE—life insurance that is payable to the beneficiary if the insured should die, or payable directly to the insured if he or she should live beyond the period of time in which premiums are paid.

ESTATE TAX—a tax levied by the Federal Government on property valued over a certain amount, left by a person who has died.

EXCISE TAX—a tax that Federal, state, and local governments may levy on the purchase of a particular product or service.

EXEMPTION—an amount of money that cannot be taxed.

EXPORTS—goods sold to other countries.

FFFFFFFFFFFFFFFFFFFFFFFFFFFFFFFF

FACTORS OF PRODUCTION—economic resources (natural, capital, and labor) used to produce goods and services.

FAMILY INCOME POLICY—an insurance policy that pays the beneficiary for a specific period of time monthly payments equal to a certain percentage of the face value of the policy. At the end of the period, the entire value of the policy is paid to the beneficiary.

FAMILY LIFE INSURANCE—a combination policy that protects all members of the family.

FEDERAL RESERVE BANK—one of 12 district banks backed by the Federal Government.

FEDERAL RESERVE SYSTEM—a nationwide banking plan created by the Federal Government, which keeps bank deposits safe and helps manage the nation's money supply.

FIXED AMOUNT OPTION—a type of settlement in which the beneficiary is paid a specific sum of money until the entire fund is used up.

FIXED CAPITAL RESOURCES—capital resources that can be used many times to produce other goods.

FIXED EXPENSES—expenses that must be paid at certain times and in specific amounts.

FIXED-RETURN INVESTMENT—an investment in which the amount of interest the investor receives stays the same for the life of the bond.

FLEXIBLE EXPENSES—expenses that vary as to when they have to be paid and in what amounts.

FOREIGN EXCHANGE MARKETS—markets where the monies of different countries are bought and sold.

FREE TRADE—the buying and selling of goods and services between nations without any barriers to restrict it.

FULL-SERVICE BANKS—banks that accept cash deposits for checking and savings accounts, make loans, transfer funds, provide trust services, and rent safe deposit boxes.

GGGGGGGGGGGGGGGGGGGGGGGGGGGGG

GENERAL PRICE LEVEL—the average level of prices in a country at any given time.

GENERAL SALES TAX—a kind of sales tax that a buyer pays when he or she makes a purchase.

GIFT TAX—a tax levied by the Federal Government, which must be paid on gifts of property, money, stocks, or bonds valued over a certain amount.

GOODS—products that can be seen and touched.

GRACE PERIOD—a period of time which allows for full insurance protection even though premiums have not been paid on time.

GROSS INCOME—total income received before taxes are subtracted.

GROSS NATIONAL PRODUCT—the total dollar value of all goods and services produced in a nation in one year.

GROWTH STOCKS—stocks issued by a corporation in which sales and earnings are growing faster than both the economy in general and the average for the industry.

HHHHHHHHHHHHHHHHHHHHHHHHHHHHH

HOMEOWNERS POLICY—a combination insurance policy that provides a wide range of coverage for real and personal property.

HOSPITAL INSURANCE—protection

that helps pay for room and board plus certain extras in a hospital.

||||||||||||||||||||||||||||||||||||||||||||||||||||||||||||||||||||||

IMPORT QUOTA—a legal limit placed on the amount of a particular product that can be imported during a certain period of time.

IMPORTS—goods which are bought from other countries.

IMPULSE BUYING—buying without thinking or planning, which can be costly.

INCOME DISTRIBUTION—the way in which buying income is divided among families.

INCOME TAX—a federal tax on earnings.

INCOME TAX RETURN—a form that must be filled out by every person and corporation paying federal income tax.

INDIRECT TAX—a tax that is paid to someone other than the agency that levied the tax. That party then forwards the tax to the appropriate agency.

INDUSTRIAL UNION—a union that is made up of all the workers of a plant, regardless of their occupation.

INFLATION—a rise in the average level of prices of all goods and services.

INPAYMENTS—items that bring money into a country.

INSTALLMENT CREDIT—credit that is repaid in more than one payment.

INSURANCE—a way of pooling funds so that a group of people share the economic risks of losing property and earning power.

INSURANCE AGENT—a person who sells insurance and represents an insurance company.

INSURED—the person who carries insurance.

INSURER—the company that makes insurance protection available to others.

INTEREST—the cost of using another person's money.

INTEREST OPTION—a type of settlement in which the beneficiary does not receive the full amount of an insurance policy but gets only the interest earned by the money.

INTERNATIONAL TRADE—trade conducted between countries.

INTERSTATE COMMERCE—the sale of goods and services between states.

INVENTORY—a list of property or possessions and their value.

INVESTMENT BANKS—banks that work mainly with large businesses to get them money for machinery and other capital goods.

INVESTMENT CLUB—a group of people who form a club to invest their combined money.

JJJJJJJJJJJJJJJJJJJJJJJJJJJJJJJJJJJJJJJJJJJJJ

JOINT ACCOUNT—a bank account used by two or more people.

LLLLLLLLLLLLLLLLLLLLLLLLLLLLLLLLLLLLLL

LABOR RESOURCES—the people that make up the labor force.

LABOR UNION—a group of workers who have banded together to improve their wages and working conditions.

LIMITED LIABILITY—a responsibility only for the amount of money invested in a corporation.

LIMITED-PAYMENT LIFE INSURANCE—a type of whole life insurance in which the insured pays premiums only for a stated number of years.

LOAD FUNDS—mutual funds that carry a loading charge (the difference between the asked price and the bid price of a share of mutual fund stock).

LOAN OPTION—a feature that entitles the insured to borrow any amount of money up to the cash surrender value of the insurance policy.

LOAN SHARK—a person who makes loans without a license to do so.

LOCKOUT—a management technique used to counteract a strike, which involves shutting the doors of a plant to workers and not allowing them to work.

LONG-TERM CREDIT—credit used by businesses to pay for capital goods. A business may take up to 25 years to repay this type of credit.

MMMMMMMMMMMMMMMMMMMMMMMM

MAJOR MEDICAL INSURANCE—insurance designed to pay heavy medical expenses resulting from serious injury or long illness.

MANAGEMENT TEAM—the decision-makers in an organization. They are usually divided into top-, middle-, and lower-level managers.

MARKETING—the activities that take

place in moving goods and services from producer to consumer.

MASS-PRODUCED GOODS—items made in large quantities.

MATURITY DATE—the date on which the face value of a bond is to be paid back to the investor.

MEDICAID—a health insurance protection plan provided by the state.

MEDICARE—a Government social insurance plan that combines medical and hospital insurance protection and is available to citizens over sixty-five years of age.

MERGER—the combining of two or more business firms into a single firm.

MINIMUM WAGE LAWS—laws stating that no person employed by a business covered by the laws can be paid less than a certain rate per hour.

MODIFIED LIFE POLICY—an insurance policy that allows the insured to pay a lower premium during the first few years of protection and a higher premium later on.

MONEY—anything that is generally accepted as payment for goods or services.

MONEY MANAGEMENT—planning how to use your dollars.

MONOPOLY—a single company that has full control of a product or service and can set prices and prevent competing firms from doing business.

MORTGAGE—a loan of money secured by property.

MORTGAGE BOND—a bond that is secured by a mortgage on the property of the issuing company.

MORTGAGE LOANS—loans made to help people buy homes.

MUNICIPAL BOND—a type of bond issued by a city.

MUTUAL FUND—a company that sells its stock to the public and buys stocks and/or bonds of other corporations.

NNNNNNNNNNNNNNNNNNNNNNNNNNN

NATIONAL BANK—a bank licensed to do business by the Federal Government.

NATURAL RESOURCES—materials that are provided by nature and can be used in making goods and services.

NEEDS—basic things people must have to exist.

NET INCOME—total income received after taxes are subtracted.

NO-FAULT INSURANCE—an insurance plan that pays all insured people in a car accident no matter who is at fault.

NO-LOAD FUNDS—mutual funds that sell their shares of stock directly to the public without adding a sales charge.

NONINSTALLMENT CREDIT—credit that is repaid in one payment.

NONPARTICIPATING POLICY—a policy that does not enable the insured to share in dividends or refunds from the company.

OOOOOOOOOOOOOOOOOOOOOOOOOO

OCCUPATION—a person's regular work or means of earning a living.

OPEN CHARGE ACCOUNTS—credit accounts used for everyday expenses. They must be paid in full within 10 to 20 days after billing.

OPEN HOUSING LAWS—laws that prohibit discrimination in the renting or selling of a home.

OPEN SHOP—a shop or workplace in which workers can decide whether or not to join a union.

OPEN-END MUTUAL FUND—a fund that has an unlimited number of shares of stock to sell.

ORDINARY LIFE INSURANCE—a type of whole life insurance in which the insured pays premiums throughout his or her lifetime.

ORGANIZATION CHART—a company chart showing which people fill various jobs and who has authority.

OUTPAYMENTS—items that take money out of a country.

OUTSTANDING CHECKS—checks that have been written but have not yet reached the bank to be paid.

OVERDRAWN CHECK—a check written for more money than is in the checking account.

OVER-THE-COUNTER STOCKS—stocks of about 15,000 national and local corporations that are not listed on the stock exchanges and are sold directly to investors.

PPPPPPPPPPPPPPPPPPPPPPPPPPPPP

PARTICIPATING POLICY—a policy that entitles the insured to a partial refund of premiums paid or to a dividend if the company earns money on its investments.

PARTNERSHIP—a business owned by two or more people.

PASSBOOK—a depositor's record of his or her savings account.

PAYEE—the person to whom a check is written.

PER CAPITA—for each individual person.

PERSONAL CHECKBOOK—a book of blank checks issued by a bank to a customer who has opened a checking account.

PERSONAL LIABILITY INSURANCE—insurance that offers protection against loss (injury to other persons or damage to property) due to personal negligence.

PERSONAL LOANS—loans made to individual people for various reasons.

PICKETING—the placing of union members at the entrances of a business to discourage nonstriking workers from entering.

POPULATION—the number of people living in a specific area.

POSTDATE—dating a check for a day in the future.

PREFERRED STOCK—stock that has preference over other stock in a corporation in the payment of dividends.

PREMIUM—the money paid to the insurer for insurance protection.

PRICE—the value of any product or service measured in dollars and cents.

PRICE DISCRIMINATION—occurs when a business charges customers different prices for products that are the same in grade and quality.

PRICE-EARNINGS RATIO—the figure calculated by dividing the price of a share of stock by the average earnings per share.

PRIVATE ENTERPRISE—a process that allows people the freedom to choose what business to enter and what goods or services to sell.

PRODUCER GOODS—goods used to produce other goods or services.

PRODUCTION—the process a business firm uses to change raw materials into goods and services.

PROFIT—the difference between what it costs to produce a product or service and what the product or service sells for in the free market.

PROFIT MOTIVE—the idea of people working for a profit.

PROGRESSIVE TAX—a tax with a tax rate that increases as a taxpayer's income increases.

PROMISSORY NOTE—a written promise to repay a loan by a certain date.

PROOF OF LOSS—the evidence required by the insurer of the insured in order to establish the breakdown and value of the loss, and determine the amount of repayment to be made.

PROPERTY TAX—taxes based on the value of real estate and personal property and levied by both state and local governments.

PROPERTY DAMAGE LIABILITY INSURANCE—insurance that protects against loss due to property damage caused by the insured person's car.

PROSPECTUS—a special pamphlet issued by a corporation, which describes future goals of the company and provides other information important to the potential investor.

PUBLIC UTILITY—a private enterprise that provides a very important service, such as electricity or telephone service.

PURCHASING AGENT—a person employed by a business or government who works full-time at buying the best goods and services for the least amount of money.

RRRRRRRRRRRRRRRRRRRRRRRRRRRRRR
RATE OF EXCHANGE—the price at which one country's money is converted into another country's money.

REAL ESTATE—land and those things that are permanently attached to the land.

REAL VALUE—the buying power of money in exchange for other goods.

REAL WAGES—the value of money earned in terms of what it will buy.

RECONCILING THE BANK STATEMENT—getting the checkbook balance and the bank's balance to match.

REGRESSIVE TAX—a tax with the same tax rate for all people. (It claims a greater percentage of lower incomes than it does of higher incomes.)

REGULAR CHARGE ACCOUNTS—credit accounts used by people who shop regularly at a certain store. They must be paid in full within 10 days after billing.

RESERVE REQUIREMENT—how much money member banks must keep on reserve (deposit) with the Federal Reserve.

RESTRICTIVE ENDORSEMENT—an endorsement that limits the use of a check.

RESUME—a summary of a job applicant's background and qualifications.

RETAILER—a distributor who buys goods and services from a wholesaler in order to sell them directly to consumers.

REVENUE—government dollars that come from taxes paid by the public.

REVENUE SHARING—a policy in which the tax dollars collected by the Federal Government are turned back to local and city governments for beneficial use in the community.

REVOLVING CHARGE ACCOUNT—a form of noninstallment credit in which credit limits are set when the account is opened.

RIDER—a special feature that is attached to an insurance policy.

SSSSSSSSSSSSSSSSSSSSSSSSSSSSSSS

SAFE DEPOSIT BOX—a compartment in a bank vault rented to a customer for the storage and protection of valuables and important documents.

SALES CREDIT—credit used for purchasing goods or services.

SAVINGS—the difference between the money a person earns and the money that person spends.

SAVINGS ACCOUNT—a bank account that earns interest.

SAVINGS AND LOAN ASSOCIATION—a business that makes loans mostly to people who want to buy or build homes.

SAVINGS BANKS—banks set up to accept personal savings accounts and to make loans to people who are buying or building homes.

SEAL OF APPROVAL—a consumer buying aid, which indicates that a product has been inspected or tested for quality and safety.

SECURED LOAN—a loan backed by collateral.

SERIES E SAVINGS BOND—a popular bond sold by the United States Government.

SERVICE CHARGE—a fee charged by banks for checking account services.

SERVICES—tasks done for you by other people.

SHOP STEWARD—an important union official on the local level who collects dues, handles workers' complaints, and represents the union.

SHOPPING GOODS—fairly expensive goods, which are usually bought only after a buyer compares the price, color, quality, and style of several items.

SHORT-TERM CREDIT—money borrowed to pay for everyday operating expenses. A business usually takes from 30 to 90 days to repay this type of credit.

SIGNATURE CARD—the bank's record of how a customer writes his or her name.

SIGNATURE LOAN—a loan that is made on the borrower's signing of a contract or agreement.

SINGLE-PAYMENT LOAN—a form of noninstallment credit, which is repaid at the end of 30, 60, or 90 days.

SIT-DOWN STRIKE—an illegal strike in which workers remain on the job but refuse to work.

SOCIAL INSURANCE—insurance that is provided by state and federal programs and financed largely by employers and employees.

SOCIAL SECURITY NUMBER—a special number that is assigned to each worker and helps the Government keep a record of the worker's earnings for the purpose of social security benefits.

SOCIAL SECURITY SYSTEM—a national social insurance program that entitles each citizen to certain benefits, including disability, survivors, retirement, hospital, and medical.

SOCIAL SECURITY TAX—a tax levied by the Federal Government and used to pay for a variety of benefits, including retirement and disability.

SOCIALISM—a type of economic system in which the government may own and operate many of the country's basic industries.

SOLE PROPRIETORSHIP—a business owned by one person.

SPECIAL SALES—sales used to promote special items in a store or the store name.

SPECIALTY GOODS—costly goods that have certain unusual or very special features that interest the buyer.

SPECULATIVE STOCKS—stocks that sell at a high price when compared to their previous earnings.

STANDARD OF LIVING—the amount of money, goods, and services a family normally has to use for everyday living.

STATE BANK—a bank licensed to do business by the state.

STOCK—a share of ownership in a corporation.

STOCK CERTIFICATE—an actual paper that is evidence of ownership in a corporation.

STOCKBROKERAGE—a company that handles the buying and selling of stock.

STOCKHOLDER—a person who owns stock in a corporation.

STOP-PAYMENT ORDER—a form instructing a bank not to pay a particular check.

STRIKE—what occurs when union members as a group refuse to work until some agreement is reached between management and the union.

SURGICAL INSURANCE—protection that pays various amounts for different operations.

SURPLUS—an amount or quantity greater than what is needed.

TTTTTTTTTTTTTTTTTTTTTTTTTTTTTTTT

TARIFF—a tax on imported goods, levied by the Federal Government.

TAX RATE—the amount of tax to be paid.

TERM LIFE INSURANCE—insurance that provides protection for a specific period of time.

TIME DEPOSIT—money put into a savings account.

TRADE—the buying and selling of goods and services.

TRADE ASSOCIATION—an organization that represents companies which produce similar products or services.

TRUST—a person's money and property that are managed by someone else.

UUUUUUUUUUUUUUUUUUUUUUUUUUUU

UNEMPLOYMENT INSURANCE—a social insurance plan that is operated by the state, regulated by the Federal Government, and provides weekly payments for workers temporarily unemployed.

UNINSURED MOTORIST PROTECTION—insurance that covers the insured for damages resulting from an accident caused by an uninsured motorist.

UNION CONTRACT—the written agreement between management and the union that results from collective bargaining.

UNION SHOP—a shop or workplace in which all new workers must join a union within a certain period of time.

UNI-STATEMENT—a complete accounting of all of the depositor's banking activities.

VVVVVVVVVVVVVVVVVVVVVVVVVVVVV

VOIDING A CHECK—destroying a check that has been written incorrectly.

WWWWWWWWWWWWWWWWWWWWW

WANTS—things that people would like to have but do not need in order to exist.

WHITE-COLLAR WORKERS—workers who are in professional, technical, managerial, clerical, or sales positions.

WHOLE LIFE INSURANCE—permanent life insurance that pays money when the insured dies.

WHOLESALER—a distributor who buys large quantities of goods from a producer and sells them in smaller quantities to retailers.

WILDCAT STRIKE—an illegal strike in which workers walk off the job without their union's authorization.

WORKER PRODUCTIVITY—the amount of goods and services produced per worker in an hour.

WORKING CAPITAL RESOURCES—capital resources that cannot be used again but are used up in the production process.

YYYYYYYYYYYYYYYYYYYYYYYYYYYYY

YEARLY PERCENTAGE RATE—the cost of credit in percentage terms (the cost of the loan divided by the average amount of credit in use during the life of the loan).

YELLOW DOG CONTRACT—a signed pledge by a new employee which states that he or she will not join a union.

ZZZZZZZZZZZZZZZZZZZZZZZZZZZZ

ZERO POPULATION GROWTH—a condition which occurs when the number of people born each year is exactly equal to the number of people who die.

INDEX

Noninstallment credit, 310, *See also* Charge accounts
Nuclear Regulatory Commission, 498

O

Occupational Health and Safety Act, 500–501
Occupations, classifications of, 519; educational levels and, 526–527, *table*, 527; experience and awareness in, 523–524; information on, 523, 529; major group categories of, 524–525, *table*, 524; production and, 527; skills, development of, 518–519; specific inquiries about, 530; status, 519–521; titles, *See The Dictionary of Occupational Titles*; trends in, percentages, 524–525
Office buildings, *See* Real estate
Office of Revenue Sharing, 480
Ordinary life insurance, *See* Life insurance
Organizations, management of, 82, *charts*, 83, 84, 85
Outpayments, 52, *See also* Balance of payments

P

Partnerships, advantages of, 66, 67; articles of (agreement), 66; credit rating of, 66; disadvantages of, 67, 68; general, 65; in the community, 68; income tax payment, 67; joint effort, 67; limited, 65; pooling of funds, talents in, 66; responsibilities of, 67
Pawnbrokers, 314, 315, *illus.*, 315
Personal liability, *See also* Home insurance; damages, 434; inventory of household goods, 438; payment for losses, 438–439; proof of loss, 439
Philadelphia-Baltimore Stock Exchange, 333
Pollution, 495, 547
Population, age groups and, 170–171, *table*, 171; consumer market and, 170, *table*, 170; control of, 37; economic growth and, 36, 37, 43, ta-

Population (cont'd)
ble, 36; education and, 175, *table*, 175; ethnic groups in, 172, *table*, 172; the future and, 546; job market and, 526; rural/urban, 172, 174, *illus.*, 173, *table*, 174; standard of living and, 36
Preferred stock, *See* Stocks
Premiums (insurance), 378, 379, 400; group, 429; health, 428; home, 437, *table*, 437; loan clause, 409; personal and property protection, 437–438, *table*, 437
Price discrimination, 499–500, *See also* Consumer complaints
Price fixing, 183–184, 499
Private enterprise, 29
Production, businesses and, 40–42; factors in, 19; Gross National Product and, 39–42, *table*, 39, *graph*, 40; increased, benefits of, 41–42; mass, 17; per capita, 40–41, *table*, 40–41; resources, use of, 18–20
Profits, in business, 7; in a capitalistic economy, 29–30; limiting of, 33; taxes on, 14
Progressive tax, *See* Taxes
Promissory note, 316–317, *illus.*, 316
Property, rights to, ownership of, 29, *See also* Capitalism
Property insurance, *See* Home insurance
Property taxes, *See* Taxes
Prospectus, corporation, 329
Public utilities, government certification of, 496; government regulation of, 33; monopolies in, 469
Public Utility Commission, 469

R

Rate of exchange, *See* Foreign exchange
Real estate, apartment houses, buying of, 369; assessed value of, 485–486; differing property values in, 367; estimated taxes, 486; *illus.*, 365; investing in, advantages of, 366, 370; investment risks in, 368; land, purchase of, 368–369; office buildings, factors in purchase of, 369; resale of, 366–367; tax base for, 486

Regressive taxes, *See* Taxes
Resources, capital, 19, 47; human, 20, 47; natural, 19, 47
Resume, writing of a, *See* Job vacancies
Retailer, 164, *See also* Marketing
Risks, automobile insurance, 443, 444; credit, 302; economic, 434–435; to income, 389; life insurance, 389–390; real estate, 368; stock investment, 337
Robinson-Patman Act, *See* Law

S

Safe deposit boxes, 236
Sales Management, 530
Sales tax, 486–487, *See also* Taxes; city and state, 486; fairness of, 486
San Francisco Mining Exchange, 333
Savings account, account number, 273; advantages of, 271; Christmas clubs, 276; compound interest on, 277, *table*, 277; deposit ticket, 272, *illus.*, 272; features of, 276; interest on, 276–277; monthly income plans, 276; passbook, 273–274, *illus.*, 273; protection of, 278; quarterly statements, 274, *illus.*, 274; restricted (time), 276; savings certificates, 276; signature card, 272, *illus.*, 272; source of ready cash (regular), 278; uni-statement, 275, *illus.*, 275; vacation clubs, 276; withdrawal ticket, 273, *illus.*, 273
Savings and loan associations, 311–312
Savings banks, 233, 234
Savings bonds, *See* United States savings bonds
Seals of approval, *See* Consumer buying aids
Securities and Exchange Commission 329, 498
Services, *See* Goods and services
Sherman Antitrust Act, *See* Law
Signature card, *See* Checking and Savings accounts

A 5
B 6
C 7
D 8
E 9
F 0
G 1
H 2
I 3
J 4